Open Books:

Literature in the Curriculum, Kindergarten through Grade Two

By Carol Otis Hurst

PROFESSIONAL GROWTH SERIES®

A Publication of THE BOOK REPORT & LIBRARY TALK
Professional Growth Series

Linworth Publishing, Inc.
Worthington, Ohio

With many thanks to Barbara Kines.

Library of Congress Cataloging-in-Publication Data

Published by Linworth Publishing, Inc.
480 East Wilson Bridge Road, Suite L
Worthington, Ohio 43085

Copyright©1999 by Linworth Publishing, Inc.

Series Information:
        From The Professional Growth Series

ISBN 0-938865-77-3

5 4 3 2 1

Table of Contents

Table of Contents continued

Introduction

Thousands of children's book titles are available every year, so it isn't surprising that educators often have trouble separating the wheat from the chaff. The purpose of this book is to make the winnowing process easier for educators by highlighting very good books which can stand alone or become part of the curriculum. I've concentrated on picture books because many are so wonderful and so full of information that they must not be missed, and also because if we rush children into novels—even short novels—in the early grades, they may never get a chance to relish picture books.

One of the primary reasons for using picture books with young children is pure enjoyment. Even so, children are learning as they experience a good picture book. Some are hearing stories read aloud for the first time and are getting a sense of what a story is. Others are learning the conventions of print. Others begin to pick out letters, words and phrases and attach meaning to them. The illustrations in a picture book are, for many children, their first exposure to art.

One of the best lessons I ever saw took place in a kindergarten class on the first day of school. The teacher had the children seated in a circle on the floor. In the center of the circle was a very large pile of books. When the teacher had the children's attention, she announced, "It's reading time." She then reached into the pile and took a book, seated herself back in the circle and began to read the book to herself, carefully examining each page. The kids watched. One child asked, "Aren't you going to read it to us?" The teacher said, "No, but there are other books in the pile," and pointed to them. Another child asked, "Aren't you even going to show us the pictures?" Again, she said no and indicated the pile of books. Some children just watched her. Others took books from the pile and began to look at them. At the end of three minutes, she said, "Oh, that was a good book. It's all about . . ." and she gave them a brief summary of the story. That was it. The lesson was over and they went on to other things.

Look what she had shown them—how the act of reading was done and that she got meaning from doing it. Each day she increased "reading time" by one minute until the reading period was 20 minutes.

Besides reading for pleasure and reading in order to learn to read better, we use picture books in the classroom to approach and then teach other areas of the curriculum. Within the covers of both fiction and nonfiction picture books is information that can answer some questions and inspire others. There are picture books to supplement and amplify any subject in the primary curriculum of any school.

The first section of this book is devoted to themes in social studies, natural and physical science, math, music, art, and, of course, literature. Each theme highlights one such area of the curriculum but touches on many others. Because we use literature so extensively in each theme, language arts is always a major part of this process. The themes were taken from the most commonly used textbooks in primary classrooms. Each theme features a picture book, brief descriptions of some suggested activities and a book list of other trade books to support the theme.

The second section of this book I've called "Focus Books." These books represent several genres and were chosen because they are outstanding works of art. Each focus

> Within the covers of both fiction and nonfiction picture books is information that can answer some questions and inspire others.

book is so strong that it can become a unit of study in and of itself. Because adults are, for the most part, text-oriented, we sometimes miss details in the illustrations of a picture book. For that reason, I have provided a detailed, sometimes page-by-page, look at every book. I've then taken each focus book across the curriculum, suggesting activities for which the book is particularly suited, starting with language arts and literature. A list of books that relate to the focus book concludes each selection.

The third section of this book is devoted to author/illustrator studies. I've chosen mostly familiar artists who have made extensive contributions to the field and provided a brief biography. I've then suggested ways in which their body of work can be viewed as a whole before going on to specific books. An activity is suggested for each book to act as a springboard for your own ideas.

Use this book to help you find good books for your classroom. Use it to inspire you and your students to delve into picture books and to find ways to integrate the books into the curriculum without distorting the literature. Use activities, both mine and the ones you'll think of, that can make these books more meaningful and the learning process more joyful. Have fun.

–Carol Otis Hurst

Themes

SCIENCE: Freshwater

COMMENTS

An investigation of the ecosystems in and around freshwater will include such topics as life cycles, predator/prey, and the effects of pollution on the systems, as well as efforts (if they exist) to reduce or eliminate pollution. Although a natural science theme, this subject can cross over into physical science when the water supply is involved and into history when local freshwater areas are studied.

PICTURE BOOK STARTER

One of the strongest picture books for this theme is **Voices of the Wild**, by Jonathan London (Crown Books for Young Readers, 1993, ISBN 0 517 59217 7). Here a man is seen paddling his kayak along a river in the wilderness. He is observed by the creatures that live in and around the river: a beaver, a bear, a moose, a lynx, a deer, an owl, and a turtle. Each identifies itself in relationship to both the man and the environment. The man saves his speech until the end, when, sitting near an old totem pole, his emphasis is on appreciating and being part of where he is and what he sees.

ACTIVITIES

Language Arts

BUILDING VOCABULARY

▶ Read **Raven and River** (see book list). Then, make a list of the animals in both books. Beside each animal make a list of descriptive words: Describe its color, shape, habits, and special adaptations. Use those lists to make up new similes. For instance, "The bear is as black as a moonless night," etc.

CHANGING POINT OF VIEW

▶ Read the book **Voices of the Wild** and then have students tell the story from the point of view of one of the animals along the river. Talk about what you see and what you think of the man in the boat.

▶ Close your eyes and visualize yourself in one of those areas. Are you in a boat? On the shore? In the water? What season of the year is it? What are you wearing? Think about what you see, feel and hear as you sit quietly in that spot. Now think about each of the animals and how it would feel about your presence there. Write about it.

DRAMATIZING

▶ Read **Tuesday** (see book list). Then, imagine the reaction of the other animals of the pond after the frogs' adventure. Role-play a conversation about their adventure.

Science

▶ Brainstorm and list freshwater areas: pond, lake, river, etc. List as many facts as you can think of that apply to those bodies of water in your area. Then, list animals, insects and plants that can be found in and around those areas. Categorize the list in as many ways as possible.

▶ Categorize the "facts" from above as "We Are Sure of This," "We Aren't Sure of This," "We Need to Know More About This."

▶ List possible sources for information about freshwater environments.

▶ Browse through some of the books listed and then add to the list above.

▶ Make frequent field trip visits to a local freshwater area. Each person should pick out a tree or small area on which to concentrate his observations. Use magnifying glasses to notice minute things such as insect eggs and trails, evidence of decay, growth, bird and animal droppings, etc. Carefully note and record differences since the last time you visited there.

▶ Take water samples from your freshwater area. Examine them under a microscope. If possible, send them to a local laboratory for testing.

▶ Find out where your drinking water comes from. Take a field trip to the local water treatment plant.

▶ Find out about sewage treatment in your area. How is the water cleaned? How clean is the water when it's released? Where is it released?

▶ Make a series of circle stories such as the one below:

A fish died, so . . .
The mosquito larva that fish would have eaten matured, so . . .
There were lots more mosquitoes in the area, so . . .

People couldn't sit outdoors in the evening, so . . .
They sprayed lots of insecticides to kill the mosquitoes, so . . .
The water in the lake got polluted, so . . .
A fish died.

▶ Use pizza cardboard or cut paper circles to make large pictures of each of the animals that live in and around freshwater. Don't forget insects. Make separate circles for any separate stages of the life cycle.

▶ Play a game in which each person takes one of the above-mentioned circles. One person holds up his circle and states what it is. Other class members find a way that their animal relates to the one being held up.

▶ Place the circles on a large area of wall and connect them with yarn, showing as many relationships as possible. Use different colors of yarn to show different relationships such as predator/prey and life cycles.

Social Studies

▶ On a map of your area, identify all the fresh water areas within 50 miles of your school, within 100 miles, within 200 miles.

Art

▶ Use watercolors to make pictures of a freshwater area.

BOOK LIST
Fiction

Arnosky, Jim. _All Night Near the Water._ G. P. Putnam's Sons Books for Young Readers, 1994. ISBN 0 399 22629 X

The water is a lake, and a mother mallard leads her ducklings there on their first trip away from the nest. There they discover a sand bar and observe fireflies, frogs and bats before settling down to sleep. In the morning, they take their first swim. Arnosky's illustrations provide detailed information on the setting.

Carlstrom, Nancy White. _Raven and River._ Little, Brown & Co., Children's Books, 1997. ISBN 0 316 12894 5

Beautiful illustrations show the animals that live around the still ice-bound river. On each page a simile is used to compare that animal to the river.

Cristini, Ermanno. _In the Pond._ Picture Book Studio, 1985. ISBN 0 907234 43 7

In this wordless book, a marsh explodes with life both above and below the surface of the water.

Lasky, Kathryn. _Pond Year._ Candlewick Press, 1995. ISBN 1 56402 187 4

Based on the author's memories of a friendship in her childhood, this book tells of how the narrator and her friend, Carole, enjoyed a neighboring pond throughout the year. The focus is on the pond and the changes the seasons create. This is a beautiful book which celebrates the life cycles in that ecosystem.

Locker, Thomas. _Where the River Begins._ Dial Books for Young Readers, 1987. ISBN 0 8037 0089 X

Two boys who live on the banks of a river ask their grandfather to take them to its source. This involves a camping trip during which they witness a thunderstorm in the high meadows.

Provensen, Alice. _Shaker Lane._ Viking Children's Books, 1987. ISBN 0 670 81568 3

The neighborhood called Shaker Lane, so named because it first contains a Shaker meetinghouse, changes through the years. The people who take up residence there have few funds, and many folks in town, it is said, would be happy to see the whole area disappear. When the townsfolk decide to build a reservoir, it is inevitable that it will be located at the end of Shaker Lane. There's a strong correlation here with the book **Letting Swift River Go.**

Tafuri, Nancy. _Have You Seen My Duckling?_ Greenwillow Books, 1984. ISBN 0 688 02798 9

We hunt for a missing duckling and find it before the mother does, and along the way, we see much of the life of the pond.

Wiesner, David. _Tuesday._ Clarion Books, 1991. ISBN 0 395 55113 7

We start in the pond with a turtle who notices something strange. Then the frogs start rising on their lily pads, and the next thing you know, they're zooming all over town.

Yolen, Jane. _Letting Swift River Go._ Illustrated by Barbara Cooney. Little, Brown & Co., Children's Books, 1992. ISBN 0 316 96899 4

This story is the fictionalized account of an actual event. Several small towns were completely flooded in order to create a water supply for the city of Boston.

Poetry

Lewis, J. Patrick. _Earth Verses and Water Rhymes._ Illustrated by Robert Sabuda. Atheneum Books for Young Readers, 1991. ISBN 0 689 31693 3

There are 17 poems in this anthology which is grouped by seasons. Several involve water life.

Yolen, Jane. _Water MUSIC._ Boyds Mills Press, 1995. ISBN 1 56397 336 7

Many moods of water are explored through color photographs and poems.

Nonfiction

Bang, Molly. *Chattanooga Sludge.* Harcourt Brace & Co., 1996. ISBN 0 15 216345 X

Bang concentrates on a real-life hero in one of her few nonfiction works. First, she shows us the forces that lead to the creation of the Chattanooga Creek, and then, she shows us how various manufacturers filled it with toxic waste. Enter hero John Todd who has a machine and a collection of bacteria designed to eat away the sludge clogging the creek.

Cherry, Lynne. *A River Ran Wild.* Harcourt Brace & Co., 1992. ISBN 0 15 200542 0

We view history and progress through the changes in a river (the Nashua River in New Hampshire.) We see it first in its pristine glory, and the text is framed with illustrations of the wildlife that thrived in and around it. As humans arrive, they take things from the river, and these things are shown around the text, as well. Progress continues as first farms and then mills are constructed near the river, and, for awhile, we lose sight of the price the river pays for human progress. When we do look at it, it seems hopelessly polluted, but one woman starts a campaign to clean up the Nashua. The last picture shows it much improved, although it will never again be what it once was.

Dorros, Arthur. *Follow the Water from Brook to Ocean.* Harper Trophy, 1993. ISBN 0 06 445115 1

This book provides a clear description of the earthly part of the water cycle, starting with melting mountain snow and ending in the ocean. Along the way we take note of erosion and water pollution, as well as various reservoirs and dams.

Kalman, Bobbie. *The Gristmill.* Crabtree Publishing Co., 1991. ISBN 0 86505 486 X

This book looks at the pioneers and the construction of mills on the rivers.

Murphy, Bryan. *Experiment with Water.* Lerner Publishing Group, 1992. ISBN 0 8225 2453 8

This book offers ideas for activities that investigate the properties of water. The author explores the various forms of water first and then gives clear directions for investigating the water cycle, water pressure and surface tension among other things.

Reidel, Marlene. *From Ice to Rain.* Carolrhoda Books, 1981. ISBN 0 87614 157 2

This book follows the entire water cycle, starting with children skating on winter ice and ending up with a summer rain. It nicely combines seasons and elements.

Savage, Stephen. *Frog.* Thomson Learning, 1995. ISBN 1 56847 326 5

Large, full-color illustrations and brief, easy-to-read text combine to make an informative, accessible life science book on frogs.

Schwartz, David M. *The Hidden Life of the Pond.* Crown Books for Young Readers, 1988. ISBN 0 517 57060 2

Stunning color photos follow life in and around a pond during the course of a year. We start with a bullfrog as he frees himself from the spring mud. There's coverage of insect, bird and plant life, as well as that of the animals of the pond.

Trotter, Stuart. *First Questions and Answers about Water: Do Fish Drink?* Time-Life Books, 1993. ISBN 0 7835 0850 6

Although this book's question/answer format makes it difficult to use as a reference tool, it does provide a broad and clear introduction to water, both salt and fresh, including such physical science concepts as water flowing downhill and evaporation.

Vogel, Carole G. *The Great Midwest Flood.* Little, Brown & Co., Children's Books, 1995. ISBN 0 316 90248 9

This book provides a clear explanation of the causes and results of the flood of the Mississippi River basin in 1995.

SCIENCE: Desert

 COMMENTS

A theme study of the desert offers a chance to pursue the various unique flora and fauna of the dry areas as well as geology and weather. Broadening the theme to a study of the world's deserts allows class exploration of various cultures. We start with a book by Byrd Baylor and, indeed, this whole theme could lead into an author study of Baylor because most of her work is set in the deserts of the American Southwest. See page 178 for more information about Byrd Baylor and her books.

 PICTURE BOOK STARTER

Byrd Baylor's **I'm in Charge of Celebrations** (Simon & Schuster Books for Young Readers, 1986, ISBN 0 684 18579 2) centers on a young girl of the desert. She is asked if she is lonely, and she answers with exuberance, telling readers about the natural phenomena of the desert that she celebrates. Through her lyrical descriptions, we learn not only about the joys of the desert but about celebrating nature in small things and large.

ACTIVITIES

Language Arts
WRITING

► Read **I'm in Charge of Celebrations.** The narrator lists six celebrations of the desert. Describe one natural event in your area that you could celebrate Byrd Baylor's way.

► Read **Roxaboxen** (see book list). The children in **Roxaboxen** use things they find around the desert to build their town. If you were to build a town like that, what natural materials would you be apt to find?

► **The Three Little Javelinas** (see book list) is a desert version of "The Three Little Pigs." After sharing it, use desert creatures and situations to write a desert version of one of the other fairy tales.

► **How the Jack Rabbit Got His Ears** (see book list) is a "pourquoi" tale. That means it explains how something came to be. (See page 171 for other pourquoi tales.) Read it and then write a pourquoi tale about some other desert animal's special attribute.

Science

► List each animal and plant of the southwest American desert on individual index cards. Don't forget insects. After each animal's name, list some adjectives to describe it.

► Find out how each of those animals has adapted to life on the desert.

► Arrange the index cards described above in order of the animals' sizes.

► Make a display showing the special anatomical features of desert animals in sections labeled "Eyes of the Desert," "Feet of the Desert," and "Tongues of the Desert." Show how those features help the animals survive in the desert.

► Choose any desert animal from the index cards. Make an illustrated flow chart showing its life cycle.

► Draw the life cycle of any desert animal on a cardboard pizza plate. Place it on a bulletin board and connect it with colored yarn to a different animal life cycle. Place labels telling how those two animals relate to each other on the connecting yarn. The labels can read something like "both are egg-layers" or "this one eats that one." Keep making connections until all of the animal life cycles are connected.

► Visit a plant store or arboretum that has cacti. Take sketchpads, crayons, and pencils to make drawings of what you see.

► To demonstrate the way animals and plants of the desert conserve water, soak several sponges in water and then squeeze out the excess moisture. Place each of the sponges in a different environment: one uncovered in bright sunlight, one covered with wax paper in bright sunlight, one in shade uncovered, and one in a baggie uncovered. Find ways of measuring the amount of moisture left in each sponge after one hour.

► How much annual rainfall does a desert get? How much annual rainfall does your area get?

Social Studies

► How close to a desert are you? Mark your place and each of the world's deserts on a globe and measure with a tape measure or string.

► Find one unique feature of each of the world's deserts. Put pictures of that feature on a map of the world showing the deserts.

► www.arab.net/camels/welcome.html is a Web site that tells a lot about camels. After you've visited it, read **Ali, Child of the Desert** (see book list). On a map, find the deserts where camels are used.

Art

► Make sand pictures in bottles. Use food coloring to color the sand or use aquarium sand. Layer it in the bottle. When all the colors are laid down, carefully slide a knitting needle or knife along the sides of the glass to bring some of the colors up or down a bit.

► Look at paintings by Georgia O'Keeffe who was often inspired by the desert. Use some of the colors she used to make your own desert pictures.

► Make a large model of a saguaro cactus using cardboard and papier-mache. Use the Cactus Hotel book listed to tell you some of the animals you can place pictures of in and around the cactus.

BOOK LIST
Fiction

Albert, Richard E. *Alejandro's Gift.* Illustrated by Sylvia Long. Chronicle Books, 1994. ISBN 0 811 80436 4

An old man builds a waterhole for the animals of the southwestern American desert.

Baylor, Byrd. *Desert Voices.* Simon & Schuster Books for Young Readers, 1981. ISBN 0 684 16712 3

Each animal of the desert gets a page in this book to tell us of its life and place in the desert ecosystem.

Irbinskas, Heather. *How Jackrabbit Got His Very Long Ears.* Illustrated by Kenneth Spengler. Rising Moon Press, 1994. ISBN 0873 58566 6

This is an original pourquoi tale (a story that explains how something came to be) that features many desert animals and calls attention to their attributes.

James, Betsy. *Blow Away Soon.* G. P. Putnam's Sons Books for Young Readers, 1995. ISBN 0 399 22648 6

A little girl who lives in the desert is frightened by the wind, so her grandmother takes the opportunity to drive home a lesson about nature and life by taking the child to the top of a mountain to face the wind.

London, Jonathan. *Ali, Child of the Desert.* Illustrated by Ted Lewin. Lothrop, Lee & Shepard Books, 1997. ISBN 0 688 12560 3

The desert is the Sahara, and when Ali and his camel become lost in a dust storm, we learn a bit about the animals and people of the Sahara.

Lowell, Susan. *The Three Little Javelinas.* Northland Publishing Co., 1992. ISBN 0 87358 542 8

This tale is the southwestern version of "The Three Little Pigs," and it features a villainous coyote and three wild pigs of the desert. Nestled in the plot is a good bit of information about the area.

Lyon, George Ella. *Dreamplace.* Orchard Books, 1993. ISBN 0 531 05466 7

The desert of present-day Mesa Verde, Colorado, evokes a vision of the Anasazi who once lived there. The text is poetic; speaking of the desert, Lyon says, "and then one day when even trees were hungry [they] turned their backs and let it go." The illustrations convey the color and feeling of the desert and the author's respect for its people.

McLerran, Alice. *Roxaboxen.* Illustrated by Barbara Cooney. Puffin Books, 1992. ISBN 0 14 054475 5

Children of the desert construct a village outlined in desert stone and glass and create their own society with strict rules of behavior.

Mora, Pat. *The Desert Is My Mother: El Desierto Es Mi Madre.* Illustrated by Daniel Lechon. Arte Publico Press, 1994. ISBN 1 558 85121 6

This book's bilingual text tells us about a little girl who feels affinity for the desert in which she lives. The text is playful but contains much information about desert life and phenomena.

Steiner, Barbara A. *Desert Trip.* Illustrated by Ronald Himler. Sierra Club Books for Children, 1996. ISBN 0 871 56581 1

We go with a little girl and her mother as they enjoy a camping trip in the southwestern desert. The mother points out many of the desert plants and one beautiful flower in particular.

NONFICTION

Bash, Barbara. *Desert Giant: The World of the Saguaro.* Little, Brown & Co., Children's Books, 1989. ISBN 0 316 08301 1

Like **Cactus Hotel** (listed at right) but for a slightly older audience, this book explains the function of the cactus in the desert ecosystem.

Baylor, Byrd. *The Desert Is Theirs.* Aladdin Paperbacks, 1975. ISBN 0 689 71105 0

This is a book in praise of the desert and its people, as well as the animals that have adapted to its rugged environment. It discusses the Papago Indians who know the desert's beauty and secrets.

Buchanan, Ken. *It Rained on the Desert Today.* Rising Moon Press, 1994. ISBN 0 873 58575 5

Beautiful watercolors and poetic text show a rainstorm's approach, presence and effect on the dry land.

Dunphy, Madeleine. *Here Is the Southwestern Desert.* Hyperion Books for Children, 1995. ISBN 0 7868 0049 6

This book's rhyming text is in a "this is the house that Jack built" format, but instead of describing the process of building a house, it builds the food chain of the desert animals.

Flanagan, Alice K. *Desert Birds.* Children's Press, 1996. ISBN 0 516 01087 5

Color photographs illustrate this book about birds in the world's deserts—including polar deserts.

George, Jean Craighead. *One Day in the Desert.* HarperCollins Children's Books, 1983. ISBN 0 690 04341 4

We spend a hot July day in the Sonoran Desert of Arizona observing the mechanisms that the desert's plants and animals use to stay cool and following a wounded mountain lion who must get to water to survive.

Guiberson, Brenda. *Cactus Hotel.* Henry Holt & Co. Books for Young Readers, 1991. ISBN 0 8050 2960 5

A saguaro cactus is an ecosystem within the desert ecosystem. This book shows how each thing that happens to the cactus starts a chain of events affecting many animals and plants in and around it.

Landau, Elaine. *Desert Mammals.* Children's Press, 1997. ISBN 0 516 26097 9

Mammals in deserts around the world are shown in color photographs accompanied by clear, easy-to-read text.

Laukel, Hans Gerold. *The Desert Fox Family Book.* North-South Books, 1996. ISBN 1 558 58580 X

The desert fox of the Sahara Desert is an elusive but attractive animal and in this book we follow its family in the desert.

Lesser, Carolyn. *Storm on the Desert.* Harcourt Brace & Co., 1997. ISBN 0 15 272198 3

There are many books about the desert, but this is the only one I know of that deals with a desert storm and its effects on the wildlife.

McLerran, Alice. *The Year of the Ranch.* Viking Children's Books, 1996. ISBN 0 670 85131 0

In this story, loosely based on the deeds of the author's grandparents, we see a determined man who moves his urban family into the desert where he means to farm and lay claim to a piece of land. Adjustment is particularly hard for the wife and two of the children. The endeavor fails, but not without a spirited attempt to succeed.

Siebert, Diane. *Mojave.* HarperCollins Children's Books, 1993. ISBN 0 06 443283 1

The narrator of this book is the desert itself. The text is a poem, and the information is scientific. The illustrations provide wonderful perspectives on the desert and its life forms.

Simon, Seymour. *Deserts.* Morrow Junior Books, 1990. ISBN 0 688 07416 2

Of all the books in this list, this one is the most informative. The colored photographs of the different deserts are breathtaking, and the text offers accessible and fascinating information.

SCIENCE: Woods

 COMMENTS

A theme on the woods allows investigation of animal and plant classifications, and its connection with ecology and pollution is obvious. Because so many children's picture books have woodland creatures for characters, this theme can help children learn to distinguish between realism and fantasy or between fact and fiction.

 PICTURE BOOK STARTER

Anne Mazer's **The Salamander Room** (Alfred A. Knopf Books for Young Readers, 1984, ISBN 0 394 82945 X) is a good book to begin this study of the woods and the creatures in it because the accent here is on environment. When Brian finds a salamander in the woods, he brings it home for a pet. Determined to keep his pet happy, he builds an ever larger and more complex ecosystem in his bedroom. Eventually even the roof must be raised. The text allows us to think about the forest layer by layer.

ACTIVITIES

Language Arts
MAKING INFERENCES
▶ In **Owl Moon,** the child has been looking forward to this trip for a long time. Make a list of the clues in the book that indicate this.

WRITING
▶ **The Magpie's Nest** (see book list) is a pourquoi tale (a story that explains how something came to be; see page 168 for other pourquoi tales) that explains why birds build different kinds of nests. After sharing it, make up a pourquoi tale about some other animal's special attributes.

▶ **Counting on the Woods** (see book list) is a counting book based on things in the woods. Use it as a model to make up your own alphabet book of the woods. Use some sort of block print for your illustrations.

▶ After sharing **Owl Moon** (see book list), speculate on the fact that, if the people in **Owl Moon** were looking for a different animal in the woods, they might have had to go at a different time or during a different season. Make up a story about a different walk in the woods.

Science
▶ Adopt a tree in the woods, if possible. If not, adopt a tree someplace else. Observe the tree at least once a week. Keep a journal of your observations.

▶ Measure off a square foot of ground in the woods. Use string and stakes to mark your square foot. Visit it frequently. Take notes on everything you see in that area. Be sure to note any insect that goes through it.

►Make bark rubbings of various tree trunks. Make a display of the rubbings and leaf pictures and label them.

►Go on a bird walk. Early morning is the best time to see birds. Count the birds you see or the species of birds you see. Listen for birdcalls. How many can you recognize?

►Make pictures of as many plants and animals, including bugs, that you could find in woods nearest you. Place these pictures on the bulletin board. Use yarn to connect pictures showing predator/prey. Place labels on those strings to show how these animals are connected.

Art

►Use sponges and paint to create a mural of a forest. Paint animals in and around the woods.

►Look at the work of various artists to see how they show woods and trees. Try some of their techniques to create your own wood scenes.

BOOK LIST
Picture Books

Arnosky, Jim. **Every Autumn Comes the Bear.** *G. P. Putnam's Sons Books for Young Readers, 1993. ISBN 0 399 22508 0*

Just as this book's title suggests, the appearance of a bear on a farm in Vermont is a yearly occurrence. Every fall, a bear wanders over the farm in search of his winter den. The illustrations are realistic, and the woods are carefully portrayed.

Brown, Ruth. **The World That Jack Built.** *Dutton Children's Books, 1991. ISBN 0 525 44635 4*

This is a strong but simple story about pollution. We and a cat follow a butterfly through the fields and woods to the factory polluting it all. The text is in a "this is the house that Jack built" pattern.

Chall, Marsha Wilson. **Up North at the Cabin.** *Lothrop, Lee & Shepard Books, 1992. ISBN 0 688 09732 4*

It's summer in the woods and, in a style reminiscent of McCloskey's **Time of Wonder** (see page 41), we watch a loon and a moose in the summer light.

Cherry, Lynne. **Flute's Journey.** *Harcourt Brace & Co., 1997. ISBN 0 15 292853 7*

We follow Flute, a wood thrush, from its birth in a dogwood tree in Maryland to the rain forest in Central America and back. This is fictionalized fact.

Foster, Joanna. **The Magpie's Nest.** *Clarion Books, 1995. ISBN 0 395 62155 0*

This is a pourquoi story telling why birds build different kinds of nests. The magpie builds a complex nest and attempts to show the other birds how to do it, but each bird hears only part of the lesson before flying off to build its own nest.

Gile, John. *The First Forest.* John Gile, 1989. ISBN 0 910941 01 7

This is a pourquoi story that explains why some trees lose their leaves while others stay green.

Lyon, George Ella. *Counting on the Woods.* DK Publishing, 1998. ISBN 0 7894 2480 0

This book's text is poetic, and we count the flora and fauna of the woods using color photographs.

Manson, Christopher. *The Tree in the Wood: An Old Nursery Song.* North-South Books, 1993. ISBN 1 55858 192 8

This cumulative song about the life in and around a tree is illustrated by woodcuts.

Romanova, Natalia. *Once There Was a Tree.* Dial Books for Young Readers, 1985. ISBN 0 8037 0235 3

A woodsman cuts down a tree, and the resulting stump is claimed by a variety of animals in order to live, rest, or eat there.

Schoenherr, John. *Bear.* Philomel Books, 1991. ISBN 0 399 22177 8

A young Alaskan bear is shown searching for its mother, but the author avoids anthropomorphism. We watch him as he finally turns on the bear shadow that was following him, prepared to defend himself.

Yolen, Jane. *Owl Moon.* Illustrated by John Schoenherr. Philomel Books, 1987. ISBN 0 399 21457 7

A father and child go on a moonlit winter night to see an owl. The child has been looking forward to this for a long time and knows the rules about no talking and making your own warmth. This book is full of respect for the wild and for family tradition.

NONFICTION

Appelbaum, Diane. *Giants in the Land.* Houghton Mifflin Books for Children, 1993. ISBN 0 395 64720 7

This is a book about the culling of New England's white pine primary forest during colonial times. The trees were used as masts for British warships, a resource that was lost to the British during the Revolution.

Arnosky, Jim. *Crinkleroot's Book of Animal Tracking.* Simon & Schuster Books for Young Readers, 1989. ISBN 0 02 705851 4

We walk through the woods with Crinkleroot as he identifies animal signs: pellets, antlers and tooth marks, as well as tracks.

Arnosky, Jim. *Crinkleroot's Guide to Knowing the Trees.* Simon & Schuster Books for Young Readers, 1992. ISBN 0 02 705855 7

Crinkleroot explains the parts of a tree and then helps us identify trees using those parts.

Arnosky, Jim. *In the Forest: A Portfolio of Paintings.* Lothrop, Lee & Shepard Books, 1989. ISBN 0 688 09138 5

These paintings cover various aspects of the forest. Each painting is accompanied by a description and remarks.

Brenner, Barbara. *The Tremendous Tree Book.* Boyds Mills Press, 1998. ISBN 1 563 97718 4

This is a very useful book for young audiences. In it, we learn about the various functions of each part of a tree, as well as the ecosystems the trees create.

Burnie, David. *Tree.* Alfred A. Knopf Books for Young Readers, 1988. ISBN 0 394 99617 8

This is an Eyewitness book, and it is a wonderful source of information on all kinds of trees, their life cycles and their use to humans.

Dorros, Arthur. *A Tree Is Growing.* Scholastic, 1997. ISBN 0 590 45300 9

In a manner somewhat similar to Bert Kitchen's book **And So They Build,** trees and the animals that survive around and on them are shown accompanied by simple information on the main part of the page and more complex information in the side bars.

Frazer, Simon. **The Mushroom Hunt.** Candlewick Press, 1994. ISBN 1 56402 500 4

A family of mushroom hunters takes us through the woods. There is good information about mushrooms and clear information about poisonous ones.

George, Jean Craighead. **The Moon of the Salamanders.** HarperCollins Children's Books, 1992. ISBN 0 06 022694 3

George did a series of these "Moon" books, each of which follows a different animal. In this case it's a salamander, and we follow it from the woods to a pond. Along the way, attention is drawn to the environment and the ecosystem.

Lang, Aubrey. **Eagles.** Sierra Club Books for Children, 1990. ISBN 0 316 51383 0

The text in this book is probably beyond the understanding of many young children, but the photographs and their captions are fascinating and full of information.

Franklin Watts, Editors. **Living Tree.** Franklin Watts, 1990. ISBN 0 531 14007 5

This book is part of Watts' Watching Nature series. Color photographs illustrate it with lots of information about trees, as well as information on how to take bark rubbings.

SCIENCE: Gardens

COMMENTS

Probably the main reason for a theme of this nature is the large number of very good picture books that have been set in and around a garden. It ties in nicely with themes about the seasons and a study of plants, of course, but also allows easy connections with insect themes (see page 28). Nutrition is another obvious connection.

PICTURE BOOK STARTER

The Gardener, by Sarah Stewart and David Small (see book list), is an excellent starting point for this study of gardens because it is both visually and textually interesting. The grim, dark lines of the railroad station and of the tenements provide a wonderful contrast to the gradually blooming garden. This is a focus book (see page 118).

ACTIVITIES

(For more gardening activities see page 118.)

Language Arts
BUILDING VOCABULARY
►Start with the flowers listed in Arnold and Anita Lobel's **The Rose in My Garden** (see book list). List them and draw pictures of them. Add to that list the names and drawings of other plants mentioned in the other picture books.

►Play with the concept of "garden." How small can it be and still be a garden? How big can it be without being a crop?

MAKING COMPARISONS
►In some of the books listed the garden is the focal point of the book. In others, the characters are the main part of the story, while the garden serves as the location. Divide the books into these categories.

►Make large pictures of the gardener in each of the books listed below. Around each character place adjectives that you think describe him or her.

INTERPRETING THE TEXT
►Read **Small Green Snake** (see book list). In it, two characters scare each other. Who gets scared? Why?

MAKING INFERENCES
►In two of the books listed, the text pattern is similar to that of "This Is the House That Jack Built," but they are very different in mood. What do you think is the author's reason for writing each of these books? What does he or she want us to feel?

Math
► Sort seeds by various categories.

Science
► Plan a fantasy garden based on color. What flowers will you use? Can you design a garden that emphasizes one color?

► Look at gardening tools from the point of view of simple machines. Which ones are levers, inclined planes, etc.?

► Plant some bean seeds in a jar between

a blotter or sponge and the glass. Dampen the sponge of all but one of the jars. Put one of the jars in a sunny place, another in a dark place. Figure out other ways to conduct experiments with these seeds to get information on how plants grow.

► Visit a garden supply center to find out how plants are cared for there.

► Plant a school garden.

► Take clippings from the garden or from houseplants and care for them over a winter.

► Find ways to make the school grounds more beautiful with plants.

► How much of your nutritional requirements can you fill with food from a garden? Get a list of the minimum daily requirements or look at the food pyramid at **www.kidsfood.org/f_pyramid/pyramid. html.**

► Figure out which of those requirements could be grown in a garden. Find a way to present this information to the rest of the class. You could use puppets, posters, a play, or a mural for instance.

► Try these Web sites for further information about nutrition: **www.kidsfood.org/** and **exhibits.pacsci.org/nutrition/.**

Social Studies

► Find out about community gardens. How do they work? How do they change the community?

► If you were gardening in another country, you might not be growing the same kinds of food as we do here. Find out about some crops that might be grown in China, Israel and Guatemala for instance.

Art

► Find a medium you like and make pictures of gardens. Title your picture.

► Make a large, three-dimensional garden on a bulletin board using construction paper flowers and vegetables, as well as painted and paper greenery.

► Look for paintings of gardens such as those by Monet.

Music

► Find and sing "The Garden Song" by Dave Mallet on Pete Seeger's record **Circles and Seasons.** It was also recorded by Dave Mallet and by John Denver.

BOOK LIST
Fiction

Albert, Richard E. *Alejandro's Gift.* Chronicle Books, 1994. ISBN 0 811 80436 4

Alejandro lives alone in the desert where he plants a vegetable garden for his own pleasure. When he realizes that many animals come to drink from his irrigation furrows, he builds a sheltered water hole for them.

Appell, Kathi. *Watermelon Day.* Henry Holt & Co. Books for Young Readers, 1996. ISBN 0 8050 2304 6

In this story, we wait with one little girl as she lovingly tends a single watermelon in order to present it to her family.

Carle, Eric. *The Tiny Seed.* Picture Book Studio, 1987. ISBN 0 88708 015 4

This book isn't about a whole garden, but about seeds that are dispersed and attempting to survive.

Carlstrom, Nancy W. *Blow Me a Kiss, Miss Lilly.* HarperCollins Children's Books, 1990. ISBN 0 06 021013 3

Miss Lilly lovingly tends her garden, and Sara, who lives across the street from Miss Lilly, spends a lot of time there helping with the chores. Each time Sara leaves, she and Miss Lilly blow each other a goodbye kiss. When Miss Lilly falls ill and dies, Sara takes care of both her cat and her garden.

Cole, Henry. *Jack's Garden.* Greenwillow Books, 1995. ISBN 0 688 13501 3

Using the rhythmic pattern of "This Is the House That Jack Built," this book takes us through the steps of planting a garden. The illustrations provide additional information.

Cooney, Barbara. *Miss Rumphius.* Puffin Books, 1985. ISBN 0 14 050539 3

Miss Rumphius has fulfilled her ambitions and all the goals urged on her by her grandfather except one: that of making the world more beautiful. This she accomplishes as an old lady by scattering lupine seeds wherever she walks.

Cutler, Jane. *Mr. Carey's Garden.* Houghton Mifflin Books for Children, 1996. ISBN 0 395 68191 X

This book is about a neighborhood full of gardening experts, and they all have advice for Mr. Carey when his garden is overrun with snails. He responds to each advice giver very politely saying that he sees things in a different light. When we see him in the garden in the moonlight, we know what he means.

Darian, Shea. *Grandpa's Garden.* Dawn Publications, 1996. ISBN 1 883220 41 6

Every Saturday, a grandfather and a little girl work together in his garden. When he becomes ill, she continues to tend the garden so that the harvest, when he returns, is just what it should be.

DeFelice, Cynthia. *Mule Eggs.* Illustrated by Mike Shenon. Orchard Books, 1994. ISBN 0 531 06843 9

This book is about a con game. Patrick is a recent immigrant, and he is conned by a farmer into paying 25 dollars for a pumpkin that he is convinced is a mule egg. Patrick gets his revenge.

Gray, Libba Moore. *Small Green Snake.* Illustrated by Holly Meade. Orchard Books, 1994. ISBN 0 531 08694 1

This is a delightfully funny story of a little snake who, although warned not to do so, visits a garden where he encounters a hideous monster (a woman holding gardening shears). Each scares the other, and the little snake returns home with his scary tale, which makes his siblings anxious to see the garden, as well.

Hines, Anna Grossnickle. *Miss Emma's Wild Garden.* Greenwillow Books, 1997. ISBN 0 688 14692 9

This story is about an informal and slightly chaotic backyard garden. Chloe is alarmed at its disorder, but Miss Emma knows each plant and loves them all.

Hurd, Thacher. **The Pea Patch Jig.** *Crown Books for Young Readers, 1986. ISBN 0 06 443383 8*

There's trouble afoot in this garden as a mouse family gets ready for a party. The baby mouse falls asleep in a head of lettuce and nearly ends up in a salad. Later, she beans Grandfather with a tomato but is redeemed when she uses her peashooter to discourage a marauding fox.

Joyce, William. **The Leaf Men: And the Brave Good Bugs.** *Laura, 1997. ISBN 0 06 027237 6*

When the old woman who loves her garden becomes ill, the garden creatures combine efforts to save her while thwarting the efforts of the evil Spider Queen.

Lobel, Anita. **Alison's Zinnia.** *Greenwillow Books, 1990. ISBN 0 688 08865 1*

Alliteration abounds in this alphabet book in which each girl hands a flower to the next in line.

Lobel, Arnold. **The Rose in My Garden.** *Illustrated by Anita Lobel. Greenwillow Books, 1985. ISBN 0 688 02587 0*

This cumulative story tells of a simple garden incident. In the process we look at various beautiful flowers and read some wonderful words describing them.

Nolen, Jerdine. **Harvey Potter's Balloon Farm.** *Mulberry Books, 1989. ISBN 0 688 07887 7*

Balloons grow on Harvey Potter's farm. They swell up from the ground like any root vegetable, and the leftover stalks are gathered into bunches like corn after harvest. The tone is serious as we learn of the trials and tribulations of a balloon farmer.

Perkins, Lynne Rae. **Home Lovely.** *Greenwillow Books, 1995. ISBN 0 688 13687 7*

In this slight, tender story, Janelle and her daughter, Tiffany, have moved to an isolated trailer, and Tiffany stays there alone for some part of each day. She transplants some seedlings nearer to the trailer, hoping they are trees. Bob, the mail carrier, tells her they are tomatoes, melons and potatoes, and he brings her flowering plants to make the home more beautiful.

Ryder, Joanne. **My Father's Hands.** *Illustrated by Mark Graham. Morrow Junior Books, 1994. ISBN 0 688 09189 X*

The author's father's hands are lovingly portrayed as they gently work around the plants in the garden.

Rylant, Cynthia. **This Year's Garden.** *Illustrated by Mary Szilagyi. Bradbury Press, 1984. ISBN 0 02 777970 X*

Adults and children survey a garden and make appropriate plans for it. The adults discuss what to plant this spring while the children anticipate the fun of working in the garden. Warm weather comes at last, and the crop is readied. We follow the garden's year.

Stern, Maggie. **The Missing Sunflowers.** *Illustrated by Donna Ruff. Greenwillow Books, 1997. ISBN 0 688 14873 5*

Mrs. Potter gives a boy some sunflower seeds. He has great success with them until someone or something begins stealing the flowers.

Stewart, Sarah. **The Gardener.** *Illustrated by David Small. Farrar Strauss & Giroux Books for Young Readers, 1997. ISBN 0 374 32517 0*

This lovely book is set in the time of the Great Depression. Lydia is sent to live with her uncle and help him in the bakery. He is a grim, unsmiling man, and Lydia is determined to make him smile. She does so by transforming the roof of their tenement into a glorious garden. This is a focus book (see page 118).

Van Allsburg, Chris. **The Garden of Abdul Gasazi.** Houghton Mifflin Books for Children, 1979. ISBN 0 395 27804 X

When Alan's dog, Fritz, runs into Abdul Gasazi's garden, he is turned into a duck, or at least he might have been. Wonderful images of topiary are everywhere in this book.

Watson, Mary. **The Butterfly Seeds.** Morrow Junior Books, 1995. ISBN 0 688 14132 3

Jake's grandfather gives him a packet of butterfly seeds when Jake and his family immigrate to America. Once in the New York tenement that is now their home, he and some other immigrants build a window box in which they plant the seeds and wait for butterflies.

White, Linda. **Too Many Pumpkins.** Illustrated by Lloyd Megan. Holiday House, 1996. ISBN 0 8234 1245 8

This book is about an inadvertent garden. A woman who lives alone hates pumpkins because, when she was a child, they had to eat lots of pumpkins in order to keep from starving. Then, a pumpkin rolls off a passing truck and smashes in her yard. Appalled by the mess and what made that mess, the woman buries the evidence. Soon she has a bumper crop of pumpkins.

Wolff, Ferida. **The Emperor's Garden.** Tambourine Books, 1994. ISBN 0 688 11651 5

This folktale-like story tells about the people of old China who wanted the Emperor to notice them when he passed through their village on his way to the summer palace. They created a beautiful garden by working together, and everything was fine—until they tried to come up with a name for the garden.

Nonfiction

Creasy, Rosalind. **Blue Potatoes, Orange Tomatoes.** Sierra Club Books for Children, 1994. ISBN 0 871 56576 5

This book encourages children to plant a garden of unusually colored vegetables. Directions are included, as is an address where you can send for the seeds.

Ehlert, Lois. **Growing Vegetable Soup.** Harcourt Brace & Co., 1987. ISBN 0 15 232575 1

A father and child plant a garden together, then reap the harvest to make soup.

Heller, Ruth. **Plants That Never Ever Bloom.** Price Stern Sloan, 1984. ISBN 0 448 18964 X

Lichens, moss and mushrooms are the plants that Heller's glorious illustrations and rhyming text investigates.

Heller, Ruth. **The Reason for a Flower.** Price Stern Sloan, 1992. ISBN 0 448 41091 5

This beautiful book analyzes the parts of a flower and then shows how flowering plants reproduce.

McMillan, Bruce. **Counting Wildflowers.** Mulberry Books, 1986. ISBN 0 688 14027 0

This is a lovely photographic and counting book in which varieties of wild flowers are lovingly displayed.

Morgan, Sally. **Flowers, Trees, and Fruits.** Kingfisher, 1996. ISBN 0 7534 5032 1

This book provides an informal, easy-to-understand explanation of plants and experiments to investigate them.

SCIENCE: Mammals

 COMMENTS

This theme is big enough to take a lifetime to complete. You have to decide whether to restrict your mammal study to one area or to make it worldwide and therefore less detailed. There's no shortage of good books about mammals, and the theme provides a wonderful opportunity to compare realistic and fantastic literature, as well as fiction and nonfiction books.

 PICTURE BOOK STARTER

In **Who Is the Beast?**, by Keith Baker (Harcourt Brace & Co., 1990, ISBN 0 15 200122 0), a tiger walks through the jungle. Each creature that sees him reacts with fear because of some attribute the tiger displays. The tiger is puzzled. Who is this beast they fear? When he looks in the water, he sees no beast, only himself. The tiger returns to confront each animal that fled in fear and points out the similarities between them. The story is told in rhyme, and each page presents another point of view.

ACTIVITIES

Language Arts

BUILDING VOCABULARY

▶ Start a list of mammals. Because there are thousands of mammals, this list should grow throughout the theme. Suggest that students know a little bit about every animal they put on the list each day.

MAKING COMPARISONS

▶ Read and share **Who Is the Beast?** In it, the tiger sees similarities between himself and each animal of the jungle. Make those comparisons into sentences, such as, "The tiger is like a bee because they both have stripes." "The tiger is like a snake because they both have eyes that are green and round."

DISTINGUISHING REALISM FROM FANTASY

▶ Read **Dear Mr. Blueberry** (see book list). In it, a little girl writes to a man for information about whales because she is sure that she has seen one in a pond in her backyard. (The pond is shown to be a small wading pool.) Mr. Blueberry writes back with information about whales, assuring her that it is not possible to find a whale in a freshwater pond. The child uses the information he sends to make her whale more comfortable. Neither the text nor the illustrations negate the reality of her whale, and children may decide either to agree with her that the whale is real or let reality intrude and side with Mr. Blueberry.

►Find picture books in which animals are dressed and behave like people, and compare them to the books listed in which the same animals behave like animals. Make lists of the ways the animals in these two types of books are different.

WRITING

►On a pocket chart, place the format below. Words and pictures of attributes, and words and pictures of mammals should be available to place in the chart. Work the chart with the whole class first and then let small groups of children use it.

> I have a _____.
> I could be a _____ or a
> _____.
> But I also have a _____.
> I must be a _____.

► Suggest that each child select a mammal to investigate. Put up an information bulletin board and suggest that children leave notes about information they are looking for and information they have found that might help others.

Science

►Make pictures of mammals on cards. Use the cards for an attribute game. Place the cards face down on a surface. Players turn over two cards at a time and try to find four things their mammals have in common. If they can do it, they take the trick. If not, they replace the cards, and it's the next player's turn.

► Use the mammal picture cards to make food chains, to arrange according to size and to put in alphabetical order.

► One of the characteristics of mammals, fur, is easily identified on most mammals. Put up pictures of all kinds of animals, intermingling pictures of reptiles, mollusks and birds with mammals. Ask children to take down all the animals that do not have fur.

► The other two attributes for mammals are less readily distinguishable: the ability to give milk and the possession of three middle-ear bones. Children can begin to deduce the first with pictures of mammals feeding their young.

► With the children, make a display featuring many animals. Each should have a label like the following: This is a tiger. It has three middle-ear bones. Its fur is brown and orange. It has from two to three cubs at a time, and the mother feeds them with her own milk. It is an endangered species.

Social Studies

►Use a world map and animal stamps to show where the mammals you've talked about live. Mark the endangered species differently.

Art

►Using paint, sponges and large brushes, make background murals for jungle, desert, pond, and woodland habitats. Have children draw and cut out mammals to place in their habitats.

Physical Education

► Pick a mammal and then move as if you were that animal. Let others guess what animal you are.

BOOK LIST
Fiction

Alarcon, Karen Beaumont. *Louella Mae, She's Run Away.* Illustrated by Rosanne Litzinger. Henry Holt & Co. Books for Young Readers, 1997. ISBN 0 805 03532 X

Everyone's looking for Louella Mae, and the rhyming text encourages us to guess at the word that will complete each line. We don't discover that Louella Mae is a pig until we find her with her piglets in the tub.

Baehr, Patricia. *Mouse in the House.* Holiday House, 1994. ISBN 0 8234 1102 8

Mrs. Teapot is annoyed by the mouse in her house and seeks advice as to how to get rid of it. Everyone she asks has a different solution, and she tries each one. However, each solution creates a different problem until she decides she'll keep the mouse.

Baker, Keith. *Who Is the Beast?* Harcourt Brace & Co., 1990. ISBN 0 15 296057 0

A tiger goes through the jungle creating fear with every step. We learn about the tiger attribute by attribute before we learn that we are the tiger.

Blake, Jon. *Daley B.* Illustrated by Axel Scheffler. Candlewick Press, 1992. ISBN 1 56402 078 9

Daley B. is a rabbit but doesn't know it. In the process of his discovery, we are treated to a list of attributes and a funny story.

Brett, Jan. *Annie and the Wild Animals.* Houghton Mifflin Books for Children, 1985. ISBN 0 395 37800 1

When Annie's cat, Taffy, disappears, Annie becomes lonely and leaves corn cakes at the edge of the woods to attract another pet. Animals come, but not one of them would be suitable as a pet. Then Taffy returns with her kittens.

Casey, Patricia. *My Cat Jack.* Candlewick Press, 1994. ISBN 1 56402 660 4

This book is just a series of statements about a boy's cat, but, in reading it, we learn about many of the cat's habits and attributes.

Cowcher, Helen. *Tigress.* Farrar Strauss & Giroux Books for Young Readers, 1991. ISBN 0 374 47781 7

This story gives us glimpses of the tiger that has villagers worried about their safety and their animals' safety. The game warden wants her left alone, but the villagers want her killed. A compromise is reached.

Cowcher, Helen. *Jaguar.* Scholastic, 1997. ISBN 0 590 29937 9

This book looks at the life of a jaguar in the rain forest.

Dalgliesh, Alice. *The Bears on Hemlock Mountain.* Simon & Schuster Books for Young Readers, 1990. ISBN 0 689 70497 6

This is more of a short story than a picture book. Jonathan has to come back over the mountain after dark. He's been assured there are no bears on Hemlock Mountain, but there's at least one, and Jonathan has to hide under the cooking pot to keep him at bay.

DeRegniers, Beatrice. *So Many Cats.* Illustrated by Ellen Weiss. Houghton Mifflin Books for Children, 1988. ISBN 0 89919 700 0

This is the story of how one household came to have 12 cats. We learn each cat's story in rhyme.

Dragonwagon, Crescent. *Bat in the Dining Room.* Cavendish, 1997. ISBN 0 76145007 6

A bat gets into a crowded hotel dining room and creates havoc. One little unconventional girl, Melissa, understands that the bat is also panicked. She crawls under a table and watches the bat's frantic attempts to escape and then opens the door for it to get out.

Fox-Davies, Sarah. **Little Caribou.** Candlewick Press, 1996. ISBN 1 56402 923 9

This book's art echoes the Inuit people, and the story follows a young caribou through one year.

Franklin, Kristine. **The Wolfhound.** Illustrated by Kris Waldherr. Lothrop, Lee & Shepard Books, 1996. ISBN 0 688 13674 5

In Czarist Russia, a boy finds a wolfhound lying nearly dead in the snow. He nurses it back to health although his brother warns him that no one but a nobleman is allowed to own a wolfhound.

Hofmeyr, Dianne. **Do the Whales Still Sing?** Dial Books for Young Readers, 1995. ISBN 0 8037 1741 5

An old man tells a boy about a sea captain who hunted whales aggressively and happily until he heard the whales sing.

James, Simon. **Dear Mr. Blueberry.** Margaret K. McElderry Books, 1991. ISBN 90 689 50529 9

A little girl writes to Mr. Blueberry for information about whales because she thinks she has one in her backyard pond.

Kinsey-Warnock, Natalie. **The Bear That Heard Crying.** Cobblehill, 1993. ISBN 0 525 65103 9

This book is based on fact. A three-year-old girl was lost for four days in the woods of New Hampshire and was befriended by a bear.

London, Jonathan. **Jackrabbit.** Crown Books for Young Readers, 1996. ISBN 0 517 596571

A baby jackrabbit is rescued by a human who teaches it to survive on its own before releasing it.

London, Sara. **Firehorse Max.** HarperCollins Children's Books, 1997. ISBN 0 06 205094 X

Bubba has grown too old to pull the horse cart any longer so Grandpa buys a retired fire horse, Max. Every time Max hears the fire bell, he bolts for the fire.

Meade, Holly. **John Willy and Freddy McGee.** Cavendish, 1998. ISBN 0 7414 5033 5

John and Freddy are guinea pigs. They have a safe and boring life in a cage until the day they get out. There's a lot of adventure waiting for them, especially in the pool table. Then, chased by the cat, they run back to their cage—for a while.

Moore, Inga. **Six Dinner Sid.** Simon & Schuster Books for Young Readers, 1991. ISBN 0 671 69613 5

Each of six families on Aristotle Street thinks that Sid is their cat. Every family feeds him dinner, which is fine until he is dragged to the doctor six times and fed medicine six times.

Murphy, Jim. **The Call of the Wolves.** Demco, 1994. ISBN 0 606 06949 6

A young wolf is separated from the pack, and survival relies on getting back to it.

Ormerod, Jan. **101 Things to Do with a Baby.** Morrow Junior Books, 1984. ISBN 0 688 03802 6

In the process of reading this book's 101 things, we learn a lot about babies and how they behave.

Rathmann, Peggy. **Good Night, Gorilla.** G. P. Putnam's Sons Books for Young Readers, 1994. ISBN 0 399 22445 9

All the animals in this zoo book are mammals, except the armadillo. The text is restricted to very few words, making this delightful and very funny book ideal for first readers.

Rounds, Glen. **Once We Had a Horse.** Holiday House, 1971. ISBN 0 8234 1241 5

Two bored and isolated children spend a summer with an old horse. The drawings are funny and so is the flatly stated text.

Rylant, Cynthia. **The Old Woman Who Named Things.** *Harcourt Brace & Co., 1996. ISBN 0 15 257809 9*

An old woman has resolved to name only things that cannot die because she grieves for friends and family she has lost. She names furniture and her car, but, when a stray puppy comes to her door, she feeds him but will not name him. When he leaves, she goes to the pound to get him but must have a name in order to claim him.

Schoenherr, John. **Bear.** *Philomel Books, 1991. ISBN 0 399 22177 8*

A young Alaskan bear wakes up to find his mother gone. He tries to find her but ends up taking on the role of an adult bear after he faces down the bear shadow which pursued him.

Segal, Lore. **The Story of Mrs. Lovewright and Purrless Her Cat.** *DK Publishing, 1996. ISBN 0 679 88085 2*

Mrs. Lovewright wants a cat to sit in her lap and purr. What she gets is a cat with a mind of its own.

Seymour, Tres. **Hunting the White Cow.** *Orchard Books, 1993. ISBN 0 531 07085 9*

A family's white cow has disappeared, and Pa takes more and more people with him each day as he pursues the cow. His daughter offers to help but is refused or ignored. In very funny text we learn how she got the white cow.

Sheldon, Dyan. **The Whales' Song.** *Illustrated by Gary Blythe. Dial Books for Young Readers, 1991. ISBN 0 8037 0972 2*

Grandmother tells Lilly of a time when she was young and whales were plentiful. She used to go to the pier to hear them sing. Her uncle says that whales were useful for their meat and oil. Lilly throws a gift from the pier and listens to the whales sing in the moonlight.

Standiford, Natalie. **The Bravest Dog Ever: The True Story of Balto.** *Random House, 1989. ISBN 0 394 89695 5*

This book is about the diphtheria epidemic in Nome in 1925 and a dog sled team, led by Balto, that brought medication through the winter ice.

Thomas, Patricia. **Stand Back Said the Elephant.** *Lothrop, Lee & Shepard Books, 1990. ISBN 0 688 09338 8*

An elephant is about to sneeze and all the animals (mostly mammals) beg him not to do so, because the last time he did, great havoc resulted.

Wild, Margaret. **Big Cat Dreaming.** *Illustrated by Anne Spudvilas. Annick Press, 1997. ISBN 1 55037 493 1*

Grandma's got a big cat and a small dog. She says she thinks cats dream of being kittens and her dog dreams of being a pup. She dreams of her own childhood and tells the kids about it.

Nonfiction

Brandenburg, Jim. Scruffy: A Wolf Finds His Place in the Pack. Walker & Co., 1996. ISBN 0 802 78446 1

One young outcast wolf on Ellesmere Island finds a role for himself in the pack, and we watch him do it. This is a fascinating look at wolf behavior.

Brandenburg, Jim. An American Safari. Walker & Co., 1985. ISBN 0 8027 8319 8

A nature photographer takes us to the prairie and shows us the prairie dogs and the buffalo, among other animals.

Darling, Kathy. Lemurs: On Location. Lothrop, Lee & Shepard Books, 1998. ISBN 0 688 12539 5

This text is quite lengthy but those who get through it will get a fascinating look at the variety of lemurs who thrive in Madagascar.

Davies, Nicola. Big Blue Whale. Candlewick Press, 1997. ISBN 1 56402 895 X

Much is made of comparative sizes in this very useful book on one species of whale.

Douglas-Hamilton, Oria. The Elephant Family Book. North-South Books, 1990. ISBN 1 55858 549 4

The elephants are in Tanzania, and we learn the story of the herd from a gamekeeper there.

D'Vincent, Cynthia. The Whale Family Book. North-South Books, 1988. ISBN 1 55858 947 3

This book is about humpback whales and emphasizes their life cycle.

Earle, Ann. Zipping, Zapping, Zooming Bats. HarperCollins Children's Books, 1995. ISBN 0 06 023479 2

This book is intended for young audiences and gives precise, clear information about several kinds of bats.

Godkin, Celia. Sea Otter Inlet. Fitzhenry & Whiteside, 1997. ISBN 1 55041 080 6

This book provides a good look at how the presence or absence of one species changes a whole ecosystem. In this case, it's the sea otters that dine on sea urchins. When the hunters kill the sea otters, disaster results.

Grace, Eric S. Apes. Sierra Club Books for Children, 1995. ISBN 0 87156 365 7

As in the other Sierra books listed here, the text may be a little advanced for some kids but the information they can get from the photographs and captions is considerable.

Harris, Robie H. Happy Birth Day! Illustrated by Michael Emberley. Candlewick Press, 1996. ISBN 1 56402 424 5

In this delightful book, we see a close-up, through beautiful illustrations, of a brand-new baby on its very first day.

Heller, Ruth. Animals Born Alive and Well. Price Stern Sloan, 1993. ISBN 0 448 40453 2

Heller's rhyming text portrays the attributes of many mammals, and her pictures are very good.

Kessler, Cristina. All the King's Animals: The Return of Endangered Wildlife to Swaziland. Boyds Mills Press, 1995. ISBN 1 56397 364 2

Not all of the animals discussed in this book are mammals, of course, but most of them are, and the color photographs are excellent.

National Geographic. Book of Mammals. National Geographic Society, 1998. ISBN 0 7922 7141 6

This book is a large and encyclopedic work detailing the habits and life cycles of many mammals.

Patent, Dorothy Hinshaw. Why Mammals Have Fur. Cobblehill, 1995. ISBN 0 525 65141 1

This book's full-color photographs examine the various kinds of fur and the use of protective coloration.

Peterson, Cris. **Horsepower: The Wonder of Draft Horses.** *Boyds Mills Press, 1997. ISBN 1 56397 626 9*

Most of this photographic essay concentrates on the draft horse as show horse, but some mention is made of their past use.

Simon, Seymour. **Big Cats.** *HarperTrophy, 1994. ISBN 0 06 446119 X*

Simon's choice of full-color photographs for this book is as good as his prose, which describes snow leopards, lions, tigers, jaguars, and cheetahs.

Simon, Seymour. **Whales.** *Crowell, 1990. ISBN 0 690 04758 4*

There are 20 full-color photographs of these ocean giants in this book, including breath-taking close-ups. The text is equally fine.

Simon, Seymour. **Wolves.** *HarperCollins Children's Books, 1993. ISBN 0 06 022531 9*

Again, it's the photographs that dominate this book, but the text is well done and full of interesting facts about the animals. It also includes a plea for conservation.

Smith, Roland. **Journey of the Red Wolf.** *Cobblehill, 1996. ISBN 0 525 65162 4*

This book explains how some of the few remaining red wolves in the United States were rounded up, bred and then reintroduced to save the species from extinction. Many colored photos accompany this narrative.

Stirling, Ian. **Bears.** *Sierra Club Books for Children, 1992. ISBN 0 87156 441 6*

This is a beautiful book. Some of the text will be beyond the youngest kids, but the information in and around the photographs is wonderful.

Wakefield, Pat. **A Moose for Jessica.** *Dutton Children's Books, 1987. ISBN 0 525 44342 8*

A moose in Vermont courted a cow. It really did, and this is the story of the farmer and his cow, Jessica, that attracted not only the moose but also scores of onlookers. Color photographs illustrate the real story.

 ## Web Sites

dialspace.dial.pipex.com/agarman/ is a wonderful source of information about big cats.

www.lionresearch.org/ is a Web site about lions and is operated by the University of Minnesota.

www.lpzoo.com/animals/mammals/facts/a_leopard.html is a Web site about leopards and is operated by the Lincoln Park Zoo.

netvet.wustl.edu/wildlife.htm has a long list of links to sites about many different mammals.

SCIENCE: Bugs

 COMMENTS

We're calling this theme "Bugs" instead of "Insects" so that we can include spiders and such for comparison as well as for general study. The short life cycle of many of these creatures allows students to observe several stages in one bug.

 PICTURE BOOK STARTER

The Very Quiet Cricket, by Eric Carle (G. P. Putnam's Sons Books for Young Readers, 1997, ISBN 0 399 22684 2), is a delightful book in which a day passes for a very quiet cricket that is unable to make a sound. We are introduced to many other insects, each of which makes a sound, except for the luna moth. It's not until the cricket sees a female cricket that he can make a sound. (Which we hear because of a microchip in the book's binding.) The book gives us many kinds of insects to talk about and work with, as well as descriptions of their sounds, and suggests the idea of mating. It also includes a hint of the "never give up" motif.

As in all of Carle's work, the illustrations are gorgeous. Childlike without being childish, they delight the eye with his use of color. See page 187 for a description of the way Carle constructs his artwork.

ACTIVITIES

Language Arts

BUILDING VOCABULARY

▶ After reading the book, make a list of all the insects in **The Very Quiet Cricket.** Find pictures of and information about them in other books.

▶ Find and display Margaret Wise Brown's **"I Like Bugs"** on the overhead or easel. Read it together and then substitute other adjectives or nouns about the bugs.

WRITING

▶ Take any bug which is in **The Very Quiet Cricket** and tell what it did after it encountered the Very Quiet Cricket. Draw pictures to illustrate your story.

▶ Draw a large picture of your bug and on it, tell the story of its life.

▶ Read the poem "Ants at the Olympics" in the anthology **The Random House Book of Poetry for Children** (Random House, 1983. ISBN 0 394 85010 6). Set up rules for an Olympics for the ants that they could really compete in.

Science

▶ Go on an "insect walk." Stop and watch an insect, carefully making notes or drawings on clipboards to remember what you have observed. Be sure to record exactly where you found the bug. Collect live specimens, being careful not to get stung or bitten and not to hurt the insect.

► Bring in insect eggs on the leaf or plant on which you found them. Place them in a safe container and see if they will hatch. If they do, take daily notes on their growth and progress.

► Start a bug zoo. Set up jars and containers with screens that suit the size and type of insect within. With the children, find out the food necessary to keep the insect alive for the study.

► Use magnifying glasses to closely observe each part of the insects.

► Give children notebooks with which to draw or write their observations of the insects' behavior, physical features, eating habits, and reactions to other insects. Encourage children to share their observations at group meetings.

► Classify the bugs as fly, butterfly, beetle, ant, spider, moth, or "other." Find the bug in a field guide or identification book. (Some science museums also help in identifying bugs.)

► Listen for bugs. On a spring, summer, or fall evening, listen and make notes or recordings of the bugs you hear.

► Find out about ways of controlling insects without using pesticides.

► Use the photocopier to make pictures of the bugs on squares of cardboard. Use the squares to play an attributes game. Turn all the squares face down upon the table. Turn them over two at a time and try to name three attributes that the bugs you've uncovered have in common. If you can do it, you keep the trick. If not, turn the squares face down again on the table and let someone else take a turn.

► Make food chains for as many of the bugs as possible.

► Design an experiment to show which substances attract which bugs or which bug repellents work best.

► Is a germ a bug? What bugs cause disease?

► Make a bulletin board on which you place fascinating facts about bugs with pictures of that kind of bug.

► Make lists of the different kinds of spiders.

Music

► Create dances showing caterpillars spinning cocoons and emerging as butterflies.

► Play "The Flight of the Bumblebee" and draw, paint, or move as you listen.

► Sing the song "The Ants Go Marching" and make up new verses for other bugs.

Art

► Draw or paint pictures showing the differences between insects and arachnids. Label the body parts.

► Make papier-mache models of various insects.

► Use string that has been dipped in starch to create spider webs.

► Fold a drawing paper in half. On one side, paint a butterfly or moth wing. While the paper is still wet, carefully press it against the other side.

BOOK LIST
Picture Books

Aylesworth, Jim. **Old Black Fly.** *Henry Holt & Co. Books for Young Readers, 1992. ISBN 0 8050 1401 2*

This is a rhyming alphabet book in which a fly buzzes and bothers a baby. The phrase "shoo fly" is repeated at each letter.

Brett, Jan. **Berlioz the Bear.** *G. P. Putnam's Sons Books for Young Readers, 1991. ISBN 0 399 22248 0*

There's a buzzing sound coming from his bass viol, and Berlioz, the bear, is annoyed. Not only that, the cart which is to take the animals to their concert is stuck in the mud. Brett uses her frames to show us that the audience is already assembling for the concert. Eventually the bee is discovered and the musicians do an encore of "The Flight of the Bumblebee."

Carle, Eric. **The Grouchy Ladybug.** *HarperCollins Children's Books, 1977. ISBN 0 06 443116 9*

We see the ladybug first on a tiny leaf, but he's raring for a fight. He challenges bigger and bigger animals to fight him as the day goes on. At last, he challenges a whale, and the whale's tail flips him back to the original leaf.

Carle, Eric. **The Very Busy Spider.** *G. P. Putnam's Sons Books for Young Readers, 1989. ISBN 0 399 21592 1*

The spider is busy spinning its web, and we watch and feel it do so, strand by strand. The strands in the web are raised on the page, and the text is repetitive.

Carle, Eric. **The Very Hungry Caterpillar.** *Philomel Books, 1969. ISBN 0 399 20853 4*

This book is Carle's classic. In it, the idea of metamorphosis is well presented, although the food the caterpillar eats is hardly a staple of a real caterpillar's diet.

Carle, Eric. **The Very Lonely Firefly.** *Philomel Books, 1995. ISBN 0 399 22774 1*

Carle concentrates on light in this book. A firefly goes in search of another firefly and is attracted to many lights before she finds a group of fireflies—and their lights really do blink on and off.

Egan, Tim. **Burnt Toast on Davenport Street.** *Houghton Mifflin Books for Children,1997. ISBN 0 395 79618 0*

Arthur Crandall and his wife are granted three wishes by a fly on the condition that Arthur puts down the fly swatter. Arthur keeps burning the toast, so he wishes for a new toaster, that the crocodiles on the corner would turn into squirrels and that he and his wife could take a trip to a tropical island with natives who sing and dance. Unfortunately the fly gets it all mixed up.

Jorgensen, Gail. **Gotcha!** *Illustrated by Kerry Argent. Scholastic, 1997. ISBN 0 590 96208 6*

There are similarities between this book and **The Bear and the Fly** (see book list). A perfect birthday party is ruined when a pesky fly bothers Bertha Bear. With a cry of "Gotcha!" she plunges into the cake and misses the fly. The chase is on. Bertha stays on the chase and clobbers the other guests but the fly keeps going.

Jukes, Mavis. **Like Jake and Me.** *Alfred A. Knopf Books for Young Readers, 1987. ISBN 0 394 89263 1*

It's all a misunderstanding in this story. Alex and his new stepfather are trying to get to know each other. The trouble is Alex is talking about spiders; Jake is talking about his wife.

Lasky, Kathryn. **Cloud Eyes.** *Harcourt Brace & Co., 1994. ISBN 0 15 219168 2*

This book is composed in a folktale style and tells how a young Native American brought to his people the secret of bees, bears and honey.

Lobel, Arnold. **The Rose in My Garden.** Illustrated by Anita Lobel. Greenwillow Books, 1985. ISBN 0 688 02587 0

This is a cumulative story in which, one by one, flowers in the garden are named and described. The descriptive word use is particularly good. There's no action until near the end of the book, but it's worth the wait. A bee is on the rose. A mouse is seen among the flowers but not mentioned. Then a cat comes into the garden and nearly gets the mouse. But there's a bee, remember?

Lonborg, Rosemary. **Helpin' Bugs.** Illustrated by Diane R. Houghton. Albatross, 1995. ISBN 0 964 12852 7

Hanna's got a new family and a new house. When she spots a neighbor working in front of his house, she helps him care for the bugs he finds. Together they create a bug village, cafeteria, and hospital. I'm not sure how grateful the bugs are, but the kids have a great time.

Lord, John V. **The Giant Jam Sandwich.** Houghton Mifflin Books for Children, 1975. ISBN 0 395 16033 2

The people of Itching Down are being tormented by four million wasps. How can they get rid of them? The baker declares that he can trap the wasps in a giant sandwich. Everyone pitches in to help: bakers, truck drivers, helicopter pilots, and more. The extraordinary plan works, and the wasps are trapped. The villagers have a great celebration that day. The birds celebrate in another way.

Oppenheim, Shulamith. **Fireflies for Nathan.** Illustrated by John Ward. Tambourine Books, 1994. ISBN 0 688 12147 0

This is a sweet story of a black child and his grandparents who catch fireflies just as his daddy once did.

Philpot, Lorna. **Amazing Anthony Ant.** Random House, 1994. ISBN 0 679 85622 6

The song "The Ants Go Marching" is given many twists in this lift-the-flap book. The flaps give the singer/reader alternate rhymes for each verse. Then, there's an added challenge. Find Anthony Ant on each page.

Pinczes, Elinor. J. **One Hundred Hungry Ants.** Houghton Mifflin Books for Children, 1993. ISBN 0 395 63116 5

The math in this book goes as far as you want to take it, but the plot is delightful all by itself. One hundred hungry ants head off to a picnic, but one ant keeps reorganizing them, insisting that his new way will get them to the picnic sooner. By the time they've gotten through all the possible reorganizations, the food is gone.

Polacco, Patricia. **The Bee Tree.** Philomel Books, 1993. ISBN 0 399 21965 X

The hunt for the bee tree starts when Mary Ellen tells her grandfather that she is tired of reading. They first capture some pollen-laden bees in a jar and then release the bees, one at a time. They follow each bee until they lose it and then release another bee. One by one, other people join the hunt for the bee tree. When they find it, they smoke the bees to make them calm, and then gather the honey. Later, Grandfather compares the sweetness of the honey to the sweetness of reading.

Polacco, Patricia. **In Enzo's Splendid Garden.** Philomel Books, 1997. ISBN 0 399 23107 2

The rhyme scheme and pattern are those of "This Is the House That Jack Built." The plot concerns a boy who begins to watch a bee while dining with his family in a peaceful outdoor restaurant. This creates a chain of events that results in havoc.

Van Allsburg, Chris. **Two Bad Ants.** Houghton Mifflin Books for Children, 1988. ISBN 0 392 48668 8

We see a kitchen and the people in it from an ant's perspective as a group of ants searches for grains of sugar for their queen. Two ants think life in the kitchen might be better than that outside, so they stay behind when the others leave. The hazards they encounter may be funny to us but aren't funny for the ants.

Watson, Mary. **The Butterfly Seeds.** Morrow Junior Books, 1995. ISBN 0 688 14132 3

When Jake's family left their country to come to America at the turn of the century, his grandfather gave them a packet of "butterfly seeds." After they settle at last in New York City, Jake builds a window box and plants the seeds. Then the butterflies come.

Winter, Paula. **The Bear and the Fly.** Crown Books for Young Readers, 1987. ISBN 0 517 52605 0

This wordless book begins with a calm scene at the Bear family dinner table. A friendly little dog is watching. Suddenly, a fly enters the room through an open window. Father Bear tries to get it with a fly swatter. He misses. Confusion ensues. Father pursues the fly like a bear possessed. Mother, Little Bear and the dog have apparently been knocked unconscious. The room is a disaster area. Father continues his pursuit until he himself falls to the floor. The last page finds the elusive fly happily going out through the open window.

Young, Ed. **Night Visitors.** Philomel Books, 1995. ISBN 0 399 22731 8

This ancient Chinese folktale is murky but beautiful. A young man persuades his father not to drown an ant colony and is rewarded by being summoned to a magnificent palace. There he falls in love with and marries the king's daughter. The red army attacks the palace, but the young man masterminds its defeat, however; his wife is killed in the battle. He thinks it was all a dream, but ants lead him to great treasure.

Novels

Dahl, Roald. **James & the Giant Peach.** Illustrated by Lane Smith. Alfred A. Knopf Books for Young Readers, 1996. ISBN 0 679 98090 3

This is a newly illustrated edition of Dahl's book (the previous edition was done by Nancy Burkert), but the text is the same. An outrageous fantasy, it starts with two won-

derfully villainous aunts who are the guardians of young, orphaned James Henry Trotter. In a Cinderella-like fashion, they mistreat their young charge but get their comeuppance when James takes up residence inside a giant peach, joining some monstrously sized insects who are already plotting their escape from the barren mountain. It's one fantastic twist after another in this exciting fantasy adventure, and Dahl keeps us rapidly turning the pages.

 ## Nonfiction

Arnosky, Jim. **Crinkleroot's Guide to Knowing Butterflies & Moths.** Simon & Schuster Books for Young Readers, 1996. ISBN 0 689 80587 X

After pointing out the various parts of a butterfly's anatomy, Crinkleroot takes young readers first on a daytime and then on a nighttime walk to identify various common moths and butterflies.

Brenner, Barbara. **Thinking About Ants.** Mondo Publishing, 1997. ISBN 1 57255 210 7

This "imagine you are" type of book is reminiscent of the books by Joanne Ryder. It puts the reader into the ants' world, and, in the process, we learn a lot about ants: the various kinds, their roles in the hill, and their predators and prey.

Cole, Joanna. **Spider's Lunch.** Illustrated by Ron Broda. Grosset & Dunlap Publishers, 1995. ISBN 0 448 40224 6

Full-color drawings and an easy-to-read text make this nonfiction book about spiders useful.

Creagh, Carson. **Things with Wings: Nature Company Young Discoveries.** Time-Life Books, 1996. ISBN 0 7835 4838 9

This book deals with insects and birds that fly, and it does so on a very simple level. Foldout panels provide additional information.

Gaffney, Michael. **Secret Forests: A Collection of Hidden Creepy Crawly Bugs and Insects.** Western, 1994. ISBN 0 307 17505 7

Several bugs from one ecosystem are pictured on a full spread and accompanied by information about each bug. The next spread shows the same bugs in their habitat where they are difficult to see. The challenge, of course, is to do just that—locate and identify the bug in its environment.

Laughlin, Robin Kittrell. **Backyard Bugs.** Chronicle Books, 1996. ISBN 0 811 80907 2

This book features full-color, close-up photos of common bugs.

Parker, Nancy Winslow & Joan Richards Wright. **Bugs.** Greenwillow Books, 1987. ISBN 0 688 06623 2

This book's riddles introduce 16 bugs: a horsefly, a cicada, an ant, a tick, a flea, a slug, a spider, a moth, a mosquito, a centipede, a roach, a cricket, a termite, a louse, a firefly, and a dragonfly. The behavior, habitat and predator/prey of each bug are explained. This is an informative survey for young readers.

Parker, Philip. **Your Living Home.** Thomson Learning, 1994. ISBN 1 568 47246 3

This book may make non-insect lovers squirm a bit. From the bacteria within our bodies to the carpet mites on the floor and the bats in the attic, this book clearly and interestingly describes their life cycles and activities. Also included are ways in which these insects can be examined.

Parsons, Alexandra. **Amazing Spiders.** Random House, 1990. ISBN 0 679 90226 0

The special attributes of each type of spider are illustrated through full-color photos and drawings.

Watts, Barrie. **Ladybugs.** Franklin Watts, 1990. ISBN 0 531 14043 1

The writing in this book is simple without being simplistic. Clear, full-color photographs extend the text, which gives equally clear directions about the safest means of capturing, handling, housing, and feeding ladybugs. The author has wisely kept the information focused on those tasks, correctly assuming that you'll find more detailed information in other books.

Poetry

Florian, Douglas. **Insectlopedia: Poems and Paintings.** Harcourt Brace & Co., 1998. ISBN 0 15 201306 7

Florian's poems combine science and fancy, and the accompanying paintings add to his whimsical approach.

Greenberg, David T. **Bugs!** Illustrated by Lynn Munsinger. Little, Brown & Co., Children's Books, 1997. ISBN 0 316 32574 0

These are irreverent and slightly revolting poems about bugs of all sorts.

Lewis, J. Patrick. **The Little Buggers: Insect & Spider Poems.** Illustrated by Victoria Chess. Dial Books for Young Readers, 1998. ISBN 0 8037 1769 5

These short poems by Lewis are about just about every kind of bug. The mood is light, and the illustrations keep pace nicely with the text.

Web Sites

mgfx.com/butterfly/ is a good butterfly Web site.

Get a bee's eye view of things at **cvs.anu.edu.au/andy/beye/beyehome.html**

You can find lots of information about cockroaches at **www.nj.com/yucky/roaches/**

SCIENCE: Changes

 COMMENTS

Usually when we work with young children on the process of change, we are focusing on natural science—metamorphosis, life cycles and seasons. This time, in a physical science unit, we are really constructing an observation theme to encourage children to look carefully, note what they see and draw conclusions based on those observations in the physical world of science. This way, we can teach them not to overlook one of the most basic principles of the physical world: that the interaction between two things causes changes in each.

Numerous experiments can be done in this theme, including explorations of electricity, simple machines, simple chemistry, and physics, each of which can become a theme in and of itself.

 PICTURE BOOK STARTER

Walter Wick's **A Drop of Water: A Book of Science and Wonder** (Scholastic, 1997, ISBN 0 590 22197 3) is a fascinating book. Amazing photographs show such things as a drop of water as it falls from a faucet, changing shape as it goes. Another series of photographs shows a snowflake as it melts. At the back of the book, Wick gives some suggestions for follow-up activities, many of which will be of interest to children. The photographs should help children focus on physical changes in everyday things.

ACTIVITIES

Language Arts
DETERMINING CAUSE & EFFECT

► Make a change in the classroom every day before the children come in. At first the changes should be obvious but then can become subtler. Ask children to find the change and then make a series of other observations based on the change. For instance, the teacher's desk faces the wall now. Because of that she can't see us when she sits at her desk. Because of that, we can't raise our hands to talk to her, etc.

MAKING INFERENCES

► In Anthony Browne's picture book **Changes** (see book list), the little boy sees changes everywhere. Share the book with the kids and then speculate together: Do you think those changes really happened? Why did he think they did?

► In **Who Sank the Boat** (see book list), you can see changes in the boat every time a new animal gets in. After sharing the book, work together to decide why those changes happened.

▶ Read **The Doorbell Rang** (see book list). In it, you have to watch what the mother is doing to see one of the changes that the story doesn't mention. What is it?

▶ In **Tuesday** (see book list), after the frogs have gone back to the pond, the villagers observe many changes. After sharing the book, decide what those changes are and what you suppose the villagers think caused those changes.

WRITING

▶ Give each child a journal in which to record such changes they see or think of as the theme progresses. If possible, give children cameras with which to record changes.

Science

▶ Give each student a new crayon and a piece of paper. Have them make a single line on the paper. Ask them what object changed. Most will tell you that the paper has changed—it now has a mark on it. Direct their attention to the crayon. Is it still in exactly the condition it was before it drew? Together, make a rebus sentence on a bulletin board showing that change.

▶ Encourage children to think of other changes that occur by leading them from the crayon on paper to similar occurrences, such as: When a car stops suddenly and the tire makes black lines on the road, what has changed? Go on to more subtle changes: When a car drives down a road, what has changed? Why do roads need repairs? Why do tires wear out? Why do shoes wear out?

▶ If you have snow, sand, or mud outside, get children to make footprints and carefully observe the changes in them over a period of days.

▶ Set up an experiment table where, each day, new materials are put out for experimentation. Use rebus directions to get children started on making changes in the materials. As always, suggest that children make statements, either in writing or orally, to the group about the things they discover.

Following are some suggestions for materials and what children can observe by experimenting with them:

Dissolving Things: Containers of water and small packages of flour, salt, sugar, olive oil, and food coloring. Students can note which of these materials dissolves best, quickest, or not at all.

Moving Objects: A small but heavy weight and a small wooden ramp, several pieces of thread or string and a few blocks. Children can try pulling the weight to the top of a block pile with and without the ramp.

Light Effects: A magnifying glass; a strong light source; materials such as parquetry blocks, feathers, and leaves; and photographic and construction paper. Children can place objects on the paper and expose it to light and sunlight for varying periods of time.

Breaking Up and Bending Light: Prisms, mirrors, flexible mirrors, and shiny spoons. Children can observe the changes in a beam of light or reflections of light.

Static Electricity: A comb, a silk cloth, tissue paper, and balloons. Children can create static electricity and use it to bend a stream of water from the faucet, make their hair stand up and attract paper and dust.

Making Crystals: Containers of water, sugar and string. Children can dissolve sugar in water and suspend string in the solution so that crystals will form.

Floating and Sinking: Various wooden shapes or boats, rocks and objects of varying sizes and materials. Children can try sinking the boats by seeing how many objects they can place on them before causing them to sink. The kids can also experiment to find out which objects float.

Condensation: Ice; water; containers of glass, plastic, and metal; and magnifying glasses. Children can examine the outside of containers to see changes caused by condensation.

▶ Nature makes changes with weather, earthquakes and volcanoes, among other things. Children should be encouraged to bring in articles from newspapers and magazines about the changes created by nature.

Art

▶ Watch watercolors change on paper as they mix with other colors.

▶ Take a piece of red construction paper. Place it against pieces of paper of various other colors, including other shades of red, to see what changes occur.

BOOK LIST
Fiction

Allen, Pamela. **Who Sank the Boat?** *G. P. Putnam's Sons Books for Young Readers, 1985. ISBN 0 698 20576 6*

A group of friends of varying weights and sizes take a row in the bay. Each time one of them gets into the very small boat the title question is asked.

Browne, Anthony. **Changes.** *Alfred A. Knopf Books for Young Readers, 1990. ISBN 0 679 81029 3*

A little boy imagines familiar objects changing into other things after he's told by his father that there will be big changes around the house soon.

Browne, Eileen. **No Problem.** *Candlewick Press, 1993. ISBN 1 56402 200 5*

A group of animals receives a package containing a disassembled object. They put it back together in different ways, causing a weird assortment of changes.

Hutchins, Pat. **Changes, Changes.** *Simon & Schuster Books for Young Readers, 1971. ISBN 0 02 745870 9*

Two enterprising dolls deal with every change that occurs as they build with blocks in this wordless book.

Hutchins, Pat. **The Doorbell Rang.** *Morrow Junior Books, 1989. ISBN 0 688 09234 9*

This book is often used to demonstrate computational math, but it also works well with this theme. Change is illustrated by Mother's attempts to keep the kitchen floor clean even though each new entrant manages to dirty it more and more.

James, Betsy. **Blow Away Soon.** *G. P. Putnam's Sons Books for Young Readers, 1995. ISBN 0 399 22648 6*

In the process of showing a child how transitory some things are, we see kids experimenting with changes made by the wind.

Wiesner, David. **Tuesday.** *Clarion Books, 1992. ISBN 0 395 55113 7*

In this delightful, almost wordless book, frogs fly about the town on lily pads. When morning comes, the townspeople gather to observe the changes they've caused.

Wood, Don & Audrey. **The Napping House.** *Harcourt Brace & Co., 1984. ISBN 0 15 256711 9*

There are many changes to observe in this favorite book about a pile of sleeping animals. One change is often overlooked, however; the perspective changes as the pile is built. Watch the water pitcher on the table to observe the process. This is a focus book (see page 139).

Nonfiction

Branley, Franklyn. **Day Light, Night Light.** *HarperCollins Children's Books, 1998. ISBN 0 06 027294 5*

We explore the different kinds of light and their sources, as well as some simple experiments with light.

Dodd, Anne Wescott. **Footprints and Shadows.** *Simon & Schuster Books for Young Readers, 1992. ISBN 0 671 78716 0*

Lyric text and photographs show footprints and shadows. Footprints in the snow are particularly useful for this theme.

Gibbons, Gail. **Click: A Book about Cameras and Taking Pictures.** *Little, Brown & Co., Children's Books, 1997. ISBN 0 316 30976 1*

This simple book shows kids how to take better photographs and also gives information about how a camera works.

Haslam, Andrew. **Machines.** *Thomson Learning, 1994. ISBN 1 568 47256 0*

Readers are shown how to construct various gadgets that demonstrate the concepts of simple machines.

Heller, Ruth. **Color.** *G. P. Putnam's Sons Books for Young Readers, 1995. ISBN 0 399 22815 2*

With rhyming text and vivid artwork, the author explores color in fun and imaginative ways. This is an excellent source of information and inspiration about printing, color and vision.

Simon, Seymour. **Volcanoes.** *Mulberry Books, 1988. ISBN 0 688 14029 7*

Simon shows us how volcanoes are created, as well as the results of some of the famous eruptions. The photographs are spectacular.

Simon, Seymour. **Earthquakes.** *Mulberry Books, 1991. ISBN 0 688 14022 X*

Simon talks about the causes of earthquakes, some of the more spectacular occurrences, and the instruments used to measure and maybe predict them.

Weiss, Nicki. **An Egg Is an Egg.** *G. P. Putnam's Sons Books for Young Readers, 1997. ISBN 0 698 11398 5*

Although many of the changes explored in this book are in the field of natural science, the accent is on change: "Day is day until sunset when it is night."

Wick, Walter. **A Drop of Water: A Book of Science and Wonder.** *Scholastic, 1997. ISBN 0 590 22197 3*

See page 44.

SCIENCE: Weather

COMMENTS

A weather theme is predominantly a science theme, of course, but there are so many good books about the weather and so many interesting words connected with it that it makes a good language arts theme, as well.

PICTURE BOOK STARTER

Jack Prelutsky's book of poems about snow, **It's Snowing! It's Snowing!** (see book list), is a good one to start with because it explores so many of the moods occasioned by snow. Some of the poems extol its beauty while others talk about the nuisance it can be.

ACTIVITIES

Language Arts
BUILDING VOCABULARY
▶ In the book **Cloudy with a Chance of Meatballs** (see book list), it's said that the weather "took a turn for the worse." What's another way of saying the same thing?

▶ Make the sounds of a rainstorm by having everyone rap their fingers against a wooden desk or chair-back lightly and then harder and more rapidly. Have someone direct the storm by stating that it's beginning to sprinkle; it's raining harder; now it's a downpour, etc. Then have the storm gradually stop.

APPRECIATING POETRY
▶ Read aloud your favorite poem from **It's Snowing! It's Snowing!**, by Jack Prelutsky (see book list).

WRITING
▶ Make a list of some of the descriptive words Prelutsky uses to describe snowy weather in **It's Snowing! It's Snowing!** Then construct a list of words to describe other weather. Use some of them to write a poem or story about the weather.

▶ Read Bill Martin's **Listen to the Rain** (see book list). Make a list of the rain words he uses. Then brainstorm together for ideas for a book called **Listen to the Wind.**

▶ Talk or write about what your family does or could do during a fierce storm.

Math
▶ Measure the rain by setting a straight-sided container with a flat bottom outside to capture the rainfall. Measure the accumulation with a ruler.

Science
▶ Track a hurricane or other tropical storm.

▶ Notice the different kinds of clouds in the sky over a period of two to three weeks. Draw pictures of what you see. Find out the scientific names for the clouds.

▶ Determine wind direction with a weather vane or windsock. How does wind direction influence the weather?

▶ If you are in a place that gets snow, categorize the different kinds of snow.

► Catch a snowflake on a piece of very cold velvet and then examine it with a magnifying glass.

► Calculate the average rainfall over a period of time. Compare that with the statistics from the National Weather Service. Make a graph of those figures, marking the highs and lows for each day.

► Get the weather maps from the local newspaper. Compare it to the school map, marking the jet stream, ocean currents and typical directions for our weather.

► To demonstrate how raindrops form, conduct an experiment outlined in Walter Wick's book, **A Drop of Water** (see book list below). Place a few grains of salt on a jar lid that is raised above a saucer of water. Cover the whole thing with a larger bowl or container. Vapor will condense on the salt and eventually dissolve it into more droplets. This experiment shows how raindrops form around particles in clouds.

► Research weather disasters. Find which ones could or did happen in your state or area.

► Find out how weather affects landforms in your area.

► What do you need to learn in school in order to become a weather forecaster?

Social Studies

► Look at the way weather affects lifestyle around the world. What kinds of food can be grown? What kind of clothing is necessary? How does it affect life in other ways?

Art

► Draw your favorite seasons.

► Using art, figure out ways to show that the wind is blowing, or that it is cold or warm.

► Make snowflakes. Place them against various colors and textures to get various effects.

BOOK LIST
Picture Books

Barret, Judi. **Cloudy with a Chance of Meatballs.** *Illustrated by Ron Barrett. Aladdin Paperbacks, 1978. ISBN 0 689 70749 5*

Grandpa told the best tall-tale bedtime story ever. It was all about the town of Chewandswallow, a town with no food stores. The sky supplied all the food the people wanted. It rained soup and juice, snowed mashed potatoes and blew in storms of hamburgers. The weather report helped residents plan their next day's meal. When the weather took a turn for the worse, however, the people had to move away.

Bunting, Eve. **Ghost's Hour, Spook's Hour.** *Illustrated by Donald Carrick. Clarion Books, 1987. ISBN 0 89919 484 2*

Jake wakes during a dark and stormy night, and he and his dog, Biff, frighten themselves with their own images in a mirror. Later, Jake's parents get up and talk about their fears.

Burningham, John. **Cloudland.** *Crown Books for Young Readers, 1997. ISBN 0 517 70928 7*

Albert falls off a cliff and into a cloud. There he plays with other cloud children and enjoys the weather.

Byars, Betsy. **Tornado.** *HarperCollins Children's Books, 1996. ISBN 0 06 026449 7*

These are short, easy-to-read stories told by Pete to entertain his family as they sit in a storm cellar waiting for a tornado to pass.

Calhoun, Mary. **Flood.** *Morrow Junior Books, 1997. ISBN 0 688 13919 1*

This book is a fictional treatment of the same flood that's discussed in **The Great Midwest Flood** (see book list). We see it here through Sarajean's eyes, as she is first excited and then frightened by the rising waters.

Cole, Joanna. **The Magic School Bus Inside a Hurricane.** *Illustrated by Bruce Degen. Scholastic, 1995. ISBN 0 590 44686 X*

This story is the usual combination of facts and fancy as Ms. Frizzle takes her students on a bus that becomes a weather balloon and then a weather plane to investigate a hurricane.

Cooney, Nancy Evans. **The Umbrella Day.** *Illustrated by Melissa Bay Mathis. G. P. Putnam's Sons Books for Young Readers, 1989 ISBN 0 698 11562 7*

Missy's mother insists that this day, like every other day, is an umbrella day. Missy takes the umbrella with her under protest, but finds all sorts of creative uses for it.

Cowley, Joy. **Singing Down the Rain.** *Illustrated by Jan Spivey Gilchrist. HarperCollins Children's Books, 1997. ISBN 0 06 027602 9*

Things look pretty grim in a dry, rain-starved town until a woman drives into town in a blue pickup truck and begins to sing for rain.

dePaola, Tomie. **The Legend of the Bluebonnet: An Old Tale of Texas.** *G. P. Putnam's Sons Books for Young Readers, 1996. ISBN 0 698 11359 4*

This legend is loosely based on one from the Comanche. It tells of an orphaned child who is told that, in order to bring rain, the members of the group must give a burnt offering of their most treasured possession. When the child burns her doll, She-Who-Is-Alone makes the rain come, and the bluebonnet is grown in her honor.

Duvoisin, Roger. **Hide and Seek Fog.** *Illustrated by Alvin Tresselt. Lothrop, Lee & Shepard Books, 1988. ISBN 0 688 51169 4*

This book offers a poetic look at an East Coast fog that keeps the fishermen confined to shore for days.

Ginsburg, Mirra. **Mushroom in the Rain.** *Simon & Schuster Books for Young Readers, 1988. ISBN 0 02 736241 8*

A mushroom starts out tiny, but, as more and more critters take refuge from the rain under the mushroom, it grows big enough to accommodate them.

Gray, Libba Moore. **Is There Room on the Feather Bed?** *Illustrated by Nadine Westcott. Orchard Books, 1997. ISBN 0 531 30013 7*

When a hard rain begins to fall, farm animals beg the Teeny Tiny Woman for permission to share her bed.

Hopkinson, Deborah. **Birdie's Lighthouse.** *Illustrated by Kimberly Buicken Root. Atheneum Books for Young Readers, 1997. ISBN 0 689 81052 0*

In this picture book, based on a journal from the 1800s, Birdie must tend the light during a fierce storm in Maine.

Inkpen, Mick. **Kipper's Snowy Day.** *Harcourt Brace & Co., 1996. ISBN 0 15 201362 8*

Two friends enjoy the snow in every possible way.

James, Betsy. **Blow Away Soon.** *Illustrated by Anna Vojtech. G. P. Putnam's Sons Books for Young Readers, 1995. ISBN 0 399 22648 6*

When a little girl is frightened by the wind, her grandmother takes her to the top of a hill to face the wind and to build a tower of things for it to blow away.

Johnston, Tony. **The Last Snow of Winter.** *Morrow Junior Books, 1993. ISBN 0 688 10749 4*

A famous artist, Gaston Pompicard, lives with his dog, Louisette, in a small French town. Inspired by the beauty of the first snowfall, he creates a surprise snow sculpture for the village. Late that winter, he falls ill, and the villagers use the last snow of winter to create a snow sculpture for him.

Kalan, Robert. *Rain.* Illustrated by Donald Crews. Mulberry Books, 1991. ISBN 0 688 10479 7

This book uses graphics to great effect by showing the rain in words and pictures.

Keats, Ezra Jack. *The Snowy Day.* Viking Children's Books, 1962. ISBN 0 670 65400 0

Keats' book, with its simple story of an inner-city child enjoying the snow, is a classic.

Keller, Holly. *Geraldine's Big Snow.* Greenwillow Books, 1988. ISBN 0 688 07513 4

Geraldine anxiously waits for the first snow of winter which has been predicted as imminent. When she goes to bed, not a single snowflake has fallen—but she has her sled ready, just in case. Everyone else has made preparations for the snow, as well. In the morning, the snow has arrived.

Koscielniak, Bruce. *Geoffrey Groundhog Predicts the Weather.* Houghton Mifflin Books for Children, 1995. ISBN 0 395 88398 9

Geoffrey Groundhog wakes up on the first Groundhog's Day, doesn't see his shadow and predicts to the local newspaper that spring will soon be here. By the time next Groundhog's Day rolls around, there are so many TV journalists at the event that Geoffrey is blinded by the TV lights and can't tell whether or not he's seen his shadow.

Lasky, Kathryn. *The Gates of the Wind.* Illustrated by Janet Stevens. Harcourt Brace & Co., 1995. ISBN 0 15 204264 4

Gamma Lee leaves her safe and comfortable home in search of new experiences. She climbs a mountain and enjoys her new life facing the wind and an adventurous life.

Lewis, Kim. *First Snow.* Candlewick Press, 1993. ISBN 1 56402 194 7

Daddy is sick, and it's snowing, but the sheep on the hill must be fed. Mommy and Sarah set out to do the job, and Sarah brings her teddy bear. On the way home, Sarah realizes she has lost her teddy bear, but the sheepdog rescues it.

Lyon, George Ella. *Come a Tide.* Illustrated by Stephen Gammell. Orchard Books, 1990. ISBN 0 531 05854 9

Heavy rains are coming, and the old folks know that coping with the flood will mean everybody pitching in. Gammell's illustrations are water-drenched, and Lyon's language is wonderful.

Martin, Bill Jr. *Listen to the Rain.* Illustrated by James Endicott. Henry Holt & Co. Books for Young Readers, 1988. ISBN 0 8050 0682 6

Beautiful illustrations dominate this book which encourages the reader to listen for sounds and silences in a rainstorm.

Martin, Bill Jr. *Old Devil Wind.* Illustrated by Barry Root. Harcourt Brace & Co., 1971. ISBN 0 15 201384 9

It's a dark and stormy night, and the chantable text leads us through many actions we can take.

McCloskey, Robert. *Time of Wonder.* Puffin Books, 1989. ISBN 0 14 050201 7

This book offers a lyrical look at the end of a summer punctuated by a hurricane.

McCully, Emily. *First Snow.* HarperCollins Children's Books, 1985. ISBN 0 06 024129 2

This book is a wordless rendition of a snowstorm. When a mouse family wakes to a perfect winter morning, they pile into the truck and head for the slopes to go sliding. One little mouse perches at the top of the hill, afraid to go down. With much encouragement from the others, she finally dares to try it, and then doesn't want to stop.

McKissack, Patricia C. *Mirandy and Brother Wind.* Illustrated by Jerry Pinkney. Alfred A. Knopf Books for Young Readers, 1997. ISBN 0 679 88333 9

Mirandy seeks a partner for the cakewalk, and her target is Brother Wind.

Neitzel, Shirley. **The Jacket I Wear in the Snow.** Greenwillow Books, 1989. ISBN 0 688 08028 6

To say that the child in this story is over-dressed is an understatement, but we learn about each item of clothing in a "house that Jack built" format.

Polacco, Patricia. **Thunder Cake.** Philomel Books, 1990. ISBN 0 399 22231 6

When a little girl hears an approaching thunderstorm, she is frightened, but her grandmother comforts her with the preparation of a cake. As they assemble the ingredients, they count the time between thunder and lightning.

Poydar, Nancy. **Snip, Snip . . . SNOW!.** Holiday House, 1997. ISBN 0 8234 1328 4

Sophie's mom and dad are glad that there's been so little snow this winter, but Sophie longs for it. She makes snowflakes at school, and at last the snow comes.

Purdy, Carol. **Iva Dunnit and the Big Wind.** Illustrated by Steven Kellogg. Dial Books for Young Readers, 1985. ISBN 0 8037 0183 7

Iva Dunnit is a determined woman in pioneer days with a passel of kids who know how to stay put. When the big wind comes, they cope very nicely.

Serfozo, Mary. **Rain Talk.** Illustrated by Keiko Narahashi. Simon & Schuster Books for Young Readers, 1990. ISBN 0 689 50496 9

As a little girl and her dog walk in the rain, she notices the different sounds it makes on various surfaces.

Seuss, Dr. **Bartholomew and the Oobleck.** Random House, 1949. ISBN 0 394 80075 3

In this classic story, the king is bored by the conventional weather that falls from the sky and demands some brand new stuff. He gets oobleck, a green, sticky substance that gums up everything.

Shulevitz, Uri. **Rain Rain Rivers.** Farrar Strauss & Giroux Books for Young Readers, 1969. ISBN 0 374 46195 3

A little girl sits in her room listening to the rain and planning the things she'll do when the rain stops.

Spier, Peter. **Peter Spier's Rain.** Yearling, 1997. ISBN 0 440 41347 8

In this delightful, wordless book, two children experience the sights, sounds and feel of rain.

Steig, William. **Brave Irene.** Farrar Strauss & Giroux Books for Young Readers, 1986. ISBN 0 374 30947 7

Irene's mother has made a beautiful gown for the duchess, and it must be delivered today. Irene braves a terrible storm to take the gown to the duchess, and for awhile the wind gets the upper hand.

Stevenson, James. **Heat Wave at Mud Flat.** Greenwillow Books, 1998. ISBN 0 688 14205 2

The characters at Mud Flat are together again. This time they need rain, and Raymond, the rainmaker, promises to bring it.

Stolz, Mary. **Storm in the Night.** Illustrated by Pat Cummings. HarperCollins Children's Books, 1990. ISBN 0 06 443256 4

Thomas and his cat, Ringo, live with Grandfather. During a thunderstorm, the lights go out, and the old man tells the boy about a time when a storm frightened him. This confidence allows the boy to voice his own fear.

Van Allsburg, Chris. **The Stranger.** Houghton Mifflin Books for Children,1997. ISBN 0 395 42331 7

A Stranger is brought to Farmer Bailey's farm after a car accident. Though the Stranger seems well physically, he is mute and appears to have no memory. He stays with the family and, while he does, the weather does not change. The Stranger leaves after blowing on a green leaf, and the weather changes.

Vaughan, Marcia. **The Sea-Breeze Hotel.** Illustrated by Patricia Mullins. HarperCollins Children's Books, 1992. ISBN 0 06 443406 0

The Sea-Breeze Hotel is buffeted by wind, so all of the guests leave. The family begins to fly lots of kites, and when people see what fun they're having, the guests return to join the fun.

Wells, Rosemary. **Edward's Overwhelming Overnight.** Dial Books for Young Readers, 1995. ISBN 0 8037 1883 7

Edward is supposed to be picked up by his parents after playing at his friend Anthony's house, but a sudden snowstorm prevents it. He must stay overnight, but he's not ready for that. Anthony's parents put chains on their car tires and manage to get him home safely.

Wiesner, David. **Hurricane.** Houghton Mifflin Books for Children,1990. ISBN 0 395 54382 7

A large tree comes down during a hurricane, and two brothers enjoy an imaginative romp through its upturned roots and branches.

Yashima, Taro. **Umbrella.** Puffin Books, 1977. ISBN 0 14 050240 8

Shiny, red boots and a new, blue umbrella are waiting and so is the little girl, but the rain is a long time coming. It comes at last, and we all enjoy the experience.

Yolen, Jane. **Before the Storm.** Illustrated by Georgia Pugh. Caroline, 1995. ISBN 1 56397 240 9

Children enjoy a summer afternoon by playing in the water from a hose—until a sudden rainstorm sends them scurrying for shelter.

Yolen, Jane. **The Girl Who Loved the Wind.** Illustrated by Ed Young. HarperCollins Children's Books, 1972. ISBN 0 06 443088 X

An imprisoned princess relies on the wind to tell her tales of the world beyond her walls.

Poetry

Harrison, Michael. **A Year Full of Poems.** Oxford University Press, 1991. ISBN 0 19 276149 8

The weather that each season brings is the subject of this varied collection of poems.

Prelutsky, Jack. **It's Snowing! It's Snowing!.** Illustrated by Jedan Titherington. Greenwillow Books, 1984. ISBN 0 688 01513 1

This wonderful, small collection of snow poems reveals all of the moods snow commands.

Nonfiction

Kramer, Stephen. **Eye of the Storm: Chasing Storms with Warren Faidley.** G. P. Putnam's Sons Books for Young Readers, 1997. ISBN 0 399 23029 7

This book's color photographs show Faidley's team chasing tornadoes.

Lesser, Carolyn. **Storm on the Desert.** Illustrated by Ted Rand. Harcourt Brace & Co., 1997. ISBN 0 15 272198 3

We witness a storm on the desert and the resulting burst of plant life it generates.

Robbins, Ken. **Air.** Henry Holt & Co. Books for Young Readers, 1995. ISBN 0 8050 2292 9

The qualities and properties of air and its disturbances are shown in this book through lovely photographs and muted prose.

Simon, Seymour. **Lightning.** Morrow Junior Books, 1997. ISBN 0 688 14638 4

The explanation and exploration of lightning, its causes and effects are the focus of this book which features spectacular photographs of lightning.

Simon, Seymour. **Ride the Wind: Airborne Journeys of Animals and Plants.** Browndeer Press, 1997. ISBN 0 15 292887 1

This volume's text is longer than in most books by Simon, and there are no color photographs in this one, but his explanation of the way the wind works to disperse animals and plants is as clear as expected.

Simon, Seymour. **Storms.** Mulberry Books, 1992. ISBN 0 688 11708 2

Simon uses spectacular color photos and his usual lucent prose to describe the many causes and effects of weather.

Simon, Seymour. **Winter Across America.** Hyperion Books for Children, 1994. ISBN 0 686 80019 4

This book allows us to see winter all the way from the Arctic Circle to Baja California, through beautiful photographs and clear, scientific explanations.

Vogel, Carole G. **The Great Midwest Flood.** Little, Brown & Co., Children's Books, 1995. ISBN 0 316 90248 9

The 1993 flooding of the Mississippi River is covered clearly and with many photographs.

Wick, Walter. **A Drop of Water: A Book of Science and Wonder.** Scholastic, 1997. ISBN 0 590 22197 3

This is a fascinating book with numerous stop-action photographs revealing the nature of water. It's also used as a picture book starter in the theme on Changes (see page 34).

SCIENCE: Safety

 **PICTURE BOOK STARTER**

Officer Buckle and Gloria, by Peggy Rathmann (G. P. Putnam's Sons Books for Young Readers, 1995, ISBN 0 399 22616 8), is a good starter book—it's humor, a Caldecott Award Winner. Officer Buckle has been giving a safety lecture at Napville School for years. Each time, his words go unheeded, and the students are totally bored, even though he knows hundreds of safety tips. Then, he gets a police dog, Gloria, as his companion. The next time he speaks on safety at Napville School, the audience reacts with applause and cheers. That's because Gloria, standing just slightly upstage from Officer Buckle, has been hilariously acting out his safety tips as he speaks. Officer Buckle is surprised and delighted at this warm reception, and he

 COMMENTS

This is a theme that can involve some very good books with some useful safety information. The theme could be extended to include health and nutrition, but for our purposes that's too big a theme.

and Gloria are soon doing the safety lectures everywhere. Then a television crew films the safety lecture, and that night Officer Buckle sees what Gloria has been doing. He refuses to do another safety lecture, and Gloria alone is a failure as a speaker. The worst accident ever happens at Napville School. Then, a letter from a fan gets the man and his dog together again, and all is well.

ACTIVITIES

Language Arts

FINDING DETAILS

► Enjoy **Officer Buckle and Gloria** together. In it, Officer Buckle gets some of his safety tips from the accidents he sees. List the accidents.

CATEGORIZING

► Make a list of all the safety tips in the book. Sort them into piles according to whether or not they make sense or are useful.

MAKING INFERENCES

► Why does Officer Buckle think that the drawings of Gloria sent by the kids show a lot of imagination?

DRAWING CONCLUSIONS

► Keep records of accidents in your school after your safety campaign has started. How will you know if your campaign has had any effect?

DRAMATIZING

► You probably can't find a dog as talented as Gloria for a television show about safety, but you can use costumes and humor to make a good safety program. Televise it.

WRITING

► Take a safety walk around your school. Examine the playground equipment. Take notes on possible hazards that might cause accidents. What can be done to prevent accidents there?

▶ Conduct a safety campaign in your school. Find out what accidents have occurred there. Make posters informing others about safety.

Math

▶ What are the most common kinds of accidents for various ages of kids? Survey the students in the school as to the various kinds of accidents they have had. Make up a questionnaire to help students remember their minor as well as major accidents. Make graphs. Compare your results to the statistics you assembled.

Science

▶ Claire says that she always wears a crash helmet. Do crash helmets work? How could you find out? Should you always wear them when you ride a bike? Is there any other reason to wear a crash helmet?

▶ Investigate safety belts in automobiles. How long has your state had a law enforcing their use? Have safety belts helped decrease physical injuries?

▶ In Carol Carrick's book **Accident** (see book list), a dog is killed in a car accident. Talk to a vet about what is being done to help dogs that are injured in this way.

▶ Visit a hospital or orthopedic surgeon's office to find out what happens when someone breaks a bone.

▶ Examine some X-rays that show a broken bone in various stages of healing.

▶ Talk to whoever is in charge of personal safety in your school. Coordinate the theme with that program as much as possible.

▶ Find out how 911 works in your area. How do they know where you're calling from? How do they train people who work there?

▶ Find out about how an emergency room works. How do those people know what to do?

▶ To determine how physical condition or fatigue affects the rate of accidents, take a coordination test at the beginning of the day and again, later in the day, after vigorous exercise.

▶ Accidents often happen because things or people become off balance and fall.

▶ Experiment with some block towers and the concept of center of gravity. How high can you build a tower before something falls? Does it always fall from the top? Does the bottom of the tower have anything to do with stability? Why does something fall? Can you predict when a block tower will fall and in which direction?

▶ Balance yourself holding various weights. If you have a weight in one hand, what do you have to do with your feet and body to keep from falling over?

BOOK LIST
Fiction

Birdseye, Tom. *A Regular Flood of Mishap.* Holiday House, 1994. ISBN 0 8234 1070 6

Everything our narrator does turns into disaster, no matter how benevolently it started out. A girl was just trying to help her grandfather by rescuing his fishing pole, but that led to one accident that led to another and so on. This is a book full of chuckles.

Carrick, Carol. *The Accident.* Clarion Books, 1976. ISBN 0 89919 041 3

It's not a human but a beloved pet that is killed in a car accident, and the owner grieves.

Cole, Joanna. *The Magic School Bus Inside the Human Body.* Illustrated by Bruce Degen. Scholastic, 1989. ISBN 0 590 72633 1

Ms. Frizzle and the kids go inside Arnold to investigate the human body.

Crews, Donald. *Shortcut.* Greenwillow Books, 1992. ISBN 0 688 064361

When the author of this book was young, he and a group of boys decided to play on some railroad tracks. When the fast freight train came, they barely made it to safety.

Kellogg, Steven. *Prehistoric Pinkerton.* Dial Books for Young Readers, 1987. ISBN 0 8037 0322 8

Pinkerton, the Great Dane, chews everything in sight. That's bad enough at home, but in the Science Museum it's a disaster.

Nielsen, Laura F. *Jeremy's Muffler.* Illustrated by Christine M. Schneider. Atheneum Books for Young Readers, 1995. ISBN 0 689 80319 2

Jeremy's aunt has knitted him one very long muffler, and he wears it so as not to hurt her feelings. However, the scarf is an accident waiting to happen until it's used as a safety line.

Viorst, Judith. *Alexander and the Terrible, Horrible, No Good, Very Bad Day.* Simon & Schuster Books for Young Readers, 1972. ISBN 0 689 30072 7

To say that Alexander is accident prone is a vast understatement, at least on this single day of his life. He may have to move to Australia to recuperate.

Viorst, Judith. *Sunday Morning.* Aladdin Paperbacks, 1968. ISBN 0 689 70447 X

Parents are trying to sleep late on Sunday morning, but their kids are up and into all kinds of mischief, creating havoc.

Ward, Cindy. *Cookie's Week.* G. P. Putnam's Sons Books for Young Readers, 1988. ISBN 0 399 21498 4

Cookie, the cat, causes a disaster each day of the week. Our only hope is that he will rest on Sunday.

Zimmerman, Andrea. *The Cow Buzzed.* Illustrated by Paul Meisel. HarperTrophy, 1993. ISBN 0 06 443410 9

When the bee's cold is caught by the cow, its buzz goes with it. The cow sneezes, and the moo and the cold go to the pig, and so it goes until we get to the rabbit who covers his mouth when he sneezes.

Nonfiction

Aliki. *My Feet.* HarperTrophy, 1990. ISBN 0 06 445106 2

Each part of the foot is analyzed, and the role of the feet in moving the body is very simply explained.

Aliki. *My Hands.* HarperCollins Children's Books, 1990. ISBN 0 690 04878 5

As with the author's **My Feet**, this book analyzes the human hands, and their functions, on a very simple level.

Morgan, Sally. **Human Body.** Kingfisher, 1996.
ISBN 0 7534 5030 5

This book explains that simple activities demonstrate the concepts of how our bodies work.

Parker, Steve. **Brain Surgery for Beginners: And Other Minor Operations for Minors.** The Millbrook Press, 1993.
ISBN 1 56294 604 8

This book is full of simple, captioned drawings that explain a lot about the human body for the youngest readers.

Rowan, Dr. Pete. **Some Body!** Illustrated by John Temperton. Alfred A. Knopf Books for Young Readers, 1994.
ISBN 0 679 87043 1

This book's foldout pages and fully captioned drawings and pictures deliver simple information about the human body.

Simon, Seymour. **The Heart: Our Circulatory System.** Morrow Junior Books, 1996. ISBN 0 688 11407 5

As with all of Simon's nonfiction works, this book uses wonderful color photography, and the simple text compares the heart to things within a child's ken.

Simon, Seymour. **The Brain: Our Nervous System.** Morrow Junior Books, 1997. ISBN 0 688 14640 6

The brain and the spinal cord are the focus of this excellent, fully illustrated book.

SCIENCE: Rocks & Minerals

 COMMENTS

Many young children are fascinated with rocks and minerals, first for their beauty and sometimes for the geology they represent. This theme allows for a lot of work with the concepts of careful observation, attributes and categories, as well as looking at the effects of rocks on the earth's history.

 **PICTURE BOOK STARTER**

Byrd Baylor's book **Everybody Needs a Rock**, with illustrations by Peter Parnall (Simon & Schuster Books for Young Readers, 1974, ISBN 0 689 71051 8), is a delightful exploration of the beauty in rocks. The narrator suggests that there are 10 rules for picking out the perfect rock for you, and each of her rules entails careful observation and thought.

ACTIVITIES

Language Arts
FINDING DETAILS
▶ Before reading **Everybody Needs a Rock** or even mentioning the subject of the theme, take the children on a walk with the challenge, "Bring back the oldest thing you can carry easily." When you get back to the classroom, discuss their objects and then present a small rock if none of them have.

WRITING
▶ Make up 10 rules for choosing a leaf, a shell, a friend, a school, or a home.

EXTENDING LITERATURE
▶ Read **Everybody Needs a Rock** and follow Byrd Baylor's rules, and then display your perfect rock. Explain your choice to others.

Science
▶ Divide the class into small groups. Use magnifying glasses and strong light to carefully examine the rocks. Give each group three pieces of yarn and suggest that they make circles with the yarn into which they should place three groups of rocks. They may use any criteria they want for the grouping, but must be able to explain what each group of rocks has in common.

▶ Take one piece of yarn away from each group of children and suggest that they find two categories for the rocks. Add pieces of yarn to create additional groupings.

▶ After providing children with safety glasses, give them small hammers so that they can smash or chip at rocks and observe the results. Encourage them to note the color of the dust created and the way the rock breaks.

► Add more small rocks to the collection. Make sure there are samples going from very soft to hard, such as soapstone, gypsum, sandstone, limestone, graphite, sulfur, calcite, pyrite, and corundum.

► Some students will be ready to use an adaptation of Moh's hardness scale to further classify the rocks. The scratching with a knife should be done under close supervision.

> **HARDNESS 1.** You can scratch it easily with a fingernail.
>
> **HARDNESS 2.** You can scratch it with a fingernail, but it's hard to do so.
>
> **HARDNESS 3.** You can scratch it with a penny.
>
> **HARDNESS 4.** You can scratch it with a knife. (Limestone is this hardness.)
>
> **HARDNESS 5.** You can scratch it with a knife, but you have to bear down hard.
>
> **HARDNESS 6.** It will scratch a knife.
>
> **HARDNESS 7.** It will scratch glass.
>
> **HARDNESS 8.** It will scratch quartz.
>
> **HARDNESS 9.** It will scratch topaz.
>
> **HARDNESS 10.** Diamond—it will scratch any other rock.

► Take a field trip to a stream. Notice the effects of the rocks in the stream on wildlife, plant life and the flow of the water. Speculate on what would happen if the stream had no rocks. Make a list of the things that would change.

► Use a sand table to build streams with and without rocks. Watch the effect on water flow.

► Read **The Magic School Bus Inside the Earth** (see book list). Use the information in that book to further classify some of the rocks in the collection.

► Speculate on how the earth would be different if there were no rocks on the surface.

► For more help identifying minerals, visit sites on the Web which allow students to type in descriptions of a mineral and get possible matches, such as **mineral.galleries.com/scripts/search.exe** or **www.minerals.net**/.

► Contact your local rock and mineral association or club. The nearest science museum can probably give you that information. Ask to visit their collection, or have them come to visit you.

► Gather crystals and examine them with magnifying glasses. Note color and shape variations.

► Make crystals by saturating water with salt, sugar, or borax and then suspending a string in the saturated water.

► Build crystal gardens with coal, ammonia and food coloring.

BOOK LIST
Fiction

Baylor, Byrd. **Everybody Needs a Rock.**

See page 49.

Birchmore, Daniel A. **The Rock.** *Illustrated by Nancy Carol Willis. Cucumber Island, 1997. ISBN 1 887 81303 9*

An anthropomorphic rock stands through time, happy to observe the changes around it.

Cole, Joanna. **The Magic School Bus Inside the Earth.** *Illustrated by Bruce Degen. Scholastic, 1987. ISBN 0 590 40760 0*

Ms. Frizzle's class takes a field trip inside the earth, encountering the layers of rock as they go through them.

Kaufman, Jeff. **Milk Rock.** *Henry Holt & Co. Books for Young Readers, 1995. ISBN 0 8050 2814 5*

When a farmer finds a rock bearing a sign that says, "Care for me and I will care for you," he brings it home, and, in return, it gives him milk.

Lionni, Leo. **On My Beach There Are Many Pebbles.** *Mulberry Books, 1995. ISBN 0 688 13284 7*

The rocks on a beach are playfully examined in this picture book.

Polacco, Patricia. **My Ol' Man.** *Philomel Books, 1995. ISBN 0 399 22822 5*

Among the adventures a group of children remember having with their father is the magic rock he took them to.

Ray, Mary Lyn. **A Rumbly Tumbly Glittery Gritty Place.** *Illustrated by Douglas Florian. Harcourt Brace & Co., 1993. ISBN 0 15 292861 8*

A little girl lives across from a rock quarry, and, although others dislike the place, she finds it wonderful.

Steig, William. **Sylvester and the Magic Pebble.** *Simon & Schuster Books for Young Readers, 1988. ISBN 0 671 67144 8*

A very small rock and a large one play a role in this transformation fantasy.

Nonfiction

Gans, Roma. **Let's Go Rock Collecting.** *HarperCollins Children's Books, 1997. ISBN 0 06 027282 1*

This book discusses rocks as the oldest objects you can collect. It goes on to discuss, simply and clearly, the formation, the various kinds and the uses of rocks.

Parker, Steve. **Rocks and Minerals: Eyewitness Explorers.** *DK Publishing, 1997. ISBN 0 789 41682 4*

As with other Eyewitness texts, the pages of this book are full of illustrations and information about the subject.

Podendorf, Illa. **Rocks and Minerals.** *Children's Press, 1982. ISBN 0 516 01648 2*

This book provides a simple introduction to the subject for the youngest reader.

Siebert, Diane. **Sierra.** *HarperCollins Children's Books, 1991. ISBN 0 06 021639 5*

The mountain range is, of course, a lot of very big rocks, and this book's poetic text tells of how geologic changes made the mountain range. It then discusses the ecosystem that the mountains created.

SOCIAL STUDIES: Families

 COMMENTS

Gone are the days when every family in children's books had a mother, a father and two children who lived in a lovely little house surrounded by a green, rolling lawn. Because children's literature does and should reflect society, we now have good books depicting all sorts of family structures. While grandparents are not always part of the household, they are integral parts of many families, so we have included many books about grandparents. While the booklist on page 53 is far from all-inclusive, because we've listed only the very good books available on families, there's enough variety in family structure to allow most children to see some variation of their own.

 PICTURE BOOK STARTER

Cynthia Rylant's text and Stephen Gammell's illustrations combine to make **The Relatives Came** (see book list). This is less a story than the narration of an experience in which a large, extended family gathers to hug, laugh, sleep, do chores, and eat. The relatives are far from idealized in Stephen Gammell's illustrations: They won't win any beauty contests, and their clothes are mussed, frequently mismatched and poorly fitted, but the family's love and exuberance bounce off the page.

ACTIVITIES

Language Arts
FINDING DETAILS
► Gammell used his own family as models for some of his character illustrations in **The Relatives Came.** His father is the man cutting hair. His wife is taking pictures, and he himself plays the guitar. Find these characters.

MAKING COMPARISONS
► Make a list of the different kinds of families that appear in the books listed below. Which family setup is closest to yours?

► Look at the books that portray grandparents and decide which ones come closest to your own grandparents in appearance or in the things they like to do.

WRITING
► Start a story with the words "If I had a _____ (family member you don't have), I would . . ."

EXTENDING LITERATURE
► How can you tell that the relatives in **The Relatives Came** have come from a long way away?

Math
► Figure out how many of the people who you are related to are alive today. Don't forget cousins and second cousins. If they all came to your house for a reunion like the one in **The Relatives Came,** where would you put them all?

▶ Read Remy Charlip's book **Hooray for Me!** (see book list below). Make a chart listing every member of your family, including the ones that don't live in your house. In a second column, put your relationship to that person. For instance:

FAMILY MEMBER	MY RELATIONSHIP
Father	I am my father's son or daughter
Mother	I am my mother's son or daughter
Uncle	I am my uncle's nephew or niece

TITLE	NUMBER OF PEOPLE IN THE HOUSE	WHAT YOU KNOW ABOUT THE FAMILY	WHAT YOU KNOW ABOUT THE NEIGHBORHOOD
Amelia's Road		They pick crops They have a truck They move a lot	There are fields of crops There is one road that doesn't go anywhere

▶ Make a chart such as the one above showing the family structure in some or all of the books listed below:

Social Studies

▶ With the class, make up a questionnaire for family members designed to help you know them better. If you ask questions that can be answered yes or no, it will be easier to record their answers but you won't get as much information as you would if you asked different questions. You may want to add symbols in order to help you remember what the questions ask. Print copies.

▶ You'll want to pick a good time to ask each person in your family those questions. Brainstorm for ways to tell whether it's a good time to ask them.

▶ Plan a grandparents' day. If your own grandparents can't come, find a person to substitute for them. Bring in pictures of grandparents when they were young and see whether others can identify them by those pictures. Learn some songs they would know and could sing with you. Learn to play a game that grandparents are apt to know. Play it with them on that day. Write a story about what you'll be like when you're a grandparent and share it on that day.

BOOK LIST
Fiction

Abercrombie, Barbara. **Charlie Anderson.** *Simon & Schuster Books for Young Readers, 1990. ISBN 0 689 50486 1*

There's a parallel in this story between the cat that the sisters adopt and their own lives. Like them, the cat has two homes and two families.

Ackerman, Karen. **By the Dawn's Early Light.** *Illustrated by Catherine Stock. Simon & Schuster Books for Young Readers, 1994. ISBN 0 689 31788 3*

Rachel's mother works all night in a factory, so Rachel stays with Nina and her little brother, Josh.

Alexander, Martha. **Nobody Asked Me If I Wanted a Baby Sister.** Dial Books for Young Readers, 1971. ISBN 0 8037 6402 2

Oliver is angry about the new baby in the house. It isn't until he discovers his special talent for amusing her that he decides she's not so bad after all.

Altman, Linda Jacobs. **Amelia's Road.** Illustrated by Enrique O. Sanchez. Lee & Low Books, 1993. ISBN 1 880000 04 0

Amelia's family travels from place to place to pick vegetables and fruits. They're on the road so much that Amelia has felt she didn't belong anywhere. She hates it when her father gets out the map because she knows they'll be on the move again. This year, however, she's in a school where the teacher bothered to learn her name. She finds a way to make it a place where she belongs.

Ballard, Robin. **When I Am a Sister.** Greenwillow Books, 1998. ISBN 0 688 15397 6

The twist to this tale is that it's the child's stepmother, not mother, who's about to have a baby. Our narrator knows that the next time she visits her father's house, the new baby will be there.

Baylor, Byrd. **The Table Where Rich People Sit.** Illustrated by Peter Parnall. Scribner, 1994. ISBN 0 684 19653 0

Our narrator is upset with her family's lack of material wealth, but, at a family meeting, they tell her about the things they really value.

Best, Cari. **Getting Used to Harry.** Illustrated by Diane Palmisciano. Orchard Books, 1996. ISBN 0 531 09494 4

A new stepfather is the focus of this story that starts with the easy part—the wedding.

Birdseye, Tom. **A Regular Flood of Mishap.** Illustrated by Megan Lloyd. Holiday House, 1994. ISBN 0 8234 1070 6

Our narrator explains that she was only trying to help by retrieving her grandfather's fishing pole, but each event caused another disaster.

Brott, Ardyth. **Jeremy's Decision.** Illustrated by Michael Martchenko. Kane/Miller Books Publishers, 1990. ISBN 0 916291 65 0

Jeremy's father is a famous musician, and he often questions Jeremy about his own future and career, but Jeremy must make his own decision.

Buehner, Caralyn. **Fanny's Dream.** Dial Books for Young Readers, 1996. ISBN 0 8037 1497 1

Fanny dreams of marrying a prince—or at least the mayor's son—but she married Heber, instead, and their life together is simple but lovely.

Bunting, Eve. **The Wall.** Clarion Books, 1998. ISBN 0 395 51588 2

Bunting deals with the sensitive subject of the Vietnam War Memorial by having a father and son visit it to look for the grandfather's name. As they do so, they see many grieving and respectful visitors.

Burningham, John. **The Baby.** Candlewick Press, 1996. ISBN 1 564 02689 2

This book's illustrations add delightful details to this story about a new arrival in the family.

Caseley, Judith. **Priscilla Twice.** Greenwillow Books, 1995. ISBN 0 688 1330503

It's never easy when your folks get a divorce, even if they're being quite civil about it. Priscilla will live in two houses now, and she finally accepts it, but not before she sounds off to her friend and then to her parents.

Charlip, Remy. **Hooray for Me!.** Bicycle Press, 1996. ISBN 0 81930790 4

A child celebrates and defines his place in the family.

Conrad, Pam. **The Tub People.** Illustrated by Richard Egielski. HarperCollins Children's Books, 1989. ISBN 0 06 443306 4

The tub people are a family of toys that live on the edge of the bathtub. When a young child is caught in the drain, they're all concerned. When he's rescued, the family is moved to the bed and they're relieved. The story is simple, but illustrates the idea of family love.

Crews, Donald. **Bigmama's.** Greenwillow Books, 1992. ISBN 0 688 09950 5

Based on the author's memories, this book tells about a reunion that took place every summer on his grandparents' farm.

Cutler, Jane. **Darcy and Gran Don't Like Babies.** Scholastic, 1993. ISBN 0 590 72126 7

Grandmother reacts unconventionally and frankly when her granddaughter says she doesn't like the family's new baby. Everyone else in the family denies Darcy's feelings, but grandmother says, "Me neither."

dePaola, Tomie. **Nana Upstairs and Nana Downstairs.** G. P. Putnam's Sons Books for Young Readers, 1973. ISBN 0 399 20300 1

Family love continues, even when a grandmother becomes very, very old and then dies.

dePaola, Tomie. **Now One Foot, Now the Other.** G. P. Putnam's Sons Books for Young Readers, 1981. ISBN 0 399 20774 0

When Bobby was little his grandfather helped him learn to walk. Now Grandfather has had a stroke, and Bobby helps him learn to walk again.

dePaola, Tomie. **Tom.** G. P. Putnam's Sons Books for Young Readers, 1993. ISBN 0 698 11448 5

Tomie calls his grandfather "Tom," and they share a great deal besides their name.

Eisenberg, Phyllis Rose. **You're My Nikki.** Puffin Books, 1986. ISBN 0 14 055463 7

A little African-American girl is convinced that her mother has forgotten her special talents. We learn as she does that her mother is just tired after her first day on a job.

Ernst, Lisa Campbell. **Luckiest Kid on the Planet.** Bradbury Press, 1994. ISBN 0 02 733566 6

Lucky knows that his name is apt. One day he finds out that his real name is Herbert, and he thinks he'll have no more good luck. His grandfather convinces him otherwise.

Fair, Sylvia. **The Bedspread.** Morrow Junior Books, 1982. ISBN 0 688 00877 1

Two bedridden sisters decide to make a quilt of their memories. Each starts from a different end of the quilt. Their styles are different, and so are their memories.

Farmer, Patti. **What's He Doing Now?** Illustrated by Janet Wilson. Firefly Books, 1996. ISBN 1 55209 218 6

Parents share information with their young son about the fetus that's developing inside the mother. Each time the boy asks the title question, they respond with simple but correct information.

Fowler, Susi Gregg. **I'll See You When the Moon Is Full.** Illustrated by Jim Fowler. Greenwillow Books, 1994. ISBN 0 688 10830 X

A father travels a lot, and his son is helping him pack for the next trip. Both are sad, but the father tells the boy to watch the moon each night. By the time it's full again, he'll be back home.

Fox, Mem. **Koala Lou.** Illustrated by Pamela Lofts. Harcourt Brace & Co., 1989. ISBN 0 15 200502 1

Koala Lou's mother seems too busy to pay enough attention to her now, and the girl misses her mother's time and love.

Fox, Mem. **Night Noises.** Harcourt Brace & Co., 1989. ISBN 0 15 200543 9

An old lady, Lily Laceby, dozes by the fire. Her dog, Aggie, tries to catch a few winks herself, but there are noises in the night that turn out to be Lily's family which has come to surprise the old woman on her birthday.

Fox, Mem. **Shoes from Grandpa.** Orchard Books, 1990. ISBN 0 531 05848 4

Using a "This Is the House That Jack Built" pattern, each member of a family gives a girl gifts of clothing, starting with shoes.

Franklin, Kristine. **Iguana Beach.** Illustrated by Lori Lohstoeter. Crown Books for Young Readers, 1997. ISBN 0 517 70900 7

In Central America, a little girl, her uncle and her cousins enjoy an outing at the beach.

Gardella, Tricia. **Just Like My Dad.** Illustrated by Margot Apple. HarperTrophy, 1996. ISBN 0 06 443463 X

Our narrator and his cowboy father go about an ordinary day on the ranch.

Garland, Sherry. **My Father's Boat.** Illustrated by Ted Rand. Orchard Books, 1998. ISBN 0 531 30073 0

A Vietnamese boy goes with his father for a day of shrimp fishing.

Gibbons, Faye. **Mountain Wedding.** Illustrated by Ted Rand. Morrow Junior Books, 1996. ISBN 0 688 11348 6

Two large mountain families will merge when this marriage takes place, but the children hate each other on sight. Before the ceremony can start, the first punch is thrown, and it's downhill from there.

Gravois, Jeanne M. **Quickly, Quigley.** Illustrated by Alison Hill. Tambourine Books, 1993. ISBN 0 688 13047 X.

Quigley is a small, slow penguin as the text repeatedly tells us. Everyone urges Quigley to speed up until he gets a little brother who urges him to slow down.

Gray, Nigel. **Running Away from Home.** Illustrated by Gregory Rogers. Crown Books for Young Readers, 1995. ISBN 0 517 70923 6

Sam is furious with his father and announces that he is leaving home, and he does so after packing his backpack. When it rains, however, he takes refuge under the porch.

Griffith, Helen. **Georgia Music.** Illustrated by James Stevenson. Greenwillow Books, 1986. ISBN 0 688 0607 1

A little girl spends the summer with her grandfather in Georgia. He plays tunes on his harmonica for her and for the birds. When he gets too old to live alone, he moves in with his granddaughter and daughter in Baltimore, but he misses the farm. The girl makes music on the harmonica to recall the good times.

Griffith, Helen. **Grandaddy's Place.** Illustrated by James Stevenson. Greenwillow Books, 1987. ISBN 0 688 06254 7

Janetta visits her grandfather's farm in Georgia for the first time. The two are awkward together at first, but he soon plays music for her.

Harley, Bill. **Nothing Happened.** Tricycle Press, 1995. ISBN 1 883672 09 0

Convinced that all sorts of wonderful things happen at night while he sleeps, Jack stays up all night. The only thing he sees, however, is his father, kissing each of his sons goodnight as he whispers, "I love you."

Henkes, Kevin. **Julius, the Baby of the World.** Greenwillow Books, 1990. ISBN 0 688 08944 5

Everybody in the family declares that Julius is the baby of the world. His sister, Lilly, however, is far from convinced. She thinks he smells, is not cute and is not smart. She wishes he would go away, that is, until her cousin agrees.

Hill, Elizabeth. **Evan's Corner.** Illustrated by Sandra Speidel. Viking Children's Books, 1967. ISBN 0 670 82830 0

Evan's family is crowded in their two-room apartment, and he wants a space of his own. He gets his own corner and makes it just perfect—almost.

Hines, Anna Grossnickle. **When We Married Gary.** Greenwillow Books, 1996. ISBN 0 688 14276 1

Our narrator doesn't remember her birth father, although her big sister does. Then her mother and Gary fall in love, and the whole family marries him.

Hoffman, Mary. **Boundless Grace.** Illustrated by Caroline Binch. Dial Books for Young Readers, 1995. ISBN 0 8037 1715 6

Grace's parents are divorced, and her father lives in Gambia with his new family. Now Grace gets to go to Africa to meet her other family.

Hughes, Shirley. **All About Alfie.** Lothrop, Lee & Shepard Books, 1997. ISBN 0 688 15186 6

This is a series of stories about Alfie, a very engaging preschooler who lives with his mother, father and little sister in an attached house in England.

Johnson, Dolores. **What Will Mommy Do When I'm at School?** Simon & Schuster Books for Young Readers, 1990. ISBN 0 02 747845 9

This is a book about projection. A little girl worries about going to school for the first time and is sure that her mother will be scared and lonely, and will miss her too much.

Johnston, Tony. **The Quilt Story.** Illustrated by Tomie dePaola. G. P. Putnam's Sons Books for Young Readers, 1985. ISBN 0 399 21009 1

A modern-day child finds a quilt made long ago, and it gives her comfort as she adapts to a new home.

Johnston, Tony. **Yonder.** Dial Books for Young Readers, 1988. ISBN 0 8037 0277 9

In this family, each birth and death is commemorated with the planting of a tree.

Joose, Barbara M. **Mama, Do You Love Me?** Chronicle Books, 1991. ISBN 0 87701 759 X

An Inuit child and her mother play a game in which the child questions what would happen if she did bad things or became a series of different animals. Each time, the mother assures her that the love would be unchanged.

Kraus, Robert. **Where Are You Going, Little Mouse?** Illustrated by Ariane Dewey. Greenwillow Books, 1986. ISBN 0 688 04294 5

A little mouse is leaving his family in search of a more exciting and caring one. Then he discovers that his family loves him a lot.

Kurtz, Jane. **Pulling the Lion's Tail.** Illustrated by Floyd Cooper. Simon & Schuster Books for Young Readers, 1995. ISBN 0 689 80324 9

Set in Ethiopia, this story tells of a young girl whose father takes a new wife. Almaz tries to make friends with her new stepmother, but she is constantly rebuffed. At last she goes to her grandfather, who assigns her a seemingly impossible task: pull the hairs from a lion's tail. She does so, but only after gaining the lion's trust. The lesson is that she must show the same patience with her stepmother.

Laminack, Lester L. **The Sunsets of Miss Olivia Wiggins.** Illustrated by Constance Bergum. Peachtree Children's Books, 1998. ISBN 1 56145 139 8

Miss Olivia Wiggins is a patient in a nursing home. She seems unaware of her visitors, her daughter and great-grandson, but the child seems to get through to her with his love.

Lasky, Kathryn. **My Island Grandma.** Illustrated by Amy Schwartz. Morrow Junior Books, 1993. ISBN 0 688 07946 6

A little girl and her grandmother luxuriate on their island vacation.

Linden, Anne Marie. **Emerald Blue.** *Atheneum Books for Young Readers, 1995. ISBN 0 689 31946 0*

A little girl lived on a Caribbean island with her grandmother and tells us about a hurricane they experienced together.

Lyon, George Ella **Mama Is a Miner.** *Illustrated by Peter Catalanotto. Orchard Books, 1994. ISBN 0 531 06853 6*

A little girl talks about her mother who works underground, while we observe the action above and below the ground.

MacLachlan, Patricia. **All the Places to Love.** *Illustrated by Mike Wimmer. HarperCollins Children's Books, 1994. ISBN 0 06 021098 2*

A child leads us around the family farm and stops to show us each family member's favorite spot.

Medearis, Angela Shelf. **Poppa's New Pants.** *Holiday House, 1995. ISBN 0 8234 1155 9*

Poppa buys a new pair of pants that are too long, so he asks each of the three women in the family to cut six inches off the pants and hem them. Each woman refuses, pleading fatigue, but then, that night, each woman relents and does as she was asked.

Parish, Peggy. **Amelia Bedelia's Family Album.** *Greenwillow Books, 1988. ISBN 0 688 07677 7*

When the Rogers family decides to give a party for their slightly cockeyed maid, Amelia Bedelia, she tells them all about her strange family whose occupations are very literal.

Plounde, Lynn. **Pigs in the Mud in the Middle of the Road.** *Illustrated by John Schoenherr. Scholastic, 1997. ISBN 0 590 56863 9*

A family's trip in their Model T Ford is interrupted by the pigs, chickens, sheep, and bulls that all end up in the mud in the middle of the road.

Purdy, Carol. **Iva Dunnit and the Big Wind.** *Illustrated by Steven Kellogg. Dial Books for Young Readers, 1985. ISBN 0 8037 0183 7*

Iva Dunnit's got a lot of kids, and they know how to stay put. That ability serves them in good stead during the high winds.

Rael, Elsa Okon. **When Zaydeh Danced on Eldridge Street.** *Illustrated by Marjorie Priceman. Simon & Schuster Books for Young Readers, 1997. ISBN 0 689 0461 2*

Zeesie is visiting her grandparents on Eldridge Street. Her grandmother is sweet and kind, but her grandfather is formidable. Now she finds that she must accompany him to the synagogue to celebrate Simchas Torah. However, she discovers another side of the man as he leads the celebration and dances in the street.

Russo, Marisabina. **Waiting for Hannah.** *Greenwillow Books, 1989. ISBN 0 688 08016 2*

Hannah wants to know all about birth—her birth. When she sees a pregnant woman, Hannah asks her mother, "Did you look like that when you were going to have me?" Hannah's mother tells her what she did while waiting for Hannah. She led an active life while pregnant, and, although the birth takes only one sentence, Hannah gets the story.

Russo, Marisabina. **When Mama Gets Home.** *Greenwillow Books, 1998. ISBN 0 688 14985 5*

In a single-parent household we see the mother leaving work and heading home while her children get busy preparing supper.

Ryder, Joanne. **My Father's Hands.** *Illustrated by Mark Graham. Morrow Junior Books, 1994. ISBN 0 688 09189 X*

The narrator's father, at work in the garden, reaches out tenderly to little creatures and to his plants.

Rylant, Cynthia. **Birthday Presents.** *Illustrated by Sucie Stevenson. Orchard Books, 1987. ISBN 0 531 07026 3*

A parent tells a little girl about each of her first six birthdays.

Rylant, Cynthia. **The Relatives Came.** *Simon & Schuster Books for Young Readers, 1985. ISBN 0 02 777220 9*

A family's relatives start out very early one morning in their rattletrap car loaded down with people, luggage and food. They travel all day through the mountains until, at last, they drive into "our" yard (quite literally). From then on, it's an endless round of hugging, eating, sleeping, and enjoying each other—a true celebration of family.

Schachner, Judith Byron. **Willy and May.** Dutton Children's Books, 1995. ISBN 0 525 45347 4

May has great zest for life and she has a pet bird, Willy, who shares most of that life because he travels about on May's head. We get the story from May's grandniece who has wonderful times with May and Willy.

Scott, Ann H. **On Mother's Lap.** Illustrated by Glo Coalson. Houghton Mifflin Books for Children,1992. ISBN 0 385 58920 7

A young Inuit child is quite comfortable on his mother's lap and is quite sure that there is no room there for the new baby.

Shea, Pegi Deitz. **New Moon.** Illustrated by Cathryn Falwell. Boyds Mills Press, 1996. ISBN 1 56397 410 X

A little girl's brother gets involved with her efforts to learn to talk. Together they focus on the moon in books and the one in the sky.

Shelby, Anne. **Homeplace.** Illustrated by Wendy A. Halperin. Orchard Books, 1995. ISBN 0 531 06882 X

A grandmother tells a child her family's story, starting with the great-great-great-great-grandfather who built the house and farm where they now live.

Slawson, Michele Benoit. **Apple Picking Time.** Illustrated by Deborah Kogan Ray. Crown Books for Young Readers, 1994. ISBN 0 517 88575 1

This family has fun picking apples, although apple-picking time means a lot of hard work.

Stanley, Diane. **The Good-Luck Pencil.** Illustrated by Bruce Degen. Four Winds, 1986. ISBN 0 02 786800 1

A little girl is supposed to be writing about her family, but she finds them just too boring to write about. Then her pencil transports her to an ideal family, but they don't look so good close-up.

Steptoe, Javaka. **In Daddy's Arms I Am Tall: African Americans Celebrating Fathers.** Lee & Low Books, 1997. ISBN 1 880 00031 8

These story-poems honor fathers with beautiful, mixed-media illustrations.

Stevenson, James. **I Meant to Tell You.** Greenwillow Books, 1996. ISBN 0 688 14177 3

A father tells his daughter about what their life was like when she was young.

Stewart, Sarah. **The Gardener.** Illustrated by David Small. Farrar Strauss & Giroux Books for Young Readers, 1997. ISBN 0 374 32517 0

Lydia is sent from her family during the Great Depression to live with her uncle in New York, but her uncle always seems to be frowning. Determined to make him smile, she plants a lovely garden surprise. This is a focus book (see page 118).

Turner, Ann. **Sewing Quilts.** Illustrated by Thomas B. Allen. Simon & Schuster Books for Young Readers, 1994. ISBN 0 02 78928 59

Two girls and their mother work on quilts, and, as they do so, they celebrate the moments that go together like a quilt to make up their lives.

Turner, Ann. **Through Moon and Stars and Night Skies.** Illustrated by James G. Hale. HarperCollins Children's Books, 1990. ISBN 0 06 026190 0

A child tells us the often-repeated story of how he came to live with his new family in America.

Waddell, Martin. **Once There Were Giants.** Candlewick Press, 1995. ISBN 1 56402 612 4

The adults and older siblings are the giants in our narrator's world. First we see her as a baby and then we watch her slowly grow to become one of the giants.

Waddell, Martin. **Owl Babies.** Illustrated by Patrick Benson. Candlewick Press, 1992. ISBN 1 56402 101 7

In an owl family, the babies awake to find their mother is gone. They reassure each other that she's just gone hunting and will be back soon, but Percy proclaims, "I want my mommy!"

Watson, Nancy Dingman. **Tommy's Mommy's Fish.**
*Illustrated by Thomas Watson. Viking Children's Books, 1971.
ISBN 0 670 85681 9*

A boy wants a special gift for his mother and decides to catch her a striped bass.

Wells, Rosemary. **Hazel's Amazing Mother.** *Dial Books for Young Readers, 1985. ISBN 0 803 70209 4*

When Hazel is threatened by bullies, her amazing mother arrives in the nick of time.

Wells, Rosemary. **Stanley and Rhoda.** *Dial Books for Young Readers, 1981. ISBN 0 8037 7995 X*

Stanley's little sister is selfish, cranky and somewhat lazy, but he loves her—even though he does get a little revenge.

Weston, Martha. **Apple Juice Tea.** *Clarion Books, 1994. ISBN 0 395 65480 7*

Gran's impending visit is not met with great joy by Polly. She only vaguely remembers the woman and is not sure she ever liked her. When Gran arrives and spends a night as babysitter, Polly is even less sure. However, Gran gives a very good tea party, and the bond between the two is made.

Wild, Margaret. **Our Granny.** *Illustrated by Julie Vivas. Houghton Mifflin Books for Children,1994.
ISBN 0 395 67023 3*

This book explains and explores all kinds of grandmothers.

Williams, Vera. **A Chair for My Mother.** *Greenwillow Books, 1982. ISBN 0 688 00915 8*

This family consists of a little girl, her mother and her grandmother. Her mother works hard in a diner all day, and there is no easy chair for her to rest in when she comes home, so they save their change in a big glass jar until there's just enough to buy one.

Yolen, Jane. **Owl Moon.** *Illustrated by John Schoenherr. Philomel Books, 1987. ISBN 0 399 21457 7*

A father and child go on a moonlit winter night to see an owl. The child has been looking forward to this for a long time and knows the rules about no talking and making your own warmth. This book is respectful of the wild and of family tradition.

Novels

Lowry, Lois. **Attaboy, Sam!** *Bantam Doubleday Dell Books for Young Readers, 1993. ISBN 0 440 40816 4*

All About Sam. *Houghton Mifflin Books for Children,1988. ISBN 0 395 48662 9*

See You Around, Sam. *Houghton Mifflin Books for Children,1996. ISBN 0 395 81664 5*

In these short novels, Lowry deals with Anastasia Krupnik's younger brother, Sam. Sam's exploits are funny and right on target for expressing the emotions and actions of the child character we know from babyhood in **All About Sam** to preschooler in **See You Around, Sam.** They make excellent read-aloud suggestions for children from first grade on up.

 ## Nonfiction

Brimmer, Larry Dane. **A Migrant Family.** *Lerner Publishing Group, 1991. ISBN 0 8225 2554 2*

This photo-essay shows Juan Medina's family at work. We see the shack where his family lives and witness their backbreaking daily work. When the shack is bulldozed without warning, the family stoically accepts the loss and goes on.

Hausherr, Rosemarie. **Celebrating Families.** *Scholastic, 1997. ISBN 0 590 48937 2*

Each spread shows a different child with his or her family, and brief text tells about the different cultures they represent.

SOCIAL STUDIES: Friends

 COMMENTS

The theme of friendship can include not only the values of friendships but also the difficulties in maintaining them, as well as conflicts between friends and their resolution. Because many friendships involve people of differing ages, we can talk about the friendships between the young and old. Friendship often involves accepting and even celebrating differences between friends. This theme allows for establishing pen pals, which leads to the writing of friendly letters and even to geography, as you study the places where those friends live. Pets are often friends, and certainly provide companionship for many children, so we've included some books and activities about pets. The pets, of course, lead us back to some of the animal themes on pages 21 and 37.

 PICTURE BOOK STARTER

Chester's Way, by Kevin Henkes (see book list), makes a good introduction to a theme about friendship. Chester and Wilson are friends because they have so much in common. Each is conservative and cautious and loves routine. They enjoy things together that are best done with two people. When Lilly moves into the neighborhood, Chester and Wilson are aghast at her unconventional behavior and they reject her overtures of friendship. It isn't until Lilly's nifty disguise and confrontational behavior, scare away some bullies who are threatening Chester and Wilson that they decide to accept Lilly. The three friends exchange ideas and gifts, and enjoy each other by doing things best done by three people. Then Victor moves into the neighborhood. We know little about Victor because he appears only on the last page, chasing a butterfly, but the implication is that he will be different from Lilly, Wilson, or Chester.

ACTIVITIES

Language Arts
MAKING COMPARISONS

► Make a list of the things Chester and Wilson like to do together. Place a check mark beside each of those things that you also like to do.

► Make a list of the things Lilly likes. Place a check mark beside each of those things that you also like to do.

► Some of the friends in the books listed below are friends because they are so much alike, such as Chester and Wilson. Others are friends even though they are very different, such as Elizabeth and Larry. Make a list of the friends in those books and mark which ones are friends because they are alike and which ones are friends even though they are different.

► Why do you think Reggie acts the way he does in **Ira Says Goodbye** (see book list)? How could Ira have found out sooner what Reggie was feeling?

USING ORAL LANGUAGE

► In the Frog and Toad books by Arnold Lobel and in the books about George and Martha by James Marshall (see book list below), the friends sometimes have trouble with each other. Tell the class about a time that one of those friends had a hard time with the other one.

CONDUCTING AN INTERVIEW

► Interview the person in class that you know least about. Find out where they live, what they like to do, what they collect, what pet they have or would like to have, and at least one more thing. Write about your new friend and read what you've written to the class.

WRITING

► In **Jessica** (see book list), Ruthie has an imaginary friend. Create a perfect friend. If you had one, what would be his or her name? What would he or she be like? What would you do together? Write about it.

EXTENDING LITERATURE

► Which of the people in the books about friends listed on page 63 would you like to have for a friend? Draw a picture of you and that friend doing things together.

Social Studies

► Spend a day without a friend. Talk only when absolutely necessary. Find things to do that can be done with only one person and that take an entire day. How do you feel at the end of the day? What things did you most enjoy doing?

► Spend a day taking special notice of people's faces. Can you tell what they are feeling by the expressions on their faces? Make notes about the feelings you are aware of.

► Have a "friend exchange." Each day for a week, practice being someone else's best friend. Draw a different class member's name from a hat each day. Move your seat next to that of the new friend. Find out something about the new friend that you can share with the group. Plan some things to do together on the playground. Write notes to each other.

► Make friends with the big kids. Choose a "buddy class" from one of the upper grades. Choose one person in that class to become your buddy. Find out something that your buddy likes to do that you also like to do and do it together. Choose a buddy time each week to work and play with your buddy.

Music

► Teach a friend a song and sing it to the class together.

► Sing songs about friends, such as "The More We Get Together," "You've Got a Friend," "Side by Side," and "Friendship."

Art

► Use a large sheet of paper, paint, and big paintbrushes. Work on a picture together with two friends.

BOOK LIST
Fiction

Blegvad, Lenore. *Anna Banana and Me.* Illustrated by Erik Blegvad. Aladdin Paperbacks, 1985. ISBN 0 689 71114 X

Our narrator's friend, Anna Banana, is fearless, and he loves her for that. He also loves her for the great ideas she has of things they can do together—even if some of those things scare him a bit.

Brenner, Barbara. *Mr. Tall and Mr. Small.* Illustrated by Mike Shenon. Henry Holt & Co. Books for Young Readers, 1966. ISBN 0 8050 2757 2

A relationship between a mouse and a giraffe begins in mutual derision but ends in a loving friendship.

Crews, Donald. *Shortcut.* Greenwillow Books, 1992. ISBN 0 688 06436 1

Based on a memory from the author's childhood, this book tells of a group of friends who place themselves in great danger by taking a shortcut home on the railroad tracks. A fast-approaching freight train nearly kills them.

Egan, Tim. *Chestnut Cove.* Houghton Mifflin Books for Children,1995. ISBN 0 395 69823 5

The people in the town of Chestnut Cove loved and helped each other until the king announced a competition, and all cooperative behavior stopped.

Fleischman, Sid. *Scarebird.* Illustrated by Peter Sis. Mulberry Books, 1994. ISBN 0 688 13105 0

Lonesome John builds a "scarebird" in the garden to keep birds away. Little by little he clothes the scarebird and soon is treating it like a human being. When a young man shows up at the farm looking for work, John gradually transfers the clothes and his affection to the young man.

Henkes, Kevin. *Chester's Way.* Scholastic, 1988. ISBN 0 590 44017 9

Chester and Wilson are best friends, perhaps because they are so much alike. Both are cautious creatures of habit who have set routines for each day. Then Lilly moves into the neighborhood. Her wild and wooly ways upset the boys, and they reject her—until she rescues them from a gang of bullies.

Henkes, Kevin. *Jessica.* Greenwillow Books, 1989. ISBN 0 688 07829 X

Nobody's seen Jessica except Ruthie, but Ruthie claims that her friend Jessica is there all the time. Her parents insist that there is no Jessica, but Jessica is a lot of company for the lonely Ruthie. On the first day of school, Jessica goes too, but then, suddenly, there's a real Jessica to play with.

Henkes, Kevin. *A Weekend with Wendell.* Mulberry Books, 1996. ISBN 0 688 1 4024 6

Wendell is not a welcome guest at his cousin Sophie's house where he is to spend the weekend. Then Sophie turns the tables on her bossy and demanding guest, and everything works out just fine.

Hutchins, Pat. *The Doorbell Rang.* Mulberry Books, 1986. ISBN 0 688 09234 9

Ma has made cookies for her two children, and there should be plenty for each, but more and more friends keep dropping by to share the cookies.

Johnston, Tony. *Amber on the Mountain.* Illustrated by Robert Duncan. Dial Books for Young Readers, 1994. ISBN 0 8037 1219 7

A man comes to build a road through the remote mountains where Amber lives. He has brought his family there to stay with him for a short time, and his daughter, Anna, teaches Amber how to read. The family moved on before Anna could teach Amber how to write, but this Amber could teach herself, so a correspondence began between the two friends.

Johnston, Tony. **The Last Snow of Winter.** *Morrow Junior Books, 1993. ISBN 0 688 10749 4*

Gaston Pompicard is a famous artist who lives in the small French town with his dog, Louisette. When the first snow of winter falls, he is so inspired by its beauty that he constructs a snow sculpture for the people in town. Later, when winter is drawing to a close, Gaston becomes ill, and the people of the town use the last snow of winter to make a snow sculpture for him.

Levine, Evan. **Not the Piano, Mrs. Medley!** *Illustrated by Stephen D. Schindler. Orchard Books, 1991. ISBN 0 531 08556 2*

Mrs. Medley decides to take her grandson, Max, and her dog ,Word, to the beach, but every time they start out, Mrs. Medley thinks of something else they absolutely must bring to the beach.

Lobel, Arnold. **Frog and Toad Are Friends.** *HarperCollins Children's Books, 1987. ISBN 0 06 444020 6*

This book is just one in a series of books about Frog and Toad. The easy-to-read stories tell of a loving friendship between the two. Frog tends to be the voice of reason while Toad is often exasperating, but the friendship continues.

Marshall, James. **George and Martha.** *Houghton Mifflin Books for Children,1972. ISBN 0 395 19972 7*

This book, too, is just one of a series of books. Marshall writes about two hippopotamus friends who go through the ups and downs of friendship with love and dignity. There is also an omnibus edition available.

Sadler, Marilyn. **Elizabeth and Larry.** *Simon & Schuster Books for Young Readers, 1990. ISBN 0 671 77817 X*

This satirical look at society and convention is told through the friendship of an elderly woman and an alligator. They see nothing wrong with their close friendship, but others look at them askance.

Viorst, Judith. **Rosie and Michael.** *Illustrated by Lorna Tomei. Aladdin Paperbacks, 1974. ISBN 0 689 30439 0*

Rosie and Michael like each other a lot. On alternating pages, they tell us about the pranks they've played on each other, but they also tell us how well they understand and like each other. This funny book is about the ups and downs of friendship.

Waber, Bernard. **Ira Says Goodbye.** *Houghton Mifflin Books for Children,1988. ISBN 0 395 48315 8*

Ira's best friend, Reggie, is moving, and Ira is devastated by the coming separation. Reggie, on the other hand, seems anxious to go. He regales Ira with wonderful tales about his new home and new neighborhood. Then, when the moving van arrives, we find out how Reggie really feels.

Waber, Bernard. **Ira Sleeps Over.** *Houghton Mifflin Books for Children,1973. ISBN 0 395 13893 0*

Ira is about to stay overnight at his friend Reggie's house. The problem is, should he take his teddy bear? His sister is sure that Reggie will laugh. His parents assure him that Reggie will not laugh. Reggie doesn't laugh, because he, too, sleeps with a teddy bear.

SOCIAL STUDIES: The Farm

COMMENTS

Although the small family farm is disappearing from the American countryside, the farm is usually part of the social studies curriculum in kindergarten or first grade. It allows children to discover food sources and can lead to a more in-depth study of nutrition. A small push can take a farm unit into some economics awareness in the form of distinguishing goods and services and profit and loss. Farm animals, of course, are usually of interest to young children and this theme can help them differentiate between real and unreal portrayals of these animals.

PICTURE BOOK STARTER

Let's start with Pat Hutchins' Rosie's Walk (see book list). Rosie's walk around the farm is, for her, a leisurely one. She doesn't notice the lurking fox, and although she narrowly escapes several times, she never sees his many attempts to get her.

ACTIVITIES

Language Arts
CHANGING POINT OF VIEW
▶ Suggest that children retell the story of **Rosie's Walk,** and then tell it from the fox's point of view.

FINDING DETAILS
▶ Make a list of the buildings and landforms on the farm in **Rosie's Walk**: the hen house, the yard, the pond, the haystack, the mill, the fence, the beehives. Beside each item, write what happened to the fox when he got there.

SENQUENCING
▶ Insert into a pocket chart or similar device phrase cards and picture cards similar to the ones below. Suggest that children place the cards in the chart in the order in which they happen in the story.

ACTIVITIES *continued*

► Make flow charts for the action in one of the books. Use words or pictures or both to show the action of the story. Display your flow chart and see if other people can figure out what book you're describing.

DISTINGUISING REALISM FROM FANTASY

► In some of the books listed below, the farm animals act the way real farm animals do, but in many of the books, the animals talk or otherwise act like people. Make a list of realistic animals and another list of fanciful animals.

►Even the animal characters that behave unrealistically have some things in common with their real counterparts. Separate the books according to the animals in them. Dealing with one kind of animal at a time, use a Venn diagram or a chart such as the one below to illustrate the likenesses and dissimilarities between the animal characters and real animals.

INTERPRETING ILLUSTRATIONS

► Read **Rosie's Walk** aloud without showing the illustrations. Because the words don't mention the fox, children who aren't acquainted with the book probably will not realize that the fox is present. Read it aloud again, sharing the illustrations as you go.

EXTENDING LITERATURE

► The landmarks in the "Finding Details" activity are the ones that are mentioned in the text of **Rosie's Walk**, but there are landmarks in the illustrations that are not mentioned in the text: the barn, the silo and the cornfield. Extend the story by thinking of things that might have happened to the fox.

BOOK TITLE	CHARACTER	LIKE THE REAL ANIMAL IN THESE WAYS	UNLIKE THE REAL ANIMAL IN THESE WAYS
Rosie's Walk	Rosie	Shaped like a hen Walks around the backyard	Has designs on her body
Hattie & the Fox	Hattie	Looks like a hen Watches for danger	Talks Cares what the other animals think

Math

► Use the position words (prepositions) from **Rosie's Walk** as part of a geometry and spatial sense activity. Place pictures created by the children to represent Rosie and the various farm landmarks. As they maneuver Rosie around the farm, they accent the position words. "I'm making Rosie go *over* the haystack, *beside* the barn," etc.

Social Studies

► Make a map of the story of **Rosie's Walk**.

►Make a list of the farm animals that you find in the picture books listed on page 68.

► Add to that list the reason why each kind of animal can be found on a farm.

► Visit a variety of farms in real life or in videos. Make a chart such as the one below showing the differences among them.

► Find stories from the book list below that could have taken place on each kind of farm.

► Follow the foods. Suggest that children bring in samples of some of the foods they like best and then find out where that food might have originated. Locate those places on a map.

KIND OF FARM	ANIMALS	JOBS	FARM MACHINERY	PRODUCTS
Dairy farm	Cows Chickens Dog Cats	Milking the cows Cleaning the barn Taking the cows to pasture	Milking Machines Trucks Milk Truck	Milk Cream
Beef Farm				
Crop Farm				
Poultry Farm				

BOOK LIST

(Many of the books about gardens on page 16 could be included in this theme.)

Fiction

Ackerman, Karen. **Bingleman's Midway.** Illustrated by Barry Moser. Boyds Mills Press, 1995. ISBN 1 56397 366 9

A farm boy tells us of the wonderful time he had when a carnival came to town. His father understands his enchantment.

Alarcon, Karen Beaumont. **Louella Mae, She's Run Away.** Illustrated by Rosanne Litzinger. Henry Holt & Co. Books for Young Readers, 1997. ISBN 0 805 03532 X

We know that Louella Mae has run away, and we know that everyone is looking for her. We join the search, but it's not until the last page of this rhythmic picture book that we learn that Louella Mae is a mother pig.

Allen, Pamela. **Belinda.** Puffin Books, 1992. ISBN 0 14 055616 8

Bessie has gone away having left her husband, Tom, with a list of chores to do. First, he must milk Belinda. Because Belinda is used to being milked by Bessie, she objects when Tom tries to milk her. There follows a wild day for Tom and Belinda.

Booth, David. **The Dust Bowl.** Illustrated by Karen Reczuch. Kids Can Press, 1997. ISBN 1 55074 295 7

This story isn't about the great dust bowl time of the '30s although Grandfather remembers that time all too well. This story is about a later time of drought, and the boy's father is about to give up farming altogether. The grandfather's memories of the worse time give the family the courage to stick this one out.

Bushnell, Jack. **Sky Dancer.** Lothrop, Lee & Shepard Books, 1996. ISBN 0 688 05288 6

Jenny and a red-tailed hawk become friends, but when the hawk is thought to be killing livestock, she tries to scare it away so that it won't be shot. Fortunately for them both, the real culprit is revealed.

Chorao, Kay. **Little Farm by the Sea.** Henry Holt & Co. Books for Young Readers, 1998. ISBN 0 8050 5053 1

In this simply told story about a little farm, we watch how things change through the seasons, and we see the goods that were produced on the farm being sold at market.

Conrad, Pam. **The Rooster's Gift.** Illustrated by Eric Beddows. HarperCollins Children's Books, 1996. ISBN 0 06 023603 5

This sweet, funny fable is about a proud rooster who learns about his "gift" through the efforts and love of a small hen.

DeFelice, Cynthia. **Mule Eggs.** Illustrated by Mike Shenon. Orchard Books, 1994. ISBN 0 531 06843 9

This tale is one of trickery. Patrick is a newcomer to the countryside, and a crafty farmer convinces him that a pumpkin is a mule egg. Patrick, who needs a mule, buys the pumpkin for 25 dollars. His revenge is to trick the farmer right back.

Dunrea, Oliver. **Eppie M. Says . . .** Simon & Schuster Books for Young Readers, 1990. ISBN 0 02 733205 5

Ben Salem tells us that his big sister, Eppie M., knows everything. He believes her outrageous statements even though they often prove to be untrue.

Duvoisin, Roger. **Petunia.** Alfred A. Knopf Books for Young Readers, 1962. ISBN 0 394 90865 1

Petunia may well be the source of the expression "silly goose." She finds a book in the meadow, and because she has heard that books are the source of wisdom, she is convinced that if she carries it around, she will become wise.

Edwards, Michelle. **Chicken Man.** Lothrop, Lee & Shepard Books, 1991. ISBN 0 688 09708 1

The farm in this story is a kibbutz. Rody loves his job there with the chickens, and the egg production shows that the chickens love Rody. He makes it look like such a grand job that others covet it. Soon they demand a chance to be in charge of the chickens, so Rody is given another job. But Rody makes the best of every job he takes, and, after awhile, the farmers realize that it isn't the job that creates success, it's the man—and send him back to the chickens.

Ernst, Lisa Campbell. **When Bluebell Sang.** Aladdin Paperbacks, 1992. ISBN 0 689 71584 6

When Farmer Stevenson discovers that his cow can sing, he takes her to town to get her into show business. Soon crafty con man Big Eddie takes over, but Bluebell and Farmer Stevenson quickly discover that show biz is not where they belong.

Ernst, Lisa Campbell. **Zinnia and Dot.** Puffin Books, 1992. ISBN 0 14 054199 3

Zinnia and Dot, two hens, quarrel which allows a weasel to get all but one of their eggs. For awhile they even quarrel over whose egg it is, but then decide they'd better start mothering it.

Fleischman, Sid. **The Scarebird.** Illustrated by Peter Sis. Mulberry Books, 1984. ISBN 0 688 13105 0

Lonesome John puts up a "scarebird." As he dresses it with his own clothing, he begins to treat it as a human friend. He talks to it and even plays checkers with it. When a young man arrives on the farm looking for work, however, Lonesome John transfers his clothing and affection, little by little, from dummy to human.

Fox, Mem. **Hattie and the Fox.** Bradbury Press, 1988. ISBN 0 02 735470 9

Hattie the hen sees something in the bushes and tries to alert the other farm animals, but they sneer at her. Bit by bit the animal is revealed to us as it is to Hattie. This funny book contains repeated phrases.

Gammell, Stephen. **Once Upon MacDonald's Farm.** Simon & Schuster Books for Young Readers, 1981. ISBN 0 689 71379 7

This MacDonald doesn't have much of a farm. In fact, he has no animals, so he goes to town and buys some: a baboon, a lion and an elephant. We watch the animals' faces and body language as he attempts to milk the lion and gather eggs from the baboon. That night his animals run away. MacDonald's neighbor feels sorry for him and brings over a horse, a cow and some chickens. You think the problem is solved, but in the last picture MacDonald is plowing the fields with the chicken.

Geisert, Arthur. **Oink.** Houghton Mifflin Books for Children, 1991. ISBN 0 395 55329 6

The only word in this book is "Oink," but the detailed illustrations let us know that it's uttered (and shouted) with a variety of expressions.

Geisert, Bonnie. **Prairie Town.** Illustrated by Arthur Geisert. Houghton Mifflin Books for Children, 1998. ISBN 0 395 85907 7

A farm town on the prairie is shown throughout the course of a year. Detailed illustrations reveal many things the text never mentions such as a house that burns down and its reconstruction and the building of the town's second grain elevator.

Gibbons, Faye. **Night in the Barn.** Morrow Junior Books, 1995. ISBN 0 688 13326 6

This story describes one night spent in a barn by a group of friends who get just slightly scared.

Gray, Libba Moore. **Is There Room on the Feather Bed?** Illustrated by Nadine Bernard Westcott. Orchard Books, 1997. ISBN 0 531 30013 7

A teeny-tiny woman snuggles in her warm bed, but as the rain outside turns into a torrent, the farm animals come inside to join her, one by one.

Griffith, Helen. **Georgia Music.** *Illustrated by James Stevenson. Greenwillow Books, 1986. ISBN 0 688 0607 1*

A little girl spends a summer with her grandfather in Georgia. He plays tunes on his harmonica for her and for the birds. When he gets too old to live alone, he moves in with his granddaughter and daughter in Baltimore. But he misses the farm, so the girl makes music on the harmonica to recall the good times.

Griffith, Helen. **Grandaddy's Place.** *Illustrated by James Stevenson. Greenwillow Books, 1987. ISBN 0 688 06254 7*

Janetta visits her grandfather's farm in Georgia for the first time. The two are awkward together at first, but he soon plays music for her.

Hall, Donald. **Farm Summer, 1942.** *Illustrated by Barry Moser. Dial Books for Young Readers, 1994. ISBN 0 8037 1501 3*

Peter spends the summer of 1942 on his grandparents' farm because his father is on a ship in the Pacific, and we see the farm through his eyes.

Hall, Donald. **The Milkman's Boy.** *Illustrated by Greg Shed. Walker & Co., 1997. ISBN 0 8027 8465 8*

This book is about the changes that occurred in the first half of the 20th century on a farm in Hamden, Connecticut.

Hutchins, Pat. **Rosie's Walk.** *Simon & Schuster Books for Young Readers, 1968. ISBN 0 02 745850 4*

Rosie the hen goes for a stroll around the barnyard, unaware that a fox pursues her. Happenstance and her actions foil the fox at every turn until, still unnoticed by either Rosie or the text of the book, he's chased away by a swarm of bees.

Jackson, Ellen. **Brown Cow, Green Grass, Yellow Mellow.** *Illustrated by Victoria Raymond. Hyperion Books for Children, 1997. ISBN 0 7868 1162 5*

In this book, we follow the process for making butter for pancakes.

Kaufman, Jeff. **Milk Rock.** *Henry Holt & Co. Books for Young Readers, 1995. ISBN 0 8050 2814 5*

A poor farmer finds and feeds a rock. This brings the farmer a great fortune much to the amazement of his neighbors.

Lindbergh, Reeve. **The Midnight Farm.** *Illustrated by Susan Jeffers. Dial Books for Young Readers, 1987. ISBN 0 8037 0333 3*

A nighttime trip around the farm for a mother and young child makes a soothing bedtime journey for both.

Lobel, Arnold. **A Treeful of Pigs.** *Greenwillow Books, 1979. ISBN 0 688 84177 5*

A farmer is too lazy to get out of bed, so his wife finds a way to trick him into doing his work.

London, Jonathan. **Like Butter on Pancakes.** *Illustrated by G. Brian Karas. Viking Children's Books, 1995. ISBN 0 670 85130 2*

Poetic and lyrical text describes a day on the farm with a young boy.

MacLachlan, Patricia. **What You Know First.** *HarperCollins Children's Books, 1995. ISBN 0 06 024413 5*

It's the time of the Great Depression, and a little girl vows she will not leave the farm even though her family insists that they must.

Martin, Bill, Jr. **Barn Dance.** *Illustrated by Ted Rand. Henry Holt & Co. Books for Young Readers, 1986. ISBN 0 8050 0799 7*

This book's barn dance rhythm and delightful illustrations give us a night of magic, when only the boy with questions in his head and lots of farm animals are still awake and dancing.

Martin, Jacqueline Briggs. **Good Times on Grandfather Mountain.** *Illustrated by Susan Gaber. Orchard Books, 1992. ISBN 0 531 05977 4*

Old Washburn is an incurable optimist, and, no matter what tragedies befall this cheerful farmer, he makes the best of it. Fortunately, that spirit pays off in the end.

McFarlane, Sheryl. **Eagle Dreams.** Illustrated by Ron Lightburn. Philomel Books, 1994. ISBN 0 399 22695 8

A young farm boy finds a hurt eagle and nurses it back to health with his father's encouragement.

McPhail, David. **Farm Morning.** Harcourt Brace & Co., 1985. ISBN 0 15 227300 X

A little girl and her father take care of all the farm animals before sitting down to breakfast.

Most, Bernard. **Cock-A-Doodle-Moo.** Harcourt Brace & Co., 1996. ISBN 0 15 201252 4

The rooster has laryngitis, so the cow has to help him out with his morning routine.

Most, Bernard. **The Cow That Went Oink.** Harcourt Brace & Co., 1990. ISBN 0 152 20195 5

Suddenly, one day, a cow says "oink." It isn't until she finds a pig that says "moo" that a solution becomes apparent: each will teach the other the appropriate sound.

Myers, Christopher. **McCrephy's Field.** Illustrated by Normand Chartier. Houghton Mifflin Books for Children, 1991. ISBN 0 395 53807 6

A farm has been abandoned for many years, and we watch it go back to the wild.

Noble, Trinka Hakes. **The Day Jimmy's Boa Ate the Wash.** Illustrated by Steven Kellogg. Dial Books for Young Readers, 1980. ISBN 0 14 054623 5

A class has been on a field trip to a farm. Little by little, we get details of the havoc that occurred on the farm that day.

Nodset, Joan L. **Who Took the Farmer's Hat?** Illustrated by Fritz Siebel. HarperCollins Children's Books, 1963. ISBN 0 06 024566 2

The wind has blown away the farmer's hat, and he's in search of it. Each farm animal is asked whether it's seen the hat, but each claims it hasn't. They really have; they just called it something different.

Nolen, Jerdine. **Harvey Potter's Balloon Farm.** Illustrated by Mark Buehner. Mulberry Books, 1989. ISBN 0 688 07887 7

This book has wonderful illustrations of the growing balloons–they grow like vegetables on Harvey Potter's farm.

Palatini, Margie. **Piggie Pie.** Clarion Books, 1995. ISBN 0 395 71691 8

In this wild fantasy, a witch arrives at Old MacDonald's farm in search of piggies for piggie pie. The hiding places and disguises the piggies use to evade her are very funny and, although they fool the witch, young readers will spot them every time.

Plounde, Lynn. **Pigs in the Mud in the Middle of the Road.** Illustrated by John Schoenherr. Scholastic, 1997. ISBN 0 590 56863 9

Grandma and the rest of the family want to take a trip in her Model T Ford, but first the pigs–then the chickens, the sheep and the bulls–are all in the mud in the middle of the road.

Polacco, Patricia. **Thunder Cake.** Philomel Books, 1990. ISBN 0 399 22231 6

This book focuses is on a little girl's fear of a coming thunderstorm, but there is a lot of information about where food comes from as Grandma distracts her by searching the farm for ingredients for Thunder Cake.

Pomerantz, Charlotte. **Here Comes Henny.** Greenwillow Books, 1994. ISBN 0 688 12355 4

Word play is the focus and the fun in this story as a hen and her chicks go on a picnic.

Rush, Ken. **What About Emma?** Orchard Books, 1997. ISBN 0 531 09534 7

Hard times are forcing our narrator's family to sell off their herd of cows. It's too much to part with her favorite cow, Emma, however, so the children are allowed to keep Emma through the winter, when she will have her calf. Emma goes off to have her baby in the middle of a fierce storm.

Seymour, Tres. **Hunting the White Cow.** *Illustrated by Wendy Anderson Halperin. Orchard Books, 1993. ISBN 0 531 07085 9*

When the white cow ran off, Pa went out to catch her. When he failed, he asked other men to help—more and more each time she is spotted—but the white cow is elusive. His daughter, our narrator, keeps offering to help, but her offers are rebuffed. This funny book contains repeated phrases.

Simont, Marc. **The Goose That Almost Got Cooked.** *Scholastic, 1997. ISBN 0 590 69075 2*

Emily the goose is a nonconformist who finally falls behind the flock due to her silly tricks. When a farmer takes her in to live with his domestic geese, Emily is quite pleased to have found sanctuary. Then she finds out she's slated for dinner.

Stoeke, Janet Morgan. **Minerva Louise.** *Dutton Children's Books, 1988 ISBN 0 525 44374 6*

Minerva Louise is a hen who sees everything on the farm a bit differently than do the people who use them. This is an exercise in perception and laughter.

Turner, Ann. **Apple Valley Year.** *Simon & Schuster Books for Young Readers, 1993. ISBN 0 02 789281 6*

We watch the Clark family's apple orchard through the seasons, each of which brings its own beauty and chores.

Waddell, Martin. **Farmer Duck.** *Illustrated by Helen Oxenbury. Candlewick Press, 1991. ISBN 1 56402 009 6*

This farm is a dictatorship run by a lazy farmer. The duck is forced to do all the work—the farmer's only effort is to ask, "How goes the work?" At last a revolution occurs, and the animals take over the farm.

Waddell, Martin. **The Pig in the Pond.** *Illustrated by Jill Barton. Candlewick Press, 1992. ISBN 1 56402 604 3*

This book's repeated pattern and simple text make its story of farm animals jumping into a pond a good one for early readers.

Wells, Rosemary. **Waiting for the Evening Star.** *Illustrated by Susan Jeffers. Dial Books for Young Readers, 1993. ISBN 0 8037 1398 3*

A remote farm in Vermont is seen through the eyes of a young boy in the early 1900s. We see the farm through all four seasons.

Winch, John. **The Old Woman Who Loved to Read.** *Holiday House, 1996. ISBN 0 8234 1281 4*

An old woman who loves to read thinks that a farm in the country would be the ideal spot for reading. Then she's faced with the reality of farm work.

Wolff, Ferida. **Seven Loaves of Bread.** *Illustrated by Katie Keller. Morrow Junior Books, 1993. ISBN 0 688 11101 7*

Millie bakes bread, and each morning, she bakes a few extra loaves to deliver to her friends on a farm. Those extra loaves seem a lot to her sister, Rose, when Rose has to take over the baking. Then she discovers what happens when the bread isn't delivered to the farm.

Yolen, Jane. **Honkers.** *Illustrated by Leslie Baker. Little, Brown & Co., Children's Books, 1993. ISBN 0 316 96893 5*

Betsy is staying on her grandparent's farm while her parents prepare for the birth of a new baby. Betsy hatches a wild goose egg and cares for the garden until both are ready to go on.

Zimmerman, Andrea. **The Cow Buzzed.** *Illustrated by Paul Meisel. HarperTrophy, 1993. ISBN 0 06 443410 9*

When a cow catches a bee's cold, its buzz goes with it. The cow sneezes, and its moo and the cold go to the pig, and so it goes until we get to the rabbit, who covers his mouth when he sneezes.

Novels

Dahl, Roald. **Fantastic Mr. Fox.** Illustrated by Quentin Blake. Puffin Books, 1998. ISBN 0 14 130113 9

This short chapter book contains Dahl's trademark villains, this time in the form of three disgusting farmers and the sympathetic, very clever Mr. Fox. It makes a good first read-aloud.

Nonfiction

Gibbons, Gail. **The Milk Makers.** Simon & Schuster Books for Young Readers, 1985. ISBN 0 02 736640 5

This simple, straightforward explanation of milk production focuses on cows.

Greenlaw, M. Jean. **Welcome to the Stock Show.** Lodestar, 1997. ISBN 0 525 67525 6

This photo-essay provides lots of information about the animals at two livestock shows.

Guiberson, Brenda Z. **Winter Wheat.** Illustrated by Megan Lloyd. Henry Holt & Co. Books for Young Readers, 1995. ISBN 0 8050 1582 5

We spend a year with one farmer and his dog as a crop of winter wheat is raised and harvested.

Heller, Ruth. **Chickens Aren't the Only Ones.** G. P. Putnam's Sons Books for Young Readers, 1981. ISBN 0 448 01872 1

This excellent science book explores the various egg layers. It begins with insects, reptiles and birds, and then discusses mammals. The illustrations are particularly wonderful.

King-Smith, Dick. **All Pigs Are Beautiful.** Illustrated by Anita Jeram. Candlewick Press, 1993. ISBN 1 56402 148 3

The author has had many relationships with pigs, and he tells us about them in this book.

Lasky, Kathryn. **Sugaring Time.** Illustrated by Christopher Knight. Simon & Schuster Books for Young Readers, 1983. ISBN 0 02 75680 6

Maple sugaring is a big part of some northern farms' income, and this photo essay explains the process.

Lavis, Steve. **Cock-a-doodle-doo.** Lodestar, 1996. ISBN 0 525 67542 6

This counting book concentrates on the sounds of farm animals.

Lester, Alison. **My Farm.** Houghton Mifflin Books for Children, 1994. ISBN 0 395 68193 6

We spend a year on an Australian farm with our young narrator, watching things grow.

Llewellyn, Clare. **Tractor: And Other Farm Machines.** Dorling Kindersley, 1995. ISBN 1 56458 515 8

This book's full-color photographs dominate the text, but the book is useful for explaining how various farm machines work.

Peterson, Cris. **Harvest Year.** Boyds Mills Press, 1996. ISBN 1 56397 571 8

This photo-essay shows the process of farming in many areas of the country, season by season.

Peterson, Cris. **Horsepower: The Wonder of Draft Horses.** Boyds Mills Press, 1997. ISBN 1 56397 626 9

Although workhorses aren't common on today's farms, they are beautiful, fascinating creatures, and this photo-essay examines their place in today's world.

SOCIAL STUDIES: Towns & Cities

COMMENTS

This theme, in which towns and cities are explored, provides an opportunity to compare one's own environment with that of others. It can quickly branch off into other themes such as neighborhoods, transportation and international cities.

PICTURE BOOK STARTER

Let's start with bragging and look at Byrd Baylor's **The Best Town in the World** (see book list). In this idealized town, which the author's father remembered from his childhood, everything was perfect. The description of life in and around this town should get children comparing it to their own towns and cities—although, of course, none will be as perfect as this one.

ACTIVITIES

Language Arts
FINDING DETAILS

▶ Read the book **The Best Town in the World**. In the town the author describes, there are lots of things that children could and did do. Make a list of those things:

Swing on wild grapevines
Hunt for arrowheads
Eat sweet potato pie
Pick wild blackberries
Herd goats
Climb trees
Catch fireflies
Carry water from the well
Swim in the creek
Go to school
Eat milk and bread for supper
Eat supper in a tree
Buy candy
Shop in a store
Celebrate the Fourth of July
Eat
    Fried chicken
    Chile con carne
    Black-eyed peas
    Corn on the cob
    Cornbread sticks
    Biscuits
    Frijoles
    Squash and turnip greens
    Watermelon pickles
    Dumplings
    Fritters
    Stews
    Chocolate cake
    Pie
Tell time by the sun
Predict the weather from the stars
Tell what to plant by the moon
Fly kites
    Jump rope
    Blow whistles
    Walk on stilts
    Play with bows and arrows
    Play with rag dolls
    Spin tops
    Play bamboo flutes
    Play checkers

CATEGORIZING

▶ Divide the books listed (and other books you have found that apply to this theme) into city books and country books. Find the book that comes closest to describing the place where you live.

MAKING COMPARISONS

▶ Make copies of the list you made of things children did in that town. How many of those things can you do in your town or city?

▶ Beside each listed activity you think you can't do, put the reason why you can't.

▶ Make a list of the things that you do that the people in that town couldn't do. Remember that they were probably living at the turn of the century.

▶ In the town in this book, people celebrate Texas Independence Day and the Fourth of July. What holidays does your town celebrate? How do they celebrate them? Can you be part of that celebration?

▶ Read the book **Night City** (see book list). It contrasts directly with **The Best Little Town in the World** because it takes place in a busy city. It focuses on night workers, but still touches on much of the activity in a big city. Discuss the different lives people there might lead.

TAKING SURVEYS

▶ Use the first list you made to conduct a survey in your household. How many people living in your house have done each of those things?

Math

▶ Think of a town or a city you have heard about that is far away from where you live. Find out how far away it is from where you now live. How many days or hours would you have to travel to get there by plane, by car, by boat, or on foot?

Social Studies

▶ Choose a city that is far away from where you live that you think you might like to live in some day. Make sure that no one else in the classroom has chosen the same city. Conduct research on that place. Find it on a map then mark it on a big display map on the bulletin board. Find out what language people speak there. Look at videos and nonfiction books that describe that town or city.

▶ What are some things that your town or city could do or could acquire that would make it better? Why haven't they been done? Write letters to or visit the mayor of your town to find out whether it's possible for your town or city to do those things.

▶ Write a brochure describing your city as "The Best City in the World."

▶ List some of the jobs that could be done in a city but that couldn't be done in a small town. Make another list of jobs that can be done in a small town but that couldn't or wouldn't be done in a city. Which list is longer?

Art

▶ Cut out shapes of city buildings from newspapers. Make a mural by pasting those buildings on a background of black or red paper. Use markers to make the effect more pleasing.

▶ Then do the opposite: Use newspapers as the background of a bulletin board and use red or black paper from which to cut out shapes of city buildings. Which effect do you like best?

BOOK LIST
Fiction

Baker, Jeannie. *Home in the Sky.* Greenwillow Books, 1984. ISBN 0 688 03841 7

Mike cares for the pigeons on the roof of his apartment building in the city. One pigeon, Light, flies over the city, and we see it through Light's eyes.

Baylor, Byrd. *The Best Town in the World.* Illustrated by Ronald Himler. Simon & Schuster Books for Young Readers, 1983. ISBN 0 684 18035 9

Maybe Baylor's father exaggerated just a bit when he told her about the town he grew up in. What we get is a book describing an ideal place to live at the turn of the century.

Brett, Jan. *Town Mouse, Country Mouse.* G. P. Putnam's Sons Books for Young Readers, 1994. ISBN 0 399 22622 2

Brett adds a bit to this traditional tale: A country owl and a city cat later pick up the house-swapping idea.

Bunting, Eve. *Secret Place.* Clarion Books, 1996. ISBN 0 395 64367 8

This little bit of nature along a river is hidden within the busy city but some people and animals are nourished by it.

Burton, Virginia Lee. *The Little House.* Houghton Mifflin Books for Children,1978. ISBN 0 395 25938 X

This classic tale shows the "progress" of a city through the eyes of a little house that first stands out in the country but gradually is surrounded by the city.

Dorros, Arthur. *Abuela.* Dutton Children's Books, 1991. ISBN 0 525 44750 4

We travel with Rosalba as she imagines a flight with her grandmother over New York City.

Egan, Tim. *Chestnut Cove.* Houghton Mifflin Books for Children,1995. ISBN 0 395 69823 5

Chestnut Cove was an ideal town in which to live until the king announced a watermelon-growing contest.

Geisert, Bonnie. *Prairie Town.* Houghton Mifflin Books for Children,1998. ISBN 0 395 85907 7

We watch a prairie town through the course of one year, observing many changes as it slowly grows.

Jakobsen, Kathy. *My New York.* Little, Brown & Co., Children's Books, 1993. ISBN 0 316 45653 5

Knowing that her friend is about to move to New York City, Becky writes her a letter describing her favorite places in New York.

Johnson, Stephen T. *Alphabet City.* Viking Children's Books, 1995. ISBN 0 670 85631 2

Letters of the alphabet are found amid a cityscape.

Johnston, Tony. *The Last Snow of Winter.* Morrow Junior Books, 1993. ISBN 0 688 10749 4

This story introduces the concept of small town as large neighborhood. A famous artist comes to town and creates an artistic snowman for the village with the first snow of winter. By the time of the winter's last snow, the artist is ill, so the villagers create a snowman for him.

Keats, Ezra. *Jack Goggles!* Puffin Books, 1987. ISBN 0 140 56440 3

Peter and his friend find a pair of goggles, but some neighborhood bullies decide to take them away.

Komaiko, Leah. *On Sally Perry's Farm.* Simon & Schuster Books for Young Readers, 1996. ISBN 0 689 80083 5

It isn't until the end of this book that we find that Sally's farm is just a patch of land in a busy city.

Kovalski, Maryan. *Wheels on the Bus.* Little, Brown & Co., Children's Books, 1987. ISBN 0 316 50256 1

This book places the familiar song within a plot. A grandmother and the kids have been on a shopping excursion. As they wait for the bus, Grandma starts the song, and soon everyone joins in.

Levitin, Sonia. **Boom Town.** *Illustrated by Cat Bowman Smith. Orchard Books, 1998. ISBN 0 531 30045 9*

This story is set during the California gold rush, and Amanda's father searches for gold all week, coming home only for the weekend. Amanda begins baking pies, and her father sells them among the miners. Soon she's got a thriving business, and a whole town grows up to serve the miners.

Macaulay, David. **City: A Story of Roman Planning & Construction.** *Houghton Mifflin Books for Children, 1983. ISBN 0 395 34922 2*

We watch the planning and development of a mythical city in great detail, both visually and textually.

Macaulay, David. **Rome Antics.** *Houghton Mifflin Books for Children, 1997. ISBN 0 395 82279 3*

In this almost wordless book, we follow the flight of a pigeon through the modern city of Rome.

McCloskey, Robert. **Make Way for Ducklings.** *Puffin Books, 1941. ISBN 0 14 050171 1*

In this classic tale, Mr. and Mrs. Mallard attempt to raise their family in the city of Boston.

Ringgold, Faith. **Tar Beach.** *Crown Books for Young Readers, 1991. ISBN 0 517 58030 6*

Like Rosalba in **Abuela**, Cassie dreams of flying over New York City. She calls the rooftop of her apartment building "Tar Beach" and from it she looks down over that city.

Rogers, Paul & Emma. **Cat's Kittens.** *Illustrated by Sophy Williams. Viking Children's Books, 1996. ISBN 0 670 86255 X*

A mother cat raises her family in an alley, and one by one, each kitten goes its own way.

Sorensen, Henri. **New Hope.** *Lothrop, Lee & Shepard Books, 1995. ISBN 0 688 13925 6*

This small town, founded by a man who broke a wagon axle there, is a microcosm for the development of the West.

Wellington, Monica. **Night City.** *Dutton Children's Books, 1998. ISBN 0 525 45948 0*

The concept of time is behind this book, as a city wakes up just as we go to bed. One by one, we see several night workers through the night until dawn, when we get up.

Yolen, Jane. **Letting Swift River Go.** *Illustrated by Barbara Cooney. Little, Brown & Co., Children's Books, 1992. ISBN 0 316 96299 4*

Several small towns were flooded during a WPA project in the '30s to create a large reservoir. Based on fact, this book tells the story from the point of view of one child growing up in one of those towns.

Poetry

Greenfield, Eloise. **Night on Neighborhood Street.** *Puffin Books, 1991. ISBN 0 14 055683 4*

These short poems celebrate the city while illustrating both its pluses and minuses.

Hughes, Langston. **The Block.** *Illustrated by Romare Bearden. Viking Children's Books, 1995. ISBN 0 670 86501 X*

Bearden's paintings are like posters, interpreting the poems with bold strokes.

Yolen, Jane. **Sky Scrape/City Scrape: Poems of City Life.** *Boyds Mills Press, 1996. ISBN 1 56397 179 8*

There are many good city poems in this book.

Nonfiction

Henderson, Kathy. **A Year in the City.** *Illustrated by Paul Howard. Candlewick Press, 1996. ISBN 1 56402 872 0*

This book about the seasons shows the subtle as well as the more obvious signs of each.

Lewin, Ted. **Market!** *Lothrop, Lee & Shepard Books, 1996. ISBN 0 688 12161 6*

This book's text is brief, but its illustrations are full of details of city markets in Ecuador, Nepal, Ireland, Uganda, and the U.S.

Nikola, Lisa W. **One Hole in the Road.** *Illustrated by Dan Yaccarino. Henry Holt & Co. Books for Young Readers, 1997. ISBN 0 8050 4285 7*

This counting book shows many city workers around a construction site.

SOCIAL STUDIES: Other Places

 COMMENTS

Trade books can do what social studies text-books can't when dealing with cultures around the world. We want to help children in the lower grades see that, while there are differences between cultures and countries, there are also many things we share with people everywhere. Trade books, particularly storybooks, can help children see these things for themselves, a goal less easily accomplished by the series of facts presented in textbooks.

Although there are many picture books set in other lands and earlier times, I've chosen, for the most part, to restrict my choices

 PICTURE BOOK STARTER

Let's start with a nonfictional picture book this time, **Children Just Like Me** (see book list). In this photographic essay children from many cultures tell of their homes, families, friends, and dreams.

to books set in the here and now in order to deal with present conditions rather than past realities.

I've stayed with realistic and nonfictional sources in this theme, but it's quite possible to take this theme into folktales from around the world.

ACTIVITIES

Language Arts

INVESTIGATING LANGUAGES

► Allow each child to select one of the books for further investigation. Find out how to say something in the language spoken in that country.

► Make a list of the many ways of saying "father" and "mother" by using other languages.

FINDING DETAILS

► Encourage children to examine the illustrations in the books listed to find details providing information about the culture or land explored in the books. Have the kids point out these details to others. For instance, you can often tell about the climate or season of a country by the clothing people are wearing.

MAKING COMPARISONS

► Suggest that students choose a page from **Children Just Like Me** that describes a child or children most like themselves. They should then make a statement such as: Just like _____, I like to _____.

► Again, using **Children Just Like Me**, ask students to find an object in one of the pictures that's like one they have in their own homes.

► Put the names of the children from that book and from other books in the book list below on separate cards spread across a bulletin board. Give children yarn and labels. When they find a similarity between any two characters on the board, they should stretch a piece of yarn between them and, on the label, state what it is they have in common.

CHARTING INFORMATION

► Read and share many of the books listed. Organize the information you discover in them in a chart similar to this:

BOOK TITLE	COUNTRY	INFORMATION ABOUT THAT COUNTRY FOUND IN THE BOOK	OTHER INFORMATION ABOUT THAT COUNTRY

Social Studies

► On a large outline world map, color in each country mentioned in one of the books.

► What form of money is used in that country? Visit a bank or coin dealer to view the currency of several countries.

► Look at and collect stamps from other countries. Notice what that country is celebrating on its stamps.

► Find and make a recipe for a food commonly eaten in the country of choice. Have a tasting party where each of these foods is sampled. Place a list of the ingredients beside each food, as well as a card telling the country it came from. (Be sure to warn people with food allergies about specific foods.)

► Visit some of the following Web sites to find out more about the people in the countries you're investigating: **www.jwindow.net/KIDS/** and **jin.jcic.or.jp/kidsweb/index.html** offer information about Japan for young children.

At **www.ipl.org/youth/cquest/** we follow Parsifal Penguin and Olivia Owl as they wander around Africa, Asia, the Far East, Antarctica, Australia, Europe, the Middle East, and South and Central America.

www.africaonline.com/AfricaOnline/ coverkids.html offers information about The Ivory Coast, Ghana, Kenya, Tanzania, Uganda, and Zimbabwe.

Music

► Find and sing some songs from other countries.

► Find and play some musical instruments from other lands.

► Watch videos of dancing from other lands. Use some of those movements or rhythms to create your own dance.

BOOK LIST
Fiction

Alexander, Lloyd. _Fortune Tellers._ Illustrated by Trina Schart Hyman. Dutton Children's Books, 1992. ISBN 0 525 44849 7

This very funny story takes place in Cameroon, West Africa. The illustrations show the art and clothing of the people there.

Anderson, Laurie Halse. _Ndito Runs._ Henry Holt & Co. Books for Young Readers, 1996. ISBN 0 8050 3265 7

It's the highlands of Kenya through which Ndito runs on her way to school.

Andrews, Jan. _The Very Last First Time._ Illustrated by Ian Wallace. Atheneum Books for Young Readers, 1985. ISBN 0 689 50388 1

An Inuit child is considered old enough to walk under the ice at low tide to gather food. Lighting her way by a candle, she goes farther and farther from the hole where she enters until she is in real danger of not making it back before the tide comes in.

Bunting, Eve. _Going Home._ Illustrated by David Diaz. HarperCollins Children's Books, 1996. ISBN 0 06 026296 6

A family is headed back to their tiny village in Mexico. The children can't understand why it's so special, and, on the way there, they wonder why their parents left it if it was such a good place.

Bunting, Eve. _Market Day._ Illustrated by Holly Berry. HarperCollins Children's Books, 1996. ISBN 0 06 025364 9

It's market day in a small village in Ireland. A little girl is given a penny to spend, and she and a "Wee Boy" enjoy the day together.

Cameron, Ann. _The Most Beautiful Place in the World._ Illustrated by Thomas B. Allen. Alfred A. Knopf Books for Young Readers, 1988. ISBN 0 394 99463 9

Juan lives with his grandmother in Guatemala. His mother and stepfather have abandoned him. He earns a little money by shining shoes, but he longs to go to school.

Castaneda, Omar S. _Abuela's Weave._ Illustrated by Enrique Sanchez. Lee & Low Books, 1993. ISBN 1 880000 20 2

In Guatemala, Esperanza and her grandmother have been weaving wall hangings to sell on market day. Because grandmother's face is marred by a birthmark, people are afraid of her and call her a witch. Therefore, it is Esperanza who must sell their handiwork.

Daly, Nikki. _Not So Fast Songololo._ Atheneum Books for Young Readers, 1985. ISBN 0 689 58367 9

Tired of hand-me-downs, Malusi is enchanted by the bright red shoes he sees in a shop window in South Africa, and his grandmother buys them for him.

Delacre, Lulu. _Vejigantes Masquerade._ Scholastic, 1993. ISBN 0 590 45776 4

It's carnival time in Puerto Rico, and a little boy tells us all about it.

Edwards, Michelle. _Chicken Man._ Lothrop, Lee & Shepard Books, 1991. ISBN 0 688 09708 1

On a kibbutz in Israel, Rody performs each occupation with such love and gusto that he makes the job look wonderful. Other kibbutz workers demand his job, only to find that it's Rody's attitude that makes the task so pleasant.

Eisenberg, Phyllis Rose. _You're My Nikki._ Illustrated by Jill Kastner. Puffin Books, 1986. ISBN 0 14 055463 7

A little African girl is convinced that her mother has forgotten her, but her mother is only tired and cranky after a hard day at work.

Fleming, Candace. _Gabriella's Song._ Illustrated by Giselle Potter. Atheneum Books for Young Readers, 1997. ISBN 0 689 80973 5

In Venice, a little girl begins to hum a tune inspired by the sounds she hears in the city. Other people of the city hear the tune and begin to hum it, too. Then a great composer hears it, and it becomes a symphony.

Franklin, Kristine. **Iguana Beach.** *Illustrated by Lori Lohstoeter. Crown Books for Young Readers, 1997. ISBN 0 517 70900 7*

A little Costa Rican girl is allowed to go to the beach with her uncle and older cousins. Some of the terrain and animal life of Costa Rica is shown.

Heide, Florence Parry. **The Day of Ahmed's Secret.** *Lothrop, Lee & Shepard Books, 1990. ISBN 0 688 08894 5*

In Cairo, Ahmed's job is to deliver cooking-gas canisters. This day, however, Ahmed has a secret that he will reveal when he gets home—he has learned to write his name.

Heide, Florence Parry. **Sami and the Time of Troubles.** *Clarion Books, 1992. ISBN 0 395 55964 2*

War-torn Lebanon is the background for this story about Sami and his family, who try to keep a feeling of family and home in spite of frequent bombings.

Hoffman, Mary. **Boundless Grace.** *Illustrated by Caroline Binch. Dial Books for Young Readers, 1995. ISBN 0 8037 1715 6*

In this sequel to **Amazing Grace**, Grace goes to visit her father and his new family in Gambia where she feels stretched between two homes.

Hughes, Shirley. **All About Alfie.** *Lothrop, Lee & Shepard Books, 1997. ISBN 0 688 15186 8*

This is a collection of stories about Alfie, an engaging preschooler who lives with his mother, father and little sister in England.

Joose, Barbara M. **Mama, Do You Love Me?** *Illustrated by Barbara Lavallee. Chronicle Books, 1991. ISBN 0 87701 759 X*

An Inuit child and her mother play a game in which the child questions what would happen if she did bad things or became a series of different animals. Each time, the mother assures the girl that she would love her. The story's touch is light, but the illustrations and the text allude to many things in the Arctic world and culture.

Joseph, Lynn. **Jasmine's Parlour Day.** *Illustrated by Ann Grifalconi. Lothrop, Lee & Shepard Books, 1994. ISBN 0 688 11487 3*

It's market day in a village on the island of Trinidad, and Jasmine helps her mother set up their stall before she goes with a friend to explore the market.

Keller, Holly. **Grandfather's Dream.** *Greenwillow Books, 1994. ISBN 0 688 12339 2*

This story takes place in Vietnam. The war has been over for years, but the sarus cranes that disappeared when the canals were drained during the fighting haven't come back. Some of the villagers like the drained land because it's ideal for raising rice, but grandfather wants to rebuild the dams and entice the cranes to return.

Khan, Rukhsana. **The Roses in My Carpets.** *Illustrated by Ronald Himler. Holiday House, 1998. ISBN 0 8234 1399 3*

A little boy cares for his mother and little sister in a refugee camp outside of Afghanistan. They live on bread and water, even though he works hard from sunup to sundown and a sponsor sends some money. He uses that money to learn how to weave a carpet.

Kurtz, Jane. **Pulling the Lion's Tail.** *Illustrated by Floyd Cooper. Simon & Schuster Books for Young Readers, 1995. ISBN 0 689 80324 9*

Set in Ethiopia, this story tells of a young girl whose father takes a new wife. Almaz tries to make friends with her new stepmother, but she is constantly rebuffed. At last she goes to her grandfather, who assigns her a seemingly impossible task: pull the hairs from a lion's tail. She does so, but only after gaining the lion's trust. The lesson is that she must show the same patience with her stepmother.

Lauture, Denize. **Running the Road to ABC.** Illustrated by Reynold Ruffins. Simon & Schuster Books for Young Readers, 1996. ISBN 0 689 80507 1

This ABC book is set in Haiti where six children run down the road to school in the predawn hours.

Lester, Alison. **My Farm.** Houghton Mifflin Books for Children, 1994. ISBN 0 395 68193 6

We watch a year go by on a small Australian farm.

Lester, Alison. **When Frank Was Four.** Houghton Mifflin Books for Children, 1994. ISBN 0 395 74275 7

This is a counting book of sorts, but the accent is on an Australian family with seven kids.

Levinson, Riki. **Our Home Is the Sea.** Illustrated by Dennis Luzak. Dutton Children's Books, 1988. ISBN 0 525 44406 8

It's the last day of school for our narrator who lives with his family on a houseboat in Hong Kong. Now he can join his father and grandfather as they fish for their living.

Lewin, Ted. **The Storytellers.** Lothrop, Lee & Shepard Books, 1998. ISBN 0 688 15178 7

This story is set in present day Fez, Morocco. Abdul and his grandfather walk through the crowded marketplace with a definite destination in mind. They pass and greet many workers before arriving at their spot for storytelling.

Linden, Anne Marie. **Emerald Blue.** Atheneum Books for Young Readers, 1995. ISBN 0 689 31946 0

A little girl tells us what life was like on the Caribbean Island where she lived with her grandmother. She also tells us about the hurricane that struck the island.

London, Jonathan. **Ali, Child of the Desert.** Illustrated by Ted Lewin. Lothrop, Lee & Shepard Books, 1997. ISBN 0 688 12560 3

Ali and his camel become separated from Ali's father during a sandstorm in the Sahara desert. A Berber goatherd befriends him.

London, Jonathan. **The Village Basket Weaver.** Illustrated by George Crespo. Dutton Children's Books, 1996. ISBN 0 525 45314 8

Tavio's grandfather is the most skilled weaver in his village in Central America. He's now weaving his last project: a cassava breadbasket.

Macaulay, David. **Rome Antics.** Houghton Mifflin Books for Children, 1997. ISBN 0 395 82279 3

We watch a messenger pigeon's flight through the busy city of Rome and, in the process, get a pigeon's eye view of the ancient city.

McDonald, Megan. **My House Has Stars.** Illustrated by Peter Catalanotto. Orchard Books, 1996. ISBN 0 531 09529 0

A mother and daughter begin to think about the fact that night falls everywhere. Then each page represents a home in a different culture with stars becoming the unifying theme.

Mollel, Tololwa. **The Orphan Boy.** Illustrated by Paul Morin. Clarion Books, 1990. ISBN 0 395 72079 6

This mythical tale takes place in Tanzania and offers some information about the land and its people, as well as a good story about a betrayal of trust.

Nye, Naomi S. **Sitti's Secrets.** Illustrated by Nancy Carpenter. Simon & Schuster Books for Young Readers, 1994. ISBN 0 02 768460 1

Our narrator misses her grandmother, Sitti, who lives in a village in Palestine. Although neither spoke the other's language, they managed to communicate when the family visited. We see some of the culture of the village through the little girl's memories.

Say, Allen. **Tree of Cranes.** Houghton Mifflin Books for Children, 1991. ISBN 0 395 52024 X

A little Japanese boy gets wet at a pool in a garden, and his mother is displeased. From the room where she puts him, he sees her digging up his tree from the garden. He thinks she must be very angry to do such a thing. At last she brings him into a room where she has decorated the tree with origami cranes and made it into a Christmas tree like the ones she knew from time she spent in California.

Sis, Peter. **The Three Golden Keys.** Bantam Doubleday Dell Books for Young Readers, 1994. ISBN 0 385 47292 7

In this very challenging picture book, the author takes an imaginary trip through his native city of Prague.

Stock, Catherine. **Where Are You Going, Manyoni?** Morrow Junior Books, 1993. ISBN 0 688 10353 7

In Zimbabwe, a little girl walks steadily along her way to school, and as she does so, we are treated to a look at the countryside and some of the animals that live there.

Talbot, Hudson. **Amazon Diary: The Jungle Adventures of Alex Winters.** Illustrated by Mark Greenberg. G. P. Putnam's Sons Books for Young Readers, 1997. ISBN 0 399 22916 7

Young Alex is flying to join his parents who are anthropologists in Brazil. When his plane crashes, he is rescued by the Yanomami people, a stone-age culture living on the border of Venezuela.

Tchana, Katrin Hyman. **Oh, No, Toto!** Illustrated by Colin Bootman. Scholastic, 1997. ISBN 0 590 46585 6

A little boy in Cameroon goes with his grandmother to market where he can't resist grabbing for every bit of food he sees. While grandmother copes with him, we get to see much of the costume and custom of the country.

Valgardson, W. D. **Winter Rescue.** Illustrated by Ange Zhang. Margaret K. McElderry Books, 1995. ISBN 0 689 80094 0

Thor is a young Icelandic boy who lives with his family on Lake Winnipeg in Canada. Although he much prefers to stay at home and watch television, his grandfather takes him ice fishing, where he helps to rescue a ski-mobiler.

Van Laan, Nancy. **Mama Rocks, Papa Sings.** Alfred A. Knopf Books for Young Readers, 1995. ISBN 0 679 84016 8

In this story based on fact, a missionary couple on Haiti took in 28 children. The pictures give us most of the information about Haiti while the rhyming text adds the fun.

Yorinks, Arthur. **It Happened in Pinsk.** Illustrated by Richard Egielski. Farrar Strauss & Giroux Books for Young Readers, 1987. ISBN 0 374 33651 2

This wild story is set in the city of Pinsk. There, Irv Irving goes unhappily about the city, envying everybody. Then he literally loses his head.

Nonfiction

Grossman, Patricia. **Saturday Market.** Lothrop, Lee & Shepard Books, 1994. ISBN 0 688 12176 4

It's market day in Mexico. We visit a different stall on each page and watch the activity in the market.

Kindersley, Barnabas. **Children Just Like Me: A Unique Celebration of Children Around the World.** DK Publishing, 1995. ISBN 0 7894 0201 7

This book is an excellent source of information about how children are alike and different all over the world. The photographs are as informative as the text.

Lewin, Ted. **Market!** Lothrop, Lee & Shepard Books, 1996. ISBN 0 688 12161 6

Markets in Ecuador, Nepal, Ireland, Uganda, and the United States are shown through detailed drawings and limited text.

Say, Allen. **Grandfather's Journey.** Houghton Mifflin Books for Children, 1993. ISBN 0 395 57035 2

This book is the biography of the author's grandfather who was born in Japan and came to America as a young man. He never felt completely at home in either place, however, because when he was in America, he missed Japan, and when he was there, he wanted to be here.

Schuett, Stacey. **Somewhere in the World Right Now.** Alfred A. Knopf Books for Young Readers, 1995. ISBN 0 679 86537 3

Time around the world is the focus of this book. End papers show us the time zones, and at each place we stop in the book there's a map to show us where we are.

SOCIAL STUDIES: Work

COMMENTS

A literary theme on work quickly becomes a social studies, math, and economics theme as well: why and how people work, what products or services they provide, who pays for those services, etc. It's important that this theme include books about service workers, as well as professional people, artists, and artisans. Besides the books listed starting on page 87, many picture book biographies would fit well in this theme. See also the Art & Artists theme on page 98.

PICTURE BOOK STARTER

In Michelle Edwards' **Chicken Man** (see book list), the point is obvious but does not overpower the book. Rody loves his job of taking care of the chickens on a kibbutz. He understands the chickens, and they produce well for him. He enjoys his work so much, however, that other, less happy workers become jealous and demand that they have a chance to do Rody's job. Unfortunately for the chickens, Rody moves on to another menial job on the kibbutz, but this, too, he manages to enjoy. It's not until Rody has taken on and succeeded at many jobs that the other workers begin to understand that it's Rody's attitude, not the task itself, that makes the job so pleasant.

ACTIVITIES

Language Arts
CATEGORIZING

TITLE	JOBS	JOBS I'D LIKE
Storytellers	Storytellers, muledrivers, wool dyers, falconer, copper workers, brass workers, tanners, market sellers	Storyteller— Carla

▶ Place the books for this theme on a large table with a chart such as the one above.

▶ As students read the books, suggest that they enter the relevant information in the chart, including the name of any job mentioned in the stories that they think they'd like to try someday.

▶ Discuss the different things the work in each of the books listed below produces in terms of goods and services, perhaps through the construction of a chart such as the one below.

TITLE	WORK	PRODUCT	SERVICE	WHY PEOPLE WANT IT
Mama Is a Miner	Mining Coal	Coal		Provides energy & heat
Ducks Disappearing	Motel Maids		Clean Rooms	To have a clean places to sleep

SEQUENCING

▶ Make a flow chart of the jobs Rody took. Beside each job, tell how he made it pleasant.

MAKING COMPARISONS

▶ Look at books, such as **Chicken Man, Chicken Soup Boots** and **Mr. Griggs' Work** (see book list), that show people who enjoy their jobs. Look for ways in which they exhibit this enjoyment and then interview various people at work to see how they feel about their work. How do they show their feelings?

▶ After sharing the book **Chicken Man**, ask the children to suggest ways to make tedious or unpleasant jobs in the classroom more pleasant. Which of those ways did Rody use?

Social Studies

▶ Invite people involved in many different kinds of work to come to the class. Construct some informational charts about their work and the work of others you know or have read about, such as:

▶ To show the effect of assembly line jobs on workers, plan a craft activity such as the making of greeting cards. First let each person complete his or her own card using their own design. Next, turn the making of cards into an assembly line. Place four or five people in each line, and give each child a single, simple task in the process of making the cards. After a few have been completed, ask children to discuss which cards they enjoyed making more, as well as the positive and negative aspects of assembly line work.

▶ Take a "job walk." Give each child note-taking materials and take a walk first around the school, carefully noting each person who's doing a job for which he or she is paid. Do the same in a downtown area and on a farm. Post the jobs as people discover them, whether from real life or from the books they are reading.

▶ Where does the money to pay people come from? Look at each of the occupations from the books listed and figure out where each worker gets his or her money. Do they, in turn, create other jobs that produce money?

THE JOB	THE GOOD PART	THE BAD PART
Teaching	You get to help lots of people You work during the day time You have to be in the workplace less than 8 hours a day.	The pay isn't very good You have lots of bosses You don't always have the right materials

BOOK LIST
Fiction

Alexander, Lloyd. **Fortune Tellers.** *Illustrated by Trina Schart Hyman. Dutton Children's Books, 1992. ISBN 0 525 44849 7*

A carpenter consults a fortune teller in Cameroon to find out what his future life will be like.

Aller, Susan Biwin. **Emma and the Night Dogs.** *Illustrated by Mami Backer. Albert Whitman & Co., 1997. ISBN 0 8075 19936*

The dogs in this story are working dogs, part of a search and rescue team. When a boy is lost, Emma's aunt and her dogs go in search of him.

Altman, Linda Jacobs. **Amelia's Road.** *Illustrated by Enrique O. Sanchez. Lee & Low Books, 1993. ISBN 1 880000 04 0*

Amelia's family travels from place to place to pick vegetables and fruits, and because they're on the road so much, she has felt that she didn't belong anywhere. She hates it when her father gets out the map because she knows they'll be on the move again. This year, however, she's in a school where the teacher bothered to learn her name, and she finds a way to make it a place where she belongs.

Barrows, Allison. **The Artist's Friends.** *Lerner Publishing Group, 1997. ISBN 1 575 05054 4*

When a little girl announces that she wants to be an artist like her father, he takes her to visit all kinds of artists and to view the work they do.

Best, Cari. **Red Light, Green Light, Mama and Me.** *Illustrated by Niki Daly. Orchard Books, 1995. ISBN 0 531 08752 2*

Lizzie spends the day with her mother, a librarian in a big city library. Lizzie's observations are acute, and her comments about various people and the things she sees lighten the story's tone.

Brott, Ardyth. **Jeremy's Decision.** *Illustrated by Michael Martchenko. Kane/Miller Books Publishers, 1990. ISBN 0 916291 65 0*

Jeremy's father is a famous maestro. Many people ask Jeremy if he's going to follow in his father's footsteps, but he dreads that question because he doesn't know what he wants to be when he grows up.

Bunting, Eve. **A Day's Work.** *Illustrated by Ronald Himler. Clarion Books, 1994. ISBN 0 395 67321 6*

Francisco acts as an interpreter for his grandfather when the man seeks work as a day laborer in California. Anxious for employment, the boy tells the boss that his grandfather is a gardener because that's the only available work.

Edwards, Michelle. **Chicken Man.** *Lothrop, Lee & Shepard Books, 1991. ISBN 0 688 09708 1*

This farm is a kibbutz, and Rody loves his job there taking care of the chickens. He makes it look like such a grand job that others covet it, and soon they demand a chance to be in charge of the chickens. Rody makes the best of every job he takes, and, after awhile, the farmers realize that it isn't the job that's successful, it's the man, so they send him back to the chickens.

Gardella, Tricia. **Just Like My Dad.** *Illustrated by Margot Apple. HarperTrophy, 1996. ISBN 0 06 443463 X*

A little boy and his modern cowboy father go about their daily chores on the ranch.

Garland, Sherry. **My Father's Boat.** *Illustrated by Ted Rand. Orchard Books, 1998. ISBN 0 531 30073 0*

A boy and his father live in the United States, but they think about the boy's grandfather, who's still in Vietnam. But even though they live in different countries, they're all involved in commercial shrimp fishing.

Greenberg, Melanie Hope. **Aunt Lilly's Laundromat.** Dutton Children's Books, 1994. ISBN 0 525 45211 7

Aunt Lilly came from Haiti, and she adorns the walls of her laundromat with pictures of that island.

Grossman, Patricia. **The Night Ones.** Illustrated by Lydia Dabcovich. Harcourt Brace & Co., 1991. ISBN 0 152 57438 7

The bus moves through the city, dropping off various night workers at their workplaces and later taking them home again.

Hazen, Barbara Shook. **Mommy's Office.** Illustrated by David Soman. Atheneum Books for Young Readers, 1992. ISBN 0 689 31601 1

Emily spends the day at her mother's office and compares it to the place where she works—the school.

Hendershot, Judith. **In Coal Country.** Illustrated by Thomas Allen. Alfred A. Knopf Books for Young Readers, 1987. ISBN 0 394 98190 1

This memoir of a time when coal dust covered everything focuses on coal mining country in the 1930s.

Jennings, Dana Andrew. **Me, Dad & Number 6.** Harcourt Brace & Co., 1997. ISBN 0 15 200085 2

Our narrator's father got him interested in stock car racing. In this book, they're getting a car ready for a big race.

Kalman, Maira. **Chicken Soup, Boots.** Viking Children's Books, 1993. ISBN 0 670 85201 5

This story exhibits a whole gallery of neighbors, along with the jobs they do. The emphasis is not so much on the work itself as it is on the satisfaction people take from their jobs.

Khalsa, Dayal Kaur. **Cowboy Dreams.** Crown Books for Young Readers, 1990. ISBN 0 517 57490 X

A woman tells us of how, as a child, she thought she would like to grow up to be a cowboy. Now, as an adult, she sings cowboy songs.

Klinting, Lars. **Bruno the Carpenter.** Henry Holt & Co. Books for Young Readers, 1995. ISBN 0 8050 4501 5

We learn about the tools and skills of a carpenter through the actions of Bruno Beaver.

Klinting, Lars. **Bruno the Tailor.** Henry Holt & Co. Books for Young Readers, 1997. ISBN 0 8050 4500 7

Bruno Beaver makes an apron for himself, and we learn about the tools and skills of a tailor.

Komaiko, Leah. **On Sally Perry's Farm.** Illustrated by Cat Bowman Smith. Simon & Schuster Books for Young Readers, 1996. ISBN 0 689 8083 5

Sally's quite a farmer, and she manages to get all the neighborhood kids involved in the garden on her farm. At the end of the book we see that her "farm" is a city lot and that she is dressed for her city job.

Levinson, Riki. **Our Home Is the Sea.** Illustrated by Dennis Luzak. Dutton Children's Books, 1988. ISBN 0 525 44406 8

This story takes place in Hong Kong. A boy joins his father and grandfather as they fish for a living, but his mother hopes he will become a teacher.

Levitin, Sonia. **Boom Town.** Illustrated by Cat Bowman Smith. Orchard Books, 1998. ISBN 0 531 30045 9

Set in gold rush times in California, this story tells of a family who came seeking gold, but, thanks to their daughter's enterprise, ended up selling pies to the miners. She then encourages other people to set up their own enterprises.

Lewin, Ted. **Storytellers.** Lothrop, Lee & Shepard Books, 1998. ISBN 0 688 15178 7

Abdul and his grandfather walk through the crowded city of Fez in Morocco, observing many different people at work and then setting up their own special spot for their occupation—storytelling.

Lobel, Arnold. **On Market Street.** Illustrated by Anita Lobel. Greenwillow Books, 1981 ISBN 0 688 80309 1

In this wordless book, each vendor is constructed of the things he or she sells.

Lyon, George Ella. **Mama Is a Miner.** Orchard Books, 1994. ISBN 0 531 06853 6

A little girl tells us what her mother does for a living, and we watch the mother going about her work, first in the mines and then at home. Our narrator liked it better when her mother worked in the store because it was less dangerous.

Naylor, Phyllis Reynolds. **Ducks Disappearing.** Illustrated by Tony Maddox. Atheneum Books for Young Readers, 1997. ISBN 0 689 31902 9

Willie gets everybody at the motel involved in his quest to find out why the baby ducks who live there are disappearing. In the process many different motel jobs are named.

Nikola, Lisa, W. **One Hole in the Road.** Illustrated by Dan Yaccarino. Henry Holt & Co. Books for Young Readers, 1997. ISBN 0 8050 4285 7

This counting book counts construction workers.

Parish, Peggy. **Amelia Bedelia's Family Album.** Greenwillow Books, 1988. ISBN 0 688 07677 7

When the Rogers family decides to give a party for their slightly cockeyed maid, Amelia Bedelia, she tells them all about her strange family whose occupations are very literal.

Paulsen, Gary. **Worksong.** Illustrated by Ruth Wright Paulsen. Harcourt Brace & Co., 1997. ISBN 0 152 00980 9

The Paulsens have combined efforts to celebrate the world of work in sound and sight. The chosen workers represent both blue-collar and professional people who work hard and then return to their various homes.

Rylant, Cynthia. **Mr. Griggs' Work.** Illustrated by Julie Downing. Orchard Books, 1989. ISBN 0 531 08369 1

Here's a man who loves his work. Mr. Griggs hates that he can't go to his post office job because he's ill, and when he comes back he enjoys it all the more.

Schwartz, Amy. **Bea & Mr. Jones.** Aladdin Paperbacks, 1994. ISBN 0 689 71796 2

Bea and her father swap jobs. He goes to kindergarten and she takes on his work as an advertising executive.

Siebert, Diane. **Truck Song.** Illustrated by Byron Barton. HarperCollins Children's Books, 1987. ISBN 0 06 443 1347

This book's rhyming text describes the activities of truckers as they go about their work.

Slawson, Michele Benoit. **Apple Picking Time.** Illustrated by Deborah Ray. Dragonwagon, 1998. ISBN 0 517 88575 1

When it's apple picking time in Washington State, everyone pitches in. We spend the day with a little girl who's determined to pick her share of the apples this time.

Smucker, Anna Egan. **No Star Nights.** Illustrated by Steve Johnson. Alfred A. Knopf Books for Young Readers, 1994. ISBN 0 679 86724 4

A woman who grew up in a town dominated by the steel mill remembers the sights and sounds of the place.

Spinelli, Eileen. **Boy, Can He Dance!** Illustrated by Paul Yalowitz. Aladdin Paperbacks, 1997. ISBN 0 689 81533 6

Tony's father is a superb chef in a big hotel, and he expects that Tony will also want to be a chef. Tony, however, is a dancer. He dances any time and any place he can. Then a time comes when both dancer and chef are needed, and each takes his chosen role.

Wellington, Monica. **Night City.** Dutton Children's Books, 1998. ISBN 0 525 45948 0

Many occupations are cited as we watch what happens after a city child goes to bed and the night workers begin their activities.

Wolff, Ferida. **Seven Loaves of Bread.** Morrow Junior Books, 1993. ISBN 0 688 11101 7

Millie bakes seven loaves of bread each morning which she carefully distributes to friends around the farm. When she falls ill, her sister takes over the bread making and she cuts the order short—with bad results.

Nonfiction

Barton, Byron. **Building a House.** *Morrow Junior Books, 1981. ISBN 0 688 84291 7*

The construction of a simple house is followed from plans to completion with an accent on the jobs and skills needed.

Jones, George. **My First Book of How Things Are Made: Crayons, Jeans, Guitars, Peanut Butter, and More.** *Cartwheel Books, 1995. ISBN 0 590 48004 9*

Eight factories are visited and we learn about the assembly line process behind many products familiar to young children.

Krauss, Ronnie. **Take a Look, It's in a Book: How Television Is Made at Reading Rainbow.** *Walker & Co., 1997. ISBN 0 8027 8488 7*

The various jobs involved in creating a television show familiar to many children are the focus of the photo-essay.

Maas, Robert. **Tugboats.** *Henry Holt & Co. Books for Young Readers, 1997. ISBN 0 8050 3116 2*

This photographic essay talks about the people who operate and use the boats.

MacHotka, Hana. **Pasta Factory.** *Houghton Mifflin Books for Children, 1992. ISBN 0 395 60197 5*

A field trip to a pasta factory deals with the workers there and the various kinds of pasta produced.

Morris, Ann. **Work.** *Lothrop, Lee & Shepard Books, 1998. ISBN 0 688 14866 2*

Color photographs show people around the world at work. Further information on each place and job is available at the end of the book.

Peterson, Cris. **Extra Cheese, Please!: Mozzarella's Journey from Cow to Pizza.** *Boyds Mills Press, 1994. ISBN 1 5639 7177 1*

This photo-essay is set on a Wisconsin farm where the process begins. Though simple, this book provides impressive amounts of information about the work involved in this process.

SOCIAL STUDIES: Other Times

COMMENTS

Young children have great difficulty with the concept of time, so this theme is not an attempt to deal with any great historical concepts or with precise dates of past events. Rather, it's a chance to read and talk about people and events of the past, giving those children who are ready to deal with such things a sort of time line on which to place events in their own family's history. Therefore, many of the activities deal with placing family generations in the context of events that take place in the books listed.

The books I have chosen to work with come from a wide variety of eras, allowing students to observe styles of clothing, modes of transportation and communication and

PICTURE BOOK STARTER

Homeplace, by Anne Shelby (see book list below), is about the generations of a family that lives on a farm started two hundred years ago. A link to each generation is established. The text is simple, but the detailed illustrations provide information about the technology, clothing, and transportation of each era.

other factors in the lives of people who lived in the past. I've limited the book selections to those that deal with U.S. history, but it can be expanded into ancient and prehistoric times in other lands as well as this one. Many picture books and easy-to-read biographies also belong with this theme.

ACTIVITIES

Language Arts
FINDING DETAILS

► In **Island Boy** (see book list), many changes are made for the people on an island. Make a quiz for the rest of the class about the changes you can find in the illustrations. For instance, one challenge might be, "Find the page that shows they have indoor plumbing now."

► In **My Great-Aunt Arizona** (see book list), there are indications in the illustrations that time is passing. Make a list of those things.

► In **Ox-Cart Man** (see book list), a man takes things to town and barters other

things for them. Make a list of the things he brings home from Portsmouth and decide how life will be different next year because of what he brings home.

MAKING COMPARISONS

► In **Alice Ramsey's Grand Adventure** (see book list), Alice travels the country in her old car. Talk to someone who has recently traveled a long distance by car. Compare her or his journey to Alice's.

► Examine the book **HomePlace** with small groups of children, encouraging them to notice such things in the illustrations as the modes of transportation, machinery, water sources, toys, and clothing.

CONDUCTING AN INTERVIEW

▶ Prepare a series of questions and a way to record the answers to those questions. Then interview your parents, grandparents and someone older than your grandparents to find out what things they did for fun when they were your age. Write down the rhymes they chanted when deciding who was "it" in a game, when ball bouncing and when jumping rope. Publish those rhymes in a book for the rest of the class.

WRITING

▶ Select a book from the list that you really like. Then write something that begins with the words, "If I lived at the time of (whatever the book is), I would . . ."

Math

▶ Take a picture of the oldest thing in your household. It may be a person or it may be an object. Take it to school and tell the class how old that thing is.

▶ Pick out the oldest tree you can find. Get some one who knows about trees to estimate how old that tree is. Figure out when it must have been planted. Then find out some major events that happened at about that time.

Social Studies

▶ Display charts which show the mode of dress for men, women and children from colonial times to the present. (The charts can be made from figures in **HomePlace** or from illustrations in history books or from Web sites such as **members.tripod.com/~histclo/**, which gives portraits and photos showing changes in boys clothing through history.) Examine the charts with the class, pointing out various salient features. Divide the class into groups of three or four children, then give each group six to eight books from the list. Suggest that the children look carefully at the illustrations in their books and arrange them from the earliest to the latest period of history, and then present their arrangement to the other groups, explaining the reasons for their sequences. It's not easy to determine an era from picture book illustrations, so be sure that the emphasis is on the reasons for the decision rather than on absolute accuracy.

▶ Make a very long time line extending from 1900 to the present day. Mark off each five-year span. Write titles from the list where you think they belong on the time line. When a book's subject extends over a period of time, indicate that by writing the title horizontally on the time line to stretch over the appropriate period.

▶ In **Dandelions,** by Eve Bunting (see book list), a family lives in a sod house. Find out more about sod houses from the book **Sod Houses on the Great Plains**. Find a way of sharing what you know about sod houses with the rest of the class.

▶ **Home Place**, by Crescent Dragonwagon (see book list3), shows us evidence of a family that once lived where now there is only woods. Look at old maps and pictures of your city to see what once stood where your school now stands.

► In **Ox-Cart Man** a man barters for goods. Figure out a way to barter for something you want or need from another person. What services can you perform or what things can you trade instead of giving money for those things?

► Select a book set in another time and after reading it, write a series of statements that follow the pattern of "I used to think _____ but now I know _____."

Music

► Have a musical night in which people come dressed in clothing from other years. Plan a program of songs that represent as many eras as possible. Pass out lyrics to the songs and have a sing along.

BOOK LIST
Fiction

Brown, Don. **Alice Ramsey's Grand Adventure.** Houghton Mifflin Books for Children, 1997. ISBN 0 395 70127 9

In 1909, Alice Ramsey and two friends set off in her Maxwell touring car to drive across America. As they experience the hazards of travel at that time, we get a look at the clothing worn by respectable ladies, the car, the roads and towns, and the reactions people have to three women involved in such a hazardous trip.

Bunting, Eve. **Dandelions.** Illustrated by Greg Shed. Harcourt Brace & Co., 1995. ISBN 0 15 200050 X

Zoe and her family have settled in their sod house on the plains, but her mother is unhappy. She says that if you take one step away from the house, it blends in with the countryside and disappears. One day Zoe plants dandelions on the roof of the soddy, and the next spring, they have a roof of yellow blossoms.

Cooney, Barbara. **Island Boy.** Puffin Books, 1988. ISBN 0 14 050756 6

A young man establishes his family on a small island off the coast of Maine in the days of sailing ships. As his family grows and technology progresses, we see signs of this in their lifestyle. The youngest boy grows up to be the captain of a large sailing ship but later returns to the island to establish his own family.

Dragonwagon, Crescent. **Home Place.** Illustrated by Jerry Pinkney. Simon & Schuster Books for Young Readers, 1990. ISBN 0 02 733190 3

People strolling through the woods come upon a patch of daffodils. Knowing that these are not wild plants, they look for other signs of previous habitation. They find a cellar hole and the remains of a fireplace. Digging in the ground a bit turns up a marble, a nail and a doll's arm. Now they recreate the people who once lived there. Neither the readers nor the visitors know whether the people truly came back to life or were just imagined.

Hall, Donald. **The Farm Summer 1942.** Illustrated by Barry Moser. Dial Books for Young Readers, 1994 ISBN 0 8037 1501 3

A young boy leaves his San Francisco home to spend the summer of 1942 on a New Hampshire farm.

Hall, Donald. **Old Home Day.** Browndeer Press, 1996. ISBN 0 15 276896 3

We watch time and progress in a small area of New Hampshire, starting with the forming of the land itself and ending with the present.

Hall, Donald. **Ox-Cart Man.** Puffin Books, 1979. ISBN 0 140 50441 0

This simple story tells a lot about its time and place. A farmer in 19th-century New Hampshire puts his goods for barter on his ox-cart and goes to Portsmouth. There, he barters everything, even the ox, for goods his family will need next year.

Harvey, Brett. **Cassie's Journey: Going West in the 1860s.** Illustrated by Deborah Kogan Ray. Holiday House, 1995 ISBN 0 8234 1172 9

We see the dangerous journey west from Illinois to California through the eyes of a little girl traveling by covered wagon with her family.

Hendershot, Judith. **In Coal Country.** Alfred A. Knopf Books for Young Readers, 1987. ISBN 0 394 98190 1

Coal country in the 1930s is the background of this memoir. The chalk illustrations add to the feeling that coal dust pervades everything.

Houston, Gloria. **My Great-Aunt Arizona.** HarperCollins Children's Books, 1991. ISBN 0 06 022606 4

Arizona is born, brought up and spends her whole life in the Blue Ridge Mountains. She yearns to see other places, but things don't work out that way. She becomes a teacher and inspires others to go to the places she sees only in her mind.

Howard, Ellen. **The Log Cabin Quilt.** Holiday House, 1996. ISBN 0 8234 1247 4

Elvirey's father packed up the wagon and loaded the family into it right after his wife's funeral in Carolina. The grandmother loaded her quilt scraps, much to the father's disdain. Later, those quilt scraps were stuffed between the logs of a cabin to keep the family from freezing.

Khalsa, Dayal Kaur. **How Pizza Came to Queens.** Crown Books for Young Readers, 1989. ISBN 0 517 57126 9

In the 1950s, Mrs. Pelligrino came to Queens from Italy to live with relatives, but the family soon realized that the old lady was most unhappy. It turned out that she wanted pizza, a dish unknown by most Americans at the time.

Lasky, Kathryn. **Marven of the Great North Woods.** Illustrated by Kevin Hawkes. Harcourt Brace & Co., 1997. ISBN 0 15 200104 2

This book is loosely based on the experiences of the author's father. In 1918 he was sent to the north woods to escape the influenza epidemic in his hometown. There, he made the acquaintance of Jean-Louis, an incredible lumberjack.

Lasky, Kathryn. **She's Wearing a Dead Bird on Her Head.** Illustrated by David Catrow. Hyperion Books for Children, 1995. ISBN 0 7868 0065 8

This book's fictionalized fact deals with the establishment of the Audubon Society in 1890 as a result of the many birds killed for their plumage.

Levitin, Sonia. **Boom Town.** Illustrated by Cat Bowman Smith. Orchard Books, 1998. ISBN 0 531 30043 9

Amanda and her family have come to California in search of gold, but Amanda begins making pies for the miners and soon her business is thriving. Other people start up their own businesses, and a boom town springs up.

Lyon, George Ella. **Cecil's Story.** Illustrated by Peter Catalanotto. Orchard Books, 1991. ISBN 0 531 08512 0

The time is the Civil War, although only the illustrations tell you that. A young boy tells us how his father went off to war and was hurt. His mother goes to get him, while the boy stays with neighbors and worries.

McCloskey, Robert. **Make Way for Ducklings.** Puffin Books, 1941. ISBN 0 14 050171 1

This book was not originally intended to be historical, but by now it has become so. Written in 1941, the cars and costumes in its illustrations give us a look at 1940s Boston.

McKissack, Patricia. **Christmas in the Big House, Christmas in the Quarters.** Illustrated by John Thompson. Scholastic, 1994 ISBN 0 590 43027 0

A fictional slave plantation in 1859 is the scene of this picture book in which the celebration of Christmas shows the great contrast between slave and master.

McLerran, Alice. **The Year of the Ranch.** Illustrated by Kimberly Root. Viking Children's Books, 1996. ISBN 0 670 85131 0

In 1911, a very determined man moved his city family to the desert where he fully intended that they would adapt to ranch life. In spite of a spirited effort, however, they fail.

Rand, Gloria. **The Cabin Key.** Illustrated by Ted Rand. Harcourt Brace & Co., 1994. ISBN 0 15 213 8846

A rustic cabin in the mountains has served four generations of our narrator's family, and, as she unlocks the door, she reflects on much that has happened there.

Roop, Peter & Connie. **Buttons for General Washington.** Illustrated by Peter E. Hanson. Carolrhoda Books, 1986. ISBN 0 87614 294 3

Charles' parents are helping the rebels by delivering coded messages to their son by sewing them into the buttons on his brother John's coat.

Shelby, Anne. **Homeplace.** Illustrated by Wendy Anderson Halperin. Orchard Books, 1995. ISBN 0 531 06882 X

A grandmother tells her family's 200-year-old history. Each generation of the family is shown on a full spread accompanied by many details about its time.

Sorensen, Henri. **New Hope.** Lothrop, Lee & Shepard Books, 1995. ISBN 0 688 13925 6

One man in a wagon train broke the axle on his wagon, so he stayed where he was. Eventually, a town grew up around him.

Tunnell, Michael O. **Mailing May.** Illustrated by Ted Rand. Greenwillow Books, 1997. ISBN 0 688 12878 5

This book is based on an actual event. A little girl was sent as a "package" by train, over the Idaho mountains, to her grandmother's house. Through her story, we get a glimpse of the era's mail and train service.

Turner, Ann. **Dust for Dinner.** HarperCollins Children's Books, 1995. ISBN 0 06 023376 1

This easy-to-read book is set in the Dust Bowl era, as a family gives up and heads for California.

Turner, Ann. **Mississippi Mud: Three Prairie Journals.** HarperCollins Children's Books, 1997. ISBN 0 06 024432 1

These journals were kept by three different children in the same family as they crossed the country in a covered wagon.

Van Leeuwen, Jean. **Across the Wide Dark Sea: The Mayflower Journey.** Dial Books for Young Readers, 1995. ISBN 0 8037 1167 0

We get the story of the Mayflower journey from Love Brewster, a young boy on board.

Yolen, Jane. **Letting Swift River Go.** Illustrated by Barbara Cooney. Little, Brown & Co., Children's Books, 1992. ISBN 0 316 96899 4

Several small towns were deliberately flooded during the 1930s and 40s in order to form the reservoir that serves as the water supply for Boston. This is the story of what happened from the viewpoint of a little girl whose town is about to disappear.

Nonfiction

Blumberg, Rhoda. **Bloomers!** Illustrated by Mary Morgan. Atheneum Books for Young Readers, 1993. ISBN 0 02 711684 0

When Amelia Bloomer, the editor of a women's journal, saw Elizabeth Cady Stanton wearing trousers, she had an idea for a woman's outfit that would be less cumbersome than long skirts but not as severe as trousers. The result was bloomers, and women of the day loved them. This simple picture book deals with their invention and the effect they had on the women's rights movement.

Charleston, Gordon. **Armstrong Lands on the Moon.** Dillon, 1994. ISBN 0 875 18530 4

This book covers more than the title implies and includes a look at the space race of the 1960s.

Goble, Paul. **Death of the Iron Horse.** Simon & Schuster Books for Young Readers, 1987. ISBN 0 02 737830 6

This picture book tells about the time a group of the Cheyenne people attacked a railroad train during the Indian Wars.

Johnson, Dinah. **All Around Town: The Photographs of Richard Samuel Roberts.** Henry Holt & Co. Books for Young Readers, 1998. ISBN 0 8050 5456 1

The wonderful photographs in this book depict life in the African-American section of Columbia, South Carolina, in the '20s and '30s. Some of the photographs are exterior shots, but many are studio portraits.

Penner, Lucille Recht. **Eating the Plates: A Pilgrim Book of Food & Manners.** Simon & Schuster Books for Young Readers, 1991. ISBN 0 02 770901 9

This book provides simple explanations of what the Pilgrims ate and of the conditions under which they spent their first years in the New World.

Rounds, Glen. **Sod Houses on the Great Plains.** Holiday House, 1995. ISBN 0 8234 1162 1

Rounds' style is simple, rather comic and very sound. He tells us how sod houses were built, why they were built, and what life in them was like.

Rylant, Cynthia. **When I Was Young in the Mountains.** Illustrated by Diane Goode. Dutton Children's Books, 1982. ISBN 0 525 44198 0

This beautiful book is based on the memories of the author who went to live with her grandparents in the mountains of West Virginia. The book evokes both the time (the 1940s) and the place.

Schroeder, Alan. **Minty: A Story of Young Harriet Tubman.** Illustrated by Jerry Pinkney. Dial Books for Young Readers, 1996. ISBN 0 8037 1889 6

This beautifully illustrated biography describes the early years of Harriet Tubman's life.

Sewall, Marcia. **People of the Breaking Day.** Atheneum Books for Young Readers, 1990. ISBN 0 689 31407 8

This wonderful picture book shows the people who lived in Plymouth before the Pilgrims came. The Wampanoags lived in harmony with nature and were guided by the wisdom of Massasoit.

Sewall, Marcia. **Pilgrims of Plimoth.** Atheneum Books for Young Readers, 1986. ISBN 0 689 312504

Simple and informative watercolors and a well-written text tell about life at Plimoth Plantation for the earliest Pilgrims.

Standiford, Natalie. **The Bravest Dog Ever: The True Story of Balto.** Random House, 1989. ISBN 0 394 89695 5

It was important, in 1925, to get diphtheria serum to Nome, Alaska. It was done by dogsled, and Balto proved his heroism on the trip.

Stanley, Diane. **The True Adventure of Daniel Hall.** *Dial Books for Young Readers, 1995. ISBN 0 8037 1469 6*

Daniel Hall signed on as a cabin boy on a whaling ship in the 1800s, but, because of the cruelty of the captain, he abandoned ship, spent a year in Siberia and then worked his way home.

Stevenson, James. **Don't You Know There's a War On.** *Greenwillow Books, 1992. ISBN 0 688 11384 2*

The author's memories of childhood in America during World War II are both funny and poignant. He was one of the lucky ones, however: His father came home unharmed.

Stevenson, James. **Higher on the Door.** *Greenwillow Books, 1987. ISBN 0 688 06637 2*

Stevenson lived in the New York suburbs when he was a child in the 1930s and 40s. This series of memories revolves around the train trips he made into the city as a child.

Stevenson, James. **I Had a Lot of Wishes.** *Greenwillow Books, 1995. ISBN 0 688 13705 9*

Life in the 1930s and 40s for one little boy is shown in a series of statements and vignettes.

Vieira, Linda. **The Ever-Living Tree: The Life & Times of a Coast Redwood.** *Walker & Co., 1996. ISBN 0 8027 7477 6*

Ancient and world history are part of this book as the growth of a redwood tree is seen against the backdrop of events in human history.

Whitely, Opal. **Only Opal.** *Illustrated by Barbara Cooney. Philomel Books, 1994. ISBN 0 399 21990 0*

In the early 1900s, a little girl lives a difficult life in a lumber camp in Oregon.

Wright, Courtni C. **Jumping the Broom.** *Illustrated by Gershom Griffith. Holiday House, 1994 ISBN 0 823 41042 0*

A marriage in the slave quarters is celebrated on a plantation.

ART: Art & Artists

 COMMENTS

Exploring art and artists allows us to bring the fine arts and literature together. We can set up an art table with varied and interesting materials with which children can create their own art while investigating the art of others. It also provides a theme through which a study of illustration in kids' books, as well as fine art, is possible. In fact, I've designed this theme so that study of fine art grows out of the study of illustration work. Author/Illustrator Studies (pages 173 to 250) should be useful here.

 PICTURE BOOK STARTER

You Can't Take a Balloon Into the Metropolitan Museum, by Jacqueline Preiss Weitzman and Robin Preiss Glasser (see book list), is a wordless romp through New York City and the Metropolitan Museum. The book is textless and uses color sparingly to highlight events. A little girl and her grandmother attempt to enter the art museum, only to be told that they can't take the yellow balloon that the little girl is holding into the museum. Finally, however, the previously stern guard relents enough to tie it to a banister near the entrance, and they go inside. Unbeknownst to them, a pigeon unties the balloon and starts off with it, pursued by the guard. From that point on, every scene inside the museum is echoed by an exterior scene involving the balloon. The repeated pattern is often subtle and very funny, and it makes the art experience light and enjoyable.

ACTIVITIES

Language Arts
INVESTIGATING ILLUSTRATIONS

▶ Suggest that children find their favorite picture book and then decide what effect the illustration has on their choice. After reexamining the book with a concentration on the illustrations, suggest that they make a list of words describing the illustrations. Later, children can explain their word choices as they show the book to others.

▶ Find other books by the same illustrator as those above. Put them in the order in which they were created. Did the artist's style change? Were the same media used each time? Did the palette of color change? Why do you think she or he might have changed those things?

▶ Read aloud a picture book without showing the illustrations. (Disguise the cover so that even it is not visible.) Make a list of the events in the story that you think should appear in the illustrations. Assuming the book has only 32 pages and that four of those are taken by the title page and other informational material, how many pictures are possible if one appears on each of the remaining pages? Look through your previous list and combine, eliminate, or expand your ideas as necessary. Make a storyboard for the story with the lines from the text separated the way you think they ought to be on the pages. What mood do you think the illustrations ought to have? What colors would you use to convey that mood? If you're interested, complete your book.

▶ Visit Web sites that give information about children's book illustrators.

FINDING DETAILS

▶ Share the book **You Can't Take a Balloon into the Metropolitan Museum** by having children look at it in pairs and instructing them to "see what's going on here."

MAKING COMPARISONS

▶ After all the children have had an opportunity to do that, gather them together and look at each page together. Encourage children to make comments on what they see. Stop at the page where the first work of art, "Invitation to the Sideshow," is shown. Ask children to point out other things on the page that are similar to the painting—musicians, instruments, etc. Do the same with each work of art in the book.

EXTENDING LITERATURE

▶ After reading some of the **Harold and the Purple Crayon** books, put a strip of brown craft paper at kid height all around the room. Each child takes large purple crayon and draws and tells a story á la Harold for a short, set period. When time is up, the next child must place the crayon where the last child ended and continue the story.

Art

▶ Go through **You Can't Take a Balloon into the Metropolitan Museum** again, asking children to find a work of art that pleases them and then to find out, from the back of the book, what it is called and who created it.

▶ Search picture books for works that demonstrate the use of different media: watercolors, photography, collage, block prints, pencil, and pen-and-ink, to name a few. Arrange the books in a display that identifies the medium. Have an art table nearby on which those materials are available for experimentation by the children.

▶ View videotapes in which illustrators of children's books are visited.

▶ Start an art gallery. Post prints of works by various artists, simply framed with construction paper. Using the same type and color of frame, post works by children in which some of those techniques and palettes of color are used.

▶ Arrange to visit an art museum when it is closed to the general public. Ask for permission to give the children sketchbooks and materials and encourage them to sit on the floor in front of a painting they like and create their own artwork to commemorate it.

▶ Visit as many art studios as possible. Visit potters and other craftspeople, as well as fine artists. Interview the artist about his or her work.

Math

▶ Listen to music as you create a work of art. Later, think about how the music made you feel. Did that have an effect on your work?

▶ Maurice Sendak often listens to Mozart as he works. Play some of Mozart's music and create a work of art. Did the music make a difference?

BOOK LIST
Fiction

Agee, Jon. *Incredible Painting of Felix Clousseau.* Farrar Strauss & Giroux Books for Young Readers, 1988. ISBN 0 374 33633 4

Felix Clousseau was unknown when he entered the exhibition at the Royal Palace. Patrons were unimpressed with the simple duck he displayed. Then the duck came to life, and Felix became famous as everything he painted became real.

Carle, Eric. *Draw Me a Star.* Philomel Books, 1992. ISBN 0 399 21877 7

This book explores creativity as an artist starts with one childlike star on a piece of paper and then begins creating a universe.

Carle, Eric. *A House for Hermit Crab.* Simon & Schuster Books for Young Readers, 1988. ISBN 0 887 08050 1

Carle's collages work beautifully in this story of a crab who decorates his dwellings.

dePaola, Tomie. *Art Lesson.* G. P. Putnam's Sons Books for Young Readers, 1989. ISBN 0 399 21688 X

In this story, based on an incident in the author's past, a little boy is taught at home to treat art as a creative opportunity, but at school the lessons are structured and imitative.

Dionetti, Michelle. *Painting the Wind.* Illustrated by Kevin Hawkes. Little, Brown & Co., Children's Books, 1995. ISBN 0 316 18602 3

Vincent Van Gogh is the artist for whom a little girl's mother keeps house. While others view him as a madman, the little girl finds that his paintings help her see the world differently.

Hurd, Thacher. *Art Dog.* HarperCollins Children's Books, 1996. ISBN 0 06 024424 0

As in **Incredible Painting of Felix Clousseau** (see above), these paintings come to life as Art Dog pursues the thieves who stole the Mona Woofa.

Johnson, Angela. *Daddy Calls Me Man.* Illustrated by Rhonda Mitchell. Orchard Books, 1997. ISBN 0 531 30042 0

The son of two African-American artists tells us about his home through a series of four poems illustrated by his parents' work.

Johnson, Crocket. *Harold and the Purple Crayon.* HarperCrest, 1987. ISBN 00 60 22936 5

This story is the first in a series of books in which a little boy, clad in his pajamas, begins to draw with his only crayon—and the things he creates become real. The plot and the illustrations are delightfully simple.

Johnston, Tony. *The Last Snow of Winter.* Morrow Junior Books, 1993. ISBN 0 688 10749 4

Snow sculpture takes center stage in this story as a famous artist creates one for the villagers and is later rewarded with one from them.

Kalan, Robert. *Rain.* Illustrated by Donald Crews. Mulberry Books, 1991. ISBN 0 688 10479 7

Print becomes graphics as words are incorporated into illustrations in this exploration of rain.

Kesselman, Wendy. *Emma.* Bantam Doubleday Dell Books for Young Readers, 1980. ISBN 0 440 40847 4

When her children give Emma a painting of the village where she grew up, the lonely old lady decides to paint things the way she remembers them, and a new artist is born.

Kleven, Elisa. *The Lion and the Little Red Bird.* Puffin Books, 1992. ISBN 0 14 055809 8

Each morning when the lion emerges from his den, a little bird notices that the lion's tail is a different color. When the two become friends, the bird sees the paintings the lion has been making with his tail.

Le Tord, Bijou. *A Blue Butterfly: A Story About Claude Monet.* Doubleday, 1995. ISBN 0 385 31102 8

The colors of Monet's palette dominate this book, and there are allusions to his paintings in the illustrations. The text is poetic in this slight story about the artist.

Lionni, Leo. **Matthew's Dream.** Alfred A. Knopf Books for Young Readers, 1995. ISBN 0 679 87310 X

Matthew's parents know what he should be when he grows up: a doctor. But after Matthew visits an art museum, it's obvious that he has other plans.

Littlesugar, Amy. **Jonkonnu.** Illustrated by Ian Schoenherr. Philomel Books, 1997. ISBN 0 300 72831 4

Based on an incident when Winslow Homer stayed in Petersburg, Virginia, this book tells the story of the slave celebration he witnessed there.

Moon, Nicola. **Lucy's Picture.** Illustrated by Alex Ayliffe. Dial Books for Young Readers, 1995. ISBN 0 8037 1833 0

When the other kids at school begin painting pictures, Lucy asks for permission to make a collage instead. Carefully assembling her materials, she creates a lovely work of art. When she brings it home to her blind grandfather, we understand why collage was better than paint for this work.

Nicholson, Nicholas. **Little Girl in a Red Dress with Cat & Dog.** Illustrated by Cynthia Von Buhler. Viking Children's Books, 1989. ISBN 0 670 87183 4

With a painting from a folk art museum as inspiration, we are given the subject's point of view as a little girl tells us what it was like to sit for the painting that now hangs over her fireplace.

Polacco, Patricia. **Appelemando's Dream.** Paperstar Books, 1997. ISBN 0 698 11590 2

The village in which Appelemando lives is drab and gray, but his dreams are full of color. The children can see Appelemando's dreams and relish the color they give. When they find out how to glue his dreams to the buildings, they transform the village.

Rylant, Cynthia. **All I See.** Orchard Books, 1988. ISBN 0 531 08377 2

An artist who paints by a pond each day paints whales. When a boy asks why, the artist responds, "That's all I see."

Say, Allen. **Emma's Rug.** Houghton Mifflin Books for Children, 1996. ISBN 0 395 74294 3

A little girl can paint what she has never seen. She seems to get her visions from the small rug she sits on. When her mother washes the rug, the visions cease.

Stanley, Diane. **The Gentleman and the Kitchen Maid.** Dial Books for Young Readers, 1993. ISBN 0 8037 1320 7

In this book, again, paintings come alive. In this case, two characters from two different paintings fall in love while characters in other paintings gossip about them.

Thompson, Colin. **How to Live Forever.** Alfred A. Knopf Books for Young Readers, 1996. ISBN 0 679 87898 X

In this story full of art references, a character from one book searches through many others looking for one that will tell him how to live forever.

Walsh, Ellen Stoll. **Mouse Paint.** Harcourt Brace & Co., 1989. ISBN 0 15 256025 4

Three white mice find three jars of paint. Because the paints are the primary colors, they make color everywhere as they play.

Weitzman, Jacqueline Preiss. **You Can't Take a Balloon Into the Metropolitan Museum.** Dial Books for Young Readers, 1998. ISBN 0 8037 2301 6

In this wordless book a little girl and her grandmother view the treasures of the museum while their yellow balloon sails through the city echoing their progress.

Nonfiction

Arai, Tomie. **Just Like Me: Stories & Self-Portraits by Fourteen Artists.** Children's Press, 1997. ISBN 0 892391 499

Each artist in this book presents a statement about his or her work along with a self-portrait.

Carle, Eric. **The Art of Eric Carle.** Philomel Books, 1996. ISBN 399 22937 X

Eric Carle's autobiography is just one part of this informative book which also includes critical reviews and a chronology of his work.

Collins, Pat Lowery. **I Am an Artist.** Illustrated by Robin Brickman. The Millbrook Press, 1994. ISBN 1 56294729 X

The idea that art is a way of seeing is further defined in this book as a way of feeling. The effect is to encourage children to notice detail and to create artistic impressions of the world around them.

Geisert, Arthur. **The Etcher's Studio.** Houghton Mifflin Books for Children, 1997. ISBN 0 395 79654 3

As a boy works in his grandfather's studio, we watch how an etcher goes about creating his art.

Gibbons, Gail. **The Art Box.** Holiday House, 1998. ISBN 0 82 3413806 1

Gibbons explores the tools of art, and with simple text and pictures, explains how each is used.

Heller, Ruth. **Color.** G. P. Putnam's Sons Books for Young Readers, 1995. ISBN 0 399 22815 2

This book is an exploration of color and is enhanced with overlays. The accent is on fun.

Hoban, Tana. **Look Up, Look Down.** Greenwillow Books, 1992. ISBN 0 688 10577 7

Color photographs encourage the reader to view common objects from new and varied perspectives.

Joyce, William. **The World of William Joyce Scrapbook.** HarperCollins Children's Books, 1997. ISBN 0 06 027432 8

An illustrator shows us early examples of his work and, in a playful manner, tells about his work.

Mayers, Florence Cassen. **ABC: The Museum of Modern Art.** Harry N. Abrams, 1986. ISBN 0 810 91849 8

Art from the museum is the basis for each letter of the alphabet here.

Micklethwait, Lucy. **I Spy: An Alphabet in Art.** Greenwillow Books, 1992. ISBN 0 688 11679 5

Like the book by Mayers (above), this one uses famous artwork as the motif of an alphabet book.

Muhlberger, Richard.
What Makes a Bruegel a Bruegel? ISBN 0 670 85203 1
What Makes a Cassatt a Cassatt? ISBN 0 670 85742 4
What Makes a Degas a Degas? ISBN 0 670 85205 8
What Makes a Goya a Goya? ISBN 0 670 85743 2
What Makes a Leonardo a Leonardo?
ISBN 0 670 85744 0
What Makes a Monet a Monet? ISBN 0 670 85200 7
What Makes a Picasso a Picasso? ISBN 0 670 85741 6
What Makes a Raphael a Raphael? ISBN 0 670 85204 X
What Makes a Rembrandt a Rembrandt? Viking Press ISBN 0 670 85199 X

This series of books is an excellent resource for information about the various artists. Older readers may use the information in the text, but most younger readers will get their information from the work of the various artists in each volume.

Stanley, Diane. **Leonardo da Vinci.** Morrow Junior Books, 1996. ISBN 0 688 10437 1

Very good illustrations establish the time and the work of the artist while the text tells his life story.

Westray, Kathleen. **A Color Sampler.** Ticknor & Fields, 1993. ISBN 0 395 65940 X

Color is explored through patterns in a quilt. The explanations of color and hues and the effects of color on pattern and juxtaposition are clear, and the illustrations are ideal for the text.

LITERATURE: Fools & Tricksters

COMMENTS

Folk literature from around the world is replete with trickster tales. Some such as the Anansi tales of Africa and the Caribbean and their American derivatives, the Br'er Rabbit stories, have characters that are both trickers and "trickees." Many modern stories also revolve around a trickster and/or a fool. Often these stories are funny and sometimes they are subtle. Analyzing and categorizing these stories can be a valuable activity involving many disciplines.

PICTURE BOOK STARTER

Patricia McKissack and Rachel Isadora's **Flossie and the Fox** (Dial Books for Young Readers, 1986. ISBN 0 8037 0250 7) is a funny story in which a frequent victim, an innocent, fools the stereotyped trickster, the fox. Flossie's on her way to deliver a basket of eggs when a fox stops her on the road and asks for the eggs. Flossie claims not to believe that he is a fox, and as he tries to prove that he is, she gets nearer and nearer her neighbor's house. She finally gets close enough so that her neighbor's hounds can see the fox.

ACTIVITIES

Language Arts

READING

► Put out as many picture book trickster and fool tales as possible. Suggest that children read them; read aloud as many as you find appealing. List the books on a chart and check off the ones that have been read by at least one person in the classroom.

CATEGORIZING

► Elicit from the children various elements in the books they have read. Some possibilities:

One character doesn't have all the information.

One character isn't listening.

One character is disguised.

One character misunderstands a statement.

One character isn't being logical.

One character isn't very smart.

► Many trickster tales are folktales. Usually the author or editor tells you somehow that a story is a folktale and not an original tale written by the author. Sometimes on the title page it will say "retold by" instead of just "by." Other times the book flap or author's note tells where the tale came from. Sort the books the class has read for this theme according to whether or not it's a folktale.

CHARTING INFORMATION

▶ After sharing one of the picture books, make a flow chart with the class, such as the following.

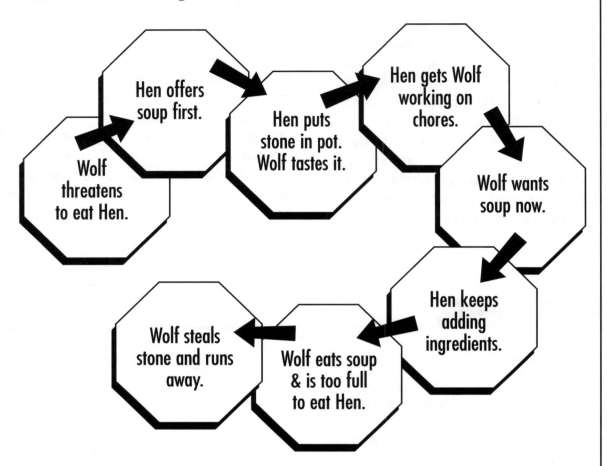

MAKING COMPARISONS

▶ During discussion circle time, tell the students about a trick that was played on you or that you played on someone else. Suggest that they share similar stories about themselves.

ASKING QUESTIONS

▶ Make large pictures of characters from the tales on poster board, cutting a child-sized face hole in each picture. Play a game where a child holds up a poster in front of him or herself without seeing the figure on the poster. The child then asks questions to identify him or herself, such as "Am I an animal?," "Am I in a Br'er Rabbit story?," "Am I bigger than a rabbit?," etc.

WRITING

▶ Divide a bulletin board into sections for each of the elements from the "Categorizing" activity. Suggest that children write or draw about an incident from one of the tales that fits one of those categories, and then place it in the proper section.

BOOK LIST
Fiction

Aardema, Verna. ***Anansi Finds a Fool.*** *Dial Books for Young Readers, 1992. ISBN 0 8037*

Anansi searches for a partner more foolish than he who will do the greatest share of the work. Bonsu agrees to do all the work if Anansi will take all the tiredness that results. Anansi, insisting that the fatigue is the worst part, insists on doing all the work instead. The watercolor illustrations show the patterns and textures of this society in Ghana.

Aardema, Verna. ***Bimwili & the Zimwi.*** *Dial Books for Young Readers, 1985. ISBN 0 8037 0212 4*

Bimwili, the youngest sister, runs back to the seashore to retrieve her shell and is captured by the Zimwi, an evil, troll-like creature. She is forced to sing from inside his drum as he travels from village to village. When she sings in her own village, her mother recognizes her voice and demands her freedom. The illustrations are watercolor with colored pencil.

Blundell, Tony. ***Beware of Boys.*** *Greenwillow Books, 1991. ISBN 0 688 10924 1*

A small boy wanders into the woods and is captured by a hungry wolf. The boy suggests a series of recipes that the wolf might use to cook him. In doing so, the boy gets the better of the wolf in this humorously clever story. The recipes involve a great deal of measurement, and the plot will remind some of **Stone Soup.**

Coplans, Peta. ***Cat and Dog.*** *Viking Children's Books, 1996. ISBN 0 670 86766 7*

A dog tricks a cat into calling out numbers, and then eats that many things from the cat's picnic.

Farmer, Nancy. ***Runnery Granary.*** *Greenwillow Books, 1996. ISBN 0 688 14187 0*

Finely detailed watercolors illustrate this tale of a granary owner who finds some grain missing. First suspecting weevils, then rats, she learns that the culprits are gnomes. Old Granny knows how to get rid of them, and the granary is free of the pests. The names of the granary family—Mrs. Runnery, Hillary Runnery, Valery Runnery, and Granny Runnery—are fun to say, as is making up additional family names.

French, Fiona. ***Anancy and Mr. Dry-Bone.*** *Little, Brown & Co., Children's Books, 1991. ISBN 0 316 29298 2*

This is a Caribbean variant of the Ananse tales of Africa. In it, Anancy, the spider, is hired to make Miss Louise laugh, a task which pits him against wealthy Mr. Dry-Bone. Stylized paintings with bold colors playing against black silhouettes.

Lobel, Arnold. ***Treeful of Pigs.*** *Greenwillow Books, 1979. ISBN 0 688 84177 5*

A very lazy farmer spends his time in bed instead of helping his wife take care of their herd of pigs. His poor wife tries lots of tricks to get the farmer to help her. Finally, she finds a trick that gets him doing her work as well as his.

Palatini, Margie. ***Piggie Pie!*** *Clarion/Houghton Mifflin, 1995. ISBN 0 395 71691 8*

Subtle this book isn't, but it is funny. A witch has all the ingredients for the piggie pie she craves except eight pigs. After consulting the Yellow Pages, she arrives at Old MacDonald's farm and announces her arrival with skywriting. The pigs disguise themselves well enough to fool the witch but not the reader.

Root, Phyllis. ***Aunt Nancy and Old Man Trouble.*** *Candlewick Press, 1996. ISBN 1 56402 347 8*

Aunt Nancy knew she was in for a bad day when the spring dried up and she lost her lucky nickel. Sure enough, it wasn't long before Old Man Trouble himself showed up. Aunt Nancy soon gets the best of him, however, by making the best of every bad thing he does. This is an engaging story told in the vernacular.

Ross, Tony. **Stone Soup.** Puffin Books, 1990.
ISBN 0 8037 0890 4

Ross puts a slightly cockeyed twist in this classic favorite by making a red hen the cook. His villain is the big bad wolf, and there's a double con game afoot.

Sierra, Judy. **Wiley and the Hairy Man.** Lodestar, 1996.
ISBN 0 525 67477 2

This tale has been done before, as a picture book by Molly Bang, but this new version of the Alabama folktale is equally good. The idea of the innocent boy and his mama outwitting the frightening Hairy Man is fun and scary.

Soto, Gary. **Chato's Kitchen.** G. P. Putnam's Sons Books for Young Readers, 1995. ISBN 0 399 22658 3

In this allegory, Chato the cat asks some mice over for dinner. He expects, of course, to eat them, and he and his friend prepare some delicious Mexican food to go with the main course. When the mice arrive, they bring with them their friend, a dog, and the feast turns out to be a meatless one. The fun in this book comes from the sly characterization of the cats, mice and dog as barrio habitues, and there is wordplay with many of the Mexican phrases.

Spooner, Michael. **Old Meshikee and the Little Crabs.** Henry Holt & Co. Books for Young Readers, 1996.
ISBN 0 8050 3487 0

This folktale from the Ojibwe is useful because of its strong kinship to Br'er Rabbit and the Briar Patch.

Strete, Craig Kee & Michelle Netten Chacon. **How the Indians Bought the Farm.** Greenwillow Books, 1996.
ISBN 0 688 14130 7

This is a funny book about an Indian chief and his wife who are forced out of their home by a government man. Ordered to live on a farm and raise sheep, pigs and cows or lose that, too, they use their only resource—their love for, and communication with, wildlife—to trick the government men.

Van Allsburg, Chris. **Widow's Broom.** Houghton Mifflin Books for Children,1992. ISBN 0 395 64051 2

This is more subtle than most of the trickster tales. When a broom loses its flying power, it is left behind at Widow Minna Shaw's home. Gradually, the Widow discovers that the broom can be taught to do many things, including playing the piano, although what it does best and prefers to do is sweep. The widow is delighted, but her neighbor, Mr. Spivey, reacts with fear and loathing, believing the broom to be the devil's tool. Eventually, he and some other neighbors demand to have the Widow's broom. Regretfully, she tells them it's in the closet and that it's sleeping. Carefully they remove the broom, tie it to a stake, and burn it. Later, the ghost of the broom is seen coming closer and closer to the Spivey's house. It's not until the Spiveys have moved away that we discover the trick the widow has played so that she and her broom can live in peace.

Wooldridge, Connie Nordhielm. **Wicked Jack.** Holiday House, 1995. ISBN 0 8234 1101 X

This retelling of a Richard Chase tale is done in a rollicking, backwoods manner. It tells of a man who outwits the devil and ends up so mean neither heaven nor hell will have him. The devil gives him a coal to start his own hell, which explains what others call marsh gas.

Wyllie, Stephen. **Flea in the Ear.** Dutton Children's Books, 1995. ISBN 0 525 45648 1

This story is about an out-foxed fox. First, the fox tricks the dog into leaving his post as chicken guard. Then, the dog turns the tables. The plot is easily absorbed and enjoyed by the very young.

MATH: Problem Solving

 COMMENTS

Many picture books revolve around a problem faced by one or more characters, which makes them all fair game for a math lesson. According to the Curriculum and Evaluation Standards of the National Council of Teachers of Math, problem solving permeates the entire math program and should provide the context for other math concepts and skills. Problem solving, of course, is not relegated only to the math program but becomes vital in science, social studies and interpreting literature. In this theme we'll touch on many of those areas of the curriculum, but we'll emphasize the mathematical whenever possible.

 PICTURE BOOK STARTER

Phyllis Reynolds Naylor's **Ducks Disappearing** (Illustrated by Tony Maddox. Atheneum Books for Young Readers, 1997, ISBN 0 689 31902 9) is a slight but delightful story. Willie and his mother arrive at a motel where they order lunch. Willie notices a mother duck outside the window with her 11 ducklings. He looks away, and when he looks back, there are only 10 ducklings. Now alarmed, Willie tries to get various hotel employees to help as more and more ducklings disappear. It's Willie who discovers that they have fallen through a grate. Even now the adults insist that it's not their problem until Willie shouts, "Well, I think they belong to all of us!" and the ducklings are rescued.

ACTIVITIES

Language Arts
INTERPRETING THE TEXT
▶ Read the story **Ducks Disappearing**. What caused the problem here? Who could have solved it? Who did solve it?

▶ In **Evan's Corner** (see book list), Evan has one problem at the beginning of the story that he solves, but then another problem is presented. What's the second problem?

Math

▶ After the children have read the story **Ducks Disappearing,** have them draw and cut out pictures of the ducklings. Place them on the bulletin board using ordinals as you do so. "Here's the first duckling. Here's the second duckling," etc.

▶ Count the number of motel employees that Willie sought help from in **Ducks Disappearing.**

▶ Alfie solves a problem himself in **Alfie Gets in First,** one of the stories in **All About Alfie** (see book list), but not before a lot of people show up outside the door. Place counters in a line to represent each person in line.

▶ In **The Salamander Room**, the mother keeps asking questions stating the problem, and the boy keeps coming up with solutions. At which point do his solutions become impractical? Do they ever become impossible?

▶ In **The Jacket I Wear in the Snow** (see book list), who solves the problem? What if she had not been available?

▶ Make a chart such as the following for the books listed.

TITLE	PROBLEM	POSSIBLE SOLUTION	AUTHOR'S SOLUTION
Ducks Disappearing	Baby ducks are trapped under a grate	Let them die. Feed them through the grate. Let the mother duck figure out what to do. Call the fire department. Call the Humane Society. Destroy the grate. Build a ramp.	

▶ Analyze the problems and their solutions in many stories. Who identifies the problem? What caused the problem—misunderstanding, not enough information, too much information? How was the problem solved—luck, a third party, time, logical thinking, or critical thinking? How often does a child solve it?

▶ Make a flow chart showing the events in the story. Highlight the moments when the problem is recognized and when it is solved.

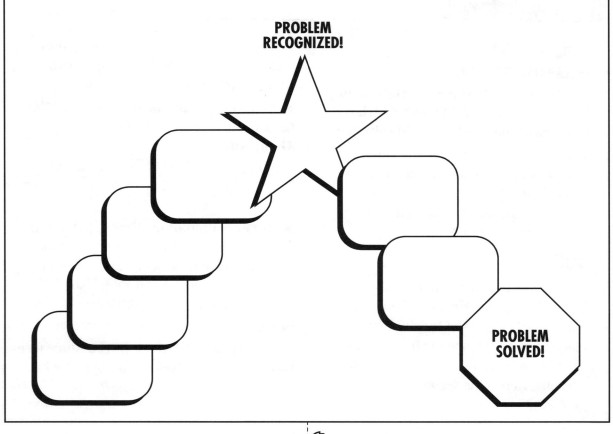

PROBLEM RECOGNIZED!

PROBLEM SOLVED!

► In **The Doorbell Rang** (see book list below), the problem is that more and more guests are arriving and there are fewer and fewer cookies for each person. Count the cookies and match them to the guests. Figure out how many cookies you'd need if twice as many guests showed up.

Science

► In **Tigress** (see book list below), villagers and wildlife advocates are in conflict over a tiger. Find out about the conflict between the ranchers and the wildlife people before and during the reintroduction of wolves to Yellowstone and other national parks. What is the problem? What are some solutions? Which solutions seem to be working?

Social Studies

► What if the setting for **Ducks Disappearing** had not been a motel courtyard but a hospital where Willie was waiting? What workers would he find there? Think of other settings for the story where there would be different workers.

► What are some of the problems in your classroom? Make a list of them and then brainstorm for possible solutions.

► In **Tigress**, a compromise is reached between those who want to save the tiger and those who want to save their herds. Find out about conflicts in your community between wildlife and people.

BOOK LIST
Picture Books

Blos, Joan W. *Old Henry.* Illustrated by Stephen Gammell. Mulberry Books, 1987. ISBN 0 688 09935 1

Old Henry wants to be left alone in his old, dilapidated house. The neighbors demand that he fix up the place because it's a disgrace. This is a focus book (see page 143).

Brisson, Pat. *Benny's Pennies.* Bantam Doubleday Dell Books for Young Readers, 1993. ISBN 0 440 41016 9

Benny has five pennies, and each member of his family has a suggestion for what he should buy. Fortunately, Benny is a creative and generous little boy.

Carle, Eric. *Papa, Please Get the Moon for Me.* Simon & Schuster Books for Young Readers, 1986. ISBN 0 887 08026 X

Monica wants the moon, so her father sets out to get it for her, but he's faced with the problem of how to get it home.

Cowcher, Helen. *Tigress.* Farrar Strauss & Giroux Books for Young Readers, 1991. ISBN 0 374 47781 7

A tigress and her cubs are in search of food. One of a village's bullocks is killed, then a camel. The villagers want to kill the tigress, but they reach a compromise with the sanctuary ranger.

Henkes, Kevin. *Lilly's Purple Plastic Purse.* Greenwillow Books, 1996. ISBN 0 688 12897 1

The problem is that Lilly just can't keep her musical purse closed at school and Mr. Slinger is annoyed. This is a focus book (see page 134).

Henkes, Kevin. **Owen.** *Greenwillow Books, 1993.*
ISBN 0 688 11449 0

Owen loves Fuzzy, his blanket, but Mrs. Tweezers, a busy-body neighbor, has lots of ways she thinks Owen and Fuzzy should be separated.

Hill, Elizabeth. **Evan's Corner.** *Illustrated by Sandra Speidel. Puffin Books, 1993. ISBN 0 140 54406 2*

Evan's problem is that he wants and needs space for himself, but his family's apartment is very small and very crowded. He solves the problem by claiming ownership of one corner of one room, but there seems to be something missing.

Hughes, Shirley. **All About Alfie.** *Lothrop, Lee & Shepard Books, 1997. ISBN 0 688 15186 8*

This book is a compilation of many smaller books about Alfie, a delightful little kid who lives with his mother, father and baby sister in a London flat.

Hutchins, Pat. **The Doorbell Rang.** *Greenwillow Books, 1986. ISBN 0 688 05251 7*

There's a lot of math in this book about some children and their mother and a plate full of cookies. Then the doorbell begins to ring.

Johnson, Paul B. **The Cow Who Wouldn't Come Down.** *Orchard Books, 1993. ISBN 0 531 05481 0*

Gertrude the cow has taken to flying and won't come down. Miss Rosemary tries lots of solutions before she thinks of a way to get Gertrude down to earth and keep her there.

Keller, Holly. **Geraldine's Blanket.** *Greenwillow Books, 1984. ISBN 0 688 02539 0*

The problem in this book is similar to the one in **Owen** (see above). Geraldine's blanket is fast deteriorating, but she solves the problem.

Levine, Evan. **What's Black & White & Came to Visit.** *Illustrated by Betty Lewin. Orchard Books, 1994. ISBN 0 531 06852 8*

It's a skunk, and Lily spies it in the rain gutter of the house. Each adult has an idea of how to get it out of the gutter, but the skunk solves the problem.

Lord, John. **The Giant Jam Sandwich.** *Houghton Mifflin Books for Children, 1974. ISBN 0 395 16033 2*

The problem for the people of Itching Down is easy to recognize: Four million wasps have descended upon them.

Mazer, Anne. **The Salamander Room.** *Illustrated by Steve Johnson. Alfred A. Knopf Books for Young Readers, 1991. ISBN 0 394 92946 4*

A boy discovers a beautiful orange salamander and wants to keep it. His mother, however, keeps asking for solutions to the various problems that keeping a salamander healthy and happy will present in their home.

Naylor, Phyllis Reynolds. **Ducks Disappearing.** *Illustrated by Tony Maddox. Atheneum Books for Young Readers, 1997. ISBN 0 689 31902 9*

Ducklings are disappearing, and Willie seems to be the only one who cares.

Neitzel, Shirley. **The Jacket I Wear in the Snow.** *Illustrated by Nancy Winslow Parker. Mulberry Books, 1994. ISBN 0 688 04587 1*

A cumulative rebus story in the style of "This Is the House That Jack Built" builds as a child is dressed for winter. Once the child's fully clothed, however, there's a problem.

Otaleye, Isaac. **Bitter Bananas.** *Illustrated by Ed Young. Puffin Books, 1994. ISBN 0 14 055710 5*

Baboons are stealing the palm sap that Yusuf needs to gather each morning. He tries several solutions to the problem before he finds one that works.

Porte, Barbara Ann. **Harry in Trouble.** Illustrated by Yossi Abolafia. Greenwillow Books, 1989. ISBN 0 688 07722 6

Harry keeps losing his library cards, or rather, he loses track of them. The librarian has a solution, however.

Pulver, Robin. **Mrs. Toggle's Zipper.** Illustrated by R. W. Alley. Aladdin Paperbacks, 1990. ISBN 0 689 71689 3

Mrs. Toggle's zipper is stuck, and everyone tries to solve the problem, but it's the janitor who finally does.

Saltzberg, Barney. **Mrs. Morgan's Lawn.** Hyperion Books for Children, 1998. ISBN 0 7868 1294 X

Mrs. Morgan is mean. When balls land on her lawn, they disappear forever. When our narrator loses his brand-new soccer ball on Mrs. Morgan's lawn, he comes up with a variety of solutions to the problem, but eventually he must face the problem itself—Mrs. Morgan.

Scieszka, Jon. **Math Curse.** Illustrated by Lane Smith. Viking Children's Books, 1995. ISBN 0 670 86194 4

This story is a bit like the legend of King Midas. Told by his teacher that she can find math anywhere, our narrator proceeds to find it.

Slobodkina, Esphyr. **Caps for Sale.** HarperCollins Children's Books, 1947. ISBN 0 06 025778 4

The problem in this old favorite is that the monkeys have stolen a man's caps.

Waddell, Martin. **Sailor Bear.** Candlewick Press, 1992. ISBN 1 56402 606 X

Sailor Bear solves a whole list of problems in this book of strong patterns.

Wood, Audrey. **King Bidgood's in the Bathtub.** Illustrated by Don Wood. Harcourt Brace & Co., 1985. ISBN 0 15 242730 9

The problem in this story is that King Bidgood is having such a wonderful time in the bathtub that he won't get out. It's the page boy who solves the problem.

SECTION 2

FOCUS BOOKS

Chicken Little

Retold and Illustrated by Steven Kellogg
Morrow Junior Books, 1985
ISBN 0 688 05690 3

SUMMARY

We see all the characters except for Sergeant Hippo Hefty on the book's title page. Foxy Loxy is busy camouflaging his poultry truck. Chicken Little is skipping down the road toward us. Henny Penny is picking flowers. Farther down the road we see Ducky Lucky jogging this way. Goosey Lucy comes pushing the baby carriage bearing Gosling Gilbert and, in the distance, Turkey Lurkey is enjoying a game of golf. In spite of the myriad characters, however, the plants in the foreground are what catch our eye. The acorn that started it all stands alone on the dedication page.

As the story gets underway, Foxy Loxy sits in his truck with a poultry cookbook on the dashboard, planning to make a chicken salad sandwich of Chicken Little as she heads for school carrying her books and a pencil. Before Foxy Loxy can pounce, however, the acorn falls from the oak tree branches over Chicken Little's head. Just as we expect her to, she screams, "The sky is falling!" and Henny Penny comes running, throwing her flowers in the air as she hears the news. She adds, "Call the police" to the repetition of "The sky is falling!"

Meanwhile, inside the poultry truck, Foxy Loxy has revised his menu. He's now planning a meal of Southern-fried chicken and is about to grab both chickens, when Ducky Lucky comes running up. He's wearing track clothes, and his jersey bears a star. He joins the cry for the police and repeats that the sky is falling. Foxy Loxy's meal plans now include Ducky Lucky, whom he intends to simmer with spices and sauce. Goosey Lucy and Gosling Gilbert join the chorus, and

COMMENTS

Many folktales make ideal stories for children in the primary grades, because they're usually straightforward narratives. Little time is spent on descriptions or setting; the characters are either the good guys or the bad guys and the stories are often funny. "Chicken Little" is a noodle-head tale, and we can all laugh at her foolishness. She's also become a symbol for alarmists in our society. Kellogg has added a whole subplot in the illustrations while taking great liberties with the ending, making this particular version of the tale even more interesting than other versions.

Foxy Loxy plans to toast the little one and put Goosey Lucy in the freezer until Christmas. Turkey Lurkey comes over, and Foxy Loxy suddenly imagines himself wearing a Pilgrim hat and sitting at an over-laden Thanksgiving table. He'd pounce on them all but, just in time, he realizes that the odds are not in his favor and that the turkey and goose look formidable. So he schemes to avoid the scuffle with a bit of trickery.

He quickly dons a policeman's jacket and hat and changes the poultry sign on his truck to a misspelled "Poulice." (His sunglasses add a nice touch.) He approaches the group with offers of help. He hustles them into his "Poulice" truck, declaring that he will take them to headquarters immediately. The frightened poultry climb inside—all except for Chicken Little. In spite of his disguise, she recognizes Foxy Loxy from a wanted poster she had seen in town. "It's Foxy Loxy!," she shrieked. "Run for your lives!" Foxy Loxy is too quick for them. He throws Chicken Little in with the others and closes the door of the truck.

Unfortunately for him, Foxy Loxy can't resist taking a moment to gloat and to reread his poultry recipes. He shows them the acorn that started it all and tosses it high in the air before climbing into his truck. The acorn flies into the propeller of a police helicopter flying overhead (and bearing Sergeant Hippo Hefty), jamming its gears. The helicopter falls into the cab of the truck. Foxy Loxy leaps from the truck and this time it's he who yells, "The sky is falling!" The other animals are ejected from the rear of the truck by the force of the wreck. They start chasing Foxy Loxy but they needn't bother. Sergeant Hefty falls on top of him and declares, "You're under arrest!" Foxy Loxy may be vanquished, but he can't resist a pun: "You mean I'm under a fat hippo."

At his trial, Foxy Loxy pleads innocent, but he is sent to prison on a vegetarian diet of green bean gruel and weed juice. Chicken Little plants the acorn near her chicken coop, and years later we see her sitting on the porch of that coop beside a huge oak tree, telling the whole story to her grandchildren as another large acorn falls.

THINGS WORTH NOTICING

► An acorn begins and ends the story.

► Foxy Loxy knows a lot about cooking.

► Each character is busy doing something else before they hear Chicken Little screaming.

► Chicken Little's foolishness starts the hysteria but it's also Chicken Little who recognizes the fox.

► Foxy Loxy isn't a very good speller or he thinks the poultry creatures are not.

► There are only two mammals in the story, the rest of the characters are poultry.

► Many details in the illustrations are not mentioned in the text.

► The ending is different from many renditions of this folktale.

ACTIVITIES

Language Arts
SPELLING
► How should Foxy Loxy have spelled "police"? Find and list other words where the "c" makes the sound of "s."

FINDING DETAILS
► Find all the characters in the story except for Sergeant Hefty on the title page. What is each one doing?

SEQUENCING
► Make a flow chart of the story.

MAKING COMPARISONS
► Read the Jataka tale **Foolish Rabbit's Big Mistake** (see book list).

Compare the events in that book with the ones in **Chicken Little.**

► Read other versions of **Chicken Little** (see book list) and compare them.

► Chicken Little is a silly character in this story. She starts the panic. Find and read other stories about silly characters from the book list below.

MAKING INFERENCES
► How do we know that Chicken Little is headed for school?

► Make a happiness graph for Foxy Loxy using the statements on the flow chart. Put those statements along the bottom of the graph. Then decide how happy Foxy Loxy was at each of those points in the story. You might show it this way:

DRAMATIZING

► Retell the story. Then act it out. Make costumes that are simple and have only one or two parts to suggest each animal.

Math

► Count the animals. Make a large picture of each animal and place all of the pictures on a bulletin board in the order in which the animals appear in the story. Put numbers underneath the characters to show that order.

► Put one item each animal is carrying beside the pictures on the bulletin board for one-to-one matching.

► Make statements such as, "The first to come was Foxy Loxy."

Science

► Can the sky fall? Why not?

► Use Venn diagrams to show what all the animals in the book have in common.

► This story names four kinds of fowl. (Chicken Little and Henny Penny are both chickens.) Are there any other kinds? If they were in the story, what names would you give them?

► Make a list of things that are true about all fowl.

HAPPINESS GRAPH FOR FOXY LOXY		
An acorn falls on Chicken Little's head.		Foxy is neither happy nor sad.
She yells that the sky is falling.		Foxy is neither happy nor sad.
Henny Penny comes and yells for the police.		Foxy is a little bit happy.
Ducky Lucky comes running up.		Foxy is quite happy.
Goosey Lucy joins them.		Foxy is quite happy.
Turkey Lurkey comes running over.		Foxy is quite happy.
Foxy Loxy disguises himself & the truck.		Foxy is quite happy.
The birds rush into the truck.		Foxy is very, very happy.
Chicken Little recognizes Foxy Loxy.		Foxy is not happy.
A helicopter crashes into the truck.		Foxy is not happy.
Sergeant Hefty falls on Foxy Loxy.		Foxy is not happy.
Foxy Loxy is sent to jail.		Foxy is very, very unhappy.
Chicken Little plants the acorn near her house.		We don't know about Foxy.
Chicken Little tells the story to her grandchildren.		We don't know about Foxy.

RELATED BOOKS

Fiction

Fox, Mem. **Hattie & the Fox.** *Illustrated by Patricia Mullins. Bradbury Press, 1988.* ISBN 0 02 735470 9

Hattie the hen sees the eyes of the fox lurking in the bushes and she warns the other animals. But even after Hattie spies more and more of the fox, the animals show nothing but disdain for Hattie—until the fox jumps out.

Froehlich, Margaret Walden. **That Kookoory.** *Illustrated by Marla Frazee. Browndeer Press, 1995. ISBN 0 152 77650 8*

A weasel is pursuing a very foolish rooster that's heading to the fair, but the weasel is foiled again and again.

Galdone, Paul. **Henny Penny.** *Houghton Mifflin Books for Children,1984. ISBN 0 899 19225 4*

The main character in this version of the tale is Henny Penny, but the tale is the same as that in **Chicken Little.**

Ginsburg, Mirra. **Across the Stream.** *Illustrated by Nancy Tafuri. Greenwillow Books, 1982. ISBN 0 688 01204 3*

A hen and her chicks are being chased by a fox and must cross a stream to escape.

Hutchins, Pat. **Rosie's Walk.** *Simon & Schuster Books for Young Readers, 1968. ISBN 0 02 745850 4*

In this story, another hen is pursued by a fox, but she's completely unaware of his presence, even though she foils him time after time.

Kasza, Keiko. **The Wolf's Chicken Stew.** *G. P. Putnam's Sons Books for Young Readers, 1987. ISBN 0 399 22000 3*

The wolf has determined to make stew of the chicken he sees on the road, but first he thinks he'll fatten her up. He leaves food for the chicken night after night, only to find that all of her chicks consider him their benefactor.

Marshall, James. **Wings: A Tale of Two Chickens.** *Viking Children's Books, 1988. ISBN 0 140 50579 2*

Two chicken sisters live together. Harriet is a reader and would know better, but nonreading Winnie doesn't hesitate a minute when a fox offers her a ride in his hot-air balloon.

Martin, Rafe. **Foolish Rabbit's Big Mistake.** *Illustrated by Ed Young. Sandcastle, 1985. ISBN 0 399 21778 9*

This story is the Jatakan version of **Chicken Little.** In it, a rabbit hears a thud behind him and becomes convinced that the earth is breaking up.

Rader, Laura. **Chicken Little.** *HarperCollins Children's Books, 1998. ISBN 0 694 01034 0*

This version of the story sticks much closer to the traditional one than Steven Kellogg's does.

Stoeke, Janet Morgan. **Minerva Louise.** *Dutton Children's Books, 1988. ISBN 0 525 44374 6*

Minerva Louise is an empty-headed chicken who perceives everything from her unique point of view. There is a series of books about her.

The Gardener

By Sarah Stewart
Illustrated by David Small
Farrar Straus & Giroux Books for Young Readers, 1997
ISBN 0 374 32517 0

SUMMARY

This story begins on the endpapers of the book. Lydia Grace and her grandmother are in a large garden. The relationship between grandmother and child is established as Lydia Grace kneels in front of her grandmother, offering a large tomato for her inspection. Grandmother's posture is that of a teacher as she points to another tomato in her hand, apparently commenting on it. The time period is established by the old cars seen on dirt roads in the background. That this is a rural area is also apparent.

The story continues on the title page, as the grandmother and Lydia Grace head back to the house. A man and woman with sagging shoulders are deep in conversation beside the house.

The story is carried, from that point on, by a series of letters written by Lydia Grace. The first is to her Uncle Jim, her mother's brother, and as we see her sad-faced grandmother helping Lydia pack, Lydia Grace's letter gives the news that she is to stay with her Uncle Jim in the city during this difficult time. (Adult readers will interpret this as the time of the Great Depression.) Her next letter to Uncle Jim (written at the railroad station) establishes three "important things" about Lydia: She knows a lot about gardening; she is anxious to help him in the bakery, but it's important that she have time to plant her seeds; and she likes to be called "Lydia Grace."

From here on, the letters are from Lydia Grace to her parents and grandmother, and we see her go through several stages in her adjustment to her new life. The wordless spread where

COMMENTS

This Caldecott Award-winning book is a treasure for its literary and visual content, as well as for the multitude of thematic avenues it can open up. Set in the time of the Great Depression, it explores the painful separation of a family necessitated by that economic crisis. There are extensive renderings of inner-city buildings (probably in New York City) and of period vehicles. The entire plot takes place through letters written by Lydia Grace, and the theme of the book is the transcendent power of beauty.

Lydia Grace stands alone in the vast railroad station establishes her vulnerability. The window boxes at her new home excite her, even as her Uncle Jim's unsmiling presence concerns her and she determines to change that frown to a smile.

As Lydia Grace's correspondence accumulates, we learn that her folks continue to send her seeds, seedlings, and bulbs, and that she has established a friendship with two of Uncle Jim's employees in the bakery, Ed and Emma Beech, and a cat named Otis. When Lydia Grace writes that she has discovered a secret place and has great plans for it, we see her on the fire escape of the apartment building, looking up. The next wordless spread shows us the barren rooftop. Emma, apparently, is helping Lydia Grace prepare a surprise for Uncle Jim in the secret place. Business at the bakery is improving, and Uncle Jim's spirits have also improved, although he still doesn't smile. Neighbors have begun referring to Lydia Grace as "the gardener" and bring containers and plants to help her plan her surprise.

On July 4, the surprise is ready, and we see a trail of flowers in all kinds of containers leading up to the roof. We see the roof as Uncle Jim does (a riot of color and life, with Lydia Grace's plants everywhere). No, Uncle Jim never does smile, but he brings his own surprise for Lydia Grace (a cake covered with flowers). As Lydia Grace leaves for home, she's first held in a fond embrace by Uncle Jim.

THINGS WORTH NOTICING

► We first see Lydia Grace on the jacket of the book, standing at the top of the fire escape. She holds a pot containing a tall, bright yellow flower. Her hand, bearing a garden trowel, is raised above her head in greeting or in triumph.

► The front endpapers show Lydia Grace and her grandmother in their thriving, rural garden. The child is kneeling in front of the woman, offering a lush, ripe tomato for her approval.

► The title page shows the pair heading back to the house bearing the garden's bounty. In the driveway, a man stands in front of his car talking to Lydia Grace's mother. Their heads lean toward each other. Both have drooping shoulders.

► Grace's room is the next scene. There are plants and flowers everywhere. A sad grandmother and Lydia Grace are packing her up to leave. A small teddy bear lies on the pillow, and we see Lydia Grace's first letter, which is to Uncle Jim. In it, there is mention of the fact that he once was a little boy who chased his sister up a tree.

► The next letter is also to Uncle Jim and mentions Lydia Grace's love of and knowledge of gardening.

► From then on, the letters are from Lydia Grace to her grandmother and parents.

► The railroad station is Penn Station in New York City, and the view of it emphasizes the gray vastness of the city, with Lydia Grace the only spot of color.

► The next scene shows a glowering Uncle Jim paying the cab driver, and Lydia Grace's letter mentions that he doesn't smile.

► Uncle Jim reads her poem, but he continues to frown.

► Lydia Grace's letter to her parents on December 25 doesn't mention that it's Christmas, although there's a Christmas tree in Uncle Jim's living room.

► We begin to get hints of Lydia Grace's "secret place," and we see a litter-strewn tenement rooftop.

► Franklin Roosevelt's picture is on the wall of the bakery.

► Times seem to be getting better, and the street in and around the bakery is full of shoppers.

► Although Lydia Grace has spent her entire stay with Uncle Jim looking forward to seeing him smile, he never does.

(See page 16 for a theme on gardening.)

Language Arts

MAKING COMPARISONS

▶ Patricia MacLachlan's book **What You Know First** (see book list) takes place at about the same time as **The Gardener**. How would you know this from looking at both books?

▶ In **What You Know First**, the people have to move. How is the little girl in that story like Lydia Grace?

▶ The families in **What You Know First, Dust for Dinner, The Dust Bowl,** and **The Gardener** are all having hard times because of the Depression. Which family is most like your own? Which child would you rather be?

MAKING INFERENCES

▶ What are some of the things in the story that tell you that Uncle Jim loves Lydia Grace?

▶ How do you know that this isn't a story that takes place in the present day?

▶ Make copies of the letters in the book. Place them under pictures of faces that show how you think Lydia Grace is feeling as she writes each letter.

▶ List the clues that tell you what the surprise for Uncle Jim is.

▶ List the clues that tell you that times are getting better.

▶ Otis, the cat, shows his feelings too. How do you know what he is feeling?

Science

▶ Plan and plant a garden like Lydia Grace's for your school. Can you use the roof? What will you use for containers? Which kind of plants will grow best there?

▶ Keep a journal of how your garden grows.

Social Studies

▶ Share gardening responsibilities with a nursing home.

▶ Find out about the Great Depression. Who do you know that would have been alive during that time? Interview them about their memories of the Great Depression

▶ There's a picture of Franklin Delano Roosevelt on the wall of the bakery. Put up a bulletin board about him, asking each member of the class to post one fact about or picture of him on the board.

▶ Find a book that shows cars of long ago. Compare them to the cars in this book to see what years they were built.

▶ We see both the inside and the outside of a train in this book. How would trains from that time differ from trains today?

▶ The family in **Dust for Dinner** (see book list) is able to stay together, but they must move to get away from the dust. Find out more about the Dust Bowl.

RELATED BOOKS

(See page 16 for other books on gardening.)

Fiction

Booth, David. ***The Dust Bowl.*** *Illustrated by Karen Reczuch. Kids Can Press, 1997.* ISBN 1 55074 295 7

The dust and drought are defeating the boy's father, but his grandfather remembers a time when the Dust Bowl overpowered everything, yet they and the farm survived.

MacLachlan, Patricia. ***What You Know First.*** *Illustrated by Barry Moser. HarperCollins Children's Books, 1995.* ISBN 0 06 024413 5

A little girl's family is moving, probably because of the Depression. She announces that she will not go with them, even if she has to stay in their old home alone.

Turner, Ann. ***Dust for Dinner.*** *Illustrated by Robert Barrett. HarperCollins Children's Books, 1995.* ISBN 0 06 023376 1

This easy-to-read book is about the Dust Bowl and a family that abandons its farm to move to California.

Nonfiction

Stein, Richard C. ***The Great Depression.*** *Children's Press, 1993. ISBN 0 516 06668 4*

The text in this book is too hard for most children in the lower grades, but the illustrations are very informative.

Gila Monsters Meet You at the Airport

By Marjorie Weinman Sharmat
Illustrated by Byron Barton
Aladdin Books, 1980
ISBN 0 688 71383 5

SUMMARY

The book's cover shows a child at the top of airplane stairs. Waiting for him at the foot of those stairs is a crowd of Gila monsters. On the title page we see a childlike street scene in a big city. The vignette on the back of the title page brings us closer in to the view of the street, and the street sign indicates that this is East 95th Street. The dedication page brings us to an apartment building on that street.

We zoom in even closer on the first page of the book to the doorway of that apartment building, where a sad looking boy stands, staring straight out at us as he speaks to us in the text. He tells us that he lives here in New York City and intends to stay here forever.

The next two pages reveal that this wish is in vain, however, as his parents are obviously moving, and he must go with them. We learn that the family is moving "Out West," and the next pages show us what the boy thinks he knows about living "Out West." He believes that nobody plays baseball because they have to chase buffalo, and we see children wearing baseball clothing and equipment chasing off a herd of buffalo. He "knows" that there are cactuses everywhere, and we see a very hot boy about to sit on a chair with a prickly cactus growing up through the seat. He "knows" that out West everybody says, "Howdy, Partner," in a long, drawn out manner, instead of "hello." And he "knows" that he must wear uncomfortable cowboy gear and ride a horse everywhere he goes. Now, he'll have to become a sheriff when he grows up, but he wants to become a subway driver.

COMMENTS

This simple picture book succeeds at expressing people's fear of the unknown. The child in the story is about to move with his parents to a new part of the country, and he believes the stereotypical information he has heard about it. The book also touches upon such themes as geographical study, friendship, and moving away from friends.

Then we learn about his best friend, Seymour, with whom he has shared salami sandwiches. Out West, he knows, he won't have any friends except for some named Slim and Tex, and he'll have to eat chili and beans for every meal.

In the second chapter, the scene switches to the interior of the airplane that's taking our hero and his mother and father to their new home. The boy's parents are reading, but he looks mournfully out of the window, "knowing" that below him is nothing but desert, where you can get lost and never rescued. We then see a map of the United States in which the words "Out West" and cactus cover half the map. In the New York City area of the map, we see the family's empty apartment building, and in the middle of the map is the airplane. He tells us that previously he could always know, when he looked at a map, that his home was on the right but that's no longer true. He's going left, left Out West.

The cover scene is repeated on the next page, and we hear about Gila monsters for the first time. Seymour told him that there are both Gila monsters and horned toads out West.

These facts are confirmed in a book, but Seymour also said that the Gila monsters meet you at the airport.

Chapter Three shows his actual arrival at the airport Out West, but there are no Gila monsters or horned toads visible. Inside the airport, he sees a boy wearing a cowboy hat and carrying a guitar. They speak and the boy tells him he is moving East. Our narrator says that's great, but the boy "knows" differently. He thinks he knows all about the East, and the next few pages illustrate what he "knows": The streets are full of gangsters, it snows all the time, airplanes zoom through your room. and everybody has to sit on somebody else because they ran out of room. He also "knows" that alligators live in the sewers. He read it in a book, so he knows it's true, and as his parents lead him away, he shouts, "Sometimes the alligators get out and they wait for you at the airport."

In Chapter Four, our main character is in a cab with his parents, heading to their new home. He sees neither buffalo nor horses, but

THINGS WORTH NOTICING

► Although this is a picture book, it's divided into chapters.

there are a few cactuses visible on people's lawns. He sees a restaurant where cooks seem to be creating food much like that in restaurants back home. He sees kids playing baseball, and when he does see a horse, he decides to ask his parents to buy him one. In front of their new house he sees two boys riding bikes and declares that he hopes one of them is named Slim. As he walks up the sidewalk to his new home, the boy says that tomorrow he will write to Seymour and tell him he is sending it by Pony Express. He thinks Seymour will believe him because, back East, they know nothing about us Westerners. Sometime during the cab ride he took off his cap and replaced it with a cowboy hat, which he tips to us as he walks into his new home.

ACTIVITIES

Language Arts
MAKING COMPARISONS
► Make a list of things you have in common with the narrator of this story.

► Read the book **Amelia's Road** (see book list below). Amelia has to move all the time. What would it be like for you to have to live like that?

WRITING
► Make a list of the things you would miss most if you had to move from the area you live in now.

► Make a brochure about your town or your school that would tell a new person things he or she might like to know before moving there.

Science
► Find out about Gila monsters. What do they look like? What do they eat? What are their enemies? Do they live all over the West or in specific areas?

► Find out about cactuses. Make a cactus garden.

Social Studies
► Interview someone who has recently moved and is now going to your school. Find out how he or she felt on their first day of school. Which people made things easier for him or her? Make a list of things to do for the next new person to make him or her more comfortable.

▶ Assume that the state the boy is moving to is Texas. Make a list of the things he thinks are true about that state. Beside each statement make a true statement about Texas on that issue.

▶ In the book, heading left on the map is equated with heading west. Look at all kinds of different maps and discover what you find out as you head west on them.

▶ In the book, a large section of the country is labeled "Out West." Is that where your state is?

▶ Take a state that you have heard about but never visited. Make a list of the things you think you know about that state. Do some research and interview someone from that state to see how many things you thought were true are not.

RELATED BOOKS
Fiction

Altman, Linda Jacobs. **Amelia's Road.** Illustrated by Enrique O. Sanchez. Lee & Low Books, 1993. ISBN 1 880000 04 0

Amelia's parents travel from place to place to pick vegetables and fruits, so she has no permanent home. This time, she really hates to move on, because her teacher knows her name and likes her work.

Asch, Frank. **Goodbye House.** Simon & Schuster Books for Young Readers, 1986. ISBN 0 671 67927 9

Baby Bear has to leave the only house he has known. His parents help him revisit all his favorite places and they say good-bye to every room.

Johnson, Angela. **The Leaving Morning.** Illustrated by David Soman. Orchard Books, 1992. ISBN 0 531 08592 9

This simple story is about the feelings of a family as they move from their apartment to their new home.

Komaiko, Leah. **Annie Bananie.** Illustrated by Laura Comeil. Harper Trophy, 1989. ISBN 0 06 443 1983

Annie Bananie is the narrator's best friend and she is moving away. We learn about all the things they used to do together.

Viorst, Judith. **Alexander, Who's Not (Do You Hear Me? I Mean It!) Going to Move.** Atheneum Books for Young Readers, 1995. ISBN 0 689 31958 4

Like the narrator in **Gila Monsters Meet You at the Airport,** Alexander really hates to move. He vows that he will not do so.

Waber, Bernard. **Ira Says Goodbye.** Houghton Mifflin Books for Children, 1988. ISBN 0 395 48315 8

Ira and Reggie have been good friends for years. Now Reggie is moving far away and he doesn't seem sorry about it at all. Ira tries to convince himself that he won't miss Reggie, but he knows he will. When the moving van finally arrives, we find out how Reggie really feels.

How to Make an Apple Pie and See the World

By Marjorie Priceman
Dragonfly, 1994
ISBN 0 679 88083 6

SUMMARY

The story is written in the second person, so "you" are the person involved in it. You learn that making an apple pie is very easy. All you have to do is go to the market, buy the ingredients, mix them together, bake them, and serve the pie. Unless, of course, the market is closed. In which case you must board a ship, learn Italian, and start a whirlwind trip around the world gathering all the necessary ingredients for the pie. After the pie is finally made, you're urged to serve it with ice cream, which you can get at the market—unless, of course, the market is closed. At that point, you, the reader, are ready for another whirlwind tour, but the author surprises you with the instruction to . . . serve it plain.

COMMENTS

This simple and funny story incorporates a lot of concepts, including some map skills often covered in social studies programs for the early grades. The book's endpapers feature a world map, and the paperback edition includes a world map with a key showing where you go in the course of the story. The story deals with the ingredients for making a pie, which sets the groundwork for a further exploration of world wide trade. This book can also serve as the beginning of a theme on food or nutrition.

The story should, I think, be read at a regular pace until the ingredients for the pie have all been gathered. At that point it's fun to read the next two pages rapidly as the pie is prepared. The return to a slower pace once the pie is ready encourages listeners to predict the ending—most likely incorrectly.

THINGS WORTH NOTICING

▶ There's a European look to the market area, but an American flag is just barely visible on the right side of the page.

▶ There are cats and dogs on many of the pages, and all the animals are fun to watch.

▶ The apple pie recipe is at the end of the book.

▶ The people who come to share the pie may have been friends you made on the trip.

▶ Notice the sign on the market door that first read, "gone fishing."

Language Arts

BUILDING VOCABULARY

► Notice all the words for "good" that are used in the story:

> Superb
>
> Elegant
>
> Finest
>
> Best
>
> Charming
>
> Rosy

► Try substituting the word "good" for each of those words in the story. Does the story still make sense? If so, why use the other words?

► Make a list of as many different kinds of apples as you can. Gather together lots of kinds of apples for a tasting. Slice the apples on different plates. Place a stack of index cards bearing the name of the apple beside each plate. Label each of four jars with one of the following: crunchiest, sweetest, sourest, best. Ask tasters to place the names of the apples they think deserve each title in the appropriate jar.

FINDING DETAILS

► Collect several recipes for apple pie. Compare them to look for ingredients in one recipe that are not in the others. Find and taste those ingredients before putting them into a pie and after the pie is made.

EXTENDING LITERATURE

► Find out about Johnny Appleseed (see book list).

► Find and read other stories about apples. Make a poster about your favorite apple book.

Math

► Make a graph showing the results of the apple tasting.

► How long would it take you to make the pie if you did all the things in the book? You'll have to figure out how long a boat trip takes from your home to Italy, how long it would take to travel by train from Italy to France, what the best way is to get from France to Sri Lanka, etc. The story doesn't tell you how you get from Sri Lanka to England, so you'll have to guess at that one.

Science

► Make a list of all the ingredients you gathered for the pie in the book. Write the name of each ingredient on a card on a bulletin board. Above each card trace what it took to make that ingredient. For instance, you needed milk for the pie:

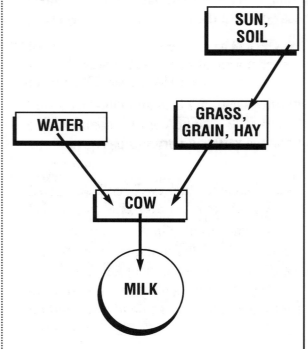

▶ Find out which food groups the ingredients of the pie belong in. Show it on a food pyramid. Which of those ingredients are best for you? Where else can you find the same nutrients?

▶ Find and try recipes using apples. Which recipes result in the healthiest food? Rate them on a scale going from healthiest to most unhealthy.

▶ Take one apple and observe it in as many ways as you can. Make notes on your observations. Gather all the apples in the room together and sort them by color. Note the results. Sort them again by size. Note the results. Sort them again using a different attribute that you decide on. Note the results.

Social Studies

▶ Learn to say "good morning" or "hello" in the language spoken in each of the places you visit in the story.

▶ Divide a large display into seven sections. Label them: home, Italy, France, Sri Lanka, England, Jamaica, and Vermont. Place a small world map in each section with the appropriate country highlighted. Find out one interesting thing about each of the places you visit in the story in addition to what the story tells you.

▶ Make a flag for each of the countries represented on the bulletin board.

Web Sites

▶ On **www.ipl.org/youth/cquest/** you follow two characters around the world.

▶ **www.un.org/Pubs/CyberSchoolBus/ menuelem.htm** offers games and puzzles about many countries.

▶ **www.supersurf.com/** features a different country each month, with puzzles and things to do.

RELATED BOOKS
Fiction

Anno, Mitsumasa. **Anno's Journey.** G. P. Putnam's Sons Books for Young Readers, 1981. ISBN 0 399 20762 7

This wordless book is about a traveler who rides across the countryside and discovers all sorts of creatures and creations from many cultures.

Brown, Don. **Alice Ramsey's Grand Adventure.** Houghton Mifflin Books for Children, 1997. ISBN 0 395 70127 9

In 1909 Alice and two companions started a trip to the West Coast in her Maxwell automobile. The trip was full of hazards but, eventually, they made it.

Carle, Eric. **Pancakes, Pancakes.** Scholastic, 1992. ISBN 0 590 44453 0

The making of these pancakes starts with cutting the wheat and then goes step by step to completion.

Cooney, Barbara. **Miss Rumphius.** Puffin Books, 1985. ISBN 0 14 050539 3

When she was a little girl, Alice Rumphius told her grandfather that, when she grew up, she wanted to travel to faraway places and to live in a house by the sea. He tells her she must also make the world more beautiful, and she accomplishes all three of these goals.

dePaola, Tomie. **Pancakes for Breakfast.** *Harcourt Brace & Co., 1978. ISBN 0 15 259455 8*

The ingredients necessary for the little old lady to make pancakes are not easy to come by, but she gets them eventually.

Houston, Gloria. **My Great-Aunt Arizona.** *Illustrated by Susan Condie Lamb. HarperCollins Children's Books, 1991. ISBN 0 06 022606 4*

Arizona has yearned to travel to faraway places since she was a little girl, but circumstances didn't allow it, so she became a teacher in the mountain community where she grew up. She encourages her students to think about the places they will surely visit someday—places she has visited only in her mind.

Jackson, Ellen. **Brown Cow, Green Grass, Yellow Mellow.** *Houghton Mifflin Books for Children, 1997. ISBN 0 7868 1162 5*

We need butter for pancakes, and this book shows us the process step by step.

Kidd, Richard. **Almost Famous Daisy!.** *Simon & Schuster Books for Young Readers, 1996. ISBN 0 689 80390 7*

Daisy, a dog artist, travels the world seeking her favorite things to paint, but she doesn't find them until she gets home.

Miranda, Anne. **To Market, To Market.** *Harcourt Brace & Co., 1997. ISBN 0 152 00035 6*

Loosely based on the nursery rhyme of the same title, this book allows us to accompany a very harried shopper as she makes frequent trips to the supermarket.

Slawson, Michele Benoit. **Apple Picking Time.** *Illustrated by Deborah Kogan Ray. Dragonfly, 1998. ISBN 0 517 88575 1*

Everyone in town gets involved during apple harvest time in Washington State. Anna is determined to fill her basket for the first time.

Stevenson, James. **All Aboard!.** *Greenwillow Books, 1995. ISBN 0 688 12438 0*

Hubie and his family are heading for the 1939 New York World's Fair, but they become separated when Hubie boards the wrong train. Because California was not where he wanted to go, he takes a plane for the return trip.

Nonfiction

Hartman, Gail. **As the Roadrunner Runs: A First Book of Maps.** *Illustrated by Cathy Bobak. Simon & Schuster Books for Young Readers, 1994. ISBN 0 027 43096 8*

A map is begun as a lizard, a jackrabbit, a roadrunner, a mule, and a deer travel short but contiguous distances. At first the map is a picture map, but then it becomes a more abstract map.

Kindersley, Barnabas. **Children Just Like Me: A Unique Celebration of Children Around the World.** *DK Publishing, 1995. ISBN 0 7894 0201 7*

Beautiful photographs and concise but interesting text provide information about many different cultures.

Lindbergh, Reeve. **Johnny Appleseed.** *Illustrated by Kathy Jakobsen. Little, Brown & Co., Children's Books, 1990. ISBN 0 316 52618 5*

Folk art illustrations accompany this book's rhyming text, which relates the events of John Chapman's life.

McMillan, Bruce. **Apples, How They Grow.** *Houghton Mifflin Books for Children, 1979. ISBN 0 395 278066*

This black-and-white photo-essay follows the development of an apple.

Micucci, Charles. **The Life and Times of the Apple.** *Orchard Books, 1995. ISBN 0 531 07067 0*

The culture and the cultivation of apples are described with exuberance in this delightful and informative book.

If You Give a Mouse a Cookie

By Laura Joffe Numeroff
Illustrated by Felicia Bond
HarperCollins Children's Books, 1987
ISBN 0 06 024687 5

SUMMARY

A little boy sits on a rock in his front yard, reading and eating chocolate chip cookies. He looks up to see a mouse clad in overalls who apparently is asking him for a cookie. The cookie makes the mouse thirsty, so he wants a glass of milk and then a straw to drink it with and then a napkin, of course. Checking in the mirror to see if he's got a milk mustache shows him that he needs scissors to give his whiskers a trim, and so it goes until we come full circle with a request for a cookie. The narration is done in the second person, as the title implies. There is no direct conversation between the boy and the mouse, it's all implied.

COMMENTS

This story is a good example of a pattern book. It has a delightful plot, and the illustrations suit the text perfectly. The other two books by the same author/illustrator team, **If You Give a Moose a Muffin** and **If You Give a Pig a Pancake,** serve as logical comparisons and companions to the first. The consistent sizes in **If You Give a Mouse a Cookie** are particularly useful for mathematics activities. The pen-and-ink and watercolor illustrations are precise and use the white space on the page to emphasize the size of the mouse.

Because there are so many books about mice (see book list), it's possible to use this book as a starter book for a theme on mice.

THINGS WORTH NOTICING

► You can tell how both the mouse and the boy are feeling by their body language.

► We never know exactly what they say to each other.

► The story returns to where it started.

► We can tell where the mouse lives by looking at the picture he drew unless, of course, he was using his imagination.

Language

READING

▶ Find and display the poem "Mice," by Rose Fyleman, which is available in many anthologies. Read it aloud together and then try reading it as if you were a mouse. Then, try reading it as if you were a cat. What if you were a person who really didn't like mice but pretended you did?

BUILDING VOCABULARY

▶ For kids who need work with color words and identification, match real crayons to the ones in the pictures in the book and name the colors. Then, list the various colors of the crayons and name other things that are the same color.

SEQUENCING

▶ This is a circle story. On a large pizza cardboard, draw the events in this story in such a way that you end up back where you started on the circle. Do the same for **If You Give a Moose a Muffin** and **If You Give a Pig a Pancake**.

MAKING COMPARISONS

▶ Find and read other circle stories (see book list). Make circle cardboards for those books.

▶ Find and read other books with mice as characters (see book list). Which of the things on the list you made in the above activity do the mice in the other books do?

DISTINGUISHING BETWEEN REALISM AND FANTASY

▶ This mouse does many things that real mice wouldn't do. Make a list of those things.

WRITING

▶ Make up the conversation between the boy and the mouse on each page.

▶ Brainstorm for words to describe how each of them is feeling as the story goes on.

Math

▶ On the page where the mouse is drawing with a green crayon, the mouse (including tail) is just about the same size as the crayon. Take a new crayon and measure it against other things in the room. What else is the mouse as tall as? Measure other things with the crayon. How many crayons wide is your desk?

▶ Make a chart similar to the one below to compare sizes. Have the children draw pictures of objects from the book in the appropriate spaces.

SMALLER THAN A MOUSE	BIGGER THAN A MOUSE	SMALLER THAN A BOY	BIGGER THAN A BOY

Science

► Which of the crayons in the book have been used more? Which ones have barely been used?

► Take a new box of crayons. Use them to draw a picture of your own family. Notice the changes in the crayons you used. What else changed?

► Do mice like cookies and milk? What is the normal diet for a field mouse? How many other kinds of mice are there?

Music

► Sing the song "Three Blind Mice."

RELATED BOOKS

Fiction

OTHER BOOKS BY NUMEROFF AND BOND

Numeroff, Laura. *If You Give a Moose a Muffin.* Illustrated by Felicia Bond. HarperCollins Children's Books, 1991. ISBN 0 06 024406 2

One muffin, even with homemade jam, isn't enough for a moose, so a boy has to go to the store for more muffin mix. Then the moose needs a sweater, a needle and thread, some socks to make puppets, and so on, until we're back to the muffin.

Numeroff, Laura. *If You Give a Pig a Pancake.* Illustrated by Felicia Bond. HarperCollins Children's Books, 1998. ISBN 0 06 026687 2

In the same pattern, we see a girl give a pig a plate of pancakes. That leads to a demand for syrup, a bath, a rubber duck, to feeling homesick, to packing to go home, and on and on, until we're back to the pancakes.

OTHER CIRCLE STORIES

Ahlberg, Janet & Allan. *Each Peach Pear Plum: An I Spy Story.* Puffin Books, 1986. ISBN 0 14 050639 X

The characters in this book are from Mother Goose and common folktales. On each page, a rhyming text asks us to find them. At the end of the book, we're back where we started.

Macaulay, David. *Why the Chicken Crossed the Road.* Houghton Mifflin Books for Children, 1987. ISBN 0 395 44241 9

This story starts and ends with a chicken crossing the road. In between we witness a series of wild events that end up explaining why the chicken crossed the road.

OTHER BOOKS ABOUT MICE

Alborough, Jez. *Watch Out! Big Bro's Coming!.* Candlewick Press, 1997. ISBN 0 7636 0130 6

A mouse tells a frog that Big Bro is coming and shows him how big Big Bro is by stretching out his arms. Each succeeding animal measures Big Bro by his own arm spread.

Baehr, Patricia. *Mouse in the House.* Holiday House, 1994. ISBN 0 8234 1102 8

Mrs. Teapot has found a mouse in her house and asks for advice about getting rid of it. She follows the suggestions, but each one gets her into more difficulty.

Brett, Jan. *Town Mouse, Country Mouse.* G. P. Putnam's Sons Books for Young Readers, 1994. ISBN 0 399 22622 2

This story includes all of the elements of the familiar folktale, but Brett adds her own touch. In this case it's a house exchange, such as humans sometimes do.

Cleary, Beverly. **The Mouse and the Motorcycle.** Morrow Junior Books, 1965. ISBN 0 688 31698 0

This novel is about a mouse who becomes very adept at riding Keith's toy motorcycle and sets off for adventure.

Edwards, Pamela. **Livingstone Mouse.** HarperCollins Children's Books, 1996. ISBN 0 06 025869 1

A young mouse sets off for China. Along the way, he identifies many things differently than most of us will.

Fleming, Denise. **Lunch.** Henry Holt & Co. Books for Young Readers, 1992. ISBN 0 8050 4646 1

Bright, bold illustrations make this book stand out. It tells a story very much like the one in **The Very Hungry Caterpillar,** but about a mouse and lots of food.

Hurd, Thacher. **The Pea Patch Jig.** Crown Books for Young Readers, 1986. ISBN 0 06 443383 8

A mouse family lives at the edge of a garden and they're about to have a party. Then the baby mouse ends up in the farmer's salad. That's just the beginning of the adventures for the baby mouse.

Kraus, Robert. **Where Are You Going, Little Mouse?.** Greenwillow Books, 1986. ISBN 0 688 04294 5

In this story, the sequel to **Whose Mouse Are You?,** a little mouse sets out in search of a new, more loving family.

Lionni, Leo. **Frederick.** Pantheon Books, 1966. ISBN 0 394 91040 0

All the other mice are busy gathering food for the winter, but Frederick just sits there enjoying the day. Later, in the dark of winter, the mice treasure Frederick's poetic look at the light and the day.

McBratney, Sam. **The Dark at the Top of the Stairs.** Candlewick Press, 1996. ISBN 1 56402 640 X

Some very young mice demand a chance to deal with the monster at the top of the stairs. An older mouse volunteers to take them, and they discover that the monster is a cat.

McCully, Emily. **First Snow.** HarperCollins Children's Books, 1985. ISBN 0 06 024129 2

This book is one of a series of wordless books McCully composed about a mouse family. In this case the mouse family is having fun in the snow, except for one little mouse, who's scared.

O'Brien, Robert C. **Mrs. Frisby and the Rats of NIMH.** Simon & Schuster Books for Young Readers, 1971. ISBN 0 689 20651 8

This novel is very well done and understandable for many children in the lower grades. It concerns a group of highly educated rats who befriend Mrs. Frisby, a widowed mouse.

Reiser, Lynn. **Two Mice in Three Fables.** Greenwillow Books, 1995. ISBN 0 688 13389 4

These stories are indeed fables, but less onerous than many, and all three could stand simply as stories.

Soto, Gary. **Chato's Kitchen.** G. P. Putnam's Sons Books for Young Readers, 1995. ISBN 0 399 22658 3

Chato, the cat, invites some mice for dinner—his dinner. He and his cat friend prepare some delicious Mexican side dishes to go with the main course. When the mice arrive, they bring their dog friend. The feast turns out to be vegetarian.

Steig, William. **Abel's Island.** Farrar Strauss & Giroux Books for Young Readers, 1987. ISBN 0 374 30010 0

This story isn't a picture book, but a novel (and a very good one), about an ultra-civilized mouse marooned on an island. It will be too hard for some children in the very youngest grades, but those in second and third grades who are ready for novels may well enjoy this tale.

Steig, William. **Doctor De Soto.** *Farrar Strauss & Giroux Books for Young Readers, 1982. ISBN 0 374 31803 4*

This story pits mouse wits against fox wits as a mouse dentist treats his fox patient. Never trust a fox, except when he's in pain.

Stevenson, James. **All Aboard!.** *Greenwillow Books, 1995. ISBN 0 688 12438 0*

Hubie Mouse and his family get on the wrong train when they start out for the 1939 New York Worlds Fair, and they end up in California.

Yolen, Jane. **Little Mouse & Elephant: A Tale from Turkey.** *Simon & Schuster Books for Young Readers, 1996. ISBN 0 689 80493 8*

A very aggressive mouse insists that he will break an elephant into bits. On the way to the elephant, he meets many animals, each of which quickly leaves. Convinced that he has scared them away, the mouse goes on to meet his comeuppance.

Lilly's Purple Plastic Purse

By Kevin Henkes
Greenwillow Books, 1996
ISBN 0 688 12897 1

SUMMARY

The book's cover shows us an exuberant and action-filled Lilly in six vignettes, all surrounded by stars. The endpapers also are covered with stars, and those of us who are familiar with Lilly from **Chester's Way** and **Julius, the Baby of the World** aren't surprised—we know that she considers herself a star. We see Lilly again on the title page, where she's smiling broadly and wearing her ubiquitous, star-bedecked, red plastic boots. Her step is high and her tail, with a red ribbon on it, is up. She wears a backpack and has a flower in hand for her teacher.

The dedication page establishes Lilly's popularity, as three backpack-bearing boys (probably Victor, Chester, and Wilson) run after her calling, "Wait for us!" One wears a sweater with a big "V" on it, confirming our suspicions. The first sentence states her feelings clearly: "I love school!"

On the next spread, the things Lilly likes about school are enumerated, and the last sentence states, "And, most of all, she loved her teacher, Mr. Slinger."

We meet Mr. Slinger on the next page, and right away we sense that he's outstanding. He's first shown standing by his desk holding a globe aloft. His body language indicates a jaunty demeanor. His tail is curled. His legs are crossed and he wears sandals. A pair of pince-nez glasses are perched on his nose. His shirt is paisley, his trousers are striped, and his plain tie is bright green. A sign dangling from an apple on his desk reads, "The boss is in." We get some hint of his political views from a globe drawn on the blackboard, which

COMMENTS

Henkes' body of work is so good and so strong that his picture books could become the basis for a whole year of study. I've chosen to focus on **Lilly's Purple Plastic Purse** because it's very funny and because Lilly is a recurring character in his books, which leads us to her other books. While Lilly's self-centered behavior is consistent with that of many children her age, it also presents an opportunity to talk about manners and group dynamics. The book's school setting generates discussion of a variety of topics about school.

is surrounded by stars and bears the inscription, "Global Village—One World!" He seems not to notice or care about the trash on the floor near his foot. Lilly is gazing at him with great approval as he commands, "Listen up!" The next page gives us more information about Mr. Slinger, his attitudes, and his teaching methods. Lilly states that, when she grows up she wants to be a teacher, and Chester, Wilson, and Victor echo her sentiment.

On the next page we see Lilly at home, attempting to teach a befuddled baby Julius. She wears a Groucho Marx-type nose, mustache, and glasses as she states, "Teachers know everything!" Her parents, peering in, are surprised that she's changed her career ambition from surgeon, ambulance driver, and diva.

We learn more about Mr. Slinger's teaching methods as the scene switches back to the classroom and the "Lightbulb Lab," where students are to express their ideas. Lilly's story is about Mr. Slinger's heroism. Her perfect and enthusiastic behavior is detailed next, and she tells Mr. Slinger that she wants to be a teacher.

The problem rears up on the next page as an overjoyed Lilly comes to school bearing the treasures she bought with her Grammy over the weekend: a new pair of movie star sunglasses, with chain, and a brand-new, purple, plastic purse that plays music when you open it. Furthermore she has three shiny quarters. What bliss! Lilly clicks her heels with joy.

We hardly need the words on the next page to tell us what's happening. Mr. Slinger is reading a story, but Lilly is holding up her purse. Mr. Slinger is teaching spelling, and Lilly is waving her hand and her purse in front of him. Mr. Slinger works from a chart displaying various kinds of cheese, and Lilly stands in front of it pointing to her purse. Lilly can keep silent no longer: "Look, everyone," she says. "Look what I've got!" Like Queen Victoria, Mr. Slinger is not amused. He confiscates Lilly's purse, quarters, and sunglasses, stating that he'll keep them until the end of the day. Lilly is too upset to eat, and for a while she can't even create in the Lightbulb Lab. Then her anger becomes fury, and she draws a picture of Mr. Slinger, which we see on the next page. She labels him fat, mean, and a thief, and she writes, "I do not want to be a teacher when I grow up." She puts the picture in his book bag.

Mr. Slinger returns Lilly's things at the end of the day, admiring them all as he does so. Lilly is unrepentant. She marches defiantly out of the room. On the way home Lilly is surprised to find a note from Mr. Slinger in her purse, which reads, "Today was a difficult day. Tomorrow will be better." He's also put in a small bag of tasty snacks. Six vignettes on the page show a shrinking Lilly. Tearfully, she rushes home, where she tells her parents everything. She punishes herself by sitting in the "uncooperative chair" and vows to remain there for a million years. That night she writes a story about forgiveness and draws a very

THINGS WORTH NOTICING

► Chester, Wilson, and Victor, characters from two other books by Kevin Henkes, are in this story as well.

► Lilly's baby brother, Julius, who appears in **Julius, the Baby of the World**, is older in this book.

► The tails and the ears on the characters often reveal the characters' feelings.

► The story is told using three devices: the illustrations, the narrative, and the conversations shown in the illustrations.

► Lilly is shown on the cover wearing her cape, but she never wears it to school.

flattering picture of Mr. Slinger, on which she states, among other things, that he could be a principal. Her parents help. Her mother writes a note to Mr. Slinger, and her father bakes snacks for the class. They also reassure her that Mr. Slinger will understand why she drew the first picture.

The next day, Lilly's apologies are abject and lengthy. Mr. Slinger accepts them (and the snacks) and gives Lilly ample opportunity during Sharing Time to demonstrate the many features of her purse, her quarters, and her sunglasses. This is followed by an "interpretative dance" by Lilly and Mr. Slinger.

As the day goes on, Lilly checks frequently on her possessions, which are now inside her desk, but she doesn't touch them. Mr. Slinger serves Lilly's snacks, and Lilly concludes that Mr. Slinger's note was right—it was a better day.

Although she and all the rest of the class have proclaimed that they will all become teachers when they grow up, the last page shows Lilly acting out many careers, so her future is still in doubt.

Language Arts

BUILDING VOCABULARY

▶ Make a list of words that describe Lilly. Make another list of words that are the opposite of what Lilly is like.

FINDING DETAILS

▶ Make a list of the things that the illustrations show but the text does not mention.

SEQUENCING

▶ Look at **Chester's Way; Julius, the Baby of the World;** and **Lilly's Purple Plastic Purse.** Put them in order of when they happened. What clues did you use?

MAKING COMPARISONS

▶ Make a list of the way your classroom is like and unlike Mr. Slinger's.

▶ Read some of the books listed below that are about teachers. Make a list of each teacher's qualities. Decide which teacher you'd like most to have.

MAKING INFERENCES

▶ Notice the tails in the illustrations. What do they indicate about the way the characters feel?

▶ What clues show that three of the kids in the class are Chester, Wilson, and Victor?

▶ Why do you think Henkes uses mice as characters? Make a list of the attributes of real mice. Do any of these attributes make sense for his characters?

WRITING

▶ Write about what you think is a perfect teacher. What would he or she look like, act like, do?

Math

▶ How many kids are in the class?

Science

▶ How do such things as musical purses work? Bring in other musical devices, such as music boxes, and see if you can figure out how they work. Take a broken music box apart and examine the pieces. Can you figure out what each piece is for?

Social Studies

▶ Why is Mr. Slinger upset about Lilly's behavior? What does it do to the rest of the class? How do you know this?

▶ What rules do you think Mr. Slinger has for his classroom? What rules does your classroom have? What rules do you think should be eliminated? What rules do you think should be instated?

▶ What rules do you have in your household? Which ones do you think are reasonable? Which ones do you think are unreasonable?

▶ Make a list of rules for a kids' day at school in which the kids are in charge of the classroom. Is safety going to be a problem with those rules? Will learning be a problem with those rules? Fix them so that both safety and learning will not be a problem and then consider such things as other people's feelings, other classrooms' behavior, and the like. Have a kids' day.

▶ Lilly is interested in many careers she thinks might be fun. Make a list of careers you think you'd like to have some day. Beside each career write one good thing and one bad thing about that job.

RELATED BOOKS

(See page 205 for an author study of Kevin Henkes and a list of his books.)

Picture Books

Allard, Harry. Miss Nelson Has a Field Day. Houghton Mifflin Books for Children, 1985. ISBN 0 395 36690 9

The football coach and the team are sure that they haven't a chance in the upcoming football game, but Miss Viola Swamp soon whips the team into shape.

Allard, Harry. Miss Nelson Is Back. Illustrated by James Marshall. Houghton Mifflin Books for Children, 1982. ISBN 0 395 32956 6

Boring Principal Blandsworth substitutes for Miss Nelson when she disappears for a week.

Allard, Harry. Miss Nelson Is Missing!. Houghton Mifflin Books for Children, 1985. ISBN 0 395 25296 2

The class won't obey Miss Nelson, and havoc results. Then Miss Nelson disappears, and Miss Viola Swamp appears to make the kids wish sweet Miss Nelson were back.

Cazet, Denys. Are There Any Questions?. Orchard Books, 1992. ISBN 0 531 05451 9

A class field trip is the focus of this book, the sequel to **Never Spit on Your Shoes.**

Cazet, Denys. Born in the Gravy. Orchard Books, 1993. ISBN 0 531 05488 8

In this story, it's kindergarten and it's the first day. Our narrator's father speaks Spanish to her, but she answers in English in this funny book.

Cazet, Denys. Never Spit on Your Shoes. Orchard Books, 1990. ISBN 0 531 05847 6

This book is enjoyed by teachers and parents as much as it is by kids. Arnie has just finished his first day in first grade and tells his mother all about it.

Cole, Joanna. Magic School Bus Inside a Hurricane. Illustrated by Bruce Degan. Scholastic, 1995. ISBN 0 590 44686 X

This book is one of a wonderful series of books about the Magic School Bus. They all feature the magic and imagination of Miss Frizzle, the teacher.

dePaola, Tomie. Art Lesson. G. P. Putnam's Sons Books for Young Readers, 1989. ISBN 0 399 21688 X

Tomie loves art and has been encouraged to be creative at home. At school, however, he's told that he must restrain that creativity and copy the teacher's art.

Henkes, Kevin. Chester's Way. Scholastic, 1988. ISBN 0 590 44017 9

Chester and Wilson are just alike and live very cautiously. When Lilly moves into the neighborhood they're aghast at her unconventional ways for a while, but they grow to like her a lot.

Henkes, Kevin. Chrysanthemum. Greenwillow Books, 1991. ISBN 0 688 09700 6

Chrysanthemum loves her name until she gets to school and the other children make fun of it. Fortunately, her teacher comes to her defense with the news that her own first name is Delphinium.

Henkes, Kevin. Julius, the Baby of the World. Greenwillow Books, 1990. ISBN 0 688 08944 5

Lilly is angry and resentful of her new baby brother that her parents think is so great. It's not until Julius is criticized by Cousin Garland that Lilly's hackles rise.

Houston, Gloria. My Great Aunt Arizona. Illustrated by Susan Condie Lamb. HarperCollins Children's Books, 1991. ISBN 0 06 022606 4

Arizona longs to travel widely, but circumstances prevent it. Instead, she becomes a teacher in a country school, where she inspires her students to want to travel.

Lasky, Kathryn. **Lunch Bunnies.** Illustrated by Marylin Hafner. Little, Brown & Co., Children's Books, 1996. ISBN 0 316 51525 6

Clyde is really frightened about going to school. It's not the classroom he's afraid of, but the lunchroom.

Polacco, Patricia. **Thank You, Mr. Falker.** Philomel Books, 1998. ISBN 0 399 23166 8

In this autobiographical story, Patricia fully expects to enjoy reading, because the rest of the family does, but reading proves to be almost impossible for her. It's Mr. Falker who recognizes her learning disability and helps her deal with it.

Pulver, Robin. **Mrs. Toggle's Zipper.** Illustrated by R. W. Alley. Aladdin Paperbacks, 1990. ISBN 0 689 71689 3

When the zipper on Mrs. Toggle's winter coat gets stuck, the whole school becomes involved in the problem.

Wells, Rosemary. **Edward Unready for School.** Dial Books for Young Readers, 1995. ISBN 0 8037 1884 5

This sweet story makes a good point about people being different and being ready for different things at different times. Small bear Edward loves being home, but others feel he belongs in preschool.

The Napping House

By Don & Audrey Wood
Harcourt Brace & Co., 1984
ISBN 0 15 256708 9

SUMMARY

It's a rainy afternoon and everyone is napping. As the rain continues, one creature after another piles onto a cozy bed. The book's cumulative text describes how the sleeping pile on the bed grows higher as animals of decreasing size get on. The tiniest creature of them all, a flea, makes both the pile and the bed collapse. This information is conveyed through a delightful use of pattern and rhythm.

The book's title page shows the color palette of the story and of the rain that dominates the tale. The harshness of the points on a picket fence is ameliorated by the comfort of a rain-drenched vine which covers most of them. On the dedication page we see more of the fence, including an unlatched, welcoming gate that stands ajar. The mailbox bears the words, "Napping House" and is also slightly open.

The perspective draws back and up on the first page, which shows the house, the fenced-in yard, and the larger, rain-blurred woods. The house's bottom window shades are closed and the top ones only slightly raised, making the windows look like two sleep-laden eyes.

We're told that in the Napping House everyone is sleeping and the next page shows that indeed they are. A woman lies with her back to us. A child sleeps in a chair, the back of which bends forward, although it otherwise looks like a straight chair. At the top of the chair is the tiny flea. The head and foot of the bed also lean inward. A large dog naps on a scatter rug beside the bed, and a cat sleeps in a pet bed at the foot of the bed. Closer inspection shows a mouse asleep atop an ornate

COMMENTS

This classic book is a visual and auditory delight, a cumulative story with a predictable text. The subtle changes in perspective and coloration may evade the casual reader, but children can be led to fully appreciate those nuances.

mirror over a pitcher and bowl on a doily-covered table. Our view is that of a person standing in the doorway of the room.

The next spread talks about the snoring granny on the bed. The illustration shows that she has now turned over on her back and her mouth is wide open, but that the child is up and moving toward the bed. A pillow has fallen from the bed onto the dog, but apparently hasn't disturbed it. Our perspective has risen slightly, for we can now see the far top edge of the pitcher.

The child is now sleeping on top of the granny, who has turned on her side to face us. The text mentions the child, but the dog is up and stretching. The pillow that was on the dog is under the child's head. We're up a little higher now and can see into the pitcher a bit.

Granny's on her stomach in the next spread, the child has moved so that his head is toward the foot of the bed, and the dog lies on its back, on the bed, crosswise. The text talks about the dog, but it's the cat's stretching motion that we see as we rise a little more.

The next picture shows us that everyone on the bed has moved again. Granny lies on her back with her head at the foot, the child's head is on the pillow at the head of the bed, but his legs and feet dangle over the edge of the bed, and the dog's head faces us as the cat curls up on top of it. The mouse has climbed down onto the edge of the bowl, and we can see farther inside the pitcher, indicating that we've climbed higher.

The pile is better aligned now; all the bodies are facing away from us, with their heads at the foot of the bed, as the mouse settles on the back of the cat. The flea has left the chair and is on the rim of the pitcher, and we can see way down inside of that pitcher.

The light outside the window is slightly brighter now. Granny's on her back. The child and the dog lie with their heads toward us, the cat and mouse lie perpendicular to them, and the flea is slightly highlighted on the mouse's back. We look down into the seat of the chair and the pet bed, as well as the pitcher. We're now almost at the ceiling—as is the pile on the bed.

Now the pile begins to break apart as the mouse jumps into the air because it's been bitten by the flea. A much brighter light illuminates the bed now.

The cat is high in the air, screeching with fright, and we are slightly lower now.

We see yellow in the palette, as well as some fairly bright pinks, as sunlight shines into the room. We're lower in the room as the dog leaps up with the cat.

When the child jumps up, yellow has begun to dominate the room's color, and the pitcher is falling. When Granny, too, is dis-

THINGS WORTH NOTICING

▶ Everybody's already in the bedroom, even the first time that we look at it.

▶ The colors change as the rain stops.

▶ The perspective changes as the pile grows higher and then collapses.

▶ The creatures get on the bed in order of decreasing size.

▶ There are many synonyms for the word "sleeping."

▶ The house pictured on the first page has the same doorway as the one on the back of the book jacket.

turbed, the pitcher and bowl are in the midst of a fall. We're standing at the door again, and the yellow is brighter.

Now the pitcher has been mysteriously righted, although the bowl underneath it is inverted. Everyone's awake and laughing, and the sun shines brightly.

The last picture gives us an outside view again. A rainbow's end is just behind the house. Granny and child stand apart with their arms opened toward each other. The dog runs with a toy in it's mouth, the cat leaps with joy, and the mouse sits atop the fence post. Perhaps the flea is still on the mouse.

Language Arts

BUILDING VOCABULARY

► Make a list of all the words that describe the animals and people on the bed. Try putting the word "sleeping" in their place in the story. Does the story still make sense? Is it as much fun?

SEQUENCING

► Make a list of all the animals in the book and then make large pictures of each animal and person. Cut them out and place them in the right order on a picture of a cozy bed.

MAKING COMPARISONS

► Find and read the Mother Goose rhyme "This Is the House That Jack Built." Compare it to this story.

► Find and read some of the other cumulative books listed below. Come in dressed as one of the characters in one of the books. See if others can figure out who you are.

► Find and read other books by Don and Audrey Wood (see book list). What do you like about their books?

INTERPRETING ILLUSTRATIONS

► Even in the very first picture of the cozy bed, everybody is in the room. Can you find them all? Then, watch their positions change from picture to picture.

► There are clues in the pictures to tell you which animal is going to get on the pile next. Can you find them all?

► Can you tell whether this is a daytime or a nighttime sleep? What are the clues?

DRAMATIZING

► Act out the story.

Math

► Place counters on a sheet of paper for each person or animal on the bed.

► Cut out a series of rectangles to represent the creatures on the bed. Make sure that each rectangle is of a different size.

► Place the rectangles in the right order to represent the animals and people in the story.

► How many people and animals get on the bed? Arrange them in order from smallest to largest.

Science

► Would the pile have worked if the flea got on the bed first? Why not?

Art

► Mix tempera paint to get the same shades of blue and of yellow as Donald Wood used in the book. Paint something with those colors.

► Notice the way the perspective changes as the pile grows higher. Watch the top of the pitcher to see the changes more clearly.

RELATED BOOKS

Fiction
CUMULATIVE STORIES

Aardema, Verna. **Bringing the Rain to Kapiti Plain.** Dial Books for Young Readers, 1981. ISBN 0 8037 0904 8

Ki-pat and his herd of cattle don't leave the plains in search of water, as many of the others have. At last, he shoots an arrow into the clouds to bring rain to the plain.

Aardema, Verna. **Why Mosquitoes Buzz in People's Ears.** Dial Books for Young Readers, 1975. ISBN 0 8037 6089 2

This is a focus book (see page 168).

Cole, Henry. **Jack's Garden.** Greenwillow Books, 1995. ISBN 0 688 13501 3

The tools and steps for creating a garden are presented in a cumulative format.

Fox, Mem. **Shoes from Grandpa.** Illustrated by Patricia Mullins. Orchard Books, 1989. ISBN 0 531 05848 4

Not to be outdone by Grandpa's gift of shoes for their little girl, each family member promises another article of clothing to complete the outfit.

Lobel, Arnold. **The Rose in My Garden.** Greenwillow Books, 1985. ISBN 0 688 02587 0

A simple incident occurs in a garden filled with lovely flowers, each of which is described with beautiful language and illustrations.

Medearis, Angela. **Too Much Talk.** Candlewick Press, 1995. ISBN 1 56402 323 0

In this cumulative West African folktale, a dog begins to talk, and that starts everything.

Neitzel, Shirley. **The Bag I'm Taking to Grandma's.** Illustrated by Nancy Winslow Parker. Mulberry Books, 1995. ISBN 0 688 15840 4

This rebus cumulative tale revolves around a boy who's packing for an overnight stay at Grandma's.

Neitzel, Shirley. **The Dress I'll Wear to the Party.** Illustrated by Nancy Winslow Parker. Mulberry Books, 1992. ISBN 0 688 14261 3

A little girl is dressing (really overdressing) for a party. Fully adorned, she starts for the party, but her mother is just in time to reverse the process.

Neitzel, Shirley. **The House I'll Build for the Wrens.** Illustrated by Nancy Winslow Parker. Greenwillow Books, 1997. ISBN 0 688 14973 1

Step by step we build a birdhouse, and each step is repeated cumulatively.

Neitzel, Shirley. **The Jacket I Wear in the Snow.** Illustrated by Nancy Winslow Parker. Greenwillow Books, 1989. ISBN 0 688 08028 6

This book was Neitzel's first cumulative story. A rebus format helps to tell the tale of a little boy who's being dressed to go out in the snow.

Robart, Rose. **The Cake that Mack Ate.** Illustrated by Maryann Kovalski. Little, Brown & Co., Children's Books, 1991. ISBN 0 316 74891 9

The cake is assembled bit by bit. The surprise comes at the end, when we find out who this Mack is that we've been reading about.

Old Henry

By Joan W. Blos
Illustrated by Stephen Gammell
Mulberry Books, 1997
ISBN 0 688 09935 1

SUMMARY

We meet Old Henry on the book's cover. He leans casually against a dilapidated fence, surrounded by tall grass, and looks smilingly at a parrot that stares back at him. Henry wears a barely buttoned, flamboyantly colored shirt and a blue cap. His jeans are faded, but not torn. At his feet is a large paper bag bearing items that don't look new. On the title page Henry has begun to unpack. There are two bird cages in which three birds are sitting (one is the parrot from the cover). There's an old suitcase and some pots and pans, as well as the paper bag from the cover.

The rhyming text begins on the dedication page, and we learn that Henry is new to the neighborhood and he's moving into a house that has stood vacant for years. Apparently, he's renting, not buying, because the next page shows the narrow, three-story house with a "House for Rent" sign in the yard. The house is a "handy-man's special" with bricks falling off the chimney as we look. There's a sort of porch falling off the third story. There are remnants of a picket fence in the front, and the grass is long and unruly. It's unclear whether someone has tried several different paint jobs to improve the house or if those are just colors uncovered by time.

Henry means to stay, however, and we see the interior of the house on the next page. The walls are cracked, but seem fairly substantial, and there are many empty shelves. Henry's in his bathrobe, with his hand on the newel post of a long stairway that curves out

COMMENTS

Old Henry is a book about an eccentric character in a community that's trying to accept him even as it's trying to change him. That gives us the concepts of eccentrics and of communities to hook onto. The letter from Henry at the end of the book, offering a compromise, allows us to work on letter writing as one means of communication, while compromise itself is a concept young children need to become familiar with. The text is in rhyme and we can focus on those rhyming words as a reading skill exercise. Add Gammell's delightful illustrations to this mix, and you've got a winner for a picture book.

of sight. He's got a round table, a straight chair, and a dresser, of sorts.

On the next page Henry has begun carting things inside, and three rather plump ladies and one little girl are watching him work. The text tells us that they hope he'll soon begin fixing up the old place, but as Henry grins cheerfully from a window, the text reads, "He did not think of it."

A more panoramic view is ours on the next page, and we see Henry's house for the first time as part of a neighborhood. Two other houses are not far from his and they're neat and well cared for, as is their landscaping. The group of neighbors now includes some men, and all are looking at the old place with great consternation as they declare, "That place is a disgrace."

A black-and-white vignette on the next page shows some neighbors in their first encounter with Henry. They represent a committee that wants him to fix the place up. Henry's words are few—"Excuse me"—and he goes back to where we see him on the next page, in a big, overstuffed chair, reading. He's filled some of the shelves with books and an old vase. His parrot is in the cage hanging over his head. The bookshelves and a tattered scatter rug seem to be the sum of his interior decoration.

The next page shows Henry cooking and eating in his home. He's bought groceries, and we see them carefully shelved in cabinets from which the doors dangle. His mailbox is a pail with a red "H" on it, and a mail carrier is stuffing it full as the text details the neighbors' attempts to get Henry to shape up the place.

Henry is happy, however, and the next page shows him sketching on an easel in the wild grass outside of his house. The birdcage door sits on the table beside him, its door open, and a dog rolls in the grass. The neighbors on the facing page are increasingly unhappy: one shakes his fist at the parrot flying over his head. One disheveled little boy on a scooter seems to be looking at Henry with admiration, however, and another child seems to be laughing as he looks over the fence at Henry.

Finally, the mayor suggests that the neighbors change tactics. They take his advice, and we next see Henry standing in the snow, as books fall from his arms, facing two neighbor women bearing a large pie. But instead of accepting their gift, he says, "I'm not hungry. No, thank you. Good-bye."

Henry's shoveling snow in the next scene, while three men with shovels, who have offered to shovel for him, leave, defeated. But Henry is defeated, too. As he sits on the foot of his bed, he declares, "I never will live like the rest of them, neat and the same. I am sorry I came."

His departure is shown on the next page, as is the note he leaves on the door: "Gone to Dakota." Chimney bricks are still falling, and the house looks worse than ever as he leaves it behind.

THINGS WORTH NOTICING

► The dog only appears three times in the book.

► There's evidence that Henry doesn't find another place to live.

► Henry does make some changes in the house.

► His mailbox is an old pail, and he apparently doesn't take his mail inside very often, probably because he doesn't want to read what the neighbors are writing him.

► Bricks keep falling off the chimney, and you can see some of them in the grass near the mail box.

► Old Henry has several different outfits.

Neighbors gather apples from his tree and notice the daylilies blooming in his yard, but in the winter they peer in the windows for signs of Henry's return. The neighbors' conversion is clear on the next page as they huddle together and conclude, "Maybe, some other time, we'd get along not thinking that somebody has to be wrong."

Henry has been living outside, in the meantime. We see his bed on the ground, but he's sitting at a table, with his books and his birds, composing a letter to the mayor, which we see on the last page.

The letter offers a compromise: He'll mend the gate and shovel the snow if they won't scold his birds and let his grass grow. We don't know whether the neighbors accept his conditions, but Old Henry looks hopeful on the next page, holding his mailbox/pail and waiting for an answer, with his belongings ready to go.

Language Arts

BUILDING VOCABULARY

► Henry could be called an eccentric character. He wants to live differently than the people around him do. Make a list of the things you like and you do that are eccentric, such as foods you like that most people don't, things you collect, things you like to do when no one is watching you, etc.

► The book refers to Henry as "Old Henry." Talk to some older people to see how they would feel if someone referred to them that way. What do they like to be called?

FINDING DETAILS

► Make a list of things that are in the illustrations of this book that the words don't mention.

MAKING COMPARISONS

► Compare Old Henry with some of the eccentric characters in the books listed . Rate their eccentricities on a scale from most to least outlandish.

SUMMARIZING

► What's the problem here? Henry and the neighbors are at odds. Summarize what Henry wants and what the neighbors want in two lists.

WRITING

► Conduct an interview with someone you think of as eccentric. Find out five or six interesting things about them. Write a paragraph or story about this person.

► Old Henry writes a letter to the mayor offering a compromise. Use his letter as a model to write to someone in government. If you don't have anything to ask that person to do, ask for information or thank them for things they have done.

Math

► Stop on the page that shows Old Henry with all his things on the ground after he has moved out of the house. Brainstorm for things he or the neighbors could do to solve their problem.

Science

► Henry keeps birds as pets. Research the good and bad aspects of keeping birds as pets.

Social Studies

► What steps do these neighbors take to solve their problem with Old Henry? How does your neighborhood solve problems? Find out about the people who can help a neighborhood that has problems—people in the city government, for instance.

► Henry offers a compromise at the end of the book. What problems in your classroom have been solved when a compromise was reached? What was the problem? What did each side have to do that they didn't want to do? What did each side get to do that they wanted to do? What was the result?

► What's the difference between a compromise and a vote?

RELATED BOOKS

Picture Books

Allard, Harry. **It's So Nice to Have a Wolf Around the House.** Yearling, 1997. ISBN 0 440 41353 2

Cuthbert Q. Devine is an unconventional housemate—he's a fugitive from the law and he's a wolf. However, the Old Man finds his presence cheering and comforting until the press gets wind of it.

Cave, Kathryn. **Something Else.** Illustrated by Chris Riddell. Mondo Publishing, 1994. ISBN 1 57255 563 7

Something Else is a creature who's rejected by all his neighbors because of his odd looks and behavior. He lives alone on a mountain top until he's approached by a different sort of thing who offers friendship. At first Something Else rejects the new creature because of his odd looks and odd behavior and then he realizes what he has done.

Cutler, Jane. **Mr. Carey's Garden.** Illustrated by G. Brian Karas. Houghton Mifflin Books for Children, 1996. ISBN 0 395 68191 X

A neighborhood of gardeners all have advice for Mr. Carey, whose garden is infested with snails. He turns it all down, however, for, as he says, he sees things in a different light. It isn't until we see the snails with him in the moonlight that we understand.

Fox, Mem. **Wilfrid Gordon McDonald Partridge.** Illustrated by Julie Vivas. Kane/Miller Books Publishers, 1984. ISBN 0 916291 04 9

Wilfrid loves his long name partly because Miss Nancy Alison Delacourt Cooper lives next door at the old lady's home and likes her own long name. He enjoys many of the rather eccentric people in the home, and he tries to recreate Miss Nancy's memory for her when he hears she has lost it.

Gray, Libba Moore. **Miss Tizzy.** Illustrated by Jada Rowland. Simon & Schuster Books for Young Readers, 1993. ISBN 0 671 77590 1

The neighbors think Miss Tizzy is very peculiar, but the children love her. Each day of the week she and the kids tackle a different project, and when she becomes ill, they plan activities to help her feel better.

Kalman, Maira. **Max Makes a Million.** Viking Children's Books, 1990. ISBN 0 670 83545 5

Max the dog has many friends, and they're all a bit eccentric. They're involved in a whole lot of absurd activities, but they approach them all with gusto.

Kesselman, Wendy. **Emma.** Bantam Doubleday Dell Books for Young Readers, 1980. ISBN 0 440 40847 4

Emma is given a painting by her relatives of the area where she grew up. Convinced that the painting is inaccurate, Emma determines to paint it the way she remembers it. This starts the old lady on a new career, which delights her and dismays her relatives.

Lasky, Kathryn. **The Gates of the Wind.** Illustrated by Janet Stevens. Harcourt Brace & Co., 1995. ISBN 0 15 204264 4

Neighbors are aghast when Gamma Lee announces her decision to leave her safe, comfortable village in search of adventure. Declaring that the fish in the stream have seen more of life than they have, she sets up a home on the top of a wild mountain and becomes a living legend.

Lester, Helen. **Tacky the Penguin.** Houghton Mifflin Books for Children, 1988. ISBN 0 395 45536 7

Like Old Henry, Tacky is a messy eccentric who refuses to follow the group's lead. He wears loud clothes, sings off-key, and is disdained by the proper penguins. He's redeemed when he saves the group from some hunters.

Lyon, George Ella. **Come a Tide.** Illustrated by Stephen Gammell. Orchard Books, 1990. ISBN 0 531 05854 9

The rains are coming down on the mountain dwellers, and the flooding has begun. It happens often, apparently, and soon the whole community is pitching together to cope with the mess.

McElligott, Matthew. **Uncle Frank's Pit.** Viking Children's Books, 1998. ISBN 0 670 87737 9

Uncle Frank shows up at his family's house unexpectedly and takes up residence. Soon he begins digging an enormous pit in the back yard. He furnishes it with great creativity and ingenuity and then, unexpectedly again, he leaves.

Pinkwater, Daniel Manus. **The Big Orange Splot.** Scholastic, 1977. ISBN 0 590 44510 3

Everyone in the neighborhood in this story conforms. Their houses all look exactly alike and they treasure their conformity. Then a seagull drops a can of paint on Mr. Plumbean's house and he likes the big orange splot it leaves. He paints his house eventually, but he does it with great imagination, to match his personality. One by one the neighbors create their own designs for their houses.

Ryan, Cheryl. **Sally Arnold.** Illustrated by Bill Farnsworth. Cobblehill/Dutton, 1996. ISBN 0 525 65176 4

Jenny is afraid of Sally Arnold, the woman who lives outside of Jenny's mountain town, until she gets to know Jenny and learns to accept her eccentricities.

Rylant, Cynthia. **The Old Woman Who Named Things.** Illustrated by Kathryn Brown. Harcourt Brace & Co., 1996. ISBN 0 15 257809 9

An old woman has lost many friends and relatives that she loved, so she refuses to name anything that will not last longer than she will. She gives every household item a name, but when a puppy turns up, she refuses to give it a name until she learns a valuable lesson.

Sadler, Marilyn. **Elizabeth and Larry.** Illustrated by Roger Bollen. Simon & Schuster Books for Young Readers, 1990. ISBN 0 671 77817 X

Elizabeth and Larry have a strange but intimate friendship—even though Elizabeth is an old lady and Larry is an alligator. They live together and do very well. It's neighbors and family who give them a hard time. The solution is for Elizabeth to relocate so that she can join Larry when he goes to live among other alligators.

Saltzberg, Barney. **Mrs. Morgan's Lawn.** Hyperion Books for Children, 1998. ISBN 0 7868 1294 X

Mrs. Morgan is mean. She's obsessive about her lawn and she confiscates any ball that lands on it. When our narrator loses his new ball that way, he faces Mrs. Morgan. She's not responsive and says she's coming down with a cold. When he sees her lawn becoming unkempt, the boy rakes it for her. The next day Mrs. Morgan and all of the lost balls appear.

Schachner, Judith Bryon. **Willy and May.** Dutton Children's Books, 1995. ISBN 0 515 45347 4

This book is about another elderly person who, like Old Henry, loves life and birds. Her bird is Willy and he travels on her head. We learn about May from her niece, who tells about the good times they had together and about the Christmas blizzard that the intrepid woman braved in order to be with her family.

Spinelli, Eileen. **Somebody Loves You, Mr. Hatch.** Illustrated by Paul Yalowitz. Simon & Schuster Books for Young Readers, 1992. ISBN 0 02 786015 9

Mr. Hatch is almost the exact opposite of Old Henry, except that he, too, is a recluse. His behavior, dress, and demeanor are sedate and unvaried until he gets an anonymous Valentine box of candy with the title words on a note. Transformed by the knowledge that someone loves him, he begins sharing his time and his things with everyone until he finds out that the gift was delivered to him by mistake. He retreats to his former life, but his new-found friends rescue him.

Stevenson, James. **Yard Sale.** Greenwillow Books, 1996. ISBN 0 688 14126 9

In this story, a neighborhood of animals has a yard sale, and the event discloses a great deal about the animals' varied personalities.

Wild, Margaret. **Our Granny.** Illustrated by Julie Vivas. Houghton Mifflin Books for Children, 1994. ISBN 0 395 67023 3

Elderly people are as varied as young people, and this book catalogs all kinds of grandmothers who are involved in all sorts of careers and pastimes.

Winch, John. **The Old Man Who Loved to Sing.** Scholastic, 1995. ISBN 0 590 22640 1

When an old man moves into the Australian outback and begins to sing loudly, the animals react with dismay, but they grow to like his music. When he can no longer remember his song, they bring it back to him.

Yashima, Taro. **Crow Boy.** Puffin Books, 1976. ISBN 0 14 050172 X

Chibi is rejected by the others at school until his talent for making bird sounds is discovered. This earns him respect and a new name.

Yolen, Jane. **Miz Berlin Walks.** Illustrated by Floyd Cooper. Philomel Books, 1997. ISBN 0 399 22938 8

Miz Berlin walks along the street each day at the same time, talking and singing to herself. Intrigued by the old lady, Mary Louise first follows and then joins her, to their mutual delight.

Owl at Home

By Arnold Lobel
HarperCollins Children's Books, 1975
ISBN 0 06 444034 6

SUMMARY

We first see Owl on the cover of the book, looking wide-eyed and rather dazed. He's ready for bed and holding a candle and a rather thick book. The title page shows his snow-covered, well-lit, two-story cottage, with Owl peering out at us from the front door.

The Table of Contents page lists the titles of five stories and features an illustration of Owl, who appears to be roasting a hot dog in his fireplace.

The first story is "The Guest." Owl sits in an armchair in front of the fire, balancing a soup bowl and spoon on one knee. Unlike many illustrations in this book, this one appears in a neat rectangle against the white space rather than bleeding into it. The effect is that of containment and comfort. The text tells us that Owl's eating pea soup for supper accompanied by buttered toast. It's a cold night, we learn, and Owl is relishing the warmth and comfort of his home.

The next page is mostly text, but a small vignette shows a frightened Owl peering out the door to find out what's been banging and pounding on the door. He goes to the door again on the next page (and we see him from behind), because he has heard the sounds again.

There's no picture on the next page as Owl comes to the conclusion that it's winter who's knocking at his door, seeking the warmth of Owl's fire. He decides to let winter in.

The wind is visible on the next three pages in the form of whirling snow, and we're told that it blew out the fire in the fireplace. Owl follows closely behind Winter, admonish-

COMMENTS

Unlike the other focus books in this volume, **Owl at Home** is not truly a picture book. It falls into the category of "Easy-to-Read," which feature small, amply illustrated books written with the youngest readers in mind. These books usually have short and uncomplicated sentences, and the short chapters allow immature readers to reach the conclusion of the story rapidly. Some books in this category use words from early-reading word lists, but Lobel never did that. He used single and multisyllabic words, but in such a way that their meaning was always obvious from the context. All of Lobel's easy-to-read books are little masterpieces, and **Owl at Home** is no exception. The humor of the book is enhanced because his Owl is not at all wise, but very foolish, indeed.

This story is almost diametrically opposed to the other "owl" book in this focus book section, **Owl Moon.** This volume uses an owl character which is more human than bird. In addition, the artwork is nothing like Schoenherr's; Lobel's illustrations for **Owl at Home** are cartoonish, light, and done in two colors.

ing it to behave itself as a good guest should. At the bottom of the page we see that Owl's pea soup has turned to hard, green ice. (The text tells us it's green, although the illustration makes it look a dark orange.)

The situation deteriorates quickly, and we see Owl on his floor covered with snow as the wind whips out the door. " 'Good-bye,' called Owl, 'and do not come back!' "

Again we see a neat, rectangular picture as Owl settles back in his armchair by the fire, this time covered with a blanket as the story comes to an end.

"Strange Bumps" begins in comfort, with another neat, rectangular illustration showing Owl in bed, though he doesn't look comforted. He is staring at the bumps at the foot of the bed. The text shows him wondering what they are. As Owl becomes more and more concerned about the bumps at the foot of his bed, they appear to become larger. He discovers that the bumps move up and down when he moves his feet up and down, but he never concludes that the bumps are his feet. A rectangular picture appears again as Owl comes to the conclusion that he cannot sleep in this bed with those strange bumps. The illustrations become vignettes again as Owl becomes frenzied and destroys the bed in search of the bumps. Then, we return to the comforting, more formal, rectangular illustration as Owl settles himself in the chair by the fire, declaring that the bumps can grow as big as they wish, he will sleep here by the fire.

The opening illustration for "Tear-Water Tea" shows Owl comfortable, but sad, holding a teakettle in his lap as he sits beside the kitchen wood stove, in which a fire burns brightly. He's deliberately thinking of sad thoughts, and we see some of the sad things he envisions: chairs with broken legs, lost spoons, books with missing pages, and an unwitnessed sunrise. Owl cries as he thinks these sad thoughts, and his tears run down his cheeks into the teakettle. His sad thoughts continue until the teakettle is filled, at which point he briskly stands up and puts the kettle on the stove to boil for tea. He's happy as he drinks his tear-water tea.

"Upstairs and Downstairs" begins with Owl standing at the foot of his stairs. A solidly filled bookcase stands behind him and he holds another book in his hand. We're told that there are 20 steps in the staircase and that Owl spends time both upstairs and downstairs. However, he says, when he's upstairs he wonders about the downstairs, and vice versa. He concludes that there must be a way to be in both places at once and he proceeds to dash up the stairs and down again. After a couple of dashes, he calls to himself from the upstairs but gets no answer. A call from the downstairs gets no answer from himself upstairs, either. He concludes that he must run faster, which he does until he's too exhausted to continue. He sits on the 10th step and we leave him, chin in hands, neither up nor down.

Our first glimpse of Owl in "Owl and the Moon" shows Owl perched high on a rock watching the moon come up over the ocean. He watches it rise higher and higher in the sky and concludes that the moon must see him as he sees the moon and that, therefore, they must be friends. He tells the moon that he must be heading for home now and walks off down a forest path. Looking up he sees the moon and concludes that it is following him. He thanks the moon for trying to light his way, but tells the moon that it should go back over the ocean where it looked so pretty. As he goes over a bridge he sees the moon again. Now he worries that the moon will expect to come inside his small house and be fed, and he has neither room nor food for it. He climbs to a high hill and shouts "good-bye" at the moon. The moon goes behind some clouds and Owl concludes that the moon has heard him and feels sad at having to part with his friend. As Owl gets ready for bed, the moon emerges from the clouds and lights up the room. Owl is delighted and snuggles down for a good night's sleep with his friend the moon looking in.

THINGS WORTH NOTICING

▶ The shape of the illustrations keeps changing.

▶ Owl is anything but a wise bird.

▶ Owl is quite a reader. His home is full of books and he often has a book in hand, ready to read it.

▶ Owl's home has no electricity.

ACTIVITIES

Language Arts

MAKING COMPARISONS

▶ Read the book **Happy Birthday, Moon**, by Frank Asch (see book list). How are Owl and Bear alike? How are they different?

▶ Compare Owl in **Owl at Home** to Owl in the Winnie the Pooh books. How are they alike?

▶ Find other books in which animal characters act differently from their stereotypes: foxes who are fools rather than sly creatures, dragons who are friendly, etc.

▶ Owl becomes frightened of his own feet under the blanket. Read What's Under My Bed? (see book list) for a story about two kids who also become frightened when lying in bed.

▶ Compare Owl to the owl in **Owl Moon**, by Jane Yolen.

▶ Find and read other easy-to-read books by Arnold Lobel. Share your favorites with the rest of the class. Are there any other characters in them who are as foolish as Owl?

MAKING INFERENCES

▶ Put the 33 sentences from "Strange Bumps" on sentence strips. Display them in order one at a time. Ask the children to stand up when they figure out what's going on here. Continue to the end of the story before asking children what clues lead them to their conclusions.

▶ Make a list of the things you know about Owl after reading this book. Write these attributes on a large silhouette of Owl on the bulletin board. Make a line from each of those attributes to the outside of the silhouette and write information from the story that led you to draw that conclusion about Owl.

DRAMATIZING

▶ Role-play a conversation with Owl in which you explain all the things he worried about in the book.

WRITING

▶ Place a large teakettle on the table. Let students write other ingredients for Owl's tear-water tea on sentence strips and place them in the teakettle. Share some herbal tea as you read the ingredients together.

▶ Place another large kettle on the table and label it "Ha-Ha Soup." Ask students to place other ingredients in this kettle. Share some soup together as you read these.

EXTENDING LITERATURE

▶ Find and read the poem "Halfway Up the Stairs," by A. A. Milne, and decide how it applies to this book.

Math

► Owl's staircase has 20 steps, and when he sits on the 10th step, he's neither up nor down. What if his staircase had only 10 steps? Where would halfway be then? Draw staircases with different numbers of steps showing where halfway is.

► Define what the problem is in each of the stories in **Owl at Home**. How does Owl solve it? How would you solve it?

Science

► How do you know that Owl has no electricity in his house?

► What things do you do at home that Owl cannot do?

► Why does the moon appear to be following Owl?

► Owls are usually thought of as wise birds—at least they are portrayed that way in literature. Are they the smartest birds?

RELATED BOOKS

Picture Books

Asch, Frank. ***Happy Birthday, Moon.*** *Simon & Schuster Books for Young Readers, 1982. ISBN 0 6716645 49*

Like Owl, Bear has a one-sided conversation with the moon but Bear hears the echo of his own speech and thinks the moon is speaking to him. Bear takes the friendship deeper, even giving the moon a gift.

Lobel, Arnold. ***Frog and Toad Are Friends.*** *HarperCollins Children's Books, 1987. ISBN 0 06 44020 6*

In this easy-to-read book, Toad is the silly character, although he's not quite as silly as Owl. This book is one in a series of books about Frog and Toad by Arnold Lobel.

Lobel, Arnold. ***Grasshopper on the Road.*** *Harper Trophy, 1978. ISBN 0 06 444094 X*

Grasshopper is the sane one in this book, but, in each chapter, he meets characters who are almost as off-the-wall as Owl.

Lobel, Arnold. ***Uncle Elephant.*** *Scholastic, 1981. ISBN 0 590 32764 X*

An old elephant is the wise one here, and the relationship between the old elephant and his young nephew is close and delightful.

Stevenson, James. ***What's Under My Bed?*** *Greenwillow Books, 1983. ISBN 0 688 02325 8*

Mary Ann and Louie become frightened by what they think are monsters under their bed and they run to Grandpa for comfort. Grandpa, however, has even wilder and scarier things to tell them about.

Owl Moon

By Jane Yolen
Illustrated by John Schoenherr
Philomel Books, 1987
ISBN 0 399 21457 7

SUMMARY

This story starts on the title page as we see a child, who's dressed for winter, looking through an open door at the moonlit snow outside. An owl flies against the white dedication page, and the shadow at the bottom of that white space turns the page to snow. The first page gives us the moon's-eye view of a farm where the expanse of snow bleeds into the white space. The story is told in first person and neither the text nor the illustrations divulge the sex of the child, who's going owling for the first time. (The book blurb calls it a little girl, however.) The rich language includes metaphors and similes, but the comparisons are always to things well within the understanding of most children. As the father and child near the woods, they hear dogs howling at distant trains.

We then learn the first rule of owling: "If you go owling, you have to be quiet." We also learn that the child has been waiting to be old enough for this quest for a long, long time. When the pair reaches the line of trees, we get our first close-up of the child and man, and the father makes the sound of the Great Horned Owl, cupping his mouth as he does so. Our next view is from up in a tree, looking down at the two as they listen for owls. But, as the child says, "My brothers all said sometimes there's an owl and sometimes there isn't." Obviously, this experience is one her older siblings have already had.

As they walk on, our view changes to one below them, perhaps from the bottom of a

COMMENTS

This Caldecott Award-winning book is a lovely tale about a family's excursion into the woods at night. The story celebrates both nature and family ritual. As such, it leads nicely into themes about traditions and customs in individual families, or into an investigation of wildlife, especially owls.

mound in the snow, and the child remarks about the cold to us but not aloud. "If you go owling, you have to be quiet and make your own heat."

In the darker woods the child mentions the need to be brave, and we see the father and child holding hands. Standing in a clearing in the moonlight, the child compares the snow to the milk in a cereal bowl. Pa makes an owl call again. They listen hard, and this time they hear it coming back at them like an echo. The text notes that "Pa almost smiled." Then Pa and the owl are exchanging calls in a conversation, and the child almost smiles as well. As they watch "silently with heat in our mouths, the heat of all those words we had not spoken," the owl hoots again and Pa turns on his flashlight, catching the magnificent creature in the beam as it lands on a nearby branch. The bird and the humans stare at each other until, still soundlessly, the owl flies off. Pa speaks, the first spoken words in the book, "Time to go home." The child knows then that it's all right to talk, but doesn't, choosing the silence of a shadow on the walk home.

The Rooster's Gift

By Pam Conrad
Illustrated by Eric Beddows
HarperCollins Children's Books, 1996
ISBN 0 06 023603 6

SUMMARY

We first see the smiling rooster on the book's cover. He and a small hen are walking together. Her beak is open, as she apparently talks to him. Whatever she's saying must be complimentary because the rooster's face is smiling and his comb is erect. They are on a hill, and far below them we see a church, fields, and trees. Directly behind them is a building, the front of which is a border made of flowers.

The title page shows us the chicken coop from afar. The rooster is on the peak of the roof as the sun rises over a peaceful, gently curving terrain of fields. A stylized rising sun is shown on the dedication page.

We see a white-haired couple looking into the open door of their brand-new chicken coop. The text tells us that there are 10 tiny chicks newly hatched inside. The woman says that she hopes one of them is a rooster. On the facing page we get a chick's-eye view of the sitting hen surrounded by broken eggshells and her new chicks.

As the story continues the chicks feed and talk among themselves. One chick declares that he thinks he's a rooster and, indeed, a closer look shows the beginning of a comb on his head. The others notice that he speaks in "glickes and gorks and flonks" instead of peeps and squeaks and cheeps.

On the next page the woman points at the rooster among the now almost grown chickens. "That's our rooster, all right," she declares. And then, "Sure hope he's got the Gift." That's all we hear of the man and woman, although we will see her again.

COMMENTS

This lushly illustrated book tells a story about vanity, about finding one's own special talent, and about loyalty. It also deals with the false perception of one's own importance. Although the book's animal characters are fairly realistically portrayed in the illustrations (they're given facial expressions), the text endows them with some very human emotions and the ability to talk.

They've provided us with the first reason for the rooster to be proud (he's been singled out as something special and she's established that there's some gift he might have), but this is a chicken's story, not a human one, and we'll see the humans no longer.

On the next page red and white hens stand against the white space with no background. All eyes are turned toward the rooster who stands with his back to us, facing the hens and declaring that he thinks he's got the gift.

The next vignette shows the hens following the rooster out of the chicken coop and into the darkness, and the text tells us that he woke when it was "past late to something else" because something would not let him sleep longer. The full picture on the next page shows the hens looking up at the rooster as he climbs to the top of the chicken coop. They speculate on why he's behaving so strangely and decide that it might well be caused by the Gift.

The next page is completely black except for some white print. The magnificent and fully feathered rooster stands against the darkness with his head raised and his beak open. His first crow is not met with applause, however."

THINGS WORTH NOTICING

► Both the author and the illustrator mention owling in their dedication.

► The illustrator uses the white space on the page as part of the illustrations.

► We don't know whether the child is a boy or a girl from the story itself.

► There are many comparisons to other things.

► The child and the father sometimes walk separately, sometimes together. At the end of the story, the child is carried home.

► There are clues to the fact that the child has talked a lot about going owling before this night.

► The visual perspective changes frequently throughout the book.

ACTIVITIES

Language Arts

USING SIMILES

► Make a list of the comparisons in this book, such as:

"The trees stood still as giant statues . . ."

"A train whistle blew long and low, like a sad, sad song."

"It was as quiet as a dream . . ."

► Find other things to compare. For instance, "The trees stood still as icicles."

FINDING DETAILS

► Look for clues that it's cold.

► Find evidence that the child has been looking forward to this trip for a long time.

► Find the three other animals besides the owl in this book. Two of them the father and child only hear, and one is almost hidden.

► How old do you think this child is?

MAKING COMPARISONS

► When you were little, what are some things you wanted to do, but couldn't, that you can do now?

► What are some things you like to do with your family? Can anybody do those things? Are there some things you like to do with your family that kids younger than you can't do?

► Read **Night Driving** (see book list) for a different kind of trip that a father and child take together. Which kind of trip is more likely to take place in your family?

► Read **Goodnight, Owl** (see book list). Find and list as many differences between **Owl Moon** and **Goodnight, Owl** as you can.

► Read **The Man Who Could Call Down Owls** (see book list). Do you think this story could have happened? Why or why not?

Science

► Owls are predators, and they have eyes on the front of their faces, like most hunters (including humans). Look through other animal books and bird books to find other creatures with eyes that are similarly placed. Are they all hunters? Why do you think non-predators usually have eyes on the sides of their faces?

'Get down from there,' scolded one. 'My, my,' worried another." But Young Rooster crows on and feels "lifted up, charged, holy."

The next page is bathed in light as the chickens look toward the rising sun. The hens declare, "Look what you've done, Rooster!" He decides that he has indeed done it and believes that this is his Gift—the ability to make the new day.

Our next view is that of the interior of the chicken coop. All of the hens but one small one are dozing inside their boxes. The fairly lengthy text on this page tell us that the Young Rooster has continued the custom of getting up in the near dark and strutting onto the rooftop to make the day begin. We also learn that the hens have stopped following him. They're proud of him, but they don't need to watch any more. The smallest hen, however, feels differently.

We see her on the next page standing at the corner of the chicken coop in a driving rain, facing the east and smiling as she hears the Young Rooster crow and sees the colors appear in the sky.

On the facing page the hen and the rooster stand against the white space. The Smallest Hen is speaking to him. The text says that she thanks him every morning for starting the day. The rooster has turned his head from her. One leg is raised and he looks quite haughty. We learn that he has stopped his earlier practice of chatting with her each morning. He is very, very proud.

Much time has passed by the next page. The woman is carrying away a basket of eggs. There are new chicks in the chicken yard. Rooster no longer sleeps in the chicken coop, but Smallest Hen continues to wake up each morning to see and hear him start the day.

It's half-light on the next page. Smallest Hen sits by the outside corner of the chicken coop, but Rooster is nowhere to be seen. The next page shows her pacing in "chicken circles" worrying about who will start the day.

A startled Smallest Hen appears on the next page. She is looking east at the rising sun. " 'Well,

THINGS WORTH NOTICING

▶ The way the illustrations have a rounded, comforting look.

▶ It's the farmer's wife who first mentions "the Gift."

▶ The body language of the chickens.

I'll be plucked,' she whispered." Rooster runs up on the next page. His feathers are ruffled, his beak is open wide with alarm. He accuses Smallest Hen, "How could you go on without me?" but she has not done it and she tells him so.

It's a despondent rooster we see on the next page. His head is bent, his tail droops. She tries to reassure him: "It's much better with you." By the next page he's even sadder. He has deliberately stood on the roof without crowing and he has seen the day begin without him.

On the next page, they discuss the problem, standing alone against the white space. If making the day begin is not his Gift, Rooster asks, what is his Gift? Smallest Hen offers the suggestion that his Gift may be that he knows the day is about to begin but he rejects that. Even she knows the day is about to begin.

Comedy ensues on the next page as he and Smallest Hen stand atop the coop while he urges her to stretch her neck and she declares that she already is stretching it. He tells her to crow when it feels right. She can't crow, of course, and as the sky lightens on the next page she says, "Bok-bok ca-bok, ca-bok." Rooster looks at her with amazement. "What was that?" he asks. She can't crow, but Rooster can, and now he knows he was right about his Gift. As they talk, Smallest Hen knows it too. His Gift is to announce the day, and he does so with great pride on the next page—after which a now-emboldened Smallest Hen says, "Well done."

Language Arts
BUILDING VOCABULARY
► In this book, the word "gift" is used to mean something other than a present. List some definitions and synonyms for "gift."

► Make a list of the things you do very well. Which do you think is your special Gift?

► Look carefully at every picture of Rooster. What one word would you use to describe how he's feeling in each picture?

► Look again at the pictures of Smallest Hen. Select words to describe her feelings in each picture.

MAKING COMPARISONS
► Find and read other books in which there is a proud or very vain creature, such as **Petunia.**

Make a chart such as the one below about those characters:

► In this story, the rooster is portrayed as a proud and foolish creature. Find and read other books in which a rooster is a main character. Are they all portrayed that way? Why do you think authors use roosters in this way?

► Read **Why Mosquitoes Buzz in People's Ears** (see page 168) for a different story about an animal who causes the sun to come up. What are some of the differences between Rooster and Mother Owl?

MAKING INFERENCES
► Rooster and Smallest Hen are convinced that he has a special Gift, but the Smallest Hen may have a special talent too. What might it be?

EXTENDING LITERATURE
► Smallest Hen is a loyal friend, but most of her role in the friendship seems to be admiring the rooster. If you had a chance to talk to her, what would you tell her?

TITLE	CHARACTER	OBJECT OF PRIDE	COMEUPPANCE
The Rooster's Gift	Rooster	Ability to make the day begin	Day begins without him
Petunia	Petunia	Wise because she has a book	Can't read
Little Mouse and Elephant	Little Mouse	Thinks other animals are frightened of him	Meets the elephant

Science
► What evidence does Rooster have that he makes the day begin? What evidence makes him change his mind?

► Listen to some recordings of roosters crowing or go to a farm and hear a real one, then have a crowing contest to see who makes the best rooster noises.

Art
► Look at the many books that show roosters. Especially look at the colors the illustrators used in their rooster pictures. Use some of those colors and a slightly damp paintbrush to make your own illustrations of rooster feathers.

▶ Put up a bulletin board with facts, pictures, and other information about owls.

▶ Look in bird books and make a list of as many different kinds of owls as possible. What kind of owls live nearest to where you live?

▶ Make predator/prey pictures to show what owls eat, and what those creatures eat in turn, and so on, down to tiny creatures or plants.

▶ This owl is a great horned owl. Find out about what it eats and where it lives.

▶ Take a "bird listening walk." Try to imitate the birds you hear.

Art

▶ Mix small amounts of one shade of blue tempera with varying amounts of white paint. Use the hues you get to make nighttime snow pictures.

▶ Make feathers from torn scraps of paper from magazines, then paste them on bigger pieces of paper to make owl pictures. Which colors work best?

RELATED BOOKS

Picture Books

Bunting, Eve. **The Man Who Could Call Down Owls.** Illustrated by Charles Mikolavcak. Simon & Schuster Books for Young Readers, 1984. ISBN 0 02 715380 0

The cloak and wand of the man who can call down owls are stolen by an evil stranger, but Con, the village child, is able to get them back.

Coy, John. **Night Driving.** Illustrated by Peter McCarty. Henry Holt & Co. Books for Young Readers, 1996. ISBN 0 8050 2931 1

A boy and his father are driving through the night on their way to a campground during the 1950s.

Gates, Frieda. **Owl Eyes.** Illustrated by Yoshi Mivake. Lothrop, Lee & Shepard Books, 1994. ISBN 0 688 12472 0

In this Mohawk legend, the Master of All Spirits allows each species to choose its special attributes, but Owl keeps kibitzing until the creator gives him the opposite of what he wanted.

Hutchins, Pat. **Goodnight, Owl.** Simon & Schuster Books for Young Readers, 1972. ISBN 0 02 7459004

Owl tries to sleep during the day, but the antics of the daytime creatures disturb his rest. Later, when those daytime creatures are settling down for their rest, Owl gets his revenge.

Lobel, Arnold. **Owl at Home.** HarperCrest, 1987. ISBN 0 06 023940 2

Owl is a comic figure in this book of short, easy-to-read stories.

Polacco, Patricia. **The Bee Tree.** Philomel Books, 1993. ISBN 0 399 21965 X

The family quest in this book is for a honey tree, and, before they find it, everyone's involved.

Waddell, Martin. **Owl Babies.** Illustrated by Patrick Benson. Candlewick Press, 1992. ISBN 1 564021 01 7

Three baby owls have awakened to find their mother gone. They reassure each other in patterned phrases, but Percy won't be consoled—he wants his mommy. The illustrations are luminous.

Nonfiction

Epple, Wolfgang. **Barn Owls.** Carolrhoda Books, 1992. ISBN 0 876 147422

Color photographs and simple text describe most of the life cycle and habits of the barn owl.

Esbensen, Barbara Juster. **Tiger With Wings: The Great Horned Owl.** Illustrated by Mary Barrett Brown. Orchard Books, 1991. ISBN 0 531 05940 5

This book is full of fascinating information about the great horned owl, including the reasons for its soundless flight. The illustrations are also very informative.

RELATED BOOKS

Picture Books

Aardema, Verna. **Why Mosquitoes Buzz in People's Ears.** *Dial Books for Young Readers, 1975. ISBN 0 14 054895 6*

This is a focus book (see page 168).

Ada, Alma Flor. **The Rooster Who Went to His Uncle's Wedding: A Latin American Folktale.** *Illustrated by Kathleen Kuchera. Paperstar Books, 1998. ISBN 0 698 11682 8*

A very proud rooster muddies his beak on the way to his uncle's wedding, but each character he asks refuses to help him clean it.

Derby, Sally. **The Mouse Who Owned the Sun.** *Illustrated by Friso Henstra. Four Winds, 1993. ISBN 0 02 766965 3.*

Mouse lives alone in the deep, dark woods. He's content with his existence mostly because he believes he owns the sun. He thinks so because he gets up early every morning and asks the sun to rise, and it does. At night, when he's sleepy, he gets into bed and asks the sun to set, and it follows his orders. One day when exploring farther than he has ever been, Mouse is discovered by the King's soldiers, who believe Mouse is the owner of the sun when he commands it to be dimmed and a cloud happens to cover it. The King is convinced, too, and offers to buy the sun from Mouse. Mouse trades the ownership of the sun to the King in exchange for a map, the first he's ever seen.

Duvoisin, Roger. **Petunia.** *Alfred A. Knopf Books for Young Readers, 1962. ISBN 0 394 90865 1*

Petunia, a goose, has found a book. Because she has heard that books bestow great wisdom, she's convinced that carrying one around makes her wise.

Kajpust, Melissa. **The Peacock's Pride.** *Illustrated by JoAnne Kelly. Disney Press, 1997. ISBN 0 786 80293 6*

In this folktale from India a proud peacock is taught by a shy and modest bird that each of us is special in some way.

Meeker, Clare Hodgson. **Who Wakes the Rooster?.** *Illustrated by Megan Halsey. Atheneum Books for Young Readers, 1996. ISBN 0 689 80541 1*

Each farm animal is fast asleep because the rooster isn't crowing. When he finally does crow, the whole farm comes to life.

Yolen, Jane. **Little Mouse and Elephant: A Tale from Turkey.** *Illustrated by John Segal. Simon & Schuster Books for Young Readers, 1996. ISBN 0 689 80493 8*

A mouse sets off to find elephant, convinced that he will be able to break him into bits. Other animals that he meets along the way leave immediately, and he's convinced that it's because they're frightened of him.

The Storytellers

By Ted Lewin
Lothrop, Lee & Shepard Books, 1998
ISBN 0 688 15178 7

SUMMARY

The book's endpapers offer a panoramic view of the city of Fez, Morocco. Vegetation, including several kinds of palms, stands in the foreground, while the modern city spreads to the horizon in shades of tan.

The title page closes in on one city street. Donkeys stand patiently and people wearing loosely fitting garments walk down the narrow street. Overhead a lattice-work seems to provide some shade, although the light shows us that the sun is not yet too fierce, and to our right walks a white-bearded man clothed in red. A young boy, who's wearing white and carrying a birdcage, looks up at him as they walk away from the market crowd.

The dedication page shows the man and boy trailing long shadows while walking down a long, cobbled path which seems to be outside of the walled city. Behind them two men lead laden donkeys. There's a glossary on this page, which provides explanations for six Arabic words used in the story. Also, Lewin tells us that he and his wife, Betsy, to whom he dedicates the book, were in Fez in 1995 when they found and listened to a storyteller.

On the next page we learn that the boy is Abdul and the man is his grandfather. We also get a close-up of the two donkeys. The one in front is bearing two large boxes, and the text implies that these contain TV sets. The second donkey is bearing a more common burden: large samovars or urns. The boy and his grandfather squeeze back

COMMENTS

The different cultural setting for this luscious book is the reason for its inclusion in my book. The Moroccan market is the backdrop to this tale, and many of the vendor's occupations come briefly into focus as an old man and a boy walk through the market to their own place in it. Some of Morocco's costumes and customs are described in the story and can be further developed in the classroom. The storyteller's veneration of and delight in this culture is also a subject for discussion.

against the wall to let them pass as an angry muleteer calls out, "Balak!"

The perspective draws back on the next page as Abdul and his grandfather walk toward us with the old man's hand protectively on the boy's shoulder. In the foreground a man is twisting light-green wool in a sort of vise, and we learn from the text that he's a wool dyer squeezing the water out of wool skeins. Abdul remarks that this work is harder than theirs, giving us the first hint that he and his grandfather are on their way to work.

A close-up of an older, rather intense-looking man holding aloft a hooded falcon greets us on the next page, and we're told that this is their friend, Aziz, who's on his way to hunt in the desert. The close-up allows us to see the hat on Aziz's head, which has creatures that might be camels in the design.

At the copper and brass works on the next page, Abdul holds his hands over his ears and remarks that this is noisy work, unlike theirs. The boy has set the birdcage down, and we see a white bird inside. The grandfather is carrying a colorful mat. The brass workers include two boys about Abdul's age.

We are told that the next scene is quieter but smelly. Abdul and his grandfather take mint leaves from a pile on the street and squeeze the mint under their noses to mask the smell of a leather tannery that can be seen on a rooftop. The vats of dye make a colorful display and the men are laying out the skins to dry. Abdul says he and his grandfather work where the air is fresher than this.

The next page brings us into the deep shade of a date souk where a hawker calls out his wares. Abdul is glad they can see the sky where they work. We don't see many of the other souks, but the text tells us that there are spice, chicken, and saddle souks in the market, as well as carpenters. What we do see on that page are weavers, each of whom has a young child by her side. The yarns on the looms lead down to intricate patterns.

The results of that weaving appear on the next page in the carpet souk, which is lined with beautiful carpets. Abdul is intrigued, but his grandfather tugs at his shoulder urging him to move on. The text tells us that they have also passed a stall in which pots are sold and craftsmen are making combs.

Now they are at the old gate of the city. We see them through the arch. The text says that grandfather has donned a colorful tunic and that the pigeon from the cage now sits on Abdul's head, but we don't see any of that in the illustration. What we do see is the old man laying out the carpet and people who seem to be heading toward them through the archway.

The close-up on the next page shows what we only heard about on the previous page. Grandfather holds a beaded water-pipe in his mouth. He sits cross-legged on the mat. Beside him is a long stick and a tray bearing two glasses of amber-colored liquid. In front of him is a picture of himself as a young boy with a pigeon on his head. It's mirrored by Abdul, who sits gazing at his grandfather with the pigeon still perched on his own head. In front of the boy other pictures lay on the mat, and his own yellow, backless shoes sit on its edge. His grandfather's larger ones are near the old man. They wait for the crowd.

The next spread is a panoramic shot. A crowd has gathered, and the boy sits with arms raised, having just thrown the pigeon high into the sky to bring back a story.

We look over their shoulders in the next picture, facing the crowd. All appear rapt. Some wear western dress while others are more traditionally garbed. A young man leans on the handlebars of a bicycle. The pigeon is back on the boy's head. Grandfather has begun his story with the traditional words, "Kan ya ma kan."

We draw back again and we're above and to the left of the grandfather as he continues his story about a Bedouin prince. An even larger crowd has gathered by now, including the people we saw in the last page's close-up, who haven't moved. The shadows grow longer as the day passes.

The crowd is leaving as the next page shows the man and boy gathering up the tossed coins and placing the pigeon back in its cage. We know they'll be back tomorrow but their work is finished for the day.

As the old man and the boy head home through the gate into the walled city, Abdul declares, and his grandfather agrees, that they have the best job in the whole medina.

The back endpapers are the same as the first.

THINGS WORTH NOTICING

► Grandfather and Abdul are proud of their work.

► The crowd respects and honors their skill.

► The marketplace is full of color and pattern.

► Donkeys are used as beasts of burden, and most people are on foot.

► Most people are wearing traditional dress, but the men and boys at the copper and brass souk are wearing western clothes.

► Most of the items offered for sale at the marketplace are handcrafts, but television sets are mentioned.

► Several occupations and crafts are mentioned in the text but not pictured.

► Children are often shown learning the craft of their elders.

► Fez is a gated city.

► There are several Arabic words used in context and easily defined.

ACTIVITIES

Language Arts

BUILDING VOCABULARY

► Make a list of the Arabic words in this story and give synonyms for them in as many languages as possible.

► Find the Arabic names of the various headpieces and other items of clothing worn by the characters.

MAKING COMPARISONS

► Grandfather begins his story with the words "Kan ya ma kan," which mean "This happened or maybe it did not." Many of our folktales begin with "Once upon a time." Look in folktale books for other ways to begin a tale. Make a list of them and then use your favorites to begin your own stories.

► In this book, people of all ages gather to hear the storyteller. Where do people in your family gather to hear stories?

► You can see many photographs of Morocco at **geogweb.berkeley.edu/**
GeoImages/Miller/millerone.html.
What information is in those photos that you didn't know from reading **The Storytellers?** What information is in **The Storytellers** that you wouldn't know from just looking at that Web site?

► If Abdul were to come to this country to visit you, what would he think of your shopping mall?

INTERPRETING THE TEXT

► What job does Abdul want when he grows up? How is he getting ready for that job?

► Make a list of the things you know about Grandfather's job before he starts telling the stories.

► Make a tape recording in which the sounds Abdul describes can be heard.

INTERPRETING ILLUSTRATIONS

► Look at the designs at the carpet souk. Compare them to Native American designs.

► Count the number of children that you see in the market. What is each one doing there?

MAKING INFERENCES

► How do you know that the art of story-telling is treated with respect by the author?

WRITING

► Write to Superintendent of Documents, U.S. Government Printing Office, Washington, D.C. 20402 for further information about Morocco.

Social Studies

► What can you tell about the surrounding areas of Morocco by looking at the illustrations, especially the one that gives a view of the old gate of the city?

► Make a list of all the occupations mentioned in the book and the items for sale at this market. The people shopping in the market would obtain those items there. Where would we get similar items?

► Find out what money Moroccans use. Write to the Moroccan Embassy for some coins and further information.

► Find out about the Sahara Desert. What's special about it? How is it like and unlike American deserts?

► If the people in the market are near or in a desert, why aren't they wearing hot-weather clothing, such as shorts?

Art

► Use some of the designs in the book in a piece of artwork of your own.

RELATED BOOKS

Fiction

Bunting, Eve. **Market Day.** HarperCollins Children's Books, 1996. ISBN 0 06 025364 9

This story is set in an Irish market, and our narrator's father has given her a penny to spend there.

Castaneda, Omar S. **Abuela's Weave.** Illustrated by Enrique Sanchez. Lee & Low Books, 1993. ISBN 1 880000 20 2

This book is about a Guatemalan market. Esperanza must be the one to sell the wall hanging she and her grandmother have completed because her grandmother's face is birthmarked and people fear she's a witch.

Joseph, Lynn. **Jasmine's Parlour Day.** Illustrated by Ann Grifalconi. Lothrop, Lee & Shepard Books, 1994. ISBN 0 688 11487 3

Trinidad is the location of the market at which Jasmine helps her mother set up their stall so they can sell fish and sugar cakes.

Lobel, Arnold. **On Market Street.** Illustrated by Anita Lobel. Greenwillow Books, 1981. ISBN 0 688 80309 1

The people in this market are made up of the items they sell.

Miranda, Anne. **To Market, To Market.** Illustrated by Janet Stevens. Harcourt Brace & Co., 1997. ISBN 0 152 0035 6

This very funny picture book is based on the familiar nursery rhyme and features a very frazzled woman dashing from market to home in order to make soup.

Tchana, Katrin Hyman. **Oh, No, Toto!.** Illustrated by Colin Bootman. Scholastic, 1997. ISBN 0 590 46585 6

In a Cameroon marketplace, young Toto makes a grab for every edible item he sees.

Nonfiction

Grossman, Patricia. **Saturday Market.**
Illustrated by Enrique Sanchez. Lothrop, Lee & Shepard Books, 1994. ISBN 0 688 12176 4

The marketplace in this book is in present-day Mexico and, as in **The Storytellers,** we get a sense of the many things offered for sale there.

Hermes, Jules M. **The Children of Morocco.** *Carolrhoda Books, 1995. ISBN 0 876 14899 2*

Color photographs and brief text describe many different children living in present-day Morocco.

Stewart, Judy. **A Family in Morocco.** *Lerner Publishing Group, 1986. ISBN 0 822 51664 0*

Malika and her family live in Tangier, Morocco, and we learn about their daily life.

Tuesday

By David Wiesner
Clarion Books, 1991
ISBN 0 395 87082 8

SUMMARY

The only words in this very clever book refer to time, but the story begins wordlessly. Three panels on a page just inside the cover show three frogs on their lily pads in various stages of elevation and looking quite surprised. The illustration on the title page itself is uneventful—only a water lily and pad appear.

After that, however, come the first words: "TUESDAY EVENING, AROUND EIGHT," and we see a turtle on a log in the pond also looking surprised. The reason for its surprise becomes clear on the next page, when several frogs on their lily pads zoom over the turtle. From then on the frogs are having a wonderful time dive-bombing and scaring birds as they approach a darkened town.

At 11:21 p.m., a man having a late-night snack sees the frogs out of the corner of his eye as they fly past his kitchen window. An encounter with some clothes on a line gives

THINGS WORTH NOTICING

► The frogs are not all alike.

► The reactions of other creatures to the frogs' adventure is easy to interpret.

► There are very few words in the book.

► The time when things are happening is clearly indicated.

► As morning approaches, the frogs' flight is lower.

► Wiesner often uses panels so that he can show things happening in stages.

COMMENTS

Wiesner's story of magic flight is told without written explanation but is pure delight for the reader. The book's sparse text puts it within reach of very young children, while its subtle hints and implied events make it a challenge. Students need to be given the opportunity to examine the book at close hand in order to pick up on these subtleties and to make their own inferences. The illustrations are in rich blues and greens with varied perspectives. While retaining the "frog look," Wiesner has managed to give his characters expressions that convey many emotions.

the frogs capes for a bit, and then they're flying into the open window of a home where an old woman dozes in front of the television set. One frog manipulates the remote control with its tongue. Back outside at 4:38 a.m., a few frogs are flying low enough to be chased by a large, brown dog. Soon a horde of low-flying frogs turns the tables on it, however, and the dog flees in panic.

As the sky lightens, the lily pads drop to the ground, leaving the frogs to fend for themselves, and they do, heading back to their pond in broad daylight. The next spread shows police and emergency vehicles on a city street covered with lily pads. In the background the late-night snacker is talking to a television crew and gesturing toward the sky. The chased dog is sniffing suspiciously at one lily pad while two leashed bloodhounds wait patiently.

On the next page we see a flying shadow against a barn as the text reads, "NEXT TUESDAY, 7:58 P.M.," and on the next page pigs are tumbling and flying through the air.

Language Arts

BUILDING VOCABULARY

► There's a common expression about pigs flying. What is it and what do you think it means? Find and list some other expressions that mean things will probably never happen, such as "When hell freezes over," "It'll be a cold day in July . . .," and "Once in a blue moon."

FINDING DETAILS

► Before the class has a chance to become familiar with the book, divide the class into two groups. Seat them in chairs facing each other. Stand so that one group is facing you. Show them the cover and encourage them to talk to their partner, the person seated across from them, about what they see. Tell the children whose backs are to you that they can't turn around, but must listen to their partner tell them what they see in the book. After one or two minutes, walk to the other side of the group and show the students facing the other way the next page, again telling them to describe to their partners what they see. Continue in this manner, alternating pages, so that each of the children has seen every other page but only heard about the intervening pages from their partner. Then have the children work in pairs to figure out the whole story.

SEQUENCING

► Give each group of partners from the activity above a large sheet of newsprint and large crayons or paintbrushes and ask them to draw or paint a picture of the part of the book they liked best.

When each twosome has completed their drawings, take the class to a large expanse of wall and have them figure out the sequence of their pictures and place them in order on the wall. If more than one picture exists for the same event, place those pictures vertically in the proper place in the sequence. Check the children's sequencing against the book for accuracy and make adjustments if necessary.

► Decide together which events from the story are missing from the sequence above. Compose a simple sentence on a sentence strip for those missing events and place them in the proper sequence or ask students to create the missing pictures.

INTERPRETING THE TEXT

► Decide whether the frogs the lily pads suddenly acquire flying power. What about the pigs, then?

► What evidence did the frogs leave behind? What conclusions might the police draw?

Math

► On real clocks, create the times indicated in the book. Make such statements as: "My clock says 4:38 a.m. At this time the frogs are still flying but are very near the ground."

► Figure out how the story would have been different if the a.m. and p.m. times were reversed.

Science

► Find and post interesting facts about frogs.

► Visit a water garden and examine some lily pads. Measure and weigh them.

► The only pond animals in this story are the frogs and a turtle. Make a list of other animals that might be found in a pond.

Art

► Use wax crayons to make pictures of frogs. Be sure to bear down hard with the crayons. Use watercolors to wash-paint the whole paper. The color will not stick to the frog pictures but will fill in the

RELATED BOOKS

(See page 6 for books about ponds.)

Fiction

Joyce, William. **Bently and Egg.** HarperCollins Children's Books, 1992. ISBN 0 06 020386 2

An artistic frog named Bently becomes responsible for the care and well-being of an egg. This involves him in a series of hair-raising adventures.

Kalan, Robert. **Jump Frog Jump.** Illustrated by Byron Barton. Scholastic, 1989. ISBN 0 590 71723 5

This boldly illustrated cumulative tale shows a frog escaping from a succession of creatures.

LeGuin, Ursula. **Catwings.** Illustrated by S. D. Schindler. Scholastic, 1992. ISBN 0 590 46072 2

This book and the next are very short chapter books. Mrs. Jane Tabby is surprised to find that her new kittens have wings, but she encourages them to use those wings to find better places to live.

LeGuin, Ursula. **Catwings Returns.** Illustrated by S. D. Schindler. Orchard Books, 1989. ISBN 0 531 05803 4

Two kittens that can fly return to their former home, the slums, to find their mother. One of her new kittens also has wings, and the two older kittens bring it with them, out of danger.

Lionni, Leo. **Fish Is Fish.** Alfred A. Knopf Books for Young Readers, 1970. ISBN 0 394 82799 6

In this fable, a fish learns about the world from a frog's descriptions of it, but imagines it in a fish-like manner.

Maizlish, Lisa. **The Ring.** Greenwillow Books, 1996. ISBN 0 688 14217 6

In this wordless book, a boy is able to fly when he dons a yellow ring. His flight takes him over the city.

Mayer, Mercer. **A Boy, A Dog, a Frog and a Friend.** Dial Books for Young Readers, 1971. ISBN 0 8037 0754 1

This book is one in a series of wordless stories about a close friendship between a boy and a frog.

Smith, Lane. **Flying Jake.** Aladdin Paperbacks, 1996. ISBN 0 689 80376 1

In this wordless adventure, a boy joins his pet bird in flight.

Nonfiction

Martin, James. **Frogs.** Crown Books for Young Readers, 1997. ISBN 0 517 70905 8

The color photographs of many different kinds of frogs make this book a browsing delight.

Savage, Stephen. **Frog.** Illustrated by Phil Weare. Thomson Learning, 1995. ISBN 1 56847 326 5

This is an easy-to-read book with good illustrations about frogs.

Why Mosquitoes Buzz in People's Ears

By Verna Aardema
Illustrated by Leo & Diane Dillon
Dial Books for Young Readers, 1975
ISBN 0 8037 6089 2

SUMMARY

Based on an African folktale, this pourquoi tale explains the book's title. The artwork is strikingly beautiful. Vivid colors provide a base on which broad, white lines define pattern and design, creating an effect similar to that of cut paper.

On the cover a very large mosquito is close to a man's ear. The man looks out of the corner of his eye at the bug. In the background a sleepy sun appears to be setting behind a lovely, yellow tree. Two other animals are visible near the bottom of the cover.

On the title page we see the same man looking at a yam he has just dug. A red sun peers at him from behind a green tree, while two mosquitoes dominate the far right of the page. We're informed that this tale is from West Africa and is being retold here.

The first page of the story shows two iguanas, although the text tells us that it's really one iguana reacting with annoyance to the mosquito. The iguana on the far left holds one claw over his ear while balancing himself on the other claw. A mosquito is obviously speaking. She tells him that the farmer dug yams that were almost as big as she is, and the iguana declares that he would rather be deaf than listen to such nonsense. The "second" iguana is really the same iguana, but now he has two sticks stuck in his ears and he's walking off the page. On the right side of the page a red bird is watching the iguana, while

COMMENTS

This cumulative folktale is an example of many similar ones found in children's literature, making it a potential point of departure for themes on folktales and on cumulative stories. The book's stylized illustrations are both beautiful and comic as various animals mug to the viewer. The tale is also a pourquoi tale (a story that explains how something came to be) and, again, can serve as a prototype for that theme.

an orange sun looks sideways out at us. The last line of the text is Aardema's first use of onomatopoeia to record the iguana's angry steps: "mek, mek, mek, mek."

On the next page we appear to be seeing a python with two heads, but, again, it's the Dillons' attempt to show us an animal in motion. The snake is magnificent in shades of purple and black with large yellow eyes first staring out at the iguana in alarm and then darting into a rabbit hole. The red bird appears twice on the page, once to observe the python entering the rabbit hole and again to watch two images of the rabbit as it runs from the python. That red bird acts as both an arrow pointing to the action and as our witness to it.

A crow appears on the next page first to observe the rabbit and then to fly off to alert the rest of the forest animals, the first of which is a monkey. Again, the red bird observes the crow and then the monkey from its vantage point on a breaking limb over a nest containing four baby owls. One branch has already killed an owlet. The sun is darker now and witnesses the action with a worried look.

We see only one image of the animals on the next page, but multiple images of the sun as it sinks and fades behind the hill. In the foreground a mother owl holds her dead baby and mourns, while her two live babies reach out for her. The red bird sits in the owl's nest. In the distance the red bird appears again, on the back of one of a group of animals. The text tells us that the baby owls have told their mother that a monkey killed their sibling. We're also told that it's Mother Owl who wakes the sun each day, but she didn't because she was grieving. The night grew long.

Up to this point, the pages have all had black print on white space, but the next page bears white print on black space. King Lion has called a meeting around the council fire. Antelope has brought Mother Owl. She stands in the front center of the page frowning up at a sort of replay in which an evil monkey holds a baby owl and hits it with a large branch. The text reflects the scenario as she tells King Lion that she can't bear to wake the sun because Monkey killed her owlet. The King repeats her story, beginning with the words, "Did you hear?" The red bird sits with the other animals listening.

A humble and supplicant monkey is seen on the next dark page waving his arms as he answers the King's question: "Why did you kill one of Mother Owl's babies?" He explains that it was an accident caused by the crow's alarm. Again, the King relays the information to the council of animals: "So, it was the crow who alarmed the monkey, who killed the owlet, etc." At the upper right of the page we see the crow's arrival.

There is humor on the next page as a wide-eyed antelope mugs for the viewer. The sad-faced monkey, however, has his eyes closed. The crow explains that it was the rabbit's running that alarmed him, and now the King has another line in the pattern of repeated phrases: "It was the rabbit who startled the crow . . . ."

The fearsome python dominates the next page. His body extends across it, with his open mouth and fangs large at the far right. The other animals look frightened, but the rabbit finds the courage to tell the King that it was python's fault. The red bird occupies center front stage as it looks back at the rabbit so that we won't miss his testimony. The King adds yet another line to the series of events.

The python's appearance on the next page is different—he stands docilely in front of King Lion. The red bird stands beside the King to listen as the python explains that it was the iguana's fault. We see a fierce iguana with branches that look like fire emanating from his ears.

Many of the animals are laughing on the next page at the grumpy iguana with the sticks in his ears. King Lion pulls them out and asks the iguana why he plotted evil against the python. Iguana proclaims that he didn't, that the snake is his friend, and he explains about the mosquito's nonsense. The iguana looks happier on the next page, as the red bird on his back looks toward the mosquito at the far right of the page.

The animals aren't laughing on the next page but are demanding that the mosquito be punished. The Owl needs no further information, however. She turns toward the sun, which is rising from the far right corner of the page and already changing the light as the owl hoots.

Appropriately, the page design has reverted to black print on white space. The red bird directs our attention to the mosquito, who's hiding behind the leaf on the left side of the page and buzzes near the farmer's ear on the right. The text tells us what she buzzes: "Zeee! Is everyone still angry at me?" On the last page we get the answer. The farmer's hand is in motion, then the mosquito is crushed against his face. The red bird flies off, and the single word of text reads, "Kpao!"

THINGS WORTH NOTICING

▶ More than one image of the same animal appears on a page to indicate a sequence of events or two interpretations of the same event.

▶ The illustrations show simultaneously both what really happened and what the animals think happened.

▶ A red bird appears on every page and may represent the reader. It becomes almost an arrow pointing to the desired creature or event.

▶ An antelope sometimes stares at the reader and makes faces.

▶ The stylized illustrations are outlined in white, giving them a stained-glass or cut-paper effect.

▶ Aardema uses African words in the text to represent movement verbs or adjectives.

▶ The story is told cumulatively—each page adds more information to the story.

ACTIVITIES

Language Arts

SEQUENCING

▶ Make a cardboard poster for each animal that is part of the reason why mosquitoes buzz in people's ears. Make a face-sized hole where the animal's face would be. Tell the story from each animal's point of view, such as, "I'm the iguana. I put sticks in my ears because the mosquito was so silly."

▶ Make a flow chart of the events in the story.

DETERMINING CAUSE & EFFECT

▶ Using the same posters as in the previous activity, make statements such as, "If I had asked the snake why he was coming into my rabbit hole, I wouldn't have run away and scared the . . .."

USING ORAL LANGUAGE

▶ This kind of folktale is called a "pourquoi story" because it explains why something happens. Find and read some of the other pourquoi stories listed below and have a pourquoi storytelling circle retelling those stories.

WRITING

▶ Make a list of animals and one thing that is noticeable about each, such as:

Blue Jay	loud call
Snake	flicking tongue
Tiger	stripes
Butterfly	pretty colored wings
Woodpecker	red head

▶ Write a pourquoi story about one of the animals on your list, such as "Why the Tiger Has Stripes."

Math

▶ Retell the story using the words first, second, third, fourth, etc., as in, "The first animal to run was the snake."

Science

▶ Why do mosquitoes buzz in people's ears?

▶ If this story took place in the woods nearest your school, it probably would have some different animals in it. Make a list of the animals in the story that could be found in those woods. Keep those animals in the story but change the other animals to ones from your woods. As a result, you may have to change some of the things that happen in the story.

Social Studies

▶ Every animal's actions in this story affect someone else's actions. Make a list of the things you do that affect, even in small ways, the actions of other people in the classroom.

▶ What are the rules in the community where these animals live? What are the rules in the household where you live? In the classroom? In the school?

Art

▶ Using bright-colored paper cut out large shapes to represent the animals in the story. Use crayons or cut paper to make the animals look the way you want them to. Then cut the animal into three or four large pieces and paste them onto a larger sheet of white paper. Leave thin spaces between the pieces to achieve a look similar to the white lines in the Dillons' illustrations.

▶ The events that happen in the daytime are shown in this book on white backgrounds with black printed words. The night actions are shown on black backgrounds with white printed words. Make some day and night pictures using those techniques.

RELATED BOOKS

(For other books by Verna Aardema, see page 174.)

POURQUOI STORIES

Foster, Joanna. **The Magpie's Nest.** Clarion Books, 1995. ISBN 0 395 62155 0

The magpie is allowed to show other birds how to build their nests because hers is so complex. Each bird flies off, however, before hearing the full explanation, which is why different birds build vastly different nests.

Gates, Frieda. **Owl Eyes.** Lothrop, Lee & Shepard Books, 1994. ISBN 0 688 12472 0

When the Master of All Spirits made the animals, he left them incomplete and let each one choose its special attribute. The Owl was butting into all the discussions, so the Master of All Spirits gave him big ears to better hear his instructions, and allowed him to fly only at night.

Gerson, Mary Joan. **Why the Sky Is Far Away: A Nigerian Folktale.** Illustrated by Carle Golembe. Joy Street, 1992. ISBN 0 316 308528

Once the sky was so close that people could break off pieces of it and eat them, so they needed no other food. One day, however, a woman broke off a big piece in spite of the sky's warning, and the sky floated up to where it is today.

Hadithi, Mwenye. **Hot Hippo.** *Little, Brown & Co., Children's Books, 1986. ISBN 0 316 33718 8*

When the hippo begs to be allowed to live in the water, he's required to keep his mouth open to show that he's not eating the little fish.

Hausman, Gerald. **How Chipmunk Got Tiny Feet: Native American Animal Origin Stories.** *Illustrated by Ashley Wolff. HarperCrest, 1995. ISBN 0 06 02 29071*

Seven pourquoi tales from Navajo, Koasati Creek, and Tsimshian traditions are well told and accompanied by block-print illustrations.

Irbinskas, Heather. **How Jackrabbit Got His Very Long Ears.** *Illustrated by Kenneth J. Spengler. Rising Moon Press, 1994. ISBN 0 873 58566 6*

The jackrabbit is entrusted by the Great Spirit to guide each new animal to its home and to explain its special qualities. Jackrabbit doesn't listen well and makes up answers for the rabbit, roadrunner, and bobcat until the Great Spirit intervenes.

Rosen, Michael. **How the Animals Got Their Colors: Animal Myths from Around the World.** *Illustrated by John Clementson. Harcourt Brace & Co., 1992. ISBN 0 152 36783 7*

There are nine pourquoi stories in this collection, which includes source notes on each of them.

Van Laan, Nancy. **Rainbow Crow.** *Alfred A. Knopf Books for Young Readers, 1991. ISBN 0 679 81942 8*

The crow once had a beautiful voice and beautiful feathers. She burned them carrying fire to earth for the other animals.

Author/ Illustrator Studies

Verna Aardema

HER LIFE

Verna Aardema nee Norberg was born in New Era, Michigan, on June 6, 1911. She taught school in Michigan for 40 years while also working part-time at the Muskegon *Chronicle*. She began writing children's stories in order to keep one of her children entertained during meals. She moved to Florida in 1991. Although most of her stories are African in origin, Aardema has never been to Africa.

HER WORK

Almost without exception, Aardema uses folktales and folktale fragments, which she then expands into a more complete story. Often she uses ideophones (groups of sounds to convey an idea). They're particularly effective when describing the movement of a character. She also frequently repeats phrases in her stories, which is an element of several African languages, to emphasize or strengthen an action.

THINGS TO DO WITH HER WORK

► Many of the folktales Aardema has retold explain how or why some thing in nature came to be. Make a list of the ones that do this and then make up your own story about something you've noticed and how it might have come to be.

► Many of her books are about a chain of events. Start with a statement such as "Mosquitoes often buzz in people's ears because a baby owl died, because . . ." or "The rain came to Kapiti plain because a boy shot an arrow, because . . ."

► Find out more about any of the countries that are the sources or locations for Aardema's tales.

BOOKS & ACTIVITIES

Anansi Finds a Fool. *Illustrated by Bryna Waldman. Dial Books for Young Readers, 1992. ISBN 0 8037 1164 6*
Anansi takes human form, in this trickster tale from West Africa, in order to outwit his neighbor, Bonsu. Turn about is fair play, however, and Bonsu tricks Anansi instead.
ACTIVITY: Find and read other Anansi stories. How are they like this one? How are they different from this one?

. . . .

Borreguita & the Coyote: A Tale from Ayutla, Mexico. *Illustrated by Petra Mathers. Alfred A. Knopf Books for Young Readers, 1991. ISBN 0 679 80921 X*

Surprisingly, the coyote is the gullible one in this story about a battle of wits between a coyote and a lamb.
ACTIVITY: Find other tales about coyotes. Is the coyote a trickster or a fool in those stories?

Bringing the Rain to Kapiti Plain. *Illustrated by Beatriz Vidal. Puffin Books, 1983. ISBN 0 8037 0904 8*

This is a cumulative tale from Africa in which Kipat brings rain to the drought-ridden plain by shooting a feather into the clouds.

ACTIVITIES:

▶ Read the Mother Goose rhyme "This Is the House That Jack Built." Then read this book aloud. Are they alike? How?

▶ What happens in your community when it doesn't rain for a long time? Does your local government control water use? How?

....

Oh, Kojo! How Could You!. *Illustrated by Marc Brown. Dial Books for Young Readers, 1988. ISBN 0 8037 0449 6*

This Anansi tale from the Sudan explains how cats became superior to dogs.

ACTIVITIES:

▶ Which do you prefer, cats or dogs? Make a list of the reasons why.

▶ Read Donald Hall's **I Am the Dog; I Am the Cat** (Dial Books for Young Readers, 1994. ISBN 0 8037 1504 8) to get each animal's perspective on the world.

....

Pedro and the Padre. *Illustrated by Friso Henstra. Dial Books for Young Readers, 1991. ISBN 0 8037 0522 0*

In this Mexican folktale, Pedro is thrown out by his father, who's convinced that the boy will never learn to work. He's taken in by a padre who is, in turn, aghast at the boy's lying ways.

ACTIVITY: Find other folktales in which a character is thrown out or mistreated by his family.

....

Princess Gorilla & a New Kind of Water. *Illustrated by Victoria Chess. Dial Books for Young Readers, 1988. ISBN 0 8037 0412 7*

The "new water" in this story is vinegar. Because the Princess's father wants her to wed the bravest animal in the jungle, he proclaims that whoever can drink the "new water" can wed his daughter. This African pourquoi tale explains why monkeys live in trees.

ACTIVITY: Try some herbal vinegars on cucumbers or other salad ingredients. Conduct a poll to see which is the favorite.

Rabbit Makes a Monkey of Lion. *Illustrated by Jerry Pinkney. Dial Books for Young Readers, 1989. ISBN 0 8037 0297 3*

Rabbit wants the honey in the calabash tree and together with his friends Bush-rat and Turtle, he tries to get it. Lion feels he owns the tree and fends them off, but Rabbit uses his wits to get the best of Lion.

ACTIVITIES:

▶ Find other folktales in which a rabbit plays tricks on bigger animals. Try the Br'er Rabbit stories.

▶ What do we mean when we say "making a monkey of someone"? List other phrases with "monkey" in them, such as "monkey shines" and "monkey wrench."

....

The Riddle of the Drum. *Illustrated by Tony Chen. Macmillan Books, 1979. ISBN 0 02 700390 6*

This Mexican folktale is a cumulative story in which contestants try to win the hand of a princess by guessing the animal skin used for the King's drum.

ACTIVITY: This is one of many folktales with a motif of an impossible task. Make up an impossible task of your own, such as counting the grains of rice in a barrel, counting the stars in the sky, or singing a new note of music.

....

Traveling to Tondo. *Illustrated by Will Hillenbrand. Alfred A. Knopf Books for Young Readers, 1991. ISBN 0 679 80081 6*

In this tale from Zaire, a civet cat gathers his animal friends to make the trip to Tondo, where his bride awaits. There's wonderful language in this story, especially the verbs.

ACTIVITY: Find out more about civet cats. What do they eat? Who are their enemies? What is their habitat?

....

Why Mosquitoes Buzz in People's Ears. *Illustrated by Leo & Diane Dillon. Puffin Books, 1978. ISBN 0 8037 6088 4*

An iguana puts sticks in his ears to avoid hearing any more foolishness from a mosquito. This causes a chain of events that leads to no sunrise. The lion, who calls everyone together for an explanation, unravels the whole tale. This cumulative tale from West Africa is a focus book (see page 168).

Molly Bang

HER LIFE

Since her birth in Princeton, New Jersey, in 1943, Molly Bang has moved around a lot: She's lived in India, Mali, and Japan. She holds degrees in French and in Oriental studies. As a child she loved the illustrations of Arthur Rackham. Her first book, **The Goblins Giggle,** was a compilation of stories illustrated with black-and-white images. Since then she has retold and illustrated many folktales. She is most famous for her original work, however, especially **The Grey Lady and the Strawberry Snatcher.**

HER WORK

Bang's use of color is one of the great strengths of her work: the luscious red of those strawberries, the pure yellow of that ball on the beach. Her palette, or set of colors, differs according to the mood of her work, and she uses figure/ground to perfection in **The Grey Lady and the Strawberry Snatcher.**

THINGS TO DO WITH HER WORK

► Bang uses a different palette for each book. Make a list of the colors she uses in **Dawn.** Put a few words next to each color to describe that particular shade. Do the same with the colors she uses in **Ten, Nine, Eight.** Are there any shades of color in common? Why do you think she might have chosen those particular colors for that particular book? How would the books seem if you exchanged one set of colors for another?

► Bang writes and illustrates her own books. Which do you think she creates first, the words or the pictures? Why do you think so? Can you find out which she usually does first?

BOOKS & ACTIVITIES

Dawn. *Morrow Junior Books, 1991. ISBN 0 688 10989 6*

This is a story of love and greed. A shipbuilder tells his daughter about her mother, who was a transformed Canadian Goose. She loved the shipbuilder and wove beautiful sails for him, but he got greedy and she gave her life for him.

ACTIVITY: If you look closely at the illustrations, you will see things that show the mother is a goose. List them.

. . . .

Delphine. *Morrow Junior Books, 1988. ISBN 0 688 05636 9*

Delphine lives high in the mountains with three animal companions. When she learns that a package awaits her at the post office, she takes the long and dangerous trip to town, worrying all the way about the package (She knows what's in it. We don't until the end.).

ACTIVITY: Put together an ideal list of animals to live with. Decide why you would choose each animal and then describe your life together.

The Grey Lady and the Strawberry Snatcher.
Aladdin, 1996. ISBN 0689 80381 8

This wordless book combines the mystical with the realistic. An old lady has bought strawberries at the market. A lanky and mysterious creature pursues her. Sometimes she disappears from his view. Other times she disappears from ours. Eventually she gets home, but they both get a berry feast.

ACTIVITIES:

▶ Tell the story with sound effects made by using only your body.

▶ Make up words for the story.

·······

The Paper Crane. *Morrow Junior Books, 1987. ISBN 0 688 07333 6*

A grateful stranger gives an origami crane to the owner of a restaurant. The crane comes to life and performs for the patrons, bringing great good fortune to the host.

ACTIVITY: To make these illustrations, Molly Bang placed her origami and paper-cut images in a shadow box to get a three-dimensional effect. Try this yourself and photograph the results.

Ten, Nine, Eight. *Morrow Junior Books, 1991. ISBN 0 688 10480 0*

A little girl and her father get ready for bed, counting backwards while describing the things in her room.

ACTIVITY: Start with a larger number and count backwards. Illustrate each number in the sequence.

·······

Wiley & the Hairy Man. *Lodestar, 1996. ISBN 0 525 674772*

In this folktale from Alabama, a terrible swamp creature threatens a young boy. With his mother, Wiley devises a clever plan to outwit the Hairy Man.

ACTIVITY: How could the plan have gone wrong? Rewrite the story assuming that the first attempt didn't work.

·······

Yellow Ball. *Morrow Junior Books, 1991. ISBN 0 688 06314 4*

A boy plays with his ball at the beach. When he becomes distracted, the ball takes on a life of its own, drifting out to sea for many adventures before being cast up on another beach, where another boy awaits.

ACTIVITY: Watch the silent movie *The Red Balloon*. Compare it to this book.

Byrd Baylor

HER LIFE

Byrd Baylor was born in Texas, in 1924, but now lives outside of Tucson, Arizona. Byrd was her mother's maiden name. When she was little, Baylor spent a lot of time by herself exploring the desert or just sitting quietly on a rock and thinking her own thoughts. Her mother often worried about what would become of her. Baylor lives simply in an adobe house, which was built by herself and some friends. With her long skirts, sandals, and flowing, white hair, she looks as if she has just stepped out of the desert, even when she's speaking at conventions far from that place. She has strong views on the misuse of the environment, misuses which she sees all too frequently.

 HER WORK

Baylor's books are always lyrical and deceptively simple. Her blank verse often trails down the page in a series of short phrases, making it especially suitable for the illustrations of Peter Parnall, her most frequent illustrator. His technique of making stylized, strong-line images trail off into the desert space echoes the author's text and extends it beautifully. Baylor's book **I'm In Charge of Celebration** is a lyrical poem in praise of the southwestern desert, and Parnall uses more vivid colors in it than he typically does for her work.

Baylor doesn't shy away from incorporating her values into her books. In fact, she often preaches them: respect for nature, celebration of privacy, and respect for people, particularly Native Americans, who know the old ways of living in harmony with the land. Her reverence for life, particularly desert life, is evident in all of her writing.

 THINGS TO DO WITH HER WORK

► Take one page of one of her books and illustrate it your way.

► Find some of the books by Byrd Baylor that are not illustrated by Peter Parnall. Compare the looks and moods of the books.

► Write the text for one of her books in regular paragraph form. Place it over the column of print on that page of the book. What does the format of the text do to the book?

► Make a list of subjects she might have chosen to write about if she had lived in your area instead of the desert.

BOOKS & ACTIVITIES

Amigo. *Illustrated by Garth Williams. Simon & Schuster Books for Young Readers, 1989. ISBN 0 689 71299 5*

A desert boy and a prairie dog, each convinced that he's taming the other, become fast friends.

ACTIVITY: Find out about prairie dogs. Where and how do they live? What do they eat? What are their enemies?

. . . .

The Best Town in the World. *Illustrated by Ronald Himler. Atheneum, 1983. ISBN 0 684 18035 9*

The small town in the Texas hills where the narrator's father grew up was absolutely perfect. She lists its wonders and attributes. Camelot, indeed.

ACTIVITY: Ask your parents and grandparents to tell you about the town or neighborhood where they grew up. Was theirs as perfect as the one Baylor's father told her about?

. . . .

The Desert Is Theirs. *Illustrated by Peter Parnall. Atheneum, 1987. ISBN 0 684 13899 9*

The Papago Indians respect the desert and its creatures and are closely connected to it. Incorporated into this story are some Papago legends.

ACTIVITY: Find out about the Papago Indians. Did they always live in the desert? Where do many of them live now? Mark their place on a map.

. . . .

Desert Voices. *Illustrated by Peter Parnall. Simon & Schuster Books for Young Readers, 1981. ISBN 0 684 16712 3*

Each of the desert creatures tells us of its day and life. Taken together, they reveal the predator/prey links of the desert.

ACTIVITY: Research another ecosystem such as the woods or the beach. Make up a picture book in which each animal in that place tells about its life.

Everybody Needs a Rock. *Illustrated by Peter Parnall. Atheneum, 1987. ISBN 0 684 13899 9*

The narrator gives us 10 carefully explained rules for choosing the perfect rock. In the process she gets us to explore the attributes of many things, including rocks.

ACTIVITY: Baylor gives 10 rules for finding the perfect rock. Make up 10 rules for choosing the perfect friend.

. . . .

Guess Who My Favorite Person Is. *Illustrated by Robert Andrew Parker. Simon and Schuster, 1985. ISBN 0 689 71052 6*

A young man and a girl play a "choose your favorite thing" game. The use of their senses as they carefully delineate and describe their choices is explored.

ACTIVITY: Play the games from the book with the whole class. Poll the answers.

. . . .

Hawk, I'm Your Brother. *Illustrated by Peter Parnall. Atheneum, 1976. ISBN 0 684 14571 5*

An encounter between a Native American boy and a hawk allows the boy to declare himself one with the world of the hawk. The Native American reverence and affinity for the natural world is the focus of this book.

ACTIVITY: Find out how to identify hawks when they're in flight by the shape of their wings and body.

. . . .

I'm In Charge of Celebrations. *Illustrated by Peter Parnall. Atheneum, 1986. ISBN 0 684 18579 2*

A girl who lives in the desert enjoys its beauty and isolation and tells us of its delightful phenomena. The idea of exulting in the beauty of nature applies to many environments.

ACTIVITY: The girl in this book celebrates the desert. For the next five days, take notes on every natural event you see happening in your area. Name it and find ways to describe it for others the way she did.

If You Are a Hunter of Fossils. *Illustrated by Peter Parnall. Aladdin, 1984. ISBN 0689 70773 8*

A fossil found in the desert brings to life and into focus the time, millions of years before, when the fossil was created. Time shifts back and forth from the prehistoric to the present.

ACTIVITY: Examine some real fossils. Then make pretend fossils using plaster of Paris and plasticene.

· · · · · · ·

The Table Where Rich People Sit. *Illustrated by Peter Parnall. Simon & Schuster Books for Young Readers, 1994. ISBN 0 684 19653 0*

A girl calls her family together to discuss money—she says they don't have enough. Her parents, though, treasure the riches of the desert where they live and work, and insist that she take into account the value of these things. Soon, the girl is adding millions of dollars to their worth.

ACTIVITY: Make a list of the things in your family that you value most but that don't have any real monetary value. Then make a list of things you value that also have cash value. Which list is most important? Begin crossing out things you are willing to part with until there are only two things left. Which list are they on?

· · · · · · ·

They Put on Masks. *Illustrated by Jerry Ingram. Scribner, 1974. ISBN 0 684 13767 4*

This poetic work describes and celebrates the masks used by native peoples for their ceremonies.

ACTIVITY: Make pâpier-mâché masks by first sculpting them in plasticene.

· · · · · · ·

The Way to Start a Day. *Illustrated by Peter Parnall. Simon & Schuster Books for Young Readers, 1978. ISBN 0 684 15651 2*

This book explores the customs and beliefs of many of the world's people—including ancient Chinese, Inca, and Egyptians, as well as people in modern-day Japan, India, and New Mexico—as they greet the new day.

ACTIVITY: Write or draw about the way you start a day.

· · · · · · ·

We Walk in Sandy Places. *Photographs by Marilyn Schweitzer. Scribner, 1976. ISBN 0 684 14526 X*

Looking closely at tracks in sand, we can recreate the creature and the events that made them.

ACTIVITIES:

► Make tracks. Make them in mud, sand, snow, and anything else you can think of.

► Make tracks by making a mold of plasticene in a dish with a flat bottom. Press something into the clay surface. Remove it and grease the mold with Vaseline. Pour plaster-of-Paris into the mold. Let it set and then tear the plasticene away. Paint your "track."

· · · · · · ·

When Clay Sings. *Illustrated by Tom Bahti. Simon and Schuster, 1972. ISBN 0 684 18829 5*

This book explores and celebrates the pottery created by Indians of the Southwest and the process by which it's created.

ACTIVITIES:

► Visit a potter. Compare the way he or she makes pottery to the method Baylor describes in this book.

► Make pots. Let them dry. Bake them in a kiln and decorate them.

· · · · · · ·

Your Own Best Secret Place. *Illustrated by Peter Parnall. Scribner, 1991. ISBN 0 684 1611 7*

Some of these places are private and a few are shared with a friend, even a new one, but they're all secret. Baylor describes some that have had meaning for her.

ACTIVITY: Make up your own fantastic secret place. Draw or write about it.

Jan Brett

HER LIFE

Jan Brett was born in Massachusetts and lives there now, in the town of Norwood, with her husband, Joe Hearne. Because Joe plays in the Boston Symphony, they move to the Berkshires each summer to be near Tanglewood, where the symphony plays.

HER WORK

Brett's work is detailed and intricate. Often a sub-plot occurs in the frames around the edges of the pages. Her plots are playful and often humorous. She usually works from live models when drawing her characters.

THINGS TO DO WITH HER WORK

▶ Look at the different ways Brett uses the frames of her books to help tell the story. Try framing one of your stories that way.

▶ What clues do you use to identify a book illustrated by Brett?

▶ Brett sends out a newsletter about her work. Write to her to get your name on her mailing list.

▶ Visit Brett's Web site at **www.janbrett.com**/.

BOOKS & ACTIVITIES

Annie & the Wild Animals. Houghton Mifflin Books for Children, 1993. ISBN 0 395 37800 1

Annie's cat is missing and she badly wants another pet. She puts out corn cakes to lure other animals, but each proves undesirable. Fortunately her cat returns with kittens.

ACTIVITY: Go through the book again, this time watching the action in the frames. Make a timetable showing what's going on in the main pictures and in the frames such as the following:

Within the Frames	Taffy behaves strangely	Taffy finds a hole in a tree	Moose are near Taffy's tree
In the Main Pictures	Taffy behaves strangely	Annie misses Taffy	Annie puts out food

Berlioz the Bear. *Putnam's Sons Books for Young Readers, 1991. ISBN 0 399 22248 0*

The orchestra is going to play in the town square, and everyone's getting ready, but Berlioz is bothered by a persistent buzz in his bass. That's not the only problem–the bandwagon gets stuck in a rut, and the mule that's pulling it refuses to budge. Every attempt to move him fails until the buzz in the bass turns out to be a bee.

ACTIVITY: Listen to a bass fiddle, then listen to recordings of an orchestra and listen for the bass.

. . . .

Christmas Trolls. *G. P. Putnam's Sons Books for Young Readers, 1993. ISBN 0 399 22507 2*

Treva is hunting down objects that are missing from her home. She suspects the trolls, because they're up to all sorts of tricks in an effort to celebrate Christmas. As in her other troll books, Brett has included an underground subplot.

ACTIVITY: Compare trolls to other small people, such as elves, gnomes, fairies, and brownies.

First Dog. *Harcourt Brace & Co., 1992. ISBN 0 15 227651 3*

Paleowolf and Kip the cave boy have a working relationship in prehistoric times.

Activity: Find pictures of some of the cave paintings from France.

. . . .

Fritz and the Beautiful Horses. *Houghton Mifflin Books for Children,1987. ISBN 0 395 45356 9*

Fritz, a shaggy pony, isn't allowed inside the walled city. Only the beautiful horses can go there. When a bridge collapses, however, it's Fritz who brings children and their parents together.

ACTIVITY: Find out more about walled cities. Are there any walled cities still in existence?

Goldilocks & the Three Bears. *G. P. Putnam's Sons Books for Young Readers, 1990. ISBN 0 399 22004 6*

Brett's version of the tale has many Scandinavian touches.

ACTIVITY: Before you read this book, tell the story as you remember it. Write it down or tape-record it. After you've read the book, compare your version with the one written by Brett. Compare both versions with other written versions of the story. Which one comes closest to yours?

. . . .

The Mitten: A Ukrainian Folktale. *G. P. Putnam's Sons Books for Young Readers, 1990. ISBN 0 399 21920 X*

A little boy loses his white mitten in the snow, and various animals (each larger than the previous one) take up residence in the mitten, which stretches to accommodate them. When a mouse enters, however, the whole thing literally blows apart.

ACTIVITIES:

►The grandmother's knitting holds and stretches very well. Bring in as many mittens as possible and compare them to the one in the book. Which of yours stretch best? Can you figure out why? Would any of them stretch enough to hold a small animal? Which animal?

► Use a large mitten and models of animals to retell the story.

. . . .

Town Mouse, Country Mouse. *G. P. Putnam's Sons Books for Young Readers, 1994. ISBN 0 399 22622 2*

This familiar fable is expanded and embellished as, this time, a country mouse couple and a city mouse couple carry out a house exchange, only to find themselves displeased and frightened by their alien worlds. Two of their pursuers, an owl and a cat, end up making a similar exchange at the end of the story. Here we go again.

ACTIVITY: Make a chart in which the best and worst aspects of living in the country and in the city are compared.

The Trouble with Trolls. *G. P. Putnam's Sons Books for Young Readers, 1992. ISBN 0 399 22336 3*

Treva and her dog, Tuffi, have a lot of trouble with trolls on their winter walk over the mountain, as one very determined troll wants Tuffi for a pet. Below the snow, we see the trolls getting ready for their new arrival.

ACTIVITY: Make a time line for this book in which the events going on above the ground are compared with the events going on under the ground.

. . . .

The Twelve Days of Christmas. *G. P. Putnam's Sons Books for Young Readers, 1990. ISBN 0 399 22197 2*

This book based on the folk song is beautifully illustrated and the frames show us a lovely romance.

ACTIVITY: Sing the song, then change it. Make it the 12 days of Halloween, or Valentine's Day, or the first day of school. Brainstorm for a list of possible gifts appropriate to your chosen day. Sing your version of the song.

The Wild Christmas Reindeer. *G. P. Putnam's Sons Books for Young Readers, 1990. ISBN 0 399 22192 1*

Teeka is asked by Santa to get the reindeer ready to fly, but that's not an easy job. These are wild reindeer, and Teeka's first approach is to show them who is the boss. She learns, and so do they.

ACTIVITY: Sing the song "Rudolph the Red-nosed Reindeer." Can you change the words to suit the action of this book?

John Burningham

HIS LIFE

John Burningham was born in Surrey, England, in 1936. His father was a salesman, so the family had to move frequently. John attended 10 different schools when he was growing up, including Summerhill, a very unconventional and progressive elementary school. He wasn't a very good student except when art and drawing were involved. He spent quite a bit of time with his grandparents and particularly loved the wonderful stories his grandfather made up for him. Both his grandmother and his mother read aloud to him often.

He met his future wife, Helen Oxenbury, while both were students at the London Central School of Art and Craft. Ms. Oxenbury is also a well-known writer and illustrator of children's books. The couple has three children: Emily, Lucy and William. They live in London where their large yard includes a bell tower and bits and pieces of several churches and other old buildings.

Once Burningham received a commission to illustrate Jules Verne's **Around the World in Eighty Days** and decided to try to duplicate the voyage described in the book. Things did not go smoothly and when he landed at Heathrow Airport in London again, he knelt down on the tarmac and kissed the ground, vowing never to travel again. He loves good wine, collecting antiques, and his work.

HIS WORK

Burningham's often wispy, whimsical illustrations are full of movement and action. He works on a variety of materials, so his illustrations frequently have great texture and color although they're cartoonish in nature. The white space on his pages helps his creations look isolated and forlorn, and his character illustrations express emotion with an economy of line.

His work is characteristically understated both in text and illustrations. Often its ironic tone can be observed only by contrasting the action in the pictures with that described in the text. Many of his plots center around lonely children who are ignored or put down by adults. In **Come Away from the Water, Shirley,** Shirley's fantasy adventures are full of color and action while the juxtaposed pages showing her parents on the beach are pale and subdued. His fantasies are stated in a matter-of-fact, deadpan manner which make them funnier and more believable.

Many of Burningham's books poke fun at authority figures. In books such as **Courtney,** the animals are more adult and more competent than the older people in the story. The children also show more maturity than their parents do. Snobbishness and middle-class values are the targets in that book. In **John Patrick Norman McHennessy** Burningham's target is an overbearing teacher. His illustrations in that book are bolder and more colorful than usual.

BOOKS & ACTIVITIES
·········

Aldo. *Crown Books for Young Readers, 1992.*
ISBN 0 517 58701 7

A shy, inhibited child becomes a daring and adventurous person when she's with her imaginary rabbit friend, Aldo, a Harvey look-alike. Together they walk tightropes and take rowboat rides. Sometimes, when things are going well, she forgets about Aldo, but she knows she can always rely on him when she needs him.

ACTIVITY: Read the book Jessica, by Kevin Henkes (see page 206), about a little girl with an imaginary friend.
·········

Avocado Baby. *HarperCollins Children's Books, 1982.*
ISBN 0 690 04244 2

A weak and tiny baby suddenly begins to thrive when he's fed avocados. Soon he reaches superhuman status.

ACTIVITY: Find out what vitamins and minerals are in avocados and sample some avocado dip with cut-up vegetables.
·········

Borka: Adventures of a Goose with No Feathers. *Crown Books for Young Readers, 1994. ISBN 0 517 58020 9*

The solution to the problem of lost feathers is to wear a sweater. This is a Kate Greenaway Award-winning book.

ACTIVITY: Examine different kinds of feathers with a magnifying glass. Record your observations.
·········

Come Away from the Water, Shirley. *HarperCollins Children's Books, 1977. ISBN 0 690 01361 2*

Shirley's trip into the sea is only in her imagination as her cautious parents stay on the beach. Her mother shouts admonitions, while her father snoozes on the beach.

ACTIVITY: Compare this book to Tar Beach by Faith Ringgold.

THINGS TO DO WITH HIS WORK

► Look for places where Burningham makes jabs at authorities, especially parents and teachers.

► Notice words and expressions that are British in nature.

Courtney. *Crown Books for Young Readers, 1994.*
ISBN 0 517 59883 3

The children have begged for a dog, and in spite of their parents' instructions to get a proper one, they bring home Courtney, a mongrel. Courtney, however, is a dog of accomplishment: He cooks, plays the violin, and even rescues the baby from a fire. When he disappears, the parents conclude that you just can't rely on dogs that aren't thoroughbreds.

ACTIVITY: Courtney is certainly well-trained. Write about the kind of life you'd have if Courtney lived with you.
······

First Steps: Letters, Numbers, Colors, Opposites. *Candlewick Press, 1994. ISBN 1 56402 205 6*

Burningham's humor and twists give this concept book its unique perspectives.

ACTIVITY: Look at other counting and alphabet books and decide what the theme is for each of them.

Granpa. *Crown Books for Young Readers, 1984. ISBN 0 517 55643 X*

A little girl and her grandfather enjoy playing and being together, often sitting in his easy chair. Later, we see that the chair is empty and the little girl is sad. Still later, she's sharing some of their pursuits with a younger child. Granpa is one of Burningham's more pensive books.

ACTIVITIES:

► Decide what might have happened to Granpa.

► Compare this book to Tomie dePaola's book **Tom.**

. . . .

Hey! Get Off Our Train. *Crown Books for Young Readers, 1990. ISBN 0 517 57643 0*

A mother interrupts her son's play with a toy train and sends him off to bed where his dream involves a train trip with his dog. Along the way, many animals join them. To the command, "Hey! Get off our train!" each endangered animal pleas to be allowed onboard to escape.

ACTIVITY: Make a list of endangered animals from this book, then find out about other endangered animals that are not in this book. Make a train with your animals onboard.

. . . .

John Patrick Norman McHennessy: The Boy Who Was Always Late. *Crown Books for Young Readers, 1987. ISBN 0 517 56805 5*

The road to learning is beset with dangers, and John Patrick Norman McHennessy encounters many of them on his way to school. His teacher refuses to accept his outrageous excuses for being late and tells him that there are no such things. When he gets to school one day without incident, he finds his teacher being kidnapped by a gorilla, but he doesn't worry because he knows there are no such things.

ACTIVITY: If you were a friend of John Patrick Norman McHennessey, what advice or help would you give him?

Mr. Gumpy's Motor Car. *HarperCollins Children's Books, 1976. ISBN 0 14 050300 5*

One after another, the animals pile into Mr. Gumpy's car, but when it gets stuck in the mud, nobody wants to get out and push, and each one has a wonderful excuse.

ACTIVITY: These passengers have all sorts of excuses for not helping Mr. Gumpy. Make a list of the jobs you have to do that you don't like. Beside each item, write an excuse that just might work.

. . . .

Mr. Gumpy's Outing. *Henry Holt & Co. Books for Young Readers, 1990. ISBN 0 8050 0708 3*

In this story it's a boat the animals pile onto, and Mr. Gumpy's warnings to behave themselves go unheeded as, one after another, the animals come onboard and misbehave.

ACTIVITY: Compare this book to **Who Sank the Boat,** by Pamela Allen (G. P. Putnam's Son's Books for Young Readers, 1985. ISBN 0 698 20576 6).

. . . .

Trubloff: The Mouse Who Wanted to Play the Balalaika. *Crown Books for Young Readers, 1994. ISBN 0 517 59435 8*

This tale, set in Central Europe, centers around a mouse with musical aspirations.

ACTIVITY: Invite people to your school to play various musical instruments for you.

Eric Carle

HIS LIFE

Eric Carle was born in Syracuse, New York, in 1929. His German immigrant parents tried to make a living in America, but, in 1935, the family went back to Germany. His father was drafted into the German army, and Eric went to school in Stuttgart. The American kindergarten he had attended here in the states was lively and colorful, but the German schools at that time were dark and oppressive.

His artistic talent was obvious, however, and in 1952, he returned to the United States determined to make a living as an artist. Leo Lionni helped him get a job as a graphic designer in an advertising agency. Bill Martin Jr. saw an ad Eric had done and asked him to illustrate his new children's picture book, **Brown Bear, Brown Bear,** and Carle's picture book career was launched. At first Carle illustrated books written by others, but, after **Very Hungry Caterpillar** was created, he wrote as well as illustrated his books. He lives with his wife, Bobbie, in Northampton, Massachusetts.

HIS WORK

Carle makes his own paper for his illustrations by pasting sheets of tissue paper on white paper. He then paints and draws freely on the tissue paper, creating textures and patterns. He cuts images for his illustrations from those sheets of paper to form his collages.

Usually he finds some way of exploding our concept of a picture book as a two-dimensional creation. Sometimes he does this by making holes in the pages, as he did in **Very Hungry Caterpillar.** Other times he uses foldout pages, and in **Very Quiet Cricket** and **Very Lonely Firefly** he added sound and lights.

Most of his books explore some small creature's life, and although his plots are fantastic, the stories usually contain solid scientific information as well.

THINGS TO DO WITH HIS WORK

► Carle often uses layers of tissue paper which he has drawn or painted on to create his illustrations. Try creating your own effects using tissue paper.

► A video about Carle and his work is available from Scholastic. Watch the video and see if it helps you understand or like Carle's work even better.

► Carle has written a "Very" book about a caterpillar, a cricket and a spider. Make a storyboard (book plan) for another "Very" book you think he should try next. What animal will be the main character? What will it be trying to do? What other animals will be in the story? What facts about those animals will you need to know first? What repeated phrases will you use?

BOOKS & ACTIVITIES

·······

All Around Us. *Picture Book Studio, 1986. ISBN 0 88708 016 2*

These are three wordless picture panels in which three areas of the earth are explored: the sky, the above-ground and the below-ground. The objects shown are simple trees, ships, fish, etc.

ACTIVITY: Display the strips one day at a time. Suggest that children draw or paint their own strips showing more of the same area or a different area.

·······

Do You Want to Be My Friend? *HarperCollins Children's Books, 1987. ISBN 0 06 443127 4*

In this book for very young children, we see the tail of each animal before we turn to find out which animal the mouse wants for a friend.

ACTIVITY: In nature, which of the animals that the mouse finds would be likely to become a mouse's friend? Which ones might eat it?

·······

Dragons Dragons & Other Creatures That Never Were. *G. P. Putnam's Sons Books for Young Readers, 1991. ISBN 0 399 22105 0*

This anthology of poetry contains work by many poets all about fabulous beasts.

ACTIVITY: Find a poem in another anthology about a dragon or similar creature, and then draw or paint a picture to go with it. Then do the same thing in reverse: Draw or paint a creature, and then find a story, song, or poem that most closely fits your illustration. Which is easier?

·······

Draw Me a Star. *G. P. Putnam's Sons Books for Young Readers, 1992. ISBN 0 399 21877 7*

An artist draws a star that asks him to draw a sun, and so on, through a chain of drawings.

ACTIVITY: How do you usually draw a star? Does anyone in your classroom do it differently? Try drawing stars that have one more point than yours do. Use Carle's method to draw his kind of star.

The Grouchy Ladybug. *HarperCollins Children's Books, 1986. ISBN 0 06 443116 9*

A ladybug challenges ever-bigger animals to a fight as the time of day (exhibited on each page) goes on. Eventually a whale flips the ladybug with its tale with such strength that the ladybug ends up back on the leaf where it started.

ACTIVITY: Using large sheets of oaktag, cut out a face-sized oval on each sheet in a spot where a child's face would be. Around the ovals paint the bodies of the creatures challenged by the ladybug. Act out the story using these character cards.

·······

Have You Seen My Cat? *Picture Book Studio, 1987 ISBN 0 88708 054 5*

A boy loses his cat and sets off to find it. He sees many other large cats but none is his pet. Returning home, he finds his cat with her kittens.

ACTIVITY: Compare this story with Jan Brett's **Annie and the Wild Animals** (see page 181).

·······

A House for Hermit Crab. *Picture Book Studio, 1991. ISBN 0 88708 056 1*

It's the nature of a hermit crab to move into bigger and bigger houses (shells) as it grows. This one, however, is particularly reluctant to leave his home because his friends helped decorate it.

ACTIVITY: Send for a hermit crab from a science supply houses. These animals are not difficult to keep, but are fascinating to watch.

I See a Song. *HarperCollins Children's Books, 1973. ISBN 0 690 43307 7*

In this wordless book, a song is played, and the feelings and visions it invokes are shown.

ACTIVITY: Listen to a piece of music you like, and on a large sheet of paper, react to the music by drawing or painting as you listen.

....

The Mixed-Up Chameleon. *HarperCollins Children's Books, 1984. ISBN 0 690 04397 X*

A chameleon tries to be many animals before deciding that his original identity was the best.

ACTIVITY: If you could change into an animal, which animal would you choose? Draw a picture of yourself slowly changing into that animal.

....

One, Two, Three to the Zoo. *G. P. Putnam's Sons Books for Young Readers, 1990. ISBN 0 399 21970 6*

In this counting book, we watch a train bearing animals to a zoo.

ACTIVITY: Compare this book with other counting books you find. Which ones do you think work best? Which ones are trying to teach people about numbers? Which ones have good stories? What is this book trying to do?

....

Pancakes, Pancakes. *Scholastic, 1992. ISBN 0 590 44453 0*

A little boy wants pancakes for breakfast and will accept no substitutes.

ACTIVITY: Are pancakes good for you? What food group are they in? If the boy in this book eats pancakes for breakfast, what other things should he eat for breakfast to give him a balanced diet? Do the same thing for the foods you usually eat for breakfast. Who has the most balanced diet, you or the boy?

Papa, Please Get the Moon for Me. *Picture Book Studio, 1991. ISBN 0 88708 026 X*

A little girl wants the moon, so her father climbs a very tall ladder to get it. He gets to the moon, but finds it's too large to bring home.

ACTIVITY: Find other stories or books where characters want the moon. Do they get it? Do they get something else instead?

....

Rooster's Off to See the World. *Picture Book Studio, 1991. ISBN 0 88708 042 1*

In this counting book, animals gather to go with Rooster on his journey. One by one they come, and one by one they tire and leave.

ACTIVITY: Use this pattern to write your own counting story.

....

Secret Birthday Message. *HarperCollins Children's Books, 1986. ISBN 0 06 443099 5*

We follow the directions on a message through (often literally through) holes and shapes in the page to find a birthday surprise.

ACTIVITY: Make a set of similar directions for someone else to follow to find a surprise you made for them.

....

The Tiny Seed. *Picture Book Studio, 1991. ISBN 0 88708 015 4*

This book follows a seed from birth to flower to seed again.

ACTIVITY: Take a "seed walk." Before gathering a seed, see if you can decide how it got to that particular place.

....

Today Is Monday. *G. P. Putnam's Sons Books for Young Readers, 1993. ISBN 0 399 21966 8*

This book uses a common folksong as a backdrop for its story about animals who show up for spaghetti on Tuesday, soup on Wednesday, etc.

ACTIVITY: Make up a menu for each day of the week, listing healthy foods that you like.

The Very Busy Spider. *G. P. Putnam's Sons Books for Young Readers, 1989. ISBN 0 399 21166 7*

This book's three-dimensional look is created by the threads of the spider's web, which are raised from the page. One after another, animals ask the spider to come and play. The patterned text makes this story easy to read and worth the effort.

ACTIVITY: Study the webs of as many spiders as possible. Dip string in plaster of Paris or glue to make spider web patterns of your own.

. . . .

The Very Hungry Caterpillar. *G. P. Putnam's Sons Books for Young Readers, 1986. ISBN 0 399 21301 5*

This classic book has delighted many generations of children as they traveled through Carle's cut out and variously sized pages with a caterpillar.

ACTIVITY: Divide the children into groups and ask them to find different ways to present this book as a play. Have them use props, puppets, cut outs, or whatever else they need to make their presentations different.

The Very Quiet Cricket. *G. P. Putnam's Sons Books for Young Readers, 1990. ISBN 0 399 21885 8*

In this lovely patterned book, we watch the insects of the day and night, as a little cricket who wants to make a sound finds his voice and a mate, and we hear the sound.

ACTIVITY: Take a tape recorder to a quiet spot and push record. After fifteen minutes, listen to your recording. Can you hear insect sounds, bird sounds, people sounds?

Barbara Cooney

HER LIFE

Barbara Cooney was born in Brooklyn, New York. Her mother encouraged her artistic abilities, and she attended Smith College and then art school in New York. While she was in art school, she received her first commission to illustrate a picture book. Since then she has illustrated more than 100 books. Many of her books were written by others, but a few are all her own. She married a doctor, Charles Porter, and they raised four children in Massachusetts before moving to Damariscotta, Maine, where she now lives. She has said that her book Hattie and the Wild Waves is largely autobiographical.

 HER WORK

Cooney uses acrylics for most of her illustrations, although some of her earliest work used scratchboard techniques. She's capable of creating pictures with great depth, as in some of the landscapes in Miss Rumphius. Most of her earlier work was to illustrate books written by others. In later years, however, she has both illustrated and written several books.

 BOOKS & ACTIVITIES

BOOKS WRITTEN & ILLUSTRATED BY BARBARA COONEY

. . . .

Hattie and the Wild Waves. *Viking Children's Books, 1990. ISBN 0 670 83056 9*

A very privileged little girl tells us of her life at the turn of the century, when her extended family vacations on Coney Island and Long Island. This story is based on the life of Cooney's mother.

ACTIVITY: Find photographs of present-day Brooklyn and compare them with the illustrations in this book.

. . . .

Island Boy. *Puffin Books, 1991. ISBN 0 14 050756 6*

A man builds his home and establishes his family on an island off the coast of Maine in the 1800s. As the family grows and prospers, many travel far from their island home, but one, Matthias, returns to his birthplace to raise his own family.

ACTIVITY: This book mentions hunting birds for their feathers. Find out about when this happened and what it did to the bird population.

 THINGS TO DO WITH HER WORK

▶ Put Cooney's books in chronological order according to the date they were published. Do you see any changes in her work?

▶ Notice the way she changes her illustration style to suit the mood or the time of the books.

. . . .

Miss Rumphius. *Puffin Books, 1985. ISBN 0 14 050539 3*

The author tells us of her great Aunt Alice who, charged by her father to make the world more beautiful, finds a way to do it only when she has grown old. She scatters lupine seeds and covers the land with beauty.

ACTIVITY: Make a list of things people could do to make the world more beautiful. Which ones could you do?

BOOKS WRITTEN BY OTHER AUTHORS & ILLUSTRATED BY BARBARA COONEY

•••••••

Bedard, Michael. **Emily.** *Bantam Doubleday Dell Books for Young Readers, 1992 ISBN 0 385 30697 8*

Poet Emily Dickinson establishes a slight relationship with a new neighbor, and we glimpse the poet through this neighbor's eyes.

ACTIVITY: Find and read a poem by Dickinson that starts out "A little bird came up the walk."

•••••••

Boulton, Jane. **Only Opal.** *G. P. Putnam's Sons Books for Young Readers, 1994. ISBN 0 399 21990 0*

This book features excerpts from the diary of a very remarkable little girl who was sent to live with a foster family in a lumber camp in Oregon at the turn of the century.

Activity: Opal talks differently than you do. Try saying something about yourself the way you think Opal would.

•••••••

Brown, Margaret Wise. **The Little Fir Tree.** *HarperCollins Children's Books, 1985. ISBN 0 06 443083 9*

Every year, at Christmas, a father digs up a fir tree and takes it into the house where his whole family, including a little lame boy, enjoys and decorates it. When Christmas is over, the father replants the little fir tree. One year, no one comes to bring the tree inside, and the tree is lonely until the boy, now grown and well, brings everyone outside to admire the tree they've always loved.

ACTIVITY: Compare this story to **The Year of the Perfect Christmas Tree,** by Gloria Houston.

•••••••

Chaucer, Geoffrey. **Chanticleer and the Fox.** *HarperCollins Children's Books, 1982. ISBN 0 690 18561 8*

Cooney received the Caldecott Award for this version of Chaucer's fable "The Nun's Priest Tale."

ACTIVITY: Compare the rooster in this book to the one in **The Rooster's Gift,** by Pam Conrad.

Hall, Donald. **Ox-Cart Man.** *Puffin Books, 1983. ISBN 0 14 050441 9*

The cycle of the seasons is the focus of this gentle book about a farming family in New Hampshire in the 1800s.

ACTIVITY: Make a list of the things the Ox-Cart Man brought home from Portsmouth. Brainstorm for things the family can do with each thing he brought.

•••••••

Houston, Gloria M. **The Year of the Perfect Christmas Tree.** *Dial Books for Young Readers, 1988. ISBN 0 8037 0299 X*

This story, set in Appalachia, tells how a family kept its promise to its village and to itself by delivering the town's perfect Christmas tree.

ACTIVITY: How would you decorate that perfect Christmas tree? Would you use many different colors or just a few? Design your own perfect Christmas tree.

•••••••

Kesselman, Wendy. **Emma.** *HarperCollins Children's Books, 1985. ISBN 0 06 443077 4*

Emma's younger relatives don't see why this 72-year-old woman has to find a new dimension to her life. She finds it in painting.

ACTIVITY: Find out about other people who started new careers when they were old.

•••••••

McLerran, Alice. **Roxaboxen.** *Puffin Books, 1992 ISBN 0 14 054475 5*

Children of a previous generation, who live in the American southwest, develop their own make-believe town, with customs and laws. Later, the memory of Roxaboxen stays with them all.

ACTIVITY: Make your own town on the playground, using whatever materials you can find on the ground to create walls and roads.

*Preston, Edna M. **Squawk to the Moon, Little Goose.** Puffin Books, 1985. ISBN 0 14 050546 6*

A goose has been accused of "crying wolf" many times by the farmer, but, when she's about to become prey to a fox, she uses her fears to good advantage.

ACTIVITY: This story is fun to act out. Divide the children into groups of three or four to perform various versions of it.

·······

*Seeger, Ruth C. **American Folk Songs for Children.** Bantam Doubleday Dell Books for Young Readers, 1980. ISBN 0 385 15788 6*

This book is a collection of all types of good songs for singing.

ACTIVITY: Sing some of the songs.

*Yolen, Jane. **Letting Swift River Go.** Little, Brown & Co., Children's Books, 1992. ISBN 0 316 96899 4*

The building of Quabbin Reservoir in Massachusetts resulted in a large water supply for Boston, but also resulted in the flooding of four little towns along with Swift River.

ACTIVITY: Imagine what would happen if your town were to be destroyed as Sally Jane's was. You would, of course, be able to take your things and your furniture with you to a new place. What would you miss? What would be good about such a move?

Donald Crews

HIS LIFE

Donald Crews, one of four children, was born on August 30, 1938, in Newark, New Jersey, the son of Asa and Marahanna Crews. His father was African American and his mother was white. Marahanna Crews was a skilled craftswoman and dressmaker, and she encouraged all her children in their artistic endeavors. Crews produced his first book, We Read A to Z, while he was in the army in Germany. Crews married Ann Jonas on January 28, 1964. They met when they were both art students at Cooper Union in New York City. He and his wife both create children's picture books although they don't work on the same books. They live in the top three floors of a brownstone in Brooklyn, New York. His studio is on the top floor; hers is on the second floor. Donald and Ann have two daughters who are now grown-up. The couple's daughter Nina is also an author/illustrator of children's books.

THINGS TO DO WITH HIS WORK

▶ Looking at as many books by Crews as possible, what can you decide about what he thinks is important? Notice his use of line and color. How does he show motion?

▶ Look at the people Crews uses in the books. How many faces can you clearly see?

HIS WORK

Donald Crews' illustrations often omit some details, making them take on a poster-like appearance. Many of his books develop concepts that relate to classrom activities. Two of his books are autobiographical.

BOOKS & ACTIVITIES

Bicycle Race. *Greenwillow Books, 1985. ISBN 0 688 05171 5*

We join a crowd watching 12 bicycle racers who are clearly numbered and wearing differently colored clothing as they warm up, line up and take off. Some race to the finish without apparent difficulty, but one racer gets a flat tire. Number nine comes from behind to win.

ACTIVITY: Have a bicycle race on your playground. Have separate contests for bicycles, tricycles, scooters, and roller skates. Put numbers like the ones in the book on the backs of the contestants.

Bigmama's. *Greenwillow Books, 1991. ISBN 0 688 09950 5*

In this story, Crews remembers a trip his family made every summer to his grandparents' house in the country. The trip was made by train and always provided the excitement and satisfaction he hoped for. The last page shows Crews standing against a city landscape as he recalls times at Bigmama's house.

ACTIVITY: Compare the family reunion in this book with the one in **The Relatives Came,** by Cynthia Rylant (see page 233).

Carousel. *Greenwillow Books, 1982. ISBN 0 688 00908 5*

A merry-go-round starts up, gains speed, slows down, and stops.

ACTIVITY: In this book, Crews shows motion. Look in his other books that feature moving things. Does he indicate the motion in the same way? Why do you think he might use different techniques to show motion? Find the work of other illustrators and cartoonists, and notice the way they show that things are moving.

....

Flying. *Greenwillow Books, 1986. ISBN 0 688 04318 6*

A propeller-driven plane takes off and flies over cities and countryside before landing again at sunset.

ACTIVITY: Draw or paint airplanes from the inside looking out, from the outside looking in, or in any way you can think of.

....

Freight Train. *Morrow Junior Books, 1992. ISBN 0 688 11701 5*

Car by car, a freight train is assembled on the track. Each car is vividly colored, and the color and type of freight car is named. After the train is complete, Crews sets it in motion, and we see it through beautifully designed pages as it crosses the countryside and city landscape.

ACTIVITY: Visit a railroad station or a model train exhibit, or just look carefully at a freight train that's moving or still. When you have looked and listened carefully, write and draw pictures about trains.

....

Harbor. *Greenwillow Books, 1982. ISBN 0 688 00862 3*

Through illustration and brief text, Crews inventories all the types of boats and ships, both pleasure and business, that one might see at a busy harbor. Even better, he includes a silhouette of each kind of boat with its name in a pictorial glossary at the end of the book.

ACTIVITY: Use the silhouettes on plain playing cards to make a visual discrimination or memory game.

Parade. *Greenwillow Books, 1983. ISBN 0 688 01996 X*

We watch as participants and spectators gather for a parade. It's a full-blown parade with a color guard, drum major, marching band, floats, baton-twirlers, old cars, and bicyclists.

ACTIVITY: Play a memory game in which each participant lists one thing that could be seen in a parade. Each successive player must repeat all the things named before, in the correct order, before adding a new one.

....

School Bus. *Puffin Books, 1985. ISBN 0 14 050549 0*

The day starts with a fleet of school buses, of all sorts and types, in a parking lot. As the day continues, they move throughout the town and countryside, picking up their passengers and depositing them at school, then waiting for the school day to conclude so they can do the same thing in reverse.

ACTIVITY: Trace the route each child takes to get to school on a city map. Use different symbols to show each child's mode of transportation.

....

Shortcut. *Greenwillow Books, 1992. ISBN 0 688 06436 1*

The kids we met previously in **Bigmama's** decide to take a shortcut home even though they know the danger of walking on the railroad track. When the train comes, it terrifies everyone, even the readers.

ACTIVITY: The kids in this story took a foolish chance. What should they have done? What do you think they'll do next time? Why are train tracks sometimes more dangerous than city streets?

....

Ten Black Dots. *Greenwillow Books, 1986. ISBN 0 688 06067 6*

This book is a simple counting book.

ACTIVITY: Cut out a series of small, black circles. Paste them on drawing paper in interesting groups. Use crayons or paint to make those circles part of bigger pictures.

Truck. *Morrow Junior Books, 1991. ISBN 0 688 10481 9*

A truck is loaded and then driven across super-highways and through city streets before it reaches the place where its merchandise is unloaded.

ACTIVITY: Make a chart showing different kinds of trucks and what each of them can be used for. Bring in toy trucks and categorize them in as many ways as possible.

We Read: A to Z. *Greenwillow Books, 1984. ISBN 0 688 03843 3*

This story is Crews' alphabet book, but he's less interested in presenting the alphabet than in showing us, through geometrical shapes, what his position words mean.

ACTIVITY: Cut construction paper into geometric shapes. Place the shapes against another piece of paper to demonstrate the meaning of a word or words. See if a partner can figure out the words you are showing. Try: under, on top of, over, beneath, against, and beside. Make a list of the words that work.

Tomie dePaola

HIS LIFE

Tomie dePaola was born in Meriden, Connecticut, in 1934. He went to art school in Brooklyn and in Oakland, California. His first book was published in 1965 and since then he has published more than 180 books.

THINGS TO DO WITH HIS WORK

▶ Divide his books into as many categories as possible. Represent your categories with overlapping circles in a diagram such as the one below. Write the titles of his books in the circles. If they would fit in more than one category, try to place them where the circles overlap.

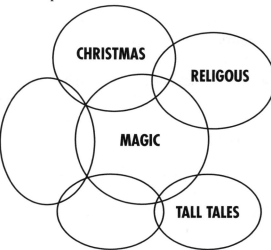

▶ Look at the books dePaola has created. Can you tell anything more about him from the books he wrote? What do you think is his favorite holiday? What things does he think are important? Where do you suppose his family came from?

HIS WORK

dePaola's artwork is easily identifiable, with strong design and stylized characters. His short, rounded characters are both comforting and comical. For his Strega Nona stories, he uses the colors and terrain of Italy. **Strega** is based on a folktale, as are several of his other books. He usually produces one Christmas book each year, as well as one religious story or legend. Some of his books, such as **The Art Lesson, Watch Out for the Chicken Feet in Your Soup,** and **Nana Upstairs and Nana Downstairs,** are autobiographical.

BOOKS & ACTIVITIES
· · · · · · ·
Andy, That's My Name. *Prentice, 1988. ISBN 0 13 036731 1*

Andy has spelled out his name with blocks which he carries in his wagon. Big boys add and subtract letters to make other words out of his name.

ACTIVITY: What words can you make out of your own name? Which person in class has the most letters in his or her first name? Is that person able to make more words?
· · · · · · ·
The Art Lesson. *G. P. Putnam's Sons Books for Young Readers, 1994. ISBN 0 399 22761 X*

Tomie loves art until he goes to school, where the art teacher's narrow definition of art conflicts with Tomie's previous experiences.

ACTIVITY: Take an "art walk" around your school, looking carefully at the art displayed there. Which artworks do you think were created Tomie's way, and which artworks were made according to strict directions?

Big Anthony and the Magic Ring. *Harcourt Brace & Co., 1979. ISBN 0 15 207124 5*

Big Anthony wants to become handsome and desirable to women, and Strega Nona's magic ring makes his wish come true, but it turns out to be a disaster because the village girls won't leave him alone.

ACTIVITY: Use this book as a source for writing your own story about getting a wish fulfilled but not liking what you get.

....

Charlie Needs a Cloak. *Simon & Schuster Books for Young Readers, 1982. ISBN 0 671 66466 2*

Charlie, the shepherd, wears a raggedy cloak. It's raggedy partly because a sheep keeps nibbling at it. Charlie sets about making himself a new cloak, and we watch each step. The actions of that same sheep and an enterprising mouse provide the humor in what might otherwise be a dull book.

ACTIVITY: Make a time line or chart showing what Charlie, the mouse and the sheep are doing on each page of the story.

....

The Cloud Book. *Holiday House, 1975. ISBN 0 8234 0259 2*

This book provides a simple explanation of the various types of clouds and the effects they create on the earth.

ACTIVITY: Go outside and look at the clouds in the sky today. Draw and label as many types as you can see. Do the same thing tomorrow. Estimate how many days you would have to watch the sky to find all the different kinds of clouds in the book.

....

The Clown of God. *Harcourt Brace & Co., 1978. ISBN 0 15 219175 5*

This legend about an artist, in this case a juggler, who offers his art as a gift is familiar, but dePaola gives it a unique twist.

ACTIVITY: Compare this story to the Christmas song "The Little Drummer Boy."

The Comic Adventures of Old Mother Hubbard and Her Dog. *Harcourt Brace & Co., 1981. ISBN 0 15 219542 4*

This nursery rhyme is usually shortened in Mother Goose books. This book, however, includes all of the verses accompanied by dePaola's humorous illustrations.

ACTIVITY: Find another Mother Goose rhyme with several verses and make your own book about it.

....

An Early American Christmas. *Holiday House, 1987. ISBN 0 8234 0617 2*

dePaola speculates on what the celebration of Christmas might have been like for a German family living in a New England village where Christmas was not celebrated by most of the villagers.

ACTIVITY: Choose a holiday which your family makes a big deal of. List the traditions that your family carries out for that holiday. Make a book or story about it.

....

The Family Christmas Tree Book. *Holiday House, 1980. ISBN 0 8234 0416 1*

This nonfiction book describes the origins of the various customs that surround the Christmas tree.

ACTIVITY: What holidays are the biggest celebrations in your family? What customs does your family share? Do you know where each custom started?

....

Fin M'Coul: The Giant of Knockmany Hill. *Holiday House, 1981. ISBN 0 8234 0384 X*

Fin and his clever wife outwit the fiercest giant in all of Ireland.

ACTIVITY: What would the fiercest giant in your community be like? What damage or good could he do to your community? Who would outwit your giant?

The First Christmas. *G. P. Putnam's Sons Books for Young Readers, 1984. ISBN 0 399 21070 9*

dePaola uses pop-up pictures to illustrate his story of the nativity.

ACTIVITY: Examine this and other pop-up books. What technique do they use to make their illustrations stand up? Try their ways with some constructions of your own. Invent your own ways.

....

Four Stories for Four Seasons. *Simon & Schuster Books for Young Readers, 1993. ISBN 0 671 88633 9*

Four friends celebrate the seasons in this gentle book.

ACTIVITY: Examine these illustrations for the seasons. Look at the work of other picture book artists who have drawn seasonal pictures. Describe to someone else how you would show winter, spring, summer, and fall. What place would you draw for each season? What objects would you put in? How would you show snow, rain and sunshine?

....

Helga's Dowry: A Troll Love Story. *Harcourt Brace & Co., 1977. ISBN 0 15 233701 6*

Helga has no dowry and she can't marry Lars without one, but the clever troll woman acquires one her way.

ACTIVITY: Look at Jan Brett's book **The Trouble with Trolls** (see page 183). Compare her trolls to Helga and the other trolls in this book.

....

The Knight & the Dragon. *G. P. Putnam's Sons Books for Young Readers, 1980. ISBN 0 399 20707 4*

An inexperienced knight and an equally inexperienced dragon are about to have a major battle. A librarian and her books save the day.

ACTIVITY: Compare the dragon in this book to **The Reluctant Dragon,** by Kenneth Grahame.

The Legend of the Bluebonnet: An Old Tale of Texas. *G. P. Putnam's Sons Books for Young Readers, 1983. ISBN 0 399 20937 9*

An Indian girl makes a sacrifice of her beloved doll for the good of the village.

ACTIVITY: Find the wildflowers that grow in your area. Decide which is the most common and/or the most beautiful. Make up a story about how it could have come to exist.

....

Nana Upstairs and Nana Downstairs. *Puffin Books, 1978. ISBN 0 14 050290 4*

Two very old grandmothers, who live in the same house, are loved by the narrator. When one dies, the sight of a falling star consoles the child.

ACTIVITY: Find out about falling stars. Watch for a meteor shower in January or August.

....

Now One Foot, Now the Other. *G. P. Putnam's Sons Books for Young Readers, 1981. ISBN 0 399 20774 0*

A child is often told how his grandfather taught him to walk. Now the old man has suffered a stroke, and it's the child who shows him how to walk.

ACTIVITY: The grandfather in this story has had a stroke, or CVA. Find out more about this condition. Can people who have suffered a stroke act differently than they did before? What can you do to help?

....

Oliver Button is a Sissy. *Harcourt Brace & Co., 1979. ISBN 0 15 257852 8*

Oliver is no athlete, and the boys at school tease him. His father calls him a sissy. But Oliver is an artist, and the teasers end up admiring his dance.

ACTIVITY: Almost everybody gets teased about something. What do people tease you about? When does the teasing hurt? Who do you tease? Do you think your teasing hurts?

Pancakes for Breakfast. Harcourt Brace & Co., 1978. ISBN 0 15 259455 8

Making pancakes seems like a simple task, but an old woman who's trying to make some keeps being interrupted.

ACTIVITY: Have a pancake breakfast at school. How many different pancake recipes can you find? Which will you use? What utensils will you need? How many people will be there?

·······

The Popcorn Book. Holiday House, 1978. ISBN 0 8234 0314 9

One twin pops corn as another reads us interesting facts about it.

ACTIVITY: Pop corn and sell it to raise money for something important in or out of your classroom.

·······

The Prince of the Dolomites. Harcourt Brace & Co., 1980. ISBN 0 15 674432 5

A storyteller in Italy tells the village children a folktale about how a prince's love for the moon princess caused the mountains to turn into the beautiful colors we see today.

ACTIVITY: The Dolomites are mountains in Italy. What mountain range is nearest to where you live? Can you make up a story about how they came to be?

The Quicksand Book. Holiday House, 1977. ISBN 0 8234 0291 6

When Jungle Girl falls into quicksand, Jungle Boy seizes the opportunity to tell us all about quicksand. He even has charts for his presentation. Meanwhile, she sinks lower and lower.

ACTIVITY: Some of what Jungle Boy says is important for Jungle Girl to know. A lot of the rest may be interesting at some other time for Jungle Girl. Which is which?

Strega Nona. Simon & Schuster Books for Young Readers, 1979. ISBN 0 671 66283 X

Strega's servant, Big Anthony, longs to create the magic that Strega is able to do. But when he sets her magic pasta pot cooking, he can't stop it, and soon the village is inundated with pasta.

ACTIVITY: Find other stories about magic which, once started, is not possible to stop.

·······

Tony's Bread. G. P. Putnam's Sons Books for Young Readers, 1989. ISBN 0 399 21693 6

Tony makes fine bread in a small village where his only worry is keeping his daughter Serafina away from all her suitors. When a nobleman falls in love with Serafina, he sets Tony up as a baker in Milano, where Tony's competition also bakes fine bread. His solution is to create a new kind of colorful bread.

ACTIVITY: Have a bread-tasting party. Bring in as many different kinds of bread as possible. Provide cheese and sandwich ingredients. Make a picture graph showing which kinds of bread are the favorites.

·······

Watch Out for the Chicken Feet in Your Soup. Prentice, 1985. ISBN 0 13 945766 6

Joey is taking his friend Eugene for lunch at his grandmother's, but he has to warn him of the Italian woman's delicious but unusual cooking.

ACTIVITY: What's the strangest food you've ever heard of? What's the strangest food you've ever tasted?

Dr. Seuss

HIS LIFE

Dr. Seuss's real name was Theodore Geisel and he was born in Springfield, Massachusetts. He lived on Mulberry Street. His father was head of the park department for the city of Springfield, and his work included managing the city zoo. Geisel worked as a cartoonist for an oil company, and his contract with that company precluded most other work that he might have been able to do outside of the company. It didn't forbid creating children's books, however, so Geisel began writing and illustrating children's books.

When he complained that the basal reading books children were learning to read with were boring, educators explained that they used a list of words which were thought at the time to be the easiest words for children to learn. Geisel took the same list and created The Cat in the Hat, proving that simple books didn't have to be dull. This began a whole series of Beginner Books which made early reading more fun.

Dr. Seuss spent much of his life in California and died there in 1991.

HIS WORK

Dr. Seuss's first book, **To Think That I Saw It on Mulberry Street,** became a prototype for a theme he revisited in many books: That of a simple object or deed becoming more and more fantastic and complicated, until it's brought back to reality at the end of the story. Another plot device Seuss pursued was that of fable. His books **Thidwick, the Big-Hearted Moose, Horton Hatches the Egg** and **Horton Hears a Who** are all fables with a stated moral. Even **Bartholomew and the Oobleck** falls into that category, as well as into the category of fairy tale. **The King's Stilts** and **The Five Hundred Hats of Bartholomew Cubbins** are also modern fairy tales.

Seuss's rhyming text and outrageous names are other trademarks of his work, as is his ability to portray vast distances within a single picture.

THINGS TO DO WITH HIS WORK

▶ If you divide his books into the categories of fables, tall tales, fairy tales, and books for beginning readers, what books would fit in each category? Are there any books left over? Are there any books that go in more than one category?

▶ One of the things Dr. Seuss does very successfully is to create the sense of distance in his illustrations. Find the picture which you think shows the greatest distance. How did he do that? Compare it with choices made by others.

▶ For his easy-to-read books, Dr. Seuss used the Dolch list of easy-to-read words. Get a copy of that list and try to make up interesting sentences using only those words. Will pictures help to make them more interesting?

▶ In many of his books, Dr. Seuss seems to be giving us rules to live by. Which ones can you find? Do you think everyone should try to live by those rules?

▶ Sometimes Geisel wrote under another pseudonym: Theo LeSieg. Spell it backwards. When did he use that pseudonym? Who illustrated those books?

BOOKS & ACTIVITIES

·······

And to Think That I Saw It on Mulberry Street.
Random House, 1937. ISBN 0 394 84494 7

This is the first book written by Seuss and its plot format is a prototype for many of his later books: A child sees something simple, imagines it in ever more exaggerated forms and then ends up with the first simple object.

ACTIVITY: Look carefully at this book. Which is the first page where you see or hear something impossible? Write your answer on a secret piece of paper. Let others do the same thing and then compare your papers. Do you agree or disagree?

·······

Bartholomew and the Oobleck. *Random House, 1949. ISBN 0 394 80075 3*

A king is tired of the same old stuff coming out of the sky, so he commands his magicians to cause some new substance to fall. They create oobleck which is sticky and causes a terrible mess. Only the page boy, Bartholomew, dares to tell the king that he must say he's sorry.

ACTIVITY: Create oobleck. Using any safe materials you can find, create a substance which is green and sticky. Write down your recipe. Can others follow it and get the same result?

·······

The Butter Battle Book. *Random House, 1986. ISBN 0 394 86580 4*

It starts out as a simple argument between cities about which is the best side to butter your bread on. The argument quickly escalates, and soon the very survival of the planet is at stake.

ACTIVITY: If you were in this book, when would you try to stop the argument? What would you say? What could you do?

The Cat in the Hat. *Random House, 1987. ISBN 0 394 89218 6*

This is the first of Seuss's easy-to-read books. A cat comes unbidden into a house where two bored children sit. He creates a terrible mess, cleans it up just in time and departs before their mother comes home.

ACTIVITY: Compare this book with Chris Van Allsburg's **Jumanji.**

············

Cat in the Hat Comes Back. *Random House, 1958. ISBN 0 394 8002 8*

The cat returns with assistant cats from A to Z who make and clean up a mess again.

ACTIVITY: This book is a sequel to **The Cat in the Hat.** Find other books that have sequels. Make a chart showing your findings. Do you like the sequels as well as the first books? Put a star beside the titles you like best. Total the winners. How many were sequels?

············

The Five Hundred Hats of Bartholomew Cubbins.
Vanguard, 1938. ISBN 08149 0388 6

Everyone knows you're supposed to take off your hat before the king, and Bartholomew tries to do so, but every time he removes a hat, another hat just like the first appears on his head. The whole bureaucracy of the castle tries to take off Bartholomew's hat, but new hats continue to arrive. Finally, the 500th hat appears and it's magnificent.

ACTIVITY: Bring in old hats. Decorate them and have a "fanciest hat" contest.

············

Green Eggs and Ham. *Random House, 1960. ISBN 0 394 80016 8*

This story is one of Seuss's early easy-to-read books, and it's among the most successful, as repeated phrases are used by Sam I Am to get the narrator to try green eggs and ham.

ACTIVITY: What's your favorite food? Can you imagine that food with a different color: purple peanut butter, green popcorn, blue apples? Color some food with food coloring. Does it change the way you feel about that food?

Horton Hatches the Egg. *Random House, 1940.*
ISBN 0 394 90077 4

Horton promises Maizie the lazy bird that he will care for her egg while she's on vacation, and so he does. Even when he and the egg he sits on are captured, brought across the sea, and sold to a circus, Horton stays faithful to his promise. When the egg hatches, it's an elephant bird.

ACTIVITY: What do you think Horton's life will be like from now on? How will he care for the elephant bird? Which things about it will be elephant-like and which will be bird-like? What will this elephant bird be able to do that other birds can't? What will this elephant bird be able to do that other elephants can't?

· · · · · · ·

Horton Hears a Who. *Random House, 1954.*
ISBN 0 394 80078 8

Horton hears a voice from a dust speck and vows to protect it because "a person's a person no matter how small." This isn't an easy task for there are many people who are angered by Horton's belief and vow to destroy the dust speck.

ACTIVITY: In this book we see many things in the Who's world. What things are the same as in your world? What things are different? How do you know that you're not a very tiny person living in a tiny world compared to that of a giant person and world? Would we know if that was true? How?

· · · · · · ·

How the Grinch Stole Christmas. *Random House, 1957.*
ISBN 0 394 80079 6

This classic Christmas story revolves around the Grinch who hates Christmas as it's celebrated by the Whos down in Whoville and sets out to destroy it. However, Christmas comes without gifts or decorations, and the Grinch is converted.

ACTIVITY: Imagine that you are a Who. Tell the story from your point of view.

If I Ran the Zoo. *Random House, 1950.*
ISBN 0 394 80081 8

Oh, the great and wonderful animals our young hero McGrew would collect if only he owned the zoo.

ACTIVITY: Make up some other preposterous creatures for a zoo. What will they eat? What will they do for amusement?

· · · · · · ·

The King's Stilts. *Random House, 1939.*
ISBN 0 394 80082 6

The kingdom is about to be flooded because the dreadful Nizzards are making holes in the dike. It's the page boy, Eric, who returns the king's stilts in time to save the kingdom.

ACTIVITY: Find or make some stilts and walk on them. Time yourself to see how long it takes you to cover a distance with and without stilts. Does practice improve your time?

· · · · · · ·

The Lorax. *Random House, 1971. ISBN 0 394 92337 5*

The old Once-ler knows what happened to the beautiful Truffula trees that once covered the land. He also knows what happened to the Lorax who tried to warn everyone what would happen if the Truffula trees disappeared.

ACTIVITY: Compare this book to Bill Peet's **The Wump World.** Are they saying the same thing? Which is the better story? Will you do anything differently as a result of reading either of these books?

· · · · · · ·

McElligott's Pool. *Random House, 1947.*
ISBN 0 394 90083 9

A boy fishes in a very small pond and imagines all the fantastic fish that could be caught there.

ACTIVITY: Find a good picture of a tropical fish. Make a copy of it and then add things of your own to make it as preposterous as the fish in McElligott's pool.

On Beyond Zebra. *Random House, 1955. ISBN 0 394 80084 2*

The alphabet doesn't go far enough for Dr. Seuss, so he invents letters that come after Z and creatures whose names start with those letters.

ACTIVITY: Investigate our alphabet. Where does it come from? Make your own alphabet of beasts.

. . . .

Scrambled Eggs Super. *Random House, 1953. ISBN 0 394 90085 5*

To make these special scrambled eggs, you need very special, exotic ingredients and must travel far to get them.

ACTIVITY: Have a breakfast at school in which omelets and scrambled eggs are the main dishes.

. . . .

The Sneetches & Other Stories. *Random House, 1961. ISBN 0 394 80089 3*

In the main story of this book, the star-bellied Sneetches and the non-star-bellied Sneetches get into a fierce competition to stay fashionably correct, but the only one who profits from the conflict is Sylvester McMonkey McBean.

ACTIVITY: What things are currently fashionable at your school for shoes, socks and hats? Do you always like to wear what everybody else is wearing? Do you know people who like to be different?

Thidwick, the Big-Hearted Moose. *Random House, 1948. ISBN 0 394 80086 9*

Thidwick's antlers look inviting to a lot of animals, and soon he's so loaded down with uninvited guests that he's in great danger, but "a host above all must be nice to his guests."

ACTIVITY: Find out about animals with antlers. What are they for? What's the difference between antlers and horns?

. . . .

Yertle the Turtle & Other Stories. *Random House, 1992. ISBN 0 679 83229 7*

Yertle declares himself to be master of all he surveys, so he figures that if he can see more, he can be ruler of more. He commands the other turtles of the pond to serve as an ever-higher throne but is unseated by the burp of the turtle at the bottom.

ACTIVITY: Compare Yertle to the king in **Bartholomew and the Oobleck.**

Kevin Henkes

HIS LIFE

Kevin Henkes was born in Racine, Wisconsin, in 1960. He remembers his childhood as particularly safe and comfortable.

HIS WORK

Henkes's picture books usually have mice as characters, and he uses their tiny ears and tails to portray a wide range of emotions. Often he places several images on a single page in a series of vignettes. Many times his characters speak to us from those illustrations more directly than through the text.

BOOKS & ACTIVITIES

. . . .

Chester's Way. *Puffin Books, 1989. ISBN 0 14 054053 9*

Chester and Wilson are the best of friends, partly because they are so much alike. Both are cautious, careful (mice) children. When Lilly, with her unconventional, zestful ways, moves into the neighborhood, Chester and Wilson shun her. However, she soon proves herself to be a good friend, and the three learn much from each other. Then Victor moves into the neighborhood.

ACTIVITY: Make a chart showing the likes and dislikes of all four characters in this book.

. . . .

Chrysanthemum. *Greenwillow Books, 1991. ISBN 0 688 09699 9*

Chrysanthemum loves her name until she goes to school and the other children make fun of it. Her music teacher, however, also has a floral name and it's as unusual as Chrysanthemum's: Delphinium.

ACTIVITIES:

► If your name could be changed, what would you like it to be.

► What's the most common first name in your school? You'll have to visit each classroom and make charts to find out.

THINGS TO DO WITH HIS WORK

► Find the characters in Henkes's books who are most like yourself, most like your best friend, and most like someone in the class you don't know very well.

► Why do you suppose Henkes uses animals that behave like people in his books?

► Find characters that appear in more than one of Henkes's books. Make a web to connect the characters who know each other.

. . . .

Grandpa & Bo. *Greenwillow Books, 1986. ISBN 0 688 04957 5*

A lovely relationship exists between Bo and Grandpa, who answers all of Bo's questions truthfully but with a touch of whimsy.

ACTIVITY: Compare this grandfather with the one in Cynthia deFelice's **When Grandpa Kissed His Elbow** or some other book that has a grandfather you like.

Jessica. *Puffin Books, 1990. ISBN 0 14 054194 2*

Ruthie has an imaginary best friend, Jessica, who does everything with her. Which is fine until Ruthie goes to kindergarten.

ACTIVITY: Create your own imaginary best friend. What will his or her name be? What will he/she be like? What can you do together?

....

Julius, the Baby of the World. *Greenwillow Books, 1990. ISBN 0 688 08943 7*

Lilly's new baby brother is much admired by the rest of the family. They call him "the baby of the world." Lilly hates him, resents him, and hopes that he'll go away soon. At his christening, however, when her cousin expresses his dislike of Julius, Lilly's hackles rise.

ACTIVITY: It isn't until Lilly's cousin makes fun of Julius that Lilly changes her mind about the baby. Do you think everyone lived happily ever after? Will Lilly love and care for Julius from now on? What makes you think that?

....

Lilly's Purple Plastic Purse. *Greenwillow Books, 1996. ISBN 0 688 12897 1*

Lilly loves everything about school but she especially loves her teacher, Mr. Slinger. She fully intends to become a teacher just like him someday. Then she brings to school her new purple plastic purse, which plays music every time she opens it, and everything changes. This is a focus book, see page 134.

ACTIVITY: Bring some musical noisemakers to school, such as music boxes. Make a display of them and listen to each one. Rate the music on a scale of one to 10.

....

Once Around the Block. *Illustrated by Victoria Chess. Greenwillow Books, 1987. ISBN 0 688 04954 0*

Bored Annie is told to take a walk around the block, so she does. On the way, she meets people and gets treats, and she arrives back home in time to share the goodies and her better mood.

ACTIVITY: Set the story in your neighborhood. What would "once around the block" allow you to do or see? Who would you be apt to meet?

....

Owen. *Greenwillow Books, 1993. ISBN 0 688 11449 0*

Owen loves his blanket, Fuzzy, and takes it with him everywhere. His parents aren't concerned until their neighbor, Mrs. Tweezers, "fills them in." None of their Tweezer-inspired wiles work to separate Owen from Fuzzy, but what will he do when he goes to kindergarten?

ACTIVITY: What would you say to Mrs. Tweezers? Role-play a conversation with her.

....

Sheila Rae, the Brave. *Puffin Books, 1988. ISBN 0 14 050835 X*

Sheila Rae and her little sister get lost, and her little sister has to lead them home again.
Activity: Find Sheila Rae's sister in most of the illustrations.

....

Shhhh. *Greenwillow Books, 1989. ISBN 0 688 07985 7*

Everyone is fast asleep except the narrator, who tiptoes around the house observing them all. Then she loudly toots her horn and startles them all awake.

ACTIVITY: Compare this book to **Noisy Nora**, by Rosemary Wells. Do you think the two girls would be friends? Could you stand to live in the same house with either of them?

....

A Weekend with Wendell. *Greenwillow Books, 1986. ISBN 0 688 06326 8*

Sophie isn't pleased when Wendell arrives for the weekend. Eventually, they come to an understanding, and things get quite pleasant.

ACTIVITY: Make up a list of things to do when a guest like Wendell comes to your house.

Pat Hutchins

HER LIFE

Pat Hutchins was born in England in 1922, one of seven children. She loved drawing from the time she was very young and was given a scholarship to art school when she was 16. At first, when she lived in London, her artwork was confined to the field of commercial art, but after she was married, she lived in New York for a while. She showed her work to some publishers there, and the very successful **Rosie's Walk** was the result.

HER WORK

Oranges, yellows, and greens are often predominant in Hutchins's work. Her decorative style is replete with patterned lines. She has a series of books about Titch and another about her monster family.

THINGS TO DO WITH HER WORK

► Divide her books into monster and non-monster books. Why do you think Hutchins uses monster characters at some times but not at others?

► Compare Hutchins's work with the work of Kevin Henkes and Rosemary Wells. How are they alike? How are they different? Which do you like best?

BOOKS & ACTIVITIES

****

Changes, Changes. *Simon & Schuster, 1987.*
ISBN 0 02 745870 9

In this wordless book, dolls cope with emergencies by using blocks imaginatively.

ACTIVITY: Use kindergarten blocks to recreate the structures in this book.

****

Clocks and More Clocks. *Aladdin, 1994.*
ISBN 0 689 71769 5

Mr. Higgins finds a beautiful clock in the attic and starts it going, but he doesn't know what time to set it at, so he buys another clock, which he puts in the bedroom. The two clocks don't agree, so he buys a third, and so on. Eventually, a watch solves his problem.

ACTIVITY: Find clocks that are more or less like the ones Mr. Higgins has. Set them at the various times mentioned in the book.

....

Don't Forget the Bacon. *Morrow Junior Books, 1989. ISBN 0 688 08743 4*

A child is sent by his mother to the store with a short mental list of things he must get. Each thing he sees on the way, however, transforms the list. What he buys at the store is nothing like the list he started with. On the way home the list returns to its original state, but the boy forgets the bacon.

ACTIVITIES:

► Make a chart which shows all the changes to the boy's list. What if he had seen other things? What changes could have been made?

► Make a different list of things for him to buy and think of things he could see that would change your list.

The Doorbell Rang. *Morrow Junior Books, 1989.*
ISBN 0 688 09234 9

Ma has made a big plate of cookies, and her two children are just about to share them when the doorbell rings. Each ring of the doorbell brings more people who must share the cookies.

ACTIVITY: Make real cookies and keep dividing them the way the children in this book do. How many cookies will you have to make for everyone to get an equal share? What if different numbers of children arrived each time? What could they do if the cookies didn't divide up equally?

· · · · · · ·

Good Night, Owl. *Simon & Schuster, 1990.*
ISBN 0 02 745900 4

Owl has a hard time sleeping, because it's daytime and the forest is full of the sounds of the diurnal animals. When nighttime comes, it's a different story, however, and Owl gets his revenge.

ACTIVITY: Make a list of daytime sleepers. Don't forget people.

· · · · · · ·

Little Pink Pig. *Greenwillow Books, 1994.*
ISBN 0 688 12014 8

Little Pink Pig's mother calls him again and again, but he's always too busy to answer. He even ignores all the other animals she gathers until they walk away. Then he calls, "Wait for me!" and they ignore him.

ACTIVITY: Brainstorm a list of excuses for not doing something. Put the list in order of their reasonableness.

My Best Friend. *Greenwillow Books, 1993.*
ISBN 0 688 11485 7

Our narrator's best friend is truly amazing. She does everything better, faster, and neater. When she sleeps over, however, she's afraid of unseen monsters, and that's when our narrator shines.

ACTIVITY: Make a list of 10 qualities you're looking for in a best friend.

· · · · · · ·

One Hunter. *Morrow Junior Books, 1986.*
ISBN 0 688 06522 8

This story is Hutchins's counting book. A hunter looks throughout the forest seeing not a single animal, but we do.

ACTIVITY: Make a similar counting book starring the same hunter but using different animals.

· · · · · · ·

Rosie's Walk. *Simon & Schuster, 1971.*
ISBN 0 02 745850 4

Rosie the hen takes a leisurely walk around the barnyard, oblivious to the fox who's constantly being foiled in his attempts to get her.

ACTIVITIES:

► Tell the story from the fox's point of view.

► Change the position words and decide what changes would have to be made in the illustrations to accommodate the changes in the text.

The Surprise Party. Aladdin, , 1991.
ISBN 0 689 71543 9

An invitation to a party starts out all right, but it gets mangled as it transfers from person to person.

ACTIVITIES:

► Play the game of "Gossip," where one person whispers a fairly long something to someone after first writing it down. The message is passed along a line of listeners in the same way. The last person in line says it out loud, and the message is compared with the written one.

► Compare this book with **Fish Fry Tonight,** by Jackie French Koller.

....

The Very Worst Monster. Morrow Junior Books, 1989.
ISBN 0 688 09038 9

Hazel isn't thrilled with the attention newborn Billy Monster is getting. Eventually she gives him away, earning her parents' attention and the title of "very worst monster."

ACTIVITY: Compare this book with **Julius, the Baby of the World,** by Kevin Henkes (see page 206).

....

What Game Shall We Play? Greenwillow Books, 1990.
ISBN 0 688 09196 2

The animals are searching for each other in order to find a good game to play. They find each other and end up playing a game of hide-and-seek which, really, they've been playing all along.

ACTIVITY: Take one game that you like to play and write up all the rules for it without using the name of the game. Hand the rules to someone else and see if they can guess the game.

Which Witch is Which? Greenwillow Books, 1989.
ISBN 0 688 06358 6

When twins choose matching witch costumes, it's hard to figure out which witch is which twin, but there are clues to follow in the text.

ACTIVITIES:

► List the clues. Which ones were hardest to follow?

► Make a list of other words which are homonyms. Make a homonym picture dictionary.

....

The Wind Blew. Penguin, 1974. ISBN 0 14 050236 X

The wind does indeed blow and it snatches something from almost everyone we see. All of the people chase their possessions, and the chain of chasers gets longer as they approach the city. When the wind drops their things, they're all mixed up.

ACTIVITIES:

► Compare this book with Patricia Polacco's **The Bee Tree** (see page 229).

► You can't see the wind, but you can see its effect. Draw some pictures that show that the wind is blowing.

Ezra Jack Keats

HIS LIFE

Ezra Jack Keats was born in Brooklyn, New York, in 1916. His mother and father were immigrants, and his father worked as a waiter. When Keats began drawing at the age of five, covering their kitchen table top with his creations, his father wasn't pleased. He'd seen too many "starving artists" on the streets of the city. While he did occasionally bring home paints for his son, he never openly encouraged him. His mother, however, was very encouraging, even covering his table cloth decorations with a protective see-through cloth. Keats was self-taught in early childhood, but he received his first formal art training in art school, after graduating from high school. He worked first as a commercial artist after serving in World War II, but then turned to children's book illustration.

His first picture book, **The Snowy Day**, received the Caldecott Award. He died in 1983.

THINGS TO DO WITH HIS WORK

► Find all the books that are connected through Peter. Make a web showing what characters these books have in common.

► Place the Peter books in order as Peter gets older.

► Make marbleized paper by dropping oil or acrylic paint on a surface of water. Swirl the paint and then lift it off the surface of the water by carefully placing and removing a piece of art paper on the water. Use the paper in your own art creations.

HIS WORK

Keats often used marbleized paper in his collages, as well as decorative papers of all sorts. His cityscapes often contained collages of newspaper and other printed material to emulate graffiti. In his later work, he largely abandoned collage and worked with acrylics.

BOOKS & ACTIVITIES

· · · · · · · · ·

Apt 3. Aladdin, 1986. ISBN 0 689 71059 3

Two boys hear music coming from somewhere in the apartment building where they live. The blind man who's creating the music becomes their friend.

ACTIVITY: Invite someone who plays the harmonica to come to school and play for you.

· · · · · · · · ·

Dreams. Aladdin Paperbacks, 1992. ISBN 0 689 71599 4

The paper mouse that appears in the book **Louie** becomes part of a dream and, as each child in the apartment building falls asleep, we watch the pattern on the window shades change.

ACTIVITY: Decide what some of the people behind those window shades might be dreaming about.

· · · · · · · · ·

Goggles. Viking, 1971. ISBN 0 670 58062 0

Peter has found some goggles, but bigger kids are trying to take them away. Willie, Peter's dog, is the hero in this book.

ACTIVITY: Try on various frames of sunglasses. Use various lenses, such as magnifying glasses, telescopes, kaleidoscopes, and microscopes, to view a variety of objects.

Hi, Cat. *Aladdin, 1988, ISBN 0 689 71258 8*

Peter's friend, Archie, finds a stray cat, which doesn't help the boys' show much.

ACTIVITY: If your classroom had a pet show, how many animals and what kind of animals would be in it?

....

Jennie's Hat. *HarperCollins Children's Books, 1985. ISBN 0 06 443072 3*

Jennie's hat is dull and uninteresting until the birds gather materials for it.

ACTIVITY: Have a "decorated hats day." Use interesting materials to decorate hats and then wear them in a parade.

....

A Letter to Amy. *HarperCollins Children's Books, 1968. ISBN 0 06 023109 2*

Peter wants Amy to come to his party, but the other guests are all boys.

ACTIVITIES:

► Look at the way Keats shows that it's raining. Compare that with other illustrators' work showing rain.

► Make your own rainy day pictures.

....

Louie. *Greenwillow Books, 1983. ISBN 0 688 02383 5*

Louie never speaks until he attends a puppet show given by the older neighborhood children, including Peter's younger sister, Susan. There he connects with one of the puppets and, eventually, is given the puppet mouse to keep.

ACTIVITY: Find Susan in **Peter's Chair**. How many years later do you think it is now?

Peter's Chair. *HarperCollins Children's Books, 1983.*

Peter doesn't welcome his new baby sister. He resents the fact that his father is painting over Peter's beloved chair until he discovers that it's too small for him now.

ACTIVITY: Bring in a toy, a piece of clothing, or a piece of furniture that once was just the right size for you, but is too small for you now.

....

Regards to the Man in the Moon. *Aladdin, 1987. ISBN 0 689 7160 3*

Louie and his friends take a make-believe trip to the moon.

ACTIVITY: Find illustrations of the moon in picture books. Then draw a picture of the moon the way you see it.

....

The Snowy Day. *Puffin Books, 1976. ISBN 0 14 050182 7*

This gentle, classic, picture book introduces us to Peter, a city boy, who experiences and enjoys the snow.

ACTIVITY: The next time your area has a snowstorm, try to do everything Peter did in the snow.

....

Whistle for Willie. *Puffin Books, 1977. ISBN 0 670 76240 7*

Peter wants to whistle for his dog, but the whistle is elusive. Eventually he gets it.

ACTIVITY: Help someone else learn to whistle.

Steven Kellogg

HIS LIFE

When he was a child, Steven Kellogg drew stories to entertain his sisters and friends, telling the stories as he drew. He was born in 1941 and grew up in Darien, Connecticut, not many miles from the town in which he now lives. He lives with his wife, Helen, in a house that was built in 1742 and is surrounded by 20 acres of woods in Sandy Hook, Connecticut. The house is furnished with antiques and has eight bedrooms. Those bedrooms came in handy, because when he and Helen met, she was the mother of six children, all of whom lived with her. Kellogg is an exuberant, almost hyperactive man who loves the work he does. He loves animals, especially Great Danes and cats, several of which have found their way into his books.

HIS WORK

Kellogg uses a variety of techniques and media to create his illustrations, but they all have an energetic, exuberant style. The details of his pictures are often humorous. Sometimes this is accomplished through tiny cartoon conversation bubbles and sometimes through the actions of minor characters. He often puts characters from one book, such as his great Dane character, Pinkerton, into several other books. He's done a series of books about Pinkerton, a series of folktales, and a series of tall tale books.

THINGS TO DO WITH HIS WORK

► Take a poll to see which of Kellogg's books is the favorite in your classroom.

► Look for characters from other books in his illustrations.

► Classify the books by Kellogg.

BOOKS & ACTIVITIES

· · · · · · · · ·

Aster Aardvark's Alphabet Adventures. *Morrow Junior Books, 1992. ISBN 0 688 11571 3*

Kellogg's usual zaniness imbues his alphabet book.

ACTIVITY: Make a survey of alphabet books. Which ones do you like best? Are your favorites the same as those of the other students in the class?

· · · · · · · · ·

Can I Keep Him? *Dial Books for Young Readers, 1976. ISBN 0 8037 1305 3*

Arnold wants a pet, and he and his mother constantly evaluate the pros and cons of the various types of pets he could get.

ACTIVITY: Make a list of the animals in this book. Which ones do you think your parents might let you keep?

Chicken Little. *Morrow Junior Books, 1985.*
ISBN 0 688 05691 1

Kellogg retains the conventional folktale in this story, but he adds a visual subplot. Foxy Loxy masquerades as a police officer to get his prey, but Sergeant Hippo Hefty inadvertently foils the villain. This is a focus book (see page 114).

ACTIVITY: Read **Foolish Rabbit's Big Mistake,** by Rafe Martin, and Paul Galdone's **Henny Penny.** How are these similar to Kellogg's book? How are they different?

·······

The Christmas Witch. *Dial Books for Young Readers, 1992. ISBN 0 8037 1268 5*

Gloria, a witch in training, is encouraged by her instructor, Madame Pestilence, to create mischief of a nasty sort, but it just isn't in Gloria to be that kind of a witch. Then an angel sends her to another planet, where a feud is going on between the Pepperwills and the Valdoons.

ACTIVITY: Compare the Pepperwills and Valdoons to the Sneetches in Dr. Seuss's story (see page 204).

·······

The Island of the Skog. *Dial Books for Young Readers, 1976. ISBN 0 8037 4122 7*

Some mice have come to an island to find a safe home, only to discover that it's inhabited by the Skog, a fierce monster.

ACTIVITY: Build a model of the Skog for your classroom.

·······

Jack and the Beanstalk. *Morrow Junior Books, 1991. ISBN 0 688 10250 6*

Kellogg tells the conventional story of Jack and his trip up the beanstalk in this book, but his illustrations add cats and a hysterical ogre.

ACTIVITY: Compare this book to other tellings of the same story.

Johnny Appleseed. *Morrow Junior Books, 1988. ISBN 0 688 06418 3*

This slightly idealized portrait of John Chapman is more legend than biography, but it shows the man from birth to his apple-strewing journey.

ACTIVITY: Can you find Pinkerton in this book?

·······

Mike Fink. *Morrow Junior Books, 1992. ISBN 0 688 07003 5*

The Mike Fink in this tall tale bears little resemblance to the actual man, who was, apparently, both cruel and ruthless. However, there's little doubt that he was an excellent keelboat man. All of the other keelboat operators are presented as cheerful, although history says they were mostly a bunch of roughnecks.

ACTIVITY: Make a display of as many different kinds of boats as you can.

·······

Much Bigger Than Martin. *Dial Books for Young Readers, 1976. ISBN 0 8037 5810 3*

Martin's little brother, Henry, yearns to be bigger, better, and smarter than Martin.

ACTIVITY: What would you say to Henry to make him feel better?

·······

The Mysterious Tadpole. *Dial Books for Young Readers, 1987. ISBN 0 8037 6245 3*

Uncle McAllister sends Louis a live animal that looks very much like a tadpole. Indeed, Louis's teacher identifies him as such, but the tadpole doesn't change into a frog–it just gets bigger and bigger. Problems galore!

ACTIVITY: This story starts out reasonably enough. Find the place where you no longer believe it could be true. Is it the same place others identify?

·······

Paul Bunyan. *Morrow Junior Books, 1986. ISBN 0 688 03849 2*

Kellogg includes several of the tall tales about the super logger in this picture book.

ACTIVITY: Paul Bunyan was a super lumberman. What qualities would a super teacher have?

Pecos Bill. *Morrow Junior Books, 1992. ISBN 0 688 09924 6*

The tall tale super cowboy gets the Kellogg touch in this story of pioneer days in the West.

ACTIVITY: Find and sing the song about Pecos Bill that was in a Walt Disney cartoon.

....

Pinkerton, Behave. *Dial Books for Young Readers, 1982. ISBN 0 8037 7250 5*

This book is the first in Kellogg's Pinkerton series. Pinkerton is certainly exuberant and he's surely big, but he always seems to do the opposite of what people want him to. One time, however, this turns out to be a good thing.

ACTIVITY: Pinkerton is a dignified name for a dog, especially a Great Dane. Find pictures of various breeds of dogs and think of names that are especially suitable for each breed.

....

A Rose for Pinkerton. *Dial Books for Young Readers, 1981. ISBN 0 8037 0060 1*

Pinkerton has further adventures in this book. This time, he has a relationship with a cat named Rose.

ACTIVITY: Compare this book to Alex and the Cat by Helen Griffiths.

BOOKS WRITTEN BY OTHER AUTHORS & ILLUSTRATED BY STEVEN KELLOGG

....

Bayer, Jane. A, ***My Name is Alice.*** *Dial Books for Young Readers, 1987. ISBN 0 8037 0130 6*

The old jump rope, ball bouncing rhyme is used in this alphabet book which features Kellogg's usual visual asides.

ACTIVITY: Make up another alphabet book, using the same pattern as this one.

Chapman, Carol. ***Barney Bipple's Magic Dandelions.*** *Dutton Children's Books, 1988. ISBN 0 525 44449 1*

Barney Bipple finds a rich lady's jewels, and she rewards him with three magic dandelions that will grant his wishes. When those wishes don't turn out the way he expects, it's okay, because there are lots more dandelions.

ACTIVITY: Draw pictures of what your three wishes would be.

....

Mahy, Margaret. ***The Boy Who Was Followed Home.*** *Dial Books for Young Readers, 1986. ISBN 0 8037 0286 8*

Twenty-seven hippos are camped on Robert's lawn, and it takes the help of a witch to get rid of them.

ACTIVITY: Compare this book to David Cleveland's **The April Rabbits.**

....

Noble, Trinka Hakes. ***The Day Jimmy's Boa Ate the Wash.*** *Dial Books for Young Readers, 1980. ISBN 0 8037 1723 7*

One disaster leads to another on a class trip to a farm.

ACTIVITY: Make a flow chart of the action in this story by setting up a series of "because" statements.

....

Lindbergh, Reeve. ***The Day the Goose Got Loose.*** *Dial Books for Young Readers, 1990. ISBN 0 8037 0408 9*

A goose creates havoc all over a farm, but a little boy knows why the goose got loose. That night the boy dreams about geese.

ACTIVITY: Compare this book to **Midnight Farm,** also by Lindbergh. Both of these books have a peaceful rhythm, but their illustrations are very different. Which one do you like best?

....

Purdy, Carol. ***Iva Dunnit and the Big Wind.*** *Dial Books for Young Readers, 1988. ISBN 0 8037 0493 3*

Iva Dunnit has a lot of children, but they know how to stay put. When, in this rollicking tall tale, the big wind comes, that ability to stay put comes in handy.

ACTIVITY: Write about a time when you didn't do exactly what you were supposed to do.

Leo Lionni

HIS LIFE

Leo Lionni was born in Amsterdam in 1910. As a child, he was greatly influenced by his uncle, who was an art collector. Lionni's uncle encouraged his drawing efforts, even giving him an art table at which to create. Lionni loved making terrariums with complicated landscapes, often including a pool for small turtles, snakes, and lizards. His family moved a great deal, and he lived in Brussels, Philadelphia, Genoa, and Zurich. He got a doctorate in economics from the University of Genoa in Italy.

Once, riding with his grandchildren on a train, he tore pieces of a magazine into small circles of color and told a story with them. Later, this became his first children's book, **Little Blue and Little Yellow.** Since that time, Lionni has written more than 30 picture books for children, two of which were named as Caldecott honor books.

Now he and his wife, Nora, divide their time between an apartment in New York City and a country home in Italy, where his studio is a short walk from the house.

HIS WORK

Lionni is one of the few authors of children's books who can get away with telling moralistic tales. This is because of his off-beat illustrations and his very light touch. Many of his illustrations use marbleized paper in a manner somewhat similar to that of Ezra Jack Keats.

THINGS TO DO WITH HIS WORK

► Many of Lionni's books are fables that contain a lesson for us all. Find the ones that seem to say that we should be happy with what we are. Find others which seem to say that we must all act together for the common good. Can you find any which seem to say that each of us has a special talent to be proud of? What other morals can you get from Lionni's work?

► Many of his books feature mice characters, and most of the mice look alike. Create your own mouse village. You can make the mice look like his if you want to.

► Lionni, like Ezra Jack Keats, often uses marbelized paper. Create some by swirling oil paint on the surface of water and gently laying on and then removing a piece of paper. Try many different kinds of paper and colors of paint until you get the best results. How will you use your creations?

BOOKS & ACTIVITIES

·······

Alexander and the Wind-Up Mouse. *Pantheon Books, 1974. ISBN 0 394 82911 5*

When Alexander finds Willie, a wind-up mouse, he envies him until he finds Willie in the junk heap. Then he sets about finding a magic pebble so that Willie can become real.

ACTIVITY: Make small cutouts of Willie (before the magic) and Alexander. Make a chart with the following words in the first column: run, eat, think, feel, hide. Place the cutouts of the correct mice beside each word. Add more words to the chart.

·······

A Busy Year. *Alfred A. Knopf Books for Young Readers, 1992. ISBN 0 679 82464 2*

Mice twins find and make friends with Woody, a talking tree. They spend a year watching and enjoying their new friend.

ACTIVITY: What if Willie and Winnie had made friends with a brook instead of a tree? How would they spend the seasons with that friend? What other friendships could they have had? Make a calendar showing one of those friendships through the year.

·······

An Extraordinary Egg. *Alfred A. Knopf Books for Young Readers, 1994. ISBN 0 679 85840 7*

Mistaking an alligator egg for a chicken egg, Jessica and Marilyn, two frog friends, call the alligator that hatches out "Little Chicken" and are amused when its mother calls it "my sweet little alligator."

ACTIVITY: Read **Chickens Aren't the Only Ones,** by Ruth Heller. Make a chart showing things you know about eggs before and after reading the book.

Fish Is Fish. *Alfred A. Knopf Books for Young Readers, 1974. ISBN 0 394 82799 6*

A frog teaches a fish to be happy with what he is.

ACTIVITY: What if the creature listening to the frog were a bird? How would a bird imagine those things?

·······

Frederick. *Alfred A. Knopf Books for Young Readers, 1973. ISBN 0 394 82614 0*

While the other mice scurry about getting ready for winter, Frederick observes and stores up the feelings of summer and fall. During the long winter, he becomes the poet who reminds the mice that the warmth will return.

ACTIVITIES:

► Read the fable "The Grasshopper and the Ants," which is available in many versions. Is Frederick like the grasshopper? In what ways?

► Find some poems that you could read in the winter to remind you of the spring, summer, and fall. Find some music you would play and some art you could look at that would do the same thing.

·······

Frederick's Fables. *Alfred A. Knopf Books for Young Readers, 1993. ISBN 0 394 87710 1*

This book is an anthology of 13 stories by Lionni. All of the text and some of the illustrations from each tale are included.

ACTIVITY: Compare this book to **Once Upon a Wood,** by Eve Rice.

·······

Inch by Inch. *Astor-Honor, 1962. ISBN 0 8392 3010 9*

Inchworm can measure anything, so the birds get him to measure everybody. Then they ask him to measure the nightingale's song.

ACTIVITY: Find out about inchworms. How long are they? How do they move? Why are they called inchworms?

Little Blue and Little Yellow. *Astor-Honor, 1959. ISBN 0 8392 3018 4*

Using torn pieces of paper, Lionni illustrates this seemingly simple story of a friendship between two characters and the reaction this blending of colors gets from their respective families.

ACTIVITY: Use pieces of colored plastic for the overhead projector to tell the story. Use color gels over flashlights shown on a screen to do the same.

....

Matthew's Dream. *Alfred A. Knopf Books for Young Readers, 1991. ISBN 0 679 81075 7*

Matthew's parents hope he'll become a doctor, but when Matthew visits an art gallery he's entranced by the art. He's also entranced by an equally artistic mouse named Nicoletta. Later he succeeds in creating beauty out of rubble.

ACTIVITY: What beauty can you create out of junk? Find some and do it.

....

Mr. McMouse. *Alfred A. Knopf Books for Young Readers, 1992. ISBSN 0 679 83890 2*

In this tale, closely related to the familiar "Country Mouse, City Mouse" fables, Timothy leaves the city to become a country mouse. Other field mice explain that he must pass some tests to get his "field mouse license," but he fails the first two. He's awarded an honorary license after saving Spinny, a friendly mouse, from a cat.

ACTIVITY: What sort of tests would you give a new kid to get a license to be a kid at your school? Could you pass them? Could your friends?

Nicolas, Where Have You Been? *Alfred A. Knopf Books for Young Readers, 1987. ISBN 0 394 98370 X*

Left with very few berries after the birds have taken their share, Nicolas the mouse goes in search of a new berry patch and is mousenapped by a big, black bird, who drops him into a nest with three baby birds. There Nicolas becomes friends with them and returns to his fellow mice with new compassion for birds.

ACTIVITY: Make a Venn diagram comparing mice and birds. Add a third circle for humans and make it a three-way comparison.

....

On My Beach There Are Many Pebbles. *Astor-Honor, 1961. ISBN 0 8392 3024 9*

This tale is a departure from Lionni's mice books. The images are almost photographic as Lionni investigates the look and structures of beach stones.

ACTIVITY: See page 49 for a whole theme about rocks and minerals.

....

Six Crows. *Alfred A. Knopf Books for Young Readers, 1988. ISBN 0 394 89572 X*

A war between a farmer and some crows escalates as the farmer builds a scarecrow and the crows build a kite to scare the "monster." The farmer makes a bigger scarecrow, the crows respond with a bigger kite. A watching owl plays the role of peacemaker.

ACTIVITY: Compare this book with **Mrs. Gaddy and the Crow.**

Swimmy. Alfred A. Knopf Books for Young Readers, 1963. ISBN 0 394 81713 3

Some smaller fish have no defense against bigger, marauding fish until Swimmy, a tiny black fish who hasn't received kindness from the others, figures out a way for them all to literally band together.

ACTIVITY: Lionni uses many different materials to make his watercolor prints for this book. Try your own hand at creating undersea images using some new materials.

....

Theodore and the Talking Mushroom. Pantheon Books, 1971. ISBN 0 685 03944 7

Theodore has convinced the other mice that he and only he has the power to interpret the talking mushroom he has found. His interpretations increase his status among the mice. Then they find a huge field of mushrooms, all of which say the same word: "Quirp!"

ACTIVITY: Compare Theodore to **Yertle the Turtle.** Find other books with other silly tyrants.

Tico and the Golden Wings. Alfred A. Knopf Books for Young Readers, 1975. ISBN 0 394 83078 4

A wingless bird is given golden wings but gives away each golden feather to other creatures in need.

ACTIVITY: If you had golden feathers, to whom would you give them? Make some golden feathers out of gold foil and show your answers in pictures.

Arnold Lobel

HIS LIFE

Arnold Lobel was born in 1933 in Los Angeles, California. His parents split up when he was very young, and he and his mother moved in with his maternal grandparents in Schenectady, New York. His mother was often away, so he was raised by his grandparents. He felt he had an unhappy childhood. He met Anita Kempler when they were both students at the Pratt Institute. They were married and had two children. They lived in a brownstone in Brooklyn, New York, where they used a large room as a shared studio in which they both worked on children's books—sometimes together. Lobel died in 1987.

HIS WORK

Lobel's illustrations are lively and informal, in direct contrast to his wife's careful, old-world style. Often a particular shade of green dominates his colors. His use of line is more dominant than his use of color and his figures often stand against white space.

THINGS TO DO WITH HIS WORK

► Compare his easy-to-read books with the books about Henry and Mudge, by Cynthia Rylant, and Dr. Seuss's easy-to-read books. How are Lobel's books different? Which do you like best? Which are easiest to read?

► Lobel created some books that his wife illustrated. How is her art work different from his?

BOOKS & ACTIVITIES

. . . .

Book of Pigericks. HarperCollins Children's Books, 1983. ISBN 0 06 023982 4

This picture book contains 38 limericks about pigs.

ACTIVITY: Limericks are among the easiest verse forms to use. Many children can make up their own limericks about pigs or other animals.

. . . .

Fables. HarperCollins Children's Books, 1983. ISBN 0 06 443046 4

Like Aesop, Lobel has written a series of short tales with morals. However, there the similarity ends, for these are funny and irreverent tales.

ACTIVITY: Lobel has chosen certain animals to be characters in his fables. Is there a reason for each choice? Would you have chosen different animals? Make a list of the animals and the characteristics they show in these fables. What changes would you make?

Frog and Toad Books ....
Days with Frog and Toad. *HarperCollins Children's Books, 1985. ISBN 0 694 00025 6* ....

Frog and Toad All Year. *HarperCollins Children's Books, 1976. ISBN 0 06 023950 6* ....

Frog and Toad Are Friends. *HarperCollins Children's Books, 1985. ISBN 0 694 00027 2* ....

Frog and Toad Together. *HarperCollins Children's Books, 1985. ISBN 0 694 00028 0*

In this series of easy-to-read books, Lobel creates a loving friendship between logical Frog and silly Toad.

ACTIVITIES:

▶ Most of what Frog and Toad do is more like people behavior than frog or toad behavior. Could Lobel have made them other animals? If he had, what things, besides the illustrations, would he have had to change?

▶ Lobel didn't really name his characters. What names would you have used?

▶ In **Frog and Toad Together,** Toad loses a button. Put as many buttons as you can gather in a box. Can you find a button that could be each of the buttons they found? Can you find the one that could be Toad's lost button? Classify the buttons in as many ways as possible.

....

Gregory Griggs and Other Nursery Rhyme People. *Morrow Junior Books, 1987. ISBN 0 688 07042 6*

Nursery rhymes you might have missed are included in this collection of folklore characters.

ACTIVITIES:

▶ Make a chart showing these Mother Goose characters and others. In one column put the names of the characters; in another column list the attributes of each character; in a third column put the interesting or silly words you see in their rhymes.

▶ Play a guessing game in which one child describes a character from the chart, and the other children have to guess which one it is.

▶ Which Mother Goose characters do you think ought to meet each other? For instance, shouldn't Little Bo Peep meet Mary? They both seem to like sheep.

....

Ming Lo Moves the Mountain. *Scholastic, 1986. ISBN 0 590 42902 7*

Ming Lo and his wife live at the foot of a large mountain and Ming Lo hates the results. The wise man tells him to dismantle his house, pack up all his things, and do the mountain moving dance–which causes Ming Lo and his wife to back up while the mountain stays in place.

ACTIVITY: This is a "noodlehead" story where we are meant to laugh at the silliness of a character. Find and read other noodlehead tales such as **Lazy Jack, No Room,** and **The Man, the Boy and the Donkey.**

....

Mouse Soup. *HarperCollins Children's Books, 1986. ISBN 0 06 444041 9*

This is a clever version of **Stone Soup** in which a mouse convinces a weasel that stones must be added to the mix in order to get perfect Mouse Soup.

ACTIVITY: Compare this story with other versions of **Stone Soup,** such as the ones by Tony Ross and John Stewig. Make up your own version.

....

Mouse Tales. *HarperCollins Children's Books, 1978. ISBN 0 06 444013 3*

Father Mouse has a tale for each of his seven children before they go to bed.

ACTIVITY: Decide what your ideal bedtime ritual would be. What would you like to do and have done for you every night before you go to bed? After you've made the list, go back and put a check mark before the ones that you think are possible. What do you think the chances are that they will happen?

On the Day Peter Stuyvesant Sailed Into Town.
HarperCollins Children's Books, 1971. ISBN 0 06 443144 4

In this rhyming picture book based on fact, Peter Stuyvesant, the governor of the colony which was to become New York, was upset when he arrived to see the dirt and clutter in town and set about ordering its cleanup.

ACTIVITY: How would Peter Stuyvesant feel about your town if he "sailed" into it today? What do you think he'd want to change first? Can it be done? Can you help?

•••••••

Owl at Home. *HarperCollins Children's Books, 1987. ISBN 0 694 00176 7*

Owl is another "noodlehead." He hears the wind rattling the door and opens the door to let the wind in. He's frightened of the bumps at the foot of his bed, which are only his feet, and he makes himself cry to produce tear-water tea. This is a focus book (see page 149 for activities about **Owl at Home**).

•••••••

The Random House Book of Mother Goose. *Random House, 1986. ISBN 0 394 86799 8*

This large anthology contains all of the standard fables, as well as some that may be less well known. All are illustrated with Lobel's comic style.

ACTIVITY: Find a rhyme you never heard before and write a newspaper headline for it.

•••••••

The Rose in My Garden. *Scholastic, 1985. ISBN 0 590 41530 1*

In this cumulative rhyming story, illustrated by Anita Lobel, a tiny drama is played out as our attention is drawn to each of the flowers in the garden.

ACTIVITY: Make a list of the flowers mentioned in this book. Find pictures of those flowers in seed catalogs and reference books and compare those pictures to the ones in this book.

Small Pig. *HarperCollins Children's Books, 1988. ISBN 0 06 444120 2*

Pig loves his mud puddle and, when the farmer's wife gets things too clean, he leaves in search of other mud.

ACTIVITY: Compare this book to **There's a Pig in the Mud in the Middle of the Road.**

•••••••

A Treeful of Pigs. *Scholastic, 1988. ISBN 0 590 41280 9*

In this tale, illustrated by Anita Lobel, the farmer's wife does all the work for her lazy husband. When he tells her he'll work when he sees a treeful of pigs, she gives him one.

ACTIVITY: What if the farmer had said he would work when he saw pigs flying? Could she have made that happen?

•••••••

The Turnaround Wind. *HarperCollins Children's Books, 1988. ISBN 0 06 023988 3*

Tiny vignettes show us 30 characters who are out to enjoy a pleasant day. When the wind blows, it turns everything upside down. Readers must do the same with the book to see all the changes the wind created.

ACTIVITY: Compare this book with **Reflections** (Greenwillow Books, 1987. ISBN 0 688 06140 0) and **Round Trip** (Greenwillow Books, 1990. ISBN 0 688 09986 6), by Ann Jonas, both of which can be viewed upside down and right side up.

James Marshall

HIS LIFE

James Marshall was born in San Antonio, Texas, where his father worked for the railroad and had a dance band. Marshall studied the viola and intended to have a musical career. Then his hand was injured during an airplane flight and his musical career was finished. He met Harry Allard, with whom he later wrote many picture books, when he was a student at Trinity College. Marshall taught Spanish in a Catholic school near Boston upon graduation from college.

His first book, **George and Martha**, was inspired by a famous play, *Who's Afraid of Virginia Woolf*, in which the main characters were named George and Martha.

For many years he divided his time between an apartment in New York City and his home in Mansfield Hollow, Connecticut. James Marshall died in 1992.

THINGS TO DO WITH HIS WORK

► Watch for the fat cats he puts in almost every book. Also notice the stacks of items that are often about to fall over, reminiscent of Dr. Seuss's books about the Cat in the Hat.

► Notice the things about Texas that he puts in the Miss Nelson series.

► Marshall's work can be categorized as fairy tale renditions and as series, such as the Cut-ups, Miss Nelson, and George and Martha. Look at many books in one series and then try to decide what Marshall is trying to tell us.

HIS WORK

Marshall's work is usually gently humorous. He has several books in series: Miss Nelson, George and Martha, the Cut-Ups, the Stupids, and the Rats, for instance. In those books, his characters change very little. His fairy tale renditions are full of sly humor.

BOOKS & ACTIVITIES

BOOKS WRITTEN & ILLUSTRATED BY JAMES MARSHALL

....

The Cut-Ups at Camp Custer. *Viking Children's Books, 1989.* ISBN 0 670 82051 2

Spud and Joe are together again. Spud's mother knows it's trouble and says as they head off, "That camp will never be the same." Then they find out that the camp director is none other than their old nemesis, school principal Mr. Spurgle, and he's ready for them. Or so he thinks.

ACTIVITIES:

► Compare Mr. Spurgle's nephew, Charles Andrew Frothingham, with the Grand Duke Wilfred in Dr. Seuss's **Five Hundred Hats of Bartholomew Cubbins.**

► With a name like Frothingham, Charles Andrew is bound to be a bit prissy. Find other stuffy names in picture books.

....

The Cut-ups Carry On. *Viking Children's Books, 1990.* ISBN 0 670 81645 0

Spud and Joe are indignant when their parents enroll them in a dance class. Then they find out about a dance contest for which the prize is a lunar walker, and their competitive spirit is aroused.

Their chances take a nosedive, however, when they see that the best girl dancer has teamed up with the dreadful Charles Andrew Frothingham.

ACTIVITY: Organize your own dance contest. Decide on and publish a list of rules, criteria for prizes, and, of course, the prizes.

·······

George and Martha. *Houghton Mifflin Books for Children, 1993. ISBN 0 395 46739 4*

In this first book about the hippo friends, five short stories give us the tale of "Split Pea Soup," "The Flying Machine," "The Tub," "The Mirror," and "The Tooth." The pair always manages to get past the minor difficulties in their close friendship.

ACTIVITY: Make a list of the events in the stories. Beside each event, draw a picture of how George and Martha feel about it.

·······

George and Martha: The Complete Stories of Two Best Friends. *Houghton Mifflin Books for Children, 1997. ISBN 0 395 85158 0*

There are 340 pages in this outsized book, but the friends are also outsized, so it seems appropriate. All of the George and Martha stories are contained in this volume.

ACTIVITY: Read through the stories and find the places where you would have been angry, annoyed, or upset if your friend was like either George or Martha. What would you have done?

·······

Rats on the Roof and Other Stories. *Dial Books for Young Readers, 1991. ISBN 0 8037 0834 3*

It's not only rats on the roof, but sheep, wolves, mice, frogs, and cats, in these funny short stories. Frog legs are a source of pride to the frog until he reads a recipe for frog legs. Birds talk a brontosaurus out of destroying an owl's nest by telling him how disgusting the owls will taste. There's humor at every turn in these tales, and all of the villains are foiled in unpredictable ways.

ACTIVITY: Read aloud your favorite tale from either of the "Rat Collections." Use a prop to introduce your reading.

Wings: A Tale of Two Chickens. *Viking Children's Books, 1988. ISBN 0 140 50579 2*

Winnie the chicken refuses to read, so she's missing some information when a fox offers her a ride in his balloon. Fortunately, her friend, Harriet, has better sense and manages to rescue her.

ACTIVITY: Compare the attitudes of Winnie with those of Petunia in the book by that name by Roger Duvoisin.

FAIRY TALES RETOLD OR ILLUSTRATED BY JAMES MARSHALL

·······

Cinderella. *Little, Brown & Co., Children's Books, 1992. ISBN 0 316 48303 6*

Karlin's text sticks pretty much to the familiar tale, although there's only one ball and the fairy godmother moves in with them at the end. It's Marshall's illustrations that make up most of the humor. Watch the dogs and the cats.

·······

Goldilocks and the Three Bears. *Puffin Books, 1998. ISBN 0 140 56366 0*

Marshall's Goldilocks is chubby and opinionated, although she follows the usual routine of breaking in to the bears' house.

·······

Hansel and Gretel. *Dial Books for Young Readers, 1990. ISBN 0 803 70827 0*

It's hard to believe that even Marshall could find humor in this grimmest of fairy tales, but he does.

·······

Red Riding Hood. *Dutton Children's Books, 1987. ISBN 0 8037 0344 9*

There's humor throughout this book, from the first words the debonair wolf addresses to the chubby little girl, to the last words of Grandma, a dedicated reader.

Three Little Pigs. *Dutton Children's Books, 1989. ISBN 0 8037 0591 3*

One of the pigs survives in this zany rendition of the familiar tale.

ACTIVITY: Find the humor in each of Marshall's renditions and chart it in a manner similar to this:

TITLE	MAIN CHARACTERS	FUNNY DETAILS IN THE ILLUSTRATIONS	FUNNY DETAILS IN THE TEXT

BOOKS WRITTEN BY OTHER AUTHORS & ILLUSTRATED BY JAMES MARSHALL

Allard, Harry. **Miss Nelson Has a Field Day.** *Houghton Mifflin Books for Children, 1985. ISBN 0 395 36690 9*

It's Viola Swamp to the rescue, just in time to help the football team of the Horace B. Smedley School shape up in time to win a game.

. . . .

Allard, Harry. **Miss Nelson Is Back.** *Houghton Mifflin Books for Children, 1982. ISBN 0 395 32956 6*

This time Miss Nelson has to go away for a week, and the kids are ready for a high old time, but Viola Swamp returns.

. . . .

Allard, Harry. **Miss Nelson Is Missing.** *Houghton Mifflin Books for Children, 1977. ISBN 0 395 25296 2*

This story is the first of the Miss Nelson books. Miss Nelson is a kind teacher, but the kids seem to have no respect for her or her rules. Then, Miss Nelson is replaced by Viola Swamp, a teacher so strict and unpleasant that the students beg for Miss Nelson's return.

ACTIVITY: You probably would have guessed who Viola Swamp really was. What were the clues you'd have used?

Allard, Harry. **The Stupids Die.** *Houghton Mifflin Books for Children, 1981. ISBN 0 395 30347 8*

When the lights go out, there's only one conclusion to be reached by the Stupid family: They must be dead.

ACTIVITY: Many people are offended when you call them "stupid." What might be better names for these people?

. . . . . .

Allard, Harry. **The Stupids Take Off.** *Houghton Mifflin Books for Children, 1989. ISBN 0 395 50068 0*

Hoping to avoid one group of boring relatives, the Stupids take off in their plane, only to encounter even more stupid relatives.

ACTIVITY: Some things about the Stupid family are like the sitcoms of "The Munsters" and "The Addams Family." Make a chart showing their likenesses and differences.

Emily Arnold McCully

HER LIFE

Emily Arnold McCully was born and in Galesburg, Illinois (the scene of her book **Popcorn at the Palace**). She grew up in Long Island, where her father worked as a radio writer and her mother was a teacher. Her early artistic efforts were greatly encouraged by her mother, and she often wrote and illustrated her own books as a child. For awhile after graduating from college, she worked as a commercial artist, but came into the children's book field when encouraged to do so by a children's book editor. She's the mother of two grown sons and lives in New York City.

HER WORK

Emily McCully's work can be categorized into biographies, wordless books, and fantasies. She received the Caldecott Award for **Mirette on the High Wire,** which represented a departure in her illustrative technique. Her work became looser and less controlled than it had been in such earlier books as Snow, for instance.

THINGS TO DO WITH HER WORK

► You can separate her books into categories: histories, wordless books, other fantasies.

► Figure out what McCully had to know before she wrote each of her historical picture books.

►McCully has also illustrated many books that were written by others. Do you see any differences in her style as she works with the stories by different authors? What are they?

BOOKS & ACTIVITIES

. . . .

The Ballot Box Battle. *Alfred A. Knopf Books for Young Readers, 1996. ISBN 0 679 87938 2*

In this book, we see Elizabeth Cady Stanton, a crusader for women's rights, through the eyes of Cordelia, a little girl who lives nearby. Mrs. Stanton tells Cordelia about her own childhood and her relationship with her father, who once said, "How I wish you were a boy." Stanton then asks Cordelia, who's more interested in horses than voting, to come with her as she attempts to vote.

ACTIVITY: Find one fact about Elizabeth Cady Stanton that Emily McCully did not use in this book. If she had used it, what would she have shown in the pictures?

. . . .

Beautiful Warrior: The Legend of the Nun's Kung Fu. *Scholastic, 1998. ISBN 0 590 37487 7*

McCully tells of more strong women in this story about two women in 17th-century China. Wu Mei was encouraged by her father to take a nontraditional role, so she studied the martial arts and became a Buddhist nun. She saves a young girl from a loveless marriage to a bandit and teaches her kung fu. Later she uses her skills to defeat the bandit.

ACTIVITY: Talk to a person who knows kung fu. Get him or her to show you some of the moves and tell you about some of the philosophy behind it.

The Bobbin Girl. *Dial Books for Young Readers, 1996. ISBN 0 8037 1827 6*

Rebecca is 10 when she enters the textile mill to work as a bobbin girl. Her mother runs a boarding house for many of the women who work at the mill. When the mill owners cut their pay, the women and Rebecca form a "turnout." Their protest fails, but they have lost only one battle.

ACTIVITY: Find out about children who worked in factories in this country long ago. How many hours a day did they work? How many days off did they have? What different jobs did they do?

....

First Snow. *HarperCollins Children's Books, 1985. ISBN 0 06 024129 2*

In this wordless book, the mouse family is out for a day in the snow. Everybody's having a wonderful time sliding down the hill, even Grandma and Grandpa. One little mouse, however, perches at the top of the hill, afraid to go down. With much encouragement from the others, she finally overcomes her fear and discovers that she loves sliding downhill. At the end of the day, it's the youngest mouse who doesn't want to go home.

ACTIVITY: When did you first notice the little mouse? How did McCully direct your attention to her? How can you tell what the little mouse is feeling?

....

Little Kit or, the Industrious Flea Circus Girl. *Dial Books for Young Readers, 1995. ISBN 0 8037 1674 6*

Little Kit sells flowers in London during Victorian times. Thinking she's a boy, Professor Malefetta hires her to help with his Industrious Flea Circus. The professor is a cruel man, but Kit and a new friend, little Nell, outwit the professor and free the fleas, and Kit is adopted by Nell's parents.

ACTIVITY: How would people see what the fleas were doing when they are so tiny?

Mirette on the High Wire. *G. P. Putnam's Sons Books for Young Readers, 1992. ISBN 0 399 22130 1*

The Great Bellini and Mirette meet at her mother's boarding house. Bellini is a high-wire artist who has lost his nerve, but Mirette persuades him to teach her the skill. When Bellini freezes midway across an expanse, Mirette climbs up to meet him. Soon they are performing together above the roofs of Paris.

ACTIVITY: Place a big, thick rope in a straight line on the floor of a gymnasium. Try walking on that rope. Try it first without a pole, stick, or umbrella, then again with one.

....

My Real Family. *Harcourt Brace & Co., 1994. ISBN 0 15 277698 2*

This is a sequel to **Speak Up, Blanche.** Sarah, the youngest bear in a performing troupe of bears, is jealous of Blanche, the sheep. When the other bears decide to adopt Blanche, it's too much. Sarah takes off to find her "real" parents in the forest. When she gets lost and the performing bears search for her, Sarah understands that they are her real family.

ACTIVITY: When did Sarah first become jealous of Blanche? How does she feel about Blanche at the end of the book? How do you know?

....

Picnic. *HarperCollins Children's Books, 1987. ISBN 0 06 024100 4*

The mouse family is on another adventure in another wordless book. This time they're off to a picnic. When the youngest mouse falls off the truck, no one misses her for a long time. Then the search is on.

ACTIVITY: Plan an ideal picnic for mice. Where would you have it? What would you serve?

Popcorn at the Palace. *Harcourt Brace & Co., 1997.
ISBN 0 15 277699 0*

This book is another of McCully's picture biographies. This one is about Olmsted Ferris, a farmer in Illinois who learned that popcorn was relatively unknown in Europe. He took a shipment to London, arranged an audience with Queen Victoria and Prince Albert, and sold his product with great success. We get the story from his daughter, who had the original idea.

ACTIVITY: Take a poll on how people in your classroom prefer their popcorn: plain, with salt, with butter, with caramel, with cheese, flavored. Have them place a sticker with their name on it in the proper column in a chart such as this:

School. *HarperCollins Children's Books, 1990.
ISBN 0 06 4432233 5*

This book is one of McCully's wordless books about the mouse family. In this story, the eight oldest mice hurry off to the first day of school. The youngest, too little to go, is bored in the suddenly quiet house and decides to see what's going on at the school.

ACTIVITY: Write six sentences to tell what happens in this story.

I PREFER MY POPCORN...					
With Salt	With Butter	With Caramel	With Cheese	Flavored	Plain

Patricia Polacco

HER LIFE

Patricia Polacco was born in Lansing, Michigan, in 1944. Her parents divorced when she was three, but both parents were very much a part of her childhood. She spent the summers with her father in Williamston, Michigan, and the rest of the year with her mother and grandparents on a farm. Both families spent a great deal of time sharing stories and memories with Patricia and her older brother, Richard. When she was seven, the children moved with their mother to Oakland, California, where she still lives, but they continued to go every summer to Michigan.

She had great difficulty learning to read because of dyslexia, a condition about which very little was known at the time, but a seventh grade teacher discovered her problem and helped her with it. Once she could read, she did so, voraciously.

Polacco published her first book in 1987. She loves the racially mixed neighborhood in which she and her husband live in Oakland. Every morning she sits in a rocking chair (she has lots of them) and collects her thoughts and plans for the day as she rocks. Sometimes she thinks through an entire story as she rocks and only later transfers it to paper.

HER WORK

There's an "Old World" look to Polacco's books, and with good reason. Her rich cultural heritage, particularly the Russian Jewish tradition, is often the background of the work such as **The Keeping Quilt** and **The Bee Tree.** Her Russian grandmother is a character in several stories. Many of Polacco's books spring from her own experiences: **My Ol' Man** comes from a childhood experience with her father, and she includes black-and-white photos of her family and, particularly, her "ol' man" on the endpapers of the book. The need for cross-cultural friendships is also evident in her books, especially **Pink & Say** and **Mrs. Katz and Tush.**

More recently, her experience during the Oakland fires appeared in one of her books. Her stories often suggest that family relationships and roots overcome difficulties and deprivations. Another common thread in her work is that, by looking closely and treasuring the ordinary, you can see the magic and miracle in it.

Often Polacco leaves her characters' faces white, though fully drawn, which contrasts with the richly patterned clothing and other detailed objects in the illustrations. Sometimes the emotion experienced by her characters is more evident in the illustrations than it is in the text.

THINGS TO DO WITH HER WORK

▶ Polacco often used incidents from her own life as the basis of her stories. Decide which books these are. Is there anything in your life similar to these stories?

▶ In some of her books, Polacco made some people or objects on the page fully colored and left others with the faces drawn but not colored. What effect does this have? Why do you think she does it?

BOOKS & ACTIVITIES

Appelemando's Dreams. *G. P. Putnam's Sons Books for Young Readers, 1991. ISBN 0 399 21800 9*

The dark town in which they live offers little for a group of children, so they cluster around Appelemando who entertains them with his colorful daydreams. When a rainstorm paints the town with the colors of those dreams, the villagers are very upset.

ACTIVITY: Using only black crayon, draw a village or city on a large sheet of paper. Use paint to color the dreams people in the buildings might be having on their houses and apartments.

Babushka's Mother Goose. *G. P. Putnam's Sons Books for Young Readers, 1995. ISBN 0 399 22747 4*

This book includes rhymes remembered from Polacco's childhood, as well as retellings of some well-known tales.

ACTIVITY: Find rhymes and stories in other books that remind you of these.

The Bee Tree. *Philomel Books, 1993. ISBN 0 399 21965 X*

There's a moral behind this hunt for a honey tree. There's also humor in the search as, one after another, the relatives join the chase.

ACTIVITY: Talk to a person who raises bees to find out if the plan suggested in this book would work. Is this the way most of our honey is found?

Chicken Sunday. *G. P. Putnam's Sons Books for Young Readers, 1992. ISBN 0 399 22133 6*

Winston and Stewart are Patricia's best friends, and after her own grandmother died, she took their grandmother, Miss Eula, as hers. Although the Baptist religion of Winston and Stewart's family wasn't hers, Patricia often attended Sunday services with them and then repaired to Miss Eula's house for chicken dinner. Accused by Mr. Kodinski, the owner of the hat shop located on their route home, of pelting his shop with eggs, Patricia used her own heritage of egg decorating to convince Mr. Kodinski of their innocence.

ACTIVITY: Paint some eggs. Use a skewer to put a hole in the top and the bottom of the egg, then stir it around a little, then blow hard through one end which will blow out the insides. You then have a very fragile but very light eggshell. String the decorated eggs on mobiles.

Firetalking. *Richard C. Owen Publishers, 1994. ISBN 1 878450 55 7*

Part of Owen's "Meet the Author" series, this short autobiography gives us photographs and accessible text about Polacco's life and work.

ACTIVITY: Polacco tells you some things about herself in this book that you can find traces of in her stories. Find them and show others.

Just Plain Fancy. *Bantam Doubleday Dell Books for Young Readers, 1990. ISBN 0 553 05884 3*

Naomi, an Amish child, longs for something fancy, and, miraculously, a peacock turns up among her chickens. Worried that the fanciness of its plumage may cause it to be shunned, she's reassured that some things are just naturally fancy.

ACTIVITY: Find and read other books about Amish and other people who live plainly.

The Keeping Quilt. *Simon & Schuster Books for Young Readers, 1988. ISBN 0 671 64963 9*

A family heirloom begins with Great-Gramma Anna's dress and babushka. Handed down for generations and used at every important occasion, it becomes tattered, faded and loved.

ACTIVITY: Use a quilt book to identify the pattern in this quilt. Look through the book and decide on your own favorite quilt patterns. Get parents and friends who own quilts to bring them to school for a quilt show. Make sure you give them a chance to talk about their quilts.

Meteor! *Grosset & Dunlap Publishers, 1992. ISBN 0 399 22407 6*

A meteor lands in the middle of a yard in Union City, Michigan, and causes great excitement.

ACTIVITY: Find out about meteors. Look for shooting stars during the winter and summer star showers.

·······

My Ol' Man. *G. P. Putnam's Sons Books for Young Readers, 1995. ISBN 0 399 22822 5*

A girl's dad is a traveling salesman, and every night he brings home wonderful stories which delight his children. His tale of a magic rock becomes poignant, however, when he loses his job.

ACTIVITY: Being a traveling salesperson would have good and bad aspects. Which parts do you think you would like and not like?

·······

My Rotten Redheaded Older Brother. *Simon & Schuster Books for Young Readers, 1994. ISBN 0 671 72751 6*

This autobiographical tale of sibling rivalry and competition takes place in Union City, Michigan. Polacco's grandmother seems unaware of how rotten Patricia's older brother, Richard, really is. The intensity and rivalry between the two are apparent, but so is their underlying love.

ACTIVITY: Where are you in your family order? Make a chart or family tree about your family.

·······

Picnic at Mudsock Meadow. *G. P. Putnam's Sons Books for Young Readers, 1992. ISBN 0 399 21811 4*

A Halloween party ends with William leaping into the swamp, because he's failed at everything else at the party. When a swamp monster appears, however, it's William who proves what it is.

ACTIVITY: In this story the weakest character turns out to be a hero. Find and tell other stories where this happens.

Rechenka's Egg. *Philomel Books, 1988. ISBN 0 399 21501 8*

Babushka wins first prize for her hand-painted eggs. Then she takes in a wounded goose. As the goose heals, it destroys all of her beautiful eggs, but then it begins to lay beautiful eggs of its own.

ACTIVITY: Paint and decorate some eggs.

············

Some Birthday. *Simon & Schuster Books for Young Readers, 1991. ISBN 0 671 72750 8*

A birthday is different when celebrated with Patricia's father, who seems to have forgotten what day it is.

ACTIVITY: If you could have an ideal celebration, what would it be like? Who would come? What would you serve? Would the celebration be ideal for all of your guests as well as yourself?

············

Thank You, Mr. Falker. *Philomel Books, 1998. ISBN 0 399 23166 8*

In this autobiographical story, Patricia fully expects to enjoy reading the way the rest of her family does, but reading proves to be almost impossible for her. It's Mr. Falker who recognizes her learning disability and helps her deal with it.

ACTIVITY: Everybody does some things well and some things not so well. Make a chart showing your strengths and your weaknesses.

············

Thunder Cake. *Philomel Books, 1990. ISBN 0 399 22231 6*

Babushka helps her granddaughter overcome her fear of thunderstorms by distracting her with the making of a thunder cake.

ACTIVITIES:

▶ Count the time lapse between thunder and lightning next time you have a thunderstorm.

▶ Make a list of the things you're afraid of. Compare your list to those of others in the class. Can you make others understand why something scares you?

Cynthia Rylant

HER LIFE

Cynthia Rylant was born on June 6, 1954, in Hopewell, Virginia, the daughter of John and Laetrel Rylant Smith. Her father was in the service, and before she was four, her family moved around a lot, even spending a year in Japan. When she was four, her mother and father divorced, and her mother took Cynthia to Cool Ridge, West Virginia, and left her with her parents while she, the mother, attended nursing school. Rylant remembers that time as one of safety and of feeling wanted and treasured. She never saw her father again, and he died when she was 13.

When she was eight, she and her mother moved to Beaver, West Virginia, about 15 miles from Cool Ridge. Rylant finished growing up there. When she was nine, she fell in love with the Beatles, especially Paul, and for several years she planned to marry him. When she graduated from college, she wanted to become an English teacher, but found a job instead in a children's library. That's when she saw her first children's books and immediately decided to write one.

Rylant writes her stories on yellow legal pads, often while sitting in her porch swing. She daydreams a lot and writes only when those daydreams give her an idea for a story. Most of her books come from incidents in her own life. She has a son, Nate.

THINGS TO DO WITH HER WORK

► Some of Rylant's books are based on her own memories, others could have happened but probably didn't, and still others couldn't have been real. Divide her books into these three categories.

HER WORK

Rylant's writing, even in her novels, is spare and economical but tremendously insightful. She says that most of her books center around the grace that comes to people in the worst of circumstances. That's particularly true of her short stories in **Children of Christmas** and in her Newbery Award-winning novel, **Missing May.** The diner which is the scene for one of the stories in **Children of Christmas,** "Half Way Home," is the diner in the Ohio town where she now lives. A restaurant is the setting for **An Angel for Solomon Singer** which, again, brings grace to a man who has little hope. In **Every Living Thing,** it's an animal which brings hope, or an epiphany, to a human.

Rural West Virginia is the setting for many of her stories because she spent so much of her life there.

Rylant had a dog named Mudge and used that name and character in the Henry and Mudge books. Henry is patterned after her own son, Nate. The Henry and Mudge books are for beginning readers, and she keeps them interesting and full of love and playfulness.

She often uses animals in her books because she believes that animals bring out the truth in people. She says that her books tell a lot about her life, but that she wrote her autobiography, **But I'll Be Back Again,** because she wanted readers to see what her life was like when she wasn't hiding behind her characters.

BOOKS & ACTIVITIES
·······

All I See. Orchard Books, 1988. ISBN 0 531 08377 2

A boy hides and watches an artist who comes to a lake every day, sets up an easel and paints whales. Eventually the two paint together, but the artist continues to paint whales because, he says, that's all that he sees.

ACTIVITY: Look out the window for a long time and then draw or paint something you didn't see but you thought of.

·······

An Angel for Solomon Singer. Illustrated by Peter Catalanotto. Orchard Books, 1992. ISBN 0 531 05978 2

A middle-aged man living in a run-down New York City hotel comes to a restaurant where the menu reads, "The Westway Cafe, where all your dreams come true." The waiter's name is Angel and he welcomes Solomon each night as the man returns to order food and wishes for things from his boyhood in Indiana. Although his wishes don't come true literally, his memories and Angel's friendliness enhance his life.

ACTIVITY: Write down one wish that you really would like to come true. Then make a list of things that might or might not happen because that wish did come true.

·······

Appalachia: The Voices of Sleeping Birds.
Illustrated by Barry Moser. Harcourt Brace & Co., 1991. ISBN 0 15 201605 8

This story's poetic text creates portraits of the people and the dogs that live in the coal mining areas of Appalachia. Moser's illustrations are also portraits and as finely detailed as the text.

ACTIVITY: What if Rylant and Moser were to write a book like this about the town where you live? What things should they be sure to include?

Best Wishes. (Meet the Author Series.) Richard C. Owen Publishers, 1992. ISBN 1 878450 20 4

This small autobiography is liberally illustrated with color photos of the author and her environs and pets. Simple enough for second graders to understand, this volume is equally useful to upper grade children who are looking for author information.

ACTIVITY: Rylant shows pictures of the place she lived in the mountains with her grandparents. Compare it to the pictures in the book **When I Was Young in the Mountains.**

·······

Birthday Presents. Orchard Books, 1987. ISBN 0 531 05705 4

A little girl's first six birthdays are lovingly and humorously recalled by her parents, and we watch her go from babyhood to a young child who can help them celebrate their birthdays.

ACTIVITY: Ask your mother or father or someone else who would know about your first six birthdays. Make up a book like this one about them.

·······

Children of Christmas: Stories for the Season. Orchard Books, 1987. ISBN 0 531 05706 2

These short stories are less about Christmas than they are about people who are isolated or alone at a time when most of us are celebrating with our families. Each story offers a glimpse of a different kind of life and the hope that sustains these characters, albeit briefly.

ACTIVITES:

► Each of these characters is alone at Christmas time. Are there any other ways in which they are alike?

► Find a book that might be the one the woman finds in the children's library.

Every Living Thing. *Simon & Schuster Books for Young Readers, 1985. ISBN 0 02 777200 4*

The 12 short stories in this book center around animals and their relationship with people.

ACTIVITY: Which of these animals have you ever come in contact with?

•••••••

Henry and Mudge and the Bedtime Thumps. *Illustrated by Sucie Stevenson. Bradbury Press, 1991. ISBN 0 02 778006 6*

Grandmother's small country house presents problems for Henry and Mudge. Mudge is too big to sleep inside, and Henry is afraid without his dog. When the crisis comes, however, a solution is arrived at quickly.

•••••••

Henry and Mudge in the Green Time. *Bradbury Press, 1987. ISBN 0 02 778003 1*

The summer is delightful, and the dream time makes it even better for Henry and Mudge.

Henry and Mudge Under the Yellow Moon. *Bradbury Press, 1987. ISBN 0 02 778004 X*

Henry and Mudge enjoy life in the autumn, right up through Thanksgiving, with Aunt Sally.

ACTIVITY: Look at and read many of the Henry and Mudge books. Find ways in which they are alike.

•••••••

Miss Maggie. *Illustrated by Thomas Di Grazia. Dutton Children's Books, 1983. ISBN 0 525 44048 8*

An Appalachian woman lives alone and is feared by children on the mountain, who spread stories about her being a witch and keeping a large snake. One young boy, however, seeing no familiar smoke coming from Miss Maggie's chimney one day, finds her ill and very un-witchy.

ACTIVITY: What do you suppose Miss Maggie has been thinking about the children all this time?

Mr. Griggs' Work. *Illustrated by Julie Downing. Franklin Watts, 1989. ISBN 0 531 08369 1*

Mr. Griggs who loves his work at the post office becomes ill and must spend a day at home. However, his brief absence only makes his job sweeter when he returns to it.

ACTIVITY: Find somebody who loves their work as much as Mr. Griggs loves his. Interview them and write about their work.

•••••••

Night in the Country. *Illustrated by Mary Szilagyi. Bradbury Press, 1986. ISBN 0 02 777210 1*

A nighttime ride in the country show us what goes on when most of us are asleep.

ACTIVITY: Compare this book to **Night Driving,** by John Coy (Henry Holt & Co. Books for Young Readers, 1997, ISBN 0 8050 2931 1).

•••••••

The Relatives Came. *Simon & Schuster Books for Young Readers, 1985. ISBN 0 02 777220 9*

The relatives come from Virginia in their rattle-trap car, drinking pop and eating sandwiches, until they arrive at the big house, whereupon they all crowd in, hugging and loving each other.

ACTIVITY: Draw pictures to show what would happen if lots of your relatives came to your house to stay for awhile.

•••••••

This Year's Garden. *Illustrated by Mary Szilagyi. Bradbury Press, 1984. ISBN 0 02 777970 X*

Adults and children survey the garden and make plans for it. The adults discuss what to plant this spring, while the children anticipate the fun of working in the garden. Warm weather comes at last, and the crop is readied. We follow the garden's year.

ACTIVITY: See page 16 for lots of activities and books about gardens.

When I Was Young in the Mountains. *Illustrated by Diane Goode. Dutton Children's Books, 1982. ISBN 0 525 42525 X*

Simply and beautifully, Rylant tells of the home in coal mining country where her grandparents lived and where she spent several years as a child. Although adults will notice the poverty experienced by the people in the picture book, the story's emphasis is on their love and hard work.

ACTIVITY: Give some older person in your family or neighborhood this book to read and then suggest that they write something that begins with the words "When I was young in _____."

The Woman Who Named Things. *Illustrated by Kathryn Brown. Harcourt Brace & Co., 1996. ISBN 0 15 257809 9*

A lonely old woman has outlived all of her friends. She gives names to many things, but refuses to give a name to anything that will not outlive her. When a puppy shows up, she feeds it but will not name it until it disappears.

ACTIVITY: Name the things in your classroom the way the old woman did in the book.

Maurice Sendak

HIS LIFE

Maurice Sendak was born in Brooklyn, New York, in 1928, the youngest of three children of Sadie and Philip Sendak who had immigrated to America from Poland. Often ill as a child, he spent a good deal of his time sitting in the window of the tenement in which he lived looking down on the children, mostly immigrant children, playing on the city streets and sidewalks below. He and his brother, Jack, were very fond of toys and gadgets, particularly those which involved Mickey Mouse. To this day, Mr. Sendak collects such toys. Sometimes Jack would write stories and Maurice would illustrate them. He loves Mozart and often plays the composer's music while he writes and draws. He's also very fond of dogs, particularly German shepherds.

Sendak has helped and inspired several upcoming picture book creators, including Peter Sis and Richard Egielski.

THINGS TO DO WITH HIS WORK

► Place Sendak's books on a table in the order of their publication. Notice how his illustrations have changed over the years.

► Three of his books—**Where the Wild Things Are, In the Night Kitchen** and **Outside Over There**—are considered by Sendak to be his trilogy of childhood. The art styles and plots vary widely in these three representative works. Take a poll on the one children like best.

HIS WORK

Perhaps more than any other author/illustrator, Maurice Sendak is responsible for the attention and respect currently given children's literature. Although much of his work is unsettling, even disturbing, it opened up new vistas for the field. Viewing each of his books as a work of art in and of itself, Sendak is less interested in writing specifically "for children" than he is using this art form as a means of self-expression. He has identified the theme in his books as being "how kids get through a day, how they survive tedium, boredom, how they cope with anger, frustration."

BOOKS & ACTIVITIES

BOOKS WRITTEN & ILLUSTRATED BY MAURICE SENDAK

• • • • • • •

Alligators All Around. HarperCollins Children's Books, 1962. ISBN 0 06 025530 7

Part of the original "Nutshell Library," this alphabet book uses alligators to demonstrate each letter's use.

ACTIVITY: Make a counting book starring the alligators.

• • • • • • •

Chicken Soup with Rice. HarperCollins Children's Books, 1962. ISBN 0 06 025535 8

Also part of the "Nutshell Library," this delightful poem finds good in every month of the year. The chant-able text makes this particularly useful in early childhood classrooms.

ACTIVITY: Make a calendar using the lines from the book.

Hector Protector. *HarperCollins Children's Books, 1965. ISBN 0 06 025485 8*

Two Mother Goose rhymes are extended and expanded in this picture book.

ACTIVITY: Find the poems in a Mother Goose anthology. How did that illustrator interpret the rhymes?

·······

In the Night Kitchen. *HarperCollins Children's Books, 1970. ISBN 0 06 025489 0*

This cartoon-like book has echoes of the earlier **Where the Wild Things Are** and contains many allusions to the author's childhood. The story features food containers and kitchen implements from the 1930s as buildings. Dedicated to Sendak's parents, there are other allusions to them in the book, as well as to Sendak's birth date. The cooks strongly resemble Oliver Hardy, and the phrase "baked while you sleep" is an advertising slogan from the period. Sendak's Mickey looks very much like Max in **Wild Things.** Mickey falls into the Night Kitchen where he emerges from dough and flies to the Milky Way before falling back into his own bed.

ACTIVITIES:

► Find some of the dates and names hidden in the illustrations and find out what they mean.

► The rhythm in the book is strong and it can be read aloud as a chant.

·······

King Grisly-Beard. *Viking Children's Books, 1978. ISBN 0 374 34133 8*

A fairy tale is being performed as a play with amusing asides from the boy and girl who watch it with us.

ACTIVITY: Act out a different fairy tale the way the kids did.

Maurice Sendak's Really Rosie. *HarperCollins Children's Books, 1986. ISBN 0 06 443138 X*

This book is based on a TV show that was based on a book. The original Sendak title was "The Sign on Rosie's Door." This version includes seven songs.

ACTIVITY: Put on the Really Rosie musical.

·······

One Was Johnny: A Counting Book. *HarperCollins Children's Books, 1962. ISBN 0 06 025540 4*

This small and simple rhyming book is part of the "Nutshell Library."

ACTIVITY: There's one part of this book that many Native Americans don't like. Can you find it? What do you think about it? Why would they object to it? How would you change it?

·······

Outside Over There. *HarperCollins Children's Books, 1981. ISBN 0 06 025523 4*

This beautiful but disturbing book revolves around Ida who turns her back on her baby brother only to have him captured by goblins. Undeterred, she bests them in their home. **Outside Over There** contains visual allusions to the Lindbergh kidnapping which occurred during the '30s and frightened many parents and children at the time. Drawn in a romantic, full color style, this work also contains a picture of Mozart whose music is beloved by Sendak.

ACTIVITIES:

► Watch the view through the window. Why do you think it changes?

► Watch the ship, the sea and the sunflowers.

► In one of the pages just before the story begins, Ida is helping the baby walk. On the last page, the baby has taken a step. How long would that have taken? Is that supposed to mean that the whole story took place in the time it took to make that step?

Pierre. *HarperCollins Children's Books, 1962. ISBN 0 06 025965 5*

This cautionary tale about a boy who says, "I won't" one time too often is the fourth book in the "Nutshell Library."

ACTIVITY: If you could talk to Pierre halfway through this story, what would you say?

....

Some Swell Pup. *Farrar Strauss Giroux Books for Young Readers, 1989. ISBN 0 374 46963 6*

Although there is a story line in this book, the book is more of a manual about taking care of a dog than it is a narrative.

ACTIVITIES:

Make posters showing how to care for any pet.

....

We Are All in the Dumps with Jack and Guy. *HarperCollins Children's Books, 1993. ISBN 0 06 205014 1*

Using two Mother Goose rhymes as anchors, in this book, Sendak tells a tale of homeless children, starting in New York and ending at an orphanage resembling Auschwitz. There are many other allusions, the Cheshire cat and Trump Tower, for instance, in this dark tale.

ACTIVITIES:

Is there any hope in this story? What do you think will happen to Jack and Guy?

....

Where the Wild Things Are. *HarperCollins Children's Books, 1964. ISBN 0 06 025521 8*

This book is Sendak's best known work. Max, who's been exiled to his room because of monstrous behavior sails away to the land of the Wild Things, where he becomes king of them all. This story contains subtle foreshadowing and other sometimes overlooked features. For instance, Max's world when he is "making mischief of one kind and another" is small, and the accompanying picture occupies a small place on the page. As he gains supremacy and control, his world as represented by the illustrations grows biggeruntil the picture occupies the entire width of the page and even spreads onto the next page. By the time the "wild rum-

pus" starts, the illustrations have proceeded down the page until they've driven off all of the text. Later, when Max smells good things to eat, the world grows smaller, but never gets as small as it once was. Sendak uses crosshatching with pen and ink over the colors he has laid down, thus creating shading and depth.

ACTIVITIES:

► With the children sitting close to you, turn the pages of the book slowly and see if they notice the increasing size of the illustrations. Brainstorm for reasons as to why Sendak did that.

► Show the pictures again, this time asking them to find any early traces of the wild things.

BOOKS WRITTEN BY OTHER AUTHORS & ILLUSTRATED BY MAURICE SENDAK

....

Minarik, Else H. **Father Bear Comes Home.** *HarperCollins Children's Books, 1959. ISBN 0 06 024231 0*

This story is just one of several Little Bear books illustrated by Sendak. These easy-to-read books are particularly charming and whimsical.

ACTIVITY: Read the other books about Little Bear by Minarik and Sendak. Which one do you like best?

....

Zolotow, Charlotte. **Mr. Rabbit and the Lovely Present.** *HarperCollins Children's Books, 1962. ISBN 0 06 026945 6*

A child wants to give her mother something special for her birthday, and a large rabbit helps her decide what it should be.

ACTIVITY: Make a list of all the things the little girl wants her present to be. Is there anything else that fits the bill?

Seymour Simon

HIS LIFE

Seymour Simon was born on August 3, 1931, in New York City, the son of David and Clara Simon. His love for writing became more pronounced during his years as a high school student at the Bronx High School of Science. One of his projects there was the grinding of his own telescope lens. After graduating from the City College of New York City, Simon taught school for more than 20 years before becoming a full-time nonfiction writer for children in 1979. By that time he had written 50 science books for young people. His first book was **Animals in Field and Laboratory.** He and his wife, Joyce, a travel agent, live in Great Neck, Long Island, New York, and are the parents of two grown sons, Robert and Michael.

HIS WORK

Simon's interest in science is exuberant and he approaches every subject with a child's eye for interesting tidbits, but he's careful not to overstate the facts. His books fascinate any reader partly because of his careful choice of dramatic photographs but also because his information is so well stated. He never leaves his readers thinking that what they've just read is the full story, or even that scientists know the full story of any subject. He always leaves the door open for future information.

THINGS TO DO WITH HIS WORK

▶ Categorize his books according to their subject.

▶ Find another book about the same subject as any of the Simon books. Compare the information he gives and the way he gives it with that of the other author.

BOOKS & ACTIVITIES

· · · · · · · · ·

Big Cats. *HarperCollins Children's Books, 1991. ISBN 0 06 021646 8*

This book points out similarities and differences among seven members of the cat family and is illustrated with full-color photographs.

ACTIVITY: Bring a pet cat to school. Observe it carefully and make comparisons to the look or action of any of the big cats in Simon's book.

· · · · · · · · ·

The Dinosaur Is the Biggest Animal That Ever Lived and Other Wrong Ideas You Thought Were True. *HarperCollins Children's Books, 1984. ISBN 006 446 533*

The title of this book is Simon's longest, but the book explodes 30 common myths about science.

ACTIVITY: Use the 30 myths in this book as a quiz for parents and others who haven't read this book.

Earthquakes. *Morrow Junior Books, 1991.*
ISBN 0 688 09633 6

Simon's look at earthquakes includes detailed information about the damage in San Francisco and Mexico City, but avoids sensationalizing the subject. Equal attention is given to the geologic causes and results of earthquakes, as well as to the effort to predict them.

ACTIVITY: Find out when the last earthquake occurred closest to your area. What damage did it do?

· · · · · · ·

How to Be an Ocean Scientist in Your Own Home. *HarperCollins Children's Books, 1988.*

There are 24 experiments and explorations with saline water in this book which can provide inspiration for many science projects.

ACTIVITY: Form groups of two and perform one of the experiments in this book, taking careful journal notes as you do so. Post your notes and compare them with others who chose the same experiment.

· · · · · · ·

Mars. *Morrow Junior Books, 1987. ISBN 0 688 06584 8*

Using color photographs and information gathered by Mariner and Viking probes, Simon tells us what is known but also what is yet unknown about this more familiar planet.

ACTIVITY: Find Mars in the night sky.

· · · · · · ·

Neptune. *Morrow Junior Books, 1991. ISBN 0 688 09631 X*

Full of interesting facts about the eighth planet from the sun, this book uses photos and information gathered by Voyager 2 as it flew by in 1989.

ACTIVITY: Make a list of the things we found out about Neptune with Voyager 2.

Snakes. *HarperCollins Children's Books, 1992.*
ISBN 0 060 225 97

Facts about snakes, their predators, their prey, the way they move, reproduce, and live are illustrated with visually stunning photographs.

ACTIVITY: Take a poll among the adults you know concerning their feelings about snakes.

· · · · · · ·

Uranus. *Morrow Junior Books, 1987. ISBN 0 688 06582 1*

Much of Uranus is still a mystery, even after the pass by Voyager 2 in 1986. Simon talks about its strange tilt and 42-year days, among other fascinating material.

ACTIVITY: What do we still not know about Uranus?

· · · · · · ·

Whales. *HarperCollins Children's Books, 1989.*
ISBN 0 690 04756 8

This book's gorgeous photographs show many kinds of whales in their natural habitat. Simon compares their size to things within a child's world. The humpback whale is "longer than a big bus and heavier than a trailer truck," for instance.

ACTIVITY: Do further research about any one of the whales mentioned in this book.

· · · · · · ·

Wolves. *HarperCollins Children's Books, 1993.*
ISBN 0 06 022531 9

Concluding with a plea to preserve and protect these beautiful animals, this book first shows us how they live, hunt and raise their young. They're compared and contrasted to their domestic relatives in an almost chatty style. Again, photographs dominate the book, but its text is clear and fascinating.

ACTIVITY: Find and bring in recent newspaper and magazine articles about the reintroduction of wolves to some areas.

Chris Van Allsburg

HIS LIFE

Chris Van Allsburg lives in a red brick house in Providence, Rhode Island, which he says looks a little like a Monopoly game hotel. Inside are many of his sculptures, including a chair with a pitched roof on its seat and tiny windows on its back and legs. He lives there with his wife, Lisa; his daughter, Sophie; and Cecil, a Siamese cat. Lisa is a radio-ad sales consultant. Van Allsburg was born on June 18, 1949, in Grand Rapids, Michigan, in a house just outside of the town where his father and uncles ran a dairy. He started his artwork with sculpture and began drawing as a hobby. His wife and picture book author/illustrator David Macaulay convinced him to try children's books. His first book, **The Garden of Abdul Gasazi,** was published in 1979 and became a Caldecott honor book. His second book, **Jumanji,** published in 1981, received the Caldecott Medal. So did **The Polar Express,** published four years later. Van Allsburg teaches at the Rhode Island School of Design. He hates to fly, so he takes the train whenever he can, instead.

THINGS TO DO WITH HIS WORK

▶ Categorize his books according to their use of color.

▶ Categorize his books according to their subject.

▶ Work with an airbrush, a medium Van Allsburg sometimes uses in his illustrations.

HIS WORK

Van Allsburg starts his books by writing the story, although the vision of certain items of the story sometimes come first: a boat hovering above the waves, a train standing still in a forest and puffing steam, or a Monopoly game where items come to life, for instance. In his books, the pictures tell as much of the story as the words do.

He says there are 12 clues to the identity of the mystery man in **The Stranger,** and many readers have enjoyed finding the dog, Fritz, in each of his books. **The Polar Express**, says Van Allsburg, is about faith. The captain in **The Wretched Stone** looks a lot like the author.

His illustrations often have a skewed or warped perspective, which some have said "show the reverse side of reality." Finding the changes in perspective often within one illustration is an art lesson in itself. Discussing the reasons for that change is a writing lesson. Someone has said that Van Allsburg's books end with a question mark rather than a period. His books are filled with mystery and wonder. Most kids seem delighted with his books, which they often describe as "weird."

BOOKS & ACTIVITIES

Bad Day at Riverbend. *Houghton Mifflin Books for Children, 1996. ISBN 0 395 67347 X*

Bad things are happening in a quiet western town: Horses, cattle and people are being struck with a greasy substance each time a bright light appears. This one-joke book plays with perspective in a unique and delightful way.

ACTIVITIES:

► When did you first figure out what was going on?

► Look through coloring books to find another that you could use make up a story like **Bad Day at Riverbend.**

Ben's Dream. *Houghton Mifflin Books for Children, 1982. ISBN 0 395 32084 4*

After studying his geography, Ben dreams that he and his friend, Margaret, have the same dream, in which they discover many famous landmarks submerged by a flood.

ACTIVITY: Make a list of the landmarks in this book and find out more about each one.

The Garden of Abdul Gasazi. *Houghton Mifflin Books for Children, 1979. ISBN 0 395 27804 X*

Alan is minding a dog, Fritz, who wanders into a magician's house and may or may not have been changed into a duck.

ACTIVITY: What is the evidence to show that this was all a dream? What is the evidence to show that this was not a dream?

Jumanji. *Houghton Mifflin Books for Children, 1981. ISBN 0 395 30448 2*

A board game comes to life, and the house is soon filled with danger as children attempt to get to the end of the game quickly.

ACTIVITY: Make the board game "Jumanji," but be careful how you play it.

The Mysteries of Harris Burdick. *Houghton Mifflin Books for Children, 1984. ISBN 0 395 35393 9*

This book contains 14 pictures with titles and captions that come from 14 stories that have never been written. It's up to us to provide the stories.

ACTIVITY: Pick out one of the pictures that intrigues you. With a partner, figure out what might have happened before the point in the story that's illustrated by this picture, and what might happen afterward.

Polar Express. *Houghton Mifflin Books for Children, 1985. ISBN 0 395 38949 6*

A boy takes a trip on a mysterious night train to the North Pole where Santa gives him a crystal bell.

ACTIVITY: Make a display of all kinds of bells. Listen to each one and find words to describe its sound.

The Stranger. *Houghton Mifflin Books for Children, 1986. ISBN 0 395 42331 7*

A mysterious stranger recuperates in a home after being struck by a car. He has no memory of who he is, but the seasons don't progress while he's there.

ACTIVITY: Who is the stranger? What makes you think so?

The Sweetest Fig. *Houghton Mifflin Books for Children, 1993. ISBN 0 395 67346 1*

An abused dog gets his revenge on his sadistic owner in this turnabout tale.

ACTIVITY: Find and read other books, such as **Martha Speaks,** by Susan Meddaugh, in which a dog does unexpected things

Two Bad Ants. *Houghton Mifflin Books for Children, 1988. ISBN 0 395 48668 8*

We see a kitchen from an ant's perspective as two of them decide to remain behind when the others in their colony leave.

ACTIVITIES:

► Identify the objects in the kitchen that the ants come in contact with.

► Look at your desk the way ants might look at it. Make drawings of the things in and around your desk from an ant's point of view.

·······

The Widow's Broom. *Houghton Mifflin Books for Children, 1992. ISBN 0 395 64051 2*

A witch's broom is left behind in a house, and a widow finds it quite useful, as it performs many tasks on its own. Unfortunately, her neighbors are afraid of it, and their fear almost results in the destruction of the broom.

ACTIVITY: What happened to the broom? Why did the Spiveys think that they had burned the broom?

The Wreck of the Zephyr. *Houghton Mifflin Books for Children, 1983. ISBN 0 395 33075 0*

A boy learns to sail above the waves, but tries to soar too high, wrecking his boat and his dream.

ACTIVITY: Compare this book to **The Silver Pony,** by Lynd Ward (Houghton Mifflin Books for Children, 1973. ISBN 0 395 14753 0).

·······

The Wretched Stone. *Houghton Mifflin Books for Children, 1991. ISBN 0 395 53307 4*

A mysteriously glowing stone hypnotizes the sailors who bring it aboard their ship until they cease to do anything but stare at it.

ACTIVITY: Find out how much time you spend each day watching television. Make a list of other fun things you could be doing during that time.

·······

The Z Was Zapped: A Play in Twenty-Six Acts. *Houghton Mifflin Books for Children, 1987. ISBN 0 395 44612 0*

The letters in this book become characters on a stage and are destroyed alphabetically.

ACTIVITY: Compare this book to other alphabet books.

Jane Yolen

HER LIFE

Jane Yolen was born in New York City, in 1939, and lived in New York, California and Virginia as a young child. Writing seems to run in her family. Her mother was a writer and a creator of crossword puzzles. Her father authored seven books and was a journalist. Her grandparents came from Russia and were great storytellers. Her brother is a journalist in Brazil. Yolen started writing plays while still in elementary school and hasn't stopped writing since. She went to high school in Connecticut and then went on to Smith College. A small group of writers work regularly with Jane. They include Patricia MacLachlan and Ann Turner.

Yolen has written more than 120 books. For the past 20 years or so she has lived on a farm in Hatfield, Massachusetts, with her husband, David Stemple, a professor of computer science at the University of Massachusetts. Hatfield is a small town in western Massachusetts. Her office, on the top floor of their large farmhouse, called Phoenix Farm, is where she writes and edits books. Their son Jason is a photographer. Their son Adam is a musician, composer and arranger and is the lead singer of the band Boiled in Lead. Daughter Heidi was a private investigator and is now a mother. All three children have worked with their mother to create children's books.

Music plays a large part in Jane's life. She plays the guitar, sings and writes music. She's also an avid bird watcher and is very active in politics. She collects unicorns, selchies, wizards, mermaids, and dragons. She can often be found in the evening "surfing the Net" on her computer.

HER WORK

Yolen is one of the most prolific writers in children's literature. She's also the successful editor of her own line of children's books. The scope of her work is wide, and her fascination with fairy tales and the Arthurian legend influences much of that work. Other inspiration for her books comes from real-life experiences: **Owl Moon** was inspired by an owl walk her husband and daughter Heidi went on. (Notice that the sex of the child in **Owl Moon** is never stated in the text or in the illustrations.) **All Those Secrets of the World** is based on a memory from her own childhood during World War II. Even the text of **Letting Swift River Go,** although set in another time, took place in an area not far from her home and with which she's very familiar. Some of her work is poetry and much of her prose, particularly in her nature books, approaches poetry in its lyric quality.

THINGS TO DO WITH HER WORK

► Categorize her books by their subject.

► Look at the poetry books Yolen has illustrated with photographs taken by her son. Which do you think came first—the poems or the photos?

BOOKS & ACTIVITIES
·······

All Those Secrets of the World. *Illustrated by Leslie Baker. Little, Brown & Co., Children's Books, 1991. ISBN 0 316 96891 9*

This is a delicate, nostalgic book about a little girl's separation from her soldier father during World War II.

ACTIVITY: Interview someone who was alive during World War II about their lives at that time.

·······

And Twelve Chinese Acrobats. *Illustrated by Jean Gralley. Philomel Books, 1995. ISBN 0 399 22691 5*

In this illustrated chapter book, Yolen relates some family stories told by her father about his older brother, Lou. In their Ukrainian village, Lou gets in such trouble that he's sent away to military school. Hating it, he runs away and is not heard from for years. Suddenly he turns up on the doorstep, accompanied by 12 Chinese acrobats.

ACTIVITY: Get your grandparents or someone of that generation to tell you about their favorite siblings and the things they did.

·······

Baby Bear's Bedtime Book. *Illustrated by Jane Dyer. Harcourt Brace & Co., 1990. ISBN 0 15 205120 1*

Goldilocks is baby-sitting Baby Bear, and he pulls out all the stops to delay bedtime, but Goldilocks is equal to the task.

ACTIVITY: Read several versions of **The Three Bears.** Which version do you like best?

Before the Storm. *Illustrated by Georgia Pugh. Boyds Mills Press, 1995. ISBN 1 56397 240 9*

A hot summer afternoon is evoked by Yolen's text in which children read and color and horse around with a garden hose. It's all interrupted by a sudden summer shower.

ACTIVITY: Compare this book to Peter Spiers's **Rain** (Yearling, 1997 ISBN 0 440 413478).

·······

Bird Watch. *Illustrated by Ted Lewin. Philomel Books, 1990. ISBN 0 399 21612 X*

This book is a bird lover's delight—hort, often beautiful, poems are juxtaposed against lovely paintings.

ACTIVITY: Go outdoors with a paintbrush, some watercolors and paper and make bird sketches.

·······

Eeny, Meeny, Miney Mole. *Illustrated by Kathryn Brown. Harcourt Brace & Co., 1992. ISBN 0 15 225350 5*

Meeny and Miney are content in their underground world, but Eeny has heard about "Up Above" and won't rest until she's seen it.

ACTIVITY: Make a chart showing each animal Eeny met and what they told her.

·······

The Emperor and the Kite. *Illustrated by Ed Young. G. P. Putnam's Sons Books for Young Readers, 1988. ISBN 0 399 21499 2*

Cut-paper illustrations adorn this Chinese legend about an emperor's loyal youngest daughter.

ACTIVITY: Find out more about Chinese kites.

·······

Encounter. *Illustrated by David Shannon. Harcourt Brace & Co., 1992. ISBN 0 15 225962 7*

The first meeting between Columbus and the people of San Salvador is told by a young Taino boy who is first intrigued and later horrified by what he sees.

ACTIVITY: Compare this book to other books about the arrival of Christopher Columbus in America.

Favorite Folktales from Around the World. *Pantheon Books, 1988. ISBN 0 394 75188 4*

This collection of tales is a valuable one. Yolen is an excellent storyteller herself and her interest in and research about folktales is a useful resource for reader and storyteller alike.

ACTIVITY: Take turns taking this book home. Choose a story you like a lot and tell it to the class.

. . . .

The Girl in the Golden Bower. *Illustrated by Jane Dyer. Little, Brown & Co., Children's Books, 1994. ISBN 0 316 96894 3*

Orphaned Curry befriends the creatures of the woods and is in turn befriended by them as she encounters a sorceress bent on obtaining a treasure.

ACTIVITY: Compare this fairy tale to **Snow White** and other stories where someone very good must fight someone very evil.

. . . .

The Girl Who Loved the Wind. *Illustrated by Ed Young. HarperCollins Children's Books, 1992. ISBN 0 690 33101 0*

Prevented by her overly protective father from experiencing sadness in any form, the princess Danina encounters the wind. It tells her about the world outside the palace walls.

ACTIVITY: Compare this story to the fairy tale **Rapunzel.**

. . . .

Good Griselle. *Illustrated by David Christiana. Harcourt Brace & Co., 1994. ISBN 0 15 231701 5*

Griselle's goodness enrages the gargoyles, so they place a bet that they can break her goodness by giving her an unlovable child. The gargoyles lose the bet, and Griselle and her ugly son receive their reward.

ACTIVITY: Compare this story to other fairy tales in which good and sweet people are pitted against evil ones.

Grandad Bill's Song. *Illustrated by Melissa Bay Mathis. Philomel Books, 1994. ISBN 0 399 21802 5*

A young boy, grieving for his grandfather, asks each family member what they did on the day Grandad died. Each one has a different memory of and reaction to the death, but they all help the narrator express his grief.

ACTIVITY: Interview your family members about some people in your family that they knew and you didn't. What are their best memories of him or her?

. . . .

Honkers. *Illustrated by Leslie Baker. Little, Brown & Co., Children's Books, 1993. ISBN 0 316 96893 5*

Betsy arrives at her grandparents lonely and frightened, but she soon becomes involved in the goslings that hatch from three abandoned eggs.

ACTIVITY: In this book, Betsy is called "Little Bit," and she doesn't seem to mind it. What nicknames are used in your classroom, and how does the person being called by that name like it?

. . . .

A Letter from Phoenix Farm. *Richard C. Owen, 1992. ISBN 1 878450 36 0*

This autobiography is readily accessible to readers in a wide age range and tells of the author's home, family and many jobs.

ACTIVITY: Find things in this book about Yolen's life that you can see in some of her work.

. . . .

Letting Swift River Go. *Illustrated by Barbara Cooney. Little, Brown & Co., Children's Books, 1992. ISBN 0 316 96800 4*

This poignant tale tells of four New England villages that were completely obliterated in order to make a large reservoir. There are no villains in this book, only people whose needs came into conflict.

ACTIVITY: In every area there's something that had to go in order for more modern things to be built. What happened in your community like that? What buildings had to be torn down? What price was paid?

The Lullaby Songbook. *Illustrated by Charles Mikolaycak. Harcourt Brace & Co., 1987. ISBN 0 15 249903 2*

This beautifully designed lap-book is good for browsing, as well as for singing.

ACTIVITY: Sing the songs in this book.

. . . .

O Jerusalem. *Scholastic, 1996. ISBN 0 590 48426 5*

This reverent picture book provides brief glimpses of Jerusalem through many guises and through many religions, and the meaning and symbolism of this city, which is about to celebrate its 3,000th anniversary, becomes clear.

ACTIVITY: Find Jerusalem on a map.

. . . .

Owl Moon. *Illustrated by John Schoenherr. G. P. Putnam's Sons Books for Young Readers, 1987. ISBN 0 399 21457 7*

In this Caldecott Award-winning book, Yolen tells of a young child's trek through the woods at night to spot an owl. An obvious rite of passage in this family, the nighttime walk is poetically and beautifully told and illustrated.

ACTIVITY: This is a focus book (see page 153).

. . . .

Picnic with Piggins. *Illustrated by Jane Dyer. Harcourt Brace & Co., 1988. ISBN 0 15 261534 2*

Yolen's second Edwardian mystery involving Piggins, the butler, has Piggins busy with the family's picnic by the river, but Rexy, one of the children, has disappeared. Leave it to Piggins to uncover the hoax.

. . . .

Piggins. *Illustrated by Jane Dyer. Harcourt Brace & Co., 1987. ISBN 0 15 261685 3*

Piggins, the butler, is the sleuth who solves the crime when Mr. and Mrs. Reynard's jewels are stolen in this picture book.

ACTIVITY: Find as many books about Piggins as you can and read them. Make a list of the things you know about Piggins.

The Seeing Stick. *Illustrated by Remy Charlip. Crowell, 1977. ISBN 0 690 00455 9*

The emperor sends for people to make his blind daughter see again, and after many try and fail, an old man provides insight, if not sight.

ACTIVITY: Many blind people use their fingers to get information. Find out some of the ways in which this is done.

. . . .

A Sip of Aesop. *Illustrated by Karen Barbour. Scholastic, 1995. ISBN 0 590 46895 8*

This book's brief tales are from Aesop, but written as poems.

ACTIVITY: Find and read the original fables on which these poems are based. Which version do you like better?

. . . .

Sky Dogs. *Illustrated by Barry Moser. Harcourt Brace & Co., 1990. ISBN 0 15 275480 6*

A tribal elder tells of the time when the Blackfoot Indians first encountered horses. A young boy is the only one brave enough to ride one and is later called "He-who-loves-horses."

ACTIVITY: Find and read the book **Doesn't Fall Off His Horse,** by Virginia Stroud.

. . . .

Sleeping Ugly. *G. P. Putnam's Sons Books for Young Readers, 1981. ISBN 0 698 20617 7*

This take-off from the tale of Sleeping Beauty is full of humor, wisdom and outrageous puns.

ACTIVITY: Find and read as many twisted fairy tales as you can.

. . . .

Street Rhymes Around the World. *Boyds Mills Press, 1992. ISBN 1 878093 53 3*

Each spread focuses on a rhyme (and its translation) that's used during counting, jumping and other games around the world.

ACTIVITY: Start a big book of jump rope, clapping and ball bouncing rhymes. After you've written down all the ones you know, get more from your parents, grandparents and other family members.

Three Bears Rhyme Book. *Illustrated by Jane Dyer. Harcourt Brace & Co., 1987. ISBN 0 15 286386 9*

Poems which use the folktale as their base give us a poet's-eye view of the life of these bears before and after the story.

ACTIVITY: Find and read as many editions of **The Three Bears** as possible. Take a survey of the class to find out which edition people like best.

Water Music. *Illustrated by Jason Stemple. Boyds Mills Press, 1995. ISBN 1 56397 336 7*

The poems in this book, which are illustrated with photographs taken by the author's son, explore the many aspects of water.

ACTIVITY: Look at Walter Wick's book **A Drop of Water.** It uses photographs, too. What does each book try to do? Which book would you like to own?

. . . .

Weather Report. *Illustrated by Annie Gusman. Boyds Mills Press, 1993. ISBN 1 56397 101 1*

The work of 30 poets is used to produce this anthology of weather poems.

ACTIVITY: Use these poems with a weather theme, such as the one on page 38.

Ed Young

HIS LIFE

Ed Young was born on November 28, 1931, in Tientsin, China, the son of Qua Ling and Yuen Teng. His father was an engineer. Because of the Japanese invasion of China in World War II, the family moved about a lot before spending considerable time in Shanghai. There they stayed until the Chinese civil war, during which the Communists took over Shanghai, at which point the family moved to Hong Kong.

Young emigrated to the United States in 1951 and became a naturalized citizen. He attended City College of San Francisco where he began as an architecture major but soon switched to art. Upon graduation, he worked in advertising before being commissioned to illustrate his first book, **The Mean Mouse and Other Mean Stories.** The book won a graphic arts award, and he began his career in illustration

THINGS TO DO WITH HIS WORK

► Categorize his work according to subject.

► Look for influences of China in his work.

► Take a survey of the class's favorite Young book.

HIS WORK

Young's work is varied, and he uses a multitude of media. Often his illustrations suggest rather than sharply delineate a mood or a character. In some of his books, the edges of the paintings are soft and blurred, which contributes to the dream-like quality of certain texts.

In **Lon Po Po,** Young divides his illustrations into sections, thereby suggesting Chinese screens. The wolf that dominates the work can be seen even as part of the landscape. For the simple story of **Donkey Trouble,** Young uses the background colors to show the time of day and the collage to define the people. The illustrations in this book are deceptively simple but full of fascinating techniques. He uses a floral border to illustrate **Dreamcatcher** which might have come from the handwork of many cultures, while the rest of his illustrations for that book concentrate on the Ojibway culture. He creates an almost three-dimensional effect in **Eyes of the Dragon,** blending colors and shadows with pastels.

Young is particularly adept in his use of color: In **Goodbye Geese,** for instance, he uses cool, almost icy shades of blue and green to contrast sharply with his warmer shades of orange that reflect fall. In **Iblis** he uses neon-bright colors to contrast sharply with his dark images of evil.

In **Little Plum,** he varies his perspective to accent the difference in size between the child and the cruel lord.

BOOKS & ACTIVITIES
BOOKS WRITTEN & ILLUSTRATED BY ED YOUNG

·········

Cat and Rat: The Legend of the Chinese Zodiac. *Henry Holt & Co. Books for Young Readers, 1995. ISBN 0 8050 2977 X*

The Jade Emperor of Heaven organizes a race to decide which animals will have a year in the Chinese calendar named for them. The competition becomes heated when two previous friends, Cat and Rat, vie for a place.

ACTIVITY: Which sign of the Zodiac were you born in? What's your sign in the Chinese Zodiac and in the Zodiac most Americans know about?

·········

Donkey Trouble. *Simon & Schuster Books for Young Readers, 1995. ISBN 0 689 31854 5*

Young beautifully illustrates this traditional tale using a variety of media. In the story, a man and his boy obey every suggestion made by passersby as to the best way to bring their donkey to the market.

ACTIVITY: What would you have done each time a suggestion was made?

·········

Little Plum. *G. P. Putnam's Sons Books for Young Readers, 1994. ISBN 0 399 22683 4*

This folktale concerns a tiny child, no bigger than a plum seed, who outwits an evil lord, saving a village.

ACTIVITY: Find other stories about tiny people, such as **Thumbelina.**

·········

Lon Po Po: A Red Riding Hood Story from China. *G. P. Putnam's Sons Books for Young Readers, 1989. ISBN 0 399 21619 7*

In this Caldecott Award-winning book, we get the story of Lon Po Po, the Granny Wolf, who pretends to be the grandmother of the three daughters left at home by their mother.

ACTIVITY: Look at the pages carefully to find images of the wolf on almost every page.

Seven Blind Mice. *G. P. Putnam's Sons Books for Young Readers, 1992. ISBN 0 399 22261 8*

In this book, the ancient fable of the blind men and the elephant is transformed into a story of the seven blind mice who each view the elephant from a different perspective.

ACTIVITY: Read the story of **The Blind Men and the Elephant.** How are the two stories alike? How are they different?

·······

Yeh Shen: A Cinderella Story from China. *G. P. Putnam's Sons Books for Young Readers, 1982. ISBN 0 399 20900 X*

As in the author/illustrator's retelling of the Chinese **Red Riding Hood**, this traditional tale is illustrated with panels and subtle images.

ACTIVITY: Find and read as many Cinderella stories from different cultures as you can find. What do they have in common?

BOOKS WRITTEN BY OTHER AUTHORS & ILLUSTRATED BY ED YOUNG

·······

Calhoun, Mary. ***While I Sleep.*** *Morrow Junior Books, 1992. ISBN 0 688 08200 9*

The theme of this book is a survey of sleepers in which a child's questions are answered, .

ACTIVITY: Find other books that tell what goes on at night.

·······

Howe, James. ***I Wish I Were a Butterfly.*** *Harcourt Brace & Co., 1987. ISBN 0 15 200470 X*

A young cricket is told by a frog that he is ugly, so he sets out to find out if it's true.

ACTIVITY: Compare this book to Leo Lionni's **Fish Is Fish.**

Martin, Rafe. **Foolish Rabbit's Big Mistake.** G. P. Putnam's Sons Books for Young Readers, 1985. ISBN 0 399 21178 0

This is the Jataka version of **Chicken Little** in which rabbit is convinced that the earth is breaking up.

ACTIVITY: See page 114.

Olaleye, Isaac. **Bitter Bananas.** Boyds Mills Press, 1994. ISBN 1 56397 039 2

Yusuf is alarmed when baboons steal the sweet palm sap he harvests for sale in this story set in the African rain forest.

ACTIVITY: See page 103 for books on trickery.

· · · · · · ·

Osofsky, Audrey. **Dreamcatcher.** Orchard Books, 1992. ISBN 0 531 08588 0

The Ojibway custom of dreamcatchers is explained in this lyrical book which centers on the life and dreams of one baby and its family.

ACTIVITY: Make dreamcatchers.

Subject Index

Author/Illustrator/Title Index